TURNING Around FAILING SCHOOLS

in memory of
John W. Osborne
as good a friend as ever there was

Joseph Murphy • Coby V. Meyers

TURNING Around FAILING SCHOOLS

Leadership Lessons From the Organizational Sciences

A Joint Publication

For information:

Corwin Press
A Sage Publications Company
2455 Teller Road
Thousand Oaks,
California 91320
www.corwinpress.com

Sage Publications Ltd.
1 Oliver's Yard
55 City Road
London EC1Y 1SP
United Kingdom

Sage Publications India Pvt. Ltd.
B 1/I 1 Mohan Cooperative
Industrial Area
Mathura Road, New Delhi 110 044
India

Sage Publications Asia-Pacific Pte. Ltd.
33 Pekin Street #02-01
Far East Square
Singapore 048763

Printed in the United States of America

Library of Congress Cataloging-in-Publication Data

Murphy, Joseph, 1949–
Turning around failing schools: leadership lessons from the organizational sciences/Joseph Murphy, Coby V. Meyers.
    p. cm.
"A Joint Publication With the National Staff Development Council and the American Association of School Administrators."
Includes bibliographical references and index.
ISBN 978-1-4129-4096-2 (cloth)
ISBN 978-1-4129-4097-9 (pbk.)
    1. School management and organization—United States. 2. School improvement programs—United States. 3. Educational leadership—United States. 4. Organizational change—United States. I. Meyers, Coby V. II. National Staff Development Council (U.S.) III. American Association of School Administrators IV. Title.

LB2805.M818 2008
371.200973—dc22   2007010019

This book is printed on acid-free paper.

07   08   09   10   11   10   9   8   7   6   5   4   3   2   1

Acquisitions Editor:	Rachel Livsey
Managing Editor:	Elizabeth Brenkus
Editorial Assistant:	Desirée Enayati and Ena Rosen
Production Editor:	Astrid Virding
Copy Editor:	Barbara Coster
Typesetter:	C&M Digitals (P) Ltd.
Proofreader:	Dennis W. Webb
Indexer:	Sheila Bodell
Cover Designer:	Scott Van Atta
Graphic Designer:	Lisa Miller

Contents

**Part V: Understanding Turnarounds
in Schools**

Preface

Two guiding principles form the basis for this book. First, we believe that understanding should precede evaluation, especially in the case of how and why schools perform at specific levels. Second, we believe that educators and education researchers can and should use examples of organizational improvement outside education as frameworks for finding new understanding in the realm of schooling. It is our hope within this volume to illuminate compelling lessons of organizational success that inspire new ideas for effecting change and turning around failing schools.

The pathway we pursue to meet those assessment and building objectives is as follows. In Part I, we construct a comprehensive framework for understanding organizational turnaround and scaffolding that we spotlight in Figure 1.1. All the central elements found in later chapters are introduced here. Parts II through IV are devoted to exploring the pieces of the framework in considerable detail, again relying on the research on organizational turnaround in a wide array of industries and in an assortment of organizations in the private, public, and nonprofit sectors of the economy. Part V attends to what is known about turnaround in the PreK–12 education industry.

We begin in Chapter 1 by examining the theoretical, empirical, and applied literature on organizational decline. We provide an overview of the concept, explore key elements, examine functions, and review models. In a similar fashion, we unpack the constructs of organizational failure and turnaround. In particular, we underscore the three distinct ways the concept of turnaround is treated in the literature— as a condition, as a process, and as a consequence. We also surface the two-phase model of turnaround that grounds the volume: retrenchment and recovery. We close the introductory chapter with an inspection of an assortment of important themes (e.g., context) that are ribboned throughout the book.

In Part II (Chapters 2–5), we offer an in-depth inspection of the period of disintegration in the turnaround story. This includes from the time when early warning signs of trouble begin to surface through the emergence of organizational crisis and failure. We explore in considerable detail the following key constructs: symptoms of decline, causes of organizational decline and failure, emergence of crisis, and dysfunctional reactions to disintegration and the accompanying negative consequences to individuals and the organization.

In Parts III and IV, we shift to the topic of reintegration and to the work of turning around troubled organizations. Phase 1 (Chapters 6 and 7) of reintegration is known most generally as the period of retrenchment. The focus here is on measures designed to prevent the final collapse of the institution. The three most critical activities in the retrenchment phase are as follows: getting the right leadership on board; diagnosing the situation; and taking emergency action, especially in terms of finances. Phase 2 of the turnaround is known as recovery. It is comprised of five sets of actions, each of which is thoroughly examined in Chapters 8 and 9: developing a focused operational vision, capturing operating efficiencies, revitalizing organizational processes, reconstructing the organizational work ethic, and improving products and services.

In the final section of the book (Part V), we review what is known about turnaround work in the PreK–12 educational sector. We begin in Chapter 10 by populating the landscape of school turnaround, acknowledging that our efforts are hindered by the recency of turnaround work in schools and the promulgation of turnaround strategies unanchored in the theoretical and empirical scholarship reviewed in Parts I–IV of this volume. Chapter 10 opens with a broad overview of turnaround in education. It then provides an analysis of the causes of decline and failure in schools. It closes with the articulation of three lenses that can be employed to view turnaround in education—type, level, and intensity. Using the same lenses, in Chapter 11 we inspect the efficacy of turnaround initiatives in schools, acknowledging at the outset that our task was made problematic by the limited supply of empirical data at hand and by the oftentimes less-than-robust methods employed to assess the impact of turnaround initiatives.

We believe that our findings will be of interest to a diverse group of educators and policymakers. All those with an interest in the impact of systemic accountability will find the book of use. So also will those who include educational reform and school improvement in their work portfolio. Colleagues in states and districts charged with crafting turnaround initiatives and tools will be drawn to the conclusions unearthed from business firms and government agencies. Finally, the large cadre of developers who work to translate scholarship into useful frames for PreK–12 educators will find an abundant supply of building material herein.

About the Authors

Joseph Murphy is Professor of Education and Associate Dean at Peabody College of Education at Vanderbilt University. He has also been a faculty member at the University of Illinois and The Ohio State University, where he was the William Ray Flesher Professor of Education.

In the public schools, he has served as an administrator at the school, district, and state levels, including an appointment as the Executive Assistant to the Chief Deputy Superintendent of Public Instruction in California. His most recent appointment was as the Founding President of the Ohio Principals Leadership Academy. At the university level, he has served as department chair and associate dean.

He is past vice president of the American Educational Research Association and was the founding chair of the Interstate School Leaders Licensure Consortium (ISLLC). He is coeditor of the AERA *Handbook on Educational Administration* (1999) and editor of the National Society for the Study of Education (NSSE) yearbook, *The Educational Leadership Challenge* (2002).

His work is in the area of school improvement, with special emphasis on leadership and policy. He has authored or coauthored 16 books in this area and edited another 11. His most recent authored volumes include *The Quest for a Center: Notes on the State of the Profession of School* (1999), *The Productive High School* (2001), *Understanding and Assessing the Charter School Movement* (2002), *Leadership for Literacy: Research-Based Practice, PreK–3* (2003), *Connecting Teacher Leadership and School Improvement* (2005), and *Preparing School Leaders: Defining a Research and Action Agenda* (2006).

Coby V. Meyers is a doctoral student in the Leadership, Policy, and Organizations program at Vanderbilt University. His current research interests include school improvement, sociology of education, and Islamic school education. Previously, he taught middle school and high school English at an Islamic school in the Chicago suburbs.

PART I

An Introduction

At some time during their history, most companies are likely to face a turnaround situation. Whether they then recover their vitality, continue to stagnate, or disappear depends on whether their management can effect the turnaround successfully. (Bibeault, 1982, p. 1)

A turnaround is a bifurcation point in the life of an organization, a point of system instability, a point at which the organization has to make a choice about its future. (Ashmos & Duchon, 1998, p. 234)

The search for some general strategic principles behind turnaround action is of some significance and considerable scholarly interest. (O'Neill, 1981, p. 1)

CHAPTER ONE

A Framework for Understanding Turnaround

The history of successful turnarounds provides many lessons for those involved in management. (Zimmerman, 1991, p. 7)

We can learn a lot from studying and analyzing failure. As with any pathology, it shows us what causes death and what to avoid. (Shuchman & White, 1995, p. 13)

In this introductory chapter, we undertake a series of assignments that are intended to illuminate the broad topic of turning around failing organizations. We begin with a short section that delineates the two guiding principles that furnish the rationale for the book and overviews some of the conceptual fuzziness we confront on our journey to understanding. The second section lays out the model of organizational turnaround that provides the scaffolding for the entire volume—a design that is forged from the raw material provided by leading academics and practitioners in the fields of organizational decline and recovery. Next, we highlight three key concepts at the heart of the model—decline, failure, and turnaround. We close with an introduction to some key themes that resurface throughout the book. In Chapters 2 and 3, we unpack the symptoms and causes of organizational decline and failure.

SETTING THE STAGE

The process of inducing major and sustained improvements in companies that are stagnating is of fundamental and lasting importance. (Grinyer & McKiernan, 1990, p. 131)

Nothing illuminates like failure. (Smith, 1963, p. 13)

Rationale

Although these studies generally are couched in the language of business and management, the issues addressed are in many ways common to any human endeavor. (Crandall, 1995, p. 17)

Two principles provide the rationale for this volume. The first is that understanding should precede evaluation and action. What makes this point so salient is that nearly all the turnaround literature in education leaps from problems (e.g., failure) to solutions (e.g., adoption of whole-school reform models) with remarkably little effort to understand the reasons schools and districts are failing. At best, solution strategies are grounded in some macro-level theory of action about reform, for example, that competition via markets (e.g., choice) will encourage (or force) failing schools to improve, and if they do not, they will find their warrant to continue operations in question if not withdrawn outright. At worst, they are unanchored answers that somehow get linked with a pressing problem (decline) with little evidence to believe that they will be effective in spearheading a turnaround in a school or district.

Our second guiding rationale is that PreK–12 education can learn a good deal about how to successfully turn around failing schools by carefully studying work afoot in other industries and organizations. Specifically, a large and growing body of literature is now available that helps us see how churches, hospitals, universities, government entities, for-profit firms, and nonprofit organizations have successfully and unsuccessfully engaged recovery efforts. Yet these insights are conspicuous by their absence from the education turnaround literature. Indeed, there is an insularity and parochialism in the turnaround literature in education that is as arrogant as it is ill advised. Our message is that there are lessons from turning around other institutions (e.g., the New York City Police Department) that can help us more effectively undertake recovery work in failing schools. This book is dedicated to ferreting out these lessons.

Current State of Understanding

Public service turnaround is a topic of huge practical significance. (Boyne, 2004, p. 102)

In this section, we examine three topics that inform our understanding of turnarounds writ large. We provide a note on the importance of investigating turnarounds. We discuss the level of conceptual clarity in the literature. And we portray the state of research knowledge on turnarounds.

Importance

We start by providing an obvious corollary from our remarks on the rationale for this volume. That is, since "most companies will experience severe adversity" (Zimmerman, 1991, p. 27) or "downturns in performance at some time in their lives" (Ford, 1985, p. 770), there is a good deal to be learned from studying turnarounds, from decline through recovery or failure. Or, as Hambrick and Schecter (1983) capture it, "turnarounds are of increasing relevance" (p. 23). To begin with, "studying failure to avoid failure . . . make[s] a lot of sense" (Bibeault, 1982, p. 7)—"the lessons learned in failure temper the personal character and abilities of us all" (p. 7). Indeed, a number of turnaround scholars and turnaround managers underscore the place that studying failure can play in the learning process. For example, Sutton, Eisenhardt, and Jucker (1986) maintain that "lessons of quality can be learned by examining failures" (p. 29). "Examining success," they assert, "encourages imitation. But examining failure encourages invention" (p. 29). And turnaround specialist Bibeault (1982) declares that "those of us entrusted with the management of a . . . business have a particular responsibility to learn from the past mistakes of others" (p. 7). Second, there is much knowledge to be gleaned from "the study of attempts to rescue failing organizations" (O'Neill, 1986b, p. 80). Finally, considerable wisdom can be culled from investigations of successful turnaround efforts (e.g., Bratton & Knobler, 1998; Gerstner, 2002).

The broad goal of all of this work is to understand the turnaround phenomenon. Specific objectives include developing strategies for "predicting failure" (Argenti, 1976, p. 122), "preventing failure before it occurs" (O'Neill, 1981, p. 19), and addressing decline and failure once the virus of organizational deterioration has spread: "We are interested in what management can do to spot and avoid declines in the first place, or turn the firm around once a decline is experienced" (Schendel, Patton, & Riggs, 1976, p. 3). The aim is the development of "some useful preventative or curative ideas" (Argenti, 1976, p. 122), "social turnaround principles" (Zimmerman, 1991, p. 289), and productive "enactment strategies" (Chesley & Huff, 1998, p. 178)—methods and insights that "are as applicable to service providers as they are to manufacturers" (Zimmerman, 1991, p. 289) and to the government sector as to the private sector.

The importance of studying and learning from turnarounds is heightened when we add the knowledge that today, despite the claims that "the history of turnarounds is an encouraging one" (Zimmerman, 1991, p. 7), "any organization can be rescued from a death spiral and then rise higher than it has ever been before" (Rindler, 1987, p. 222), and "despite impressive examples of recovery, the majority of turnaround efforts fail" (Chesley & Huff, 1998, p. 178). Specifically, the literature reveals that "traditional turnaround efforts result in failure far more often than in success" (Pearce & Robbins, 1993, p. 613) and that "most attempts to save a severely troubled business do not succeed" (Shuchman & White, 1995, p. 16). According to Slatter (1984), on average about one in four companies "manage[s] successful recovery" (p. 19; see also O'Shaughnessy, 1995, p. 5). Shuchman and White (1995) peg the success rate even lower, at about 10% (p. 16).

Conceptual Clarity

Wherever one looks in the turnaround literature, ideas and concepts appear somewhat opaque, and even "simplistic and sterile" (Greenhalgh, 1983, p. 232). As we report in more detail later, there is considerable ambiguity about the concepts at the heart of the turnaround literature. Speaking about *decline,* for example, Whetten (1988a) observes that "there is little agreement in this literature on the definition of organizational decline" (p. 33): "Confusion exists about the definition of organizational decline. The conceptual boundaries of decline . . . have been neither consensual nor clear" (Cameron, Sutton, & Whetten, 1988, p. 5) nor "consistent" (Cameron, Kim, & Whetten, 1988, p. 208). The failure to distinguish between organizational and environmental decline adds still another "source of confusion" (p. 208) to the literature on decline.

Turning to financial distress, a concept at the heart of *failure,* Renn and Kirk (1993) disclose that "there is no generally accepted definition of the term or a precise consensus as to what it means. Nor is there any recognized or reliable litmus test that can be applied to reveal a failing financial condition" (p. 20). Moreover, Anheier and Moulton affirm that "failure is a relative concept" (1999b, p. 273), that "failure is relative to notions of success as well as to organizational maintenance . . . [and] failure implies an underlying question that analysts must bring to the forefront: a failure for whom?" (1999a, p. 14). And, as we see later in this section, these same analysts exercise considerable discretion in "choos[ing] from a wide array of performance referents" (Short, Palmer, & Stimpert, 1998, p. 171) in arriving at an understanding of failure.

Redirecting the spotlight to *turnarounds,* Slatter (1984) concludes that "there is no hard-and-fast definition of what constitutes a turnaround situation" (p. 13); there is "no single definition" (p. 18). Shuchman and White (1995) deepen our understanding of this condition when they disclose that a "review of the literature in this field shows that there is no unifying theory of turnarounds, no common taxonomy or classification system or even a universally accepted lexicon of terms" (p. 14). On the backside of turnarounds, Slatter (1984) also divulges that "it is difficult to define what we mean by corporate recovery" (p. 15). According to Lohrke and Bedeian (1998), all this "vagueness in terminology has arguably obscured both the essential turnaround processes being implemented and the successfulness of the ensuing results" (p. 10). Likewise, "the definition of organizational death is not without its difficulties" (Hager, Galaskiewicz, Bielefeld, & Pins, 1999, p. 53), and its links with organizational failure are not always clear (Meyer & Zucker, 1989).

Crispness of understanding is also blurred because academics and practitioners in the turnaround field employ a large assortment of terms to cover overlapping sections of the same intellectual terrain, sometimes without helping travelers see the uniqueness of each parcel and the boundaries between and among the sections. For example, the turnaround literature is laden with concepts such as stagnation, performance downturn, troubled firm, financially distressed organization, insolvency, collapse, retrenchment, inertia, unhealthy institution, and so forth that cross back and forth among themselves (Argenti, 1976).

Seeds of confusion have also been sown to some extent because all these "phenomena are semantic (rather than natural) classifications" (Chowdhury & Lang, 1993, p. 14). They necessitate "judgment" (p. 14). Also, scholars have pulled together knowledge of turnarounds from "varied settings" (Lohrke & Bedeian, 1998, p. 10) and from organizations "facing varying conditions of decline" (p. 10). The operationalization and measurement of these concepts in varied research studies have also contributed to conceptual fuzziness (Cameron, Kim, & Whetten, 1988; Cameron, Sutton, & Whetten, 1988).

Strength of Research Foundations

Perhaps a good summative statement on the scholarship on turnarounds would read as follows: "While turnaround management is drawing increased attention from researchers and managers alike" (Chakraborty & Dixit, 1992, p. 345), and "in spite of the interest in reversing decline, the topic of turnaround has not been subjected to the rigors of systematic research as often and as carefully as the subject's importance demands" (O'Neill, 1986b, p. 80): "The ecology of organizational decline looks more like a desert than a horticultural showplace" (McKelvey, 1988, pp. 399–340). As Greenhalgh (1983) relates, "decline is possibly the least understood of the important organizational phenomena" (p. 265). Or more recently from Boyne (2004), "despite its huge practical significance the sources of organizational failure and recovery have received scant attention by public management researchers" (p. 102). Indeed, analysts reveal how researchers and practitioners "seem to have been drawn to think almost exclusively about strategic planning for strong firms—to the detriment of knowledge building on the management of troubled or declining businesses" (Pearce & Robbins, 1993, p. 614). Until recently, "organizational researchers and theorists have based their perspectives of organizations on assumptions of growth, and decline has been ignored as a phenomenon" (Cameron, 1983, p. 361): "Researchers have instead given most of their attention to organizations that are adapting well" (Greenhalgh, 1983, p. 234). Business schools in particular "have long neglected the subject of turnarounds" (Goldstein, 1988, p. 44), and until relatively recently, "very few books [were] written on the important subject of business turnarounds" (Goldstein, 1988, p. vii). Argenti (1976) first surfaced these points in his state-of-the-art portrait around 1980:

There are few serious writers in this field. The fashion in management literature for the past two decades has been to concentrate on go-go performance and how to achieve it. While it was right that this should be so, and it still is, it is nevertheless extraordinary that so little should have been written about failure and how to avoid it. (p. 22)

If a manager wishes to learn the rudiments of business finance, or the details of a sales incentive scheme, or the principles of merger planning, or the mathematics of linear programming, he may consult a dozen different books, attend a dozen different lectures, consult a dozen different experts. If he wishes to know about failure and its symptoms or causes, its prevention or cure, his choice is negligible. (p. 3)

To be sure, it is only in the last quarter century that "organizational decline and turnaround emerge[d] as subjects of systematic research" (Ford, 1985, p. 770) and the problems of the "striking lack of any integrated framework for the subject" (Argenti, 1976, p. 49) in play around 1980 began to be addressed (Cameron, Kim, & Whetten, 1988). And "although there has been an increase in scholarly interest and writing on the subject of organizational mortality or failure, little of this has dealt systematically with nonprofit organizations" (Hager et al., 1999, p. 51). More to the point here, "little academic theory or evidence on public sector organizations is available to help national bodies and local service providers in their quest for turnaround strategies" (Boyne, 2004, p. 97).

While we have progressed beyond the "rudimentary knowledge of the pathogenesis of failure, its diagnosis and its prognosis" (Argenti, 1976, p. 169) that characterized the field 30 years ago, the turnaround area is still plagued by a number of important problems. "The paucity" (Cameron, Kim, & Sutton, 1988, p. 207) of the overall research base has already been highlighted, resulting in a "state of the art in theory and research [that] appears to be quite primitive" (Greenhalgh, 1983, p. 234). As with research in many new domains of study, "the literature [here] is uneven, and to a large extent, noncumulative" (Cameron, Kim, & Sutton, 1988, p. 207): "The large majority of published studies on this subject are theoretical treatises, proposed frameworks, descriptions of the experiences of single organizations or individuals, or analyses of demographic trends"

(Cameron, Whetten, & Kim, 1987, p. 126). The extant body of research is not especially impressive (Boyne, 2004). For example, there are few "large scale studies of multiple organizations experiencing decline" (Cameron, Whetten, & Kim, 1987, p. 126). "Integration of the research has also been lacking" (Lohrke & Bedeian, 1998, p. 4). For all of these reasons, "empirical studies of turnaround contain many contradictory results" (Boyne, 2004, p. 98), and "the study of business turnaround is without a unifying theory to guide its advancement" (Pearce & Robbins, 1993, p. 614).

Not surprisingly, while the skill to turn around failing organizations is no longer seen "as a sort of black magic" (Bibeault, 1982, p. xv) and we have progressed beyond "folklore on how to revive poorly performing businesses" (Hambrick & Schecter, 1983, p. 231), the literature still "offers practicing managers limited guidance for reversing or turning around a decline in a firm's performance" (Lohrke & Bedeian, 1998, p. 4): "Few consistent prescriptions are currently available in extant turnaround research" (Lohrke & Bedeian, 1998, p. 16), beyond the general notion that "the key to successful turnarounds is the visible hand of management" (Bibeault, 1982, p. 3).

The Turnaround Framework: An Overview

The turnaround process occurs after a period of decline [and] the literature on failure exhibits some clues about the nature of the decline process. (O'Neill, 1981, p. 18)

A portrait of the turnaround narrative chronicled in the remainder of this volume is presented in Figure 1.1 (see also Armenakis & Fredenberger, 1998, p. 41; Ford, 1983, p. 15; and Pearce & Robbins, 1993, p. 624). In the model, time flows from left to right. At the top of the figure, that flow unfolds across four time zones. Period 1 represents a state of success, or at least stability. Period 2 encompasses the time when the factors that push an organization into a turnaround situation begin to occupy center stage. Period 3 includes the time when actions in response to decline, failing status, and crisis that are designed to stabilize the organization are brought into play. Period 4 is the end game in the turnaround narrative, either recovery or death. Looking at the bottom of Figure 1.1, we see that Period 2 can be described as the disintegration phase in the turnaround story, while Period 3 represents the attempted reintegration/regeneration phase of the turnaround process.

Figure 1.1 Model of Organizational Turnaround

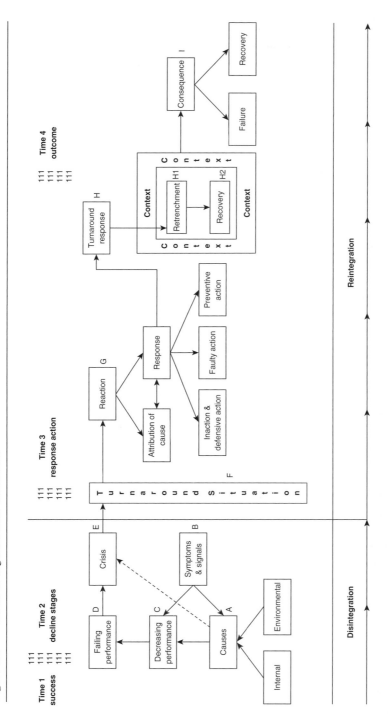

11

Turning to the dynamics of the model, the story begins at the lower left-hand corner [A] when a factor or set of factors (i.e., causes) from the organization's environment or from inside the institution pushes the organization onto the path of decline. Symptoms [B] with the potential to alert managers to the presence of problems, if not to the actual nature of the causes of the downturn, are generally visible here. These warning signals are also in play through the decline process itself. Decline [C] is defined as important decreases in performance, a condition that creates additional problems and often minor crises in the organization. Unchecked or responded to inappropriately [C→D] (e.g., faulty action), decline continues through somewhat predictable stages until performance, and the institution, can be characterized as failing [D]. Failing performance in turn produces a crisis [E], and the organization finds itself in a turnaround situation [F], a condition that has critical consequences for the organization and its members.

All previous management interventions—to alleviate symptoms, to tackle causes, or to address initial decline—were undertaken to prevent the firm from reaching a turnaround situation. Now management action is employed in an attempt to save the organization by implementing a turnaround strategy. The starting point is reaction to the troubled state of affairs [G], beginning with the attribution of causes and carrying through to responses—either potentially damaging responses (e.g., blaming and scapegoating) or more productive endeavors that we can label the turnaround strategy [H].

Turnaround strategy generally features action on two fronts, retrenchment actions [H1] to address immediate, often life-threatening, problems and recovery activities [H2] designed to restore the health of the organization. The recovery stage of turnaround is itself comprised of two dimensions, efficiency or operational actions and entrepreneurial or strategic actions. As can be seen in the square surrounding the phases of the turnaround response in Figure 1.1, context, defined in an assortment of ways, is a critical variable in the turnaround equation. Finally, turnaround activities are linked to outcomes [I]: the restoration or stabilization of the formerly troubled firm or failure, the inability of the organization to recover and survive.

DISINTEGRATION AND TURNAROUND: KEY ELEMENTS

Stagnation and turnaround is a significant topic in policy research.
(Schendel & Patton, 1976, p. 241)

Organizations that get into trouble do not cope with the serious internal challenges created by change. (Bibeault, 1982, p. 17)

Organizations fail and they fail in important ways. (Clarke & Perrow, 1999, p. 179)

Disintegration

Decline

As seen in Figure 1.1, disintegration is the period leading up to the turnaround situation, the time in which the organization confronts problems, begins to decline, and becomes a failing entity. As conveyed earlier, decline and failure as "area[s] of conceptual and empirical scholarship" (Meyer, 1988, p. 411) date from the tail end of the 1970s (Meyer, 1988; Whetten, 1988a). Starting with Greenhalgh's (1983) admonition that "a first priority for researchers . . . is to develop a satisfactory operational definition of organizational decline" (p. 266), we observe that scholars have begun to offer "a wide variety of possible definitions" (Cameron, Sutton, & Whetten, 1988, p. 5) and have started to conceive of the concept in a multitude of ways. On the first issue, the following are representative examples of definitions of organizational decline:

Organizational decline is a condition in which a substantial, absolute decrease in an organization's resource base occurs over a specified period of time. (Cameron, Kim, & Whetten, 1988, p. 209)

Organizational decline [is] a deterioration in an organization's adaptation to its microniche and the associated reduction of resources within the organization. (Cameron, Sutton, & Whetten, 1988, p. 9)

Decline is a stage in which external and internal needs are not appropriately met and signals warning of the need for a change are ignored. (Weitzel & Jonsson, 1989, p. 93)

[Organizational decline is a] downturn in organizational size or performance that is attributable to change in the size or qualitative nature (shape) of an organization's environmental niche. (McKinley, cited in Sutton, 1990, p. 208)

Decline [is] a pattern of decrease over time in a firm's internal resources as measured by an index of internal resource munificence. (D'Aveni, 1989, p. 598)

On the second front, conceptualizations of the concept, Cameron, Sutton, and Whetten (1988) and Weitzel and Jonsson (1989) provide helpful summaries. According to Cameron, Sutton, and Whetten (1988), decline can be "characterized as shrinking markets and increased competition, as budget cuts, as workforce reduction—especially layoffs, as loss of legitimacy, maladaptation to a shrinking environment, stagnation, and deteriorating and unsatisfactory organizational performance that causes members and clients to become disgruntled" (p. 6). Similarly, Weitzel and Jonsson (1989) assert that decline can be

conceived of as (1) a reduction in some organizational size measure (e.g., market share, asset(s), (2) a stage in the organization's life cycle, (3) internal stagnation, or inefficiency, (4) a failure to recognize warning signals (internal or external) about changes needed to remain competitive, and (5) a failure to adapt or change to fit external environmental demands. (p. 94)

For purposes of organization, it is productive to partition decline into two principal meanings. Here we observe that decline is used first "to denote a cutback in the size of an organization's workforce, profits, budget, clients, and so forth. In this case, an organization's command over environmental resources has been reduced as the result of either decreased competitive advantage . . . or decreased environmental munificence" (Whetten, 1988b, p. 153). This "lack of growth" (Levine, 1978, p. 317) perspective attends to two issues, "decline as stagnation and decline as cutback" (Weitzel & Jonsson, 1989, p. 93). Stagnation reflects the inability to grow or move forward (see Whetten, 1988a, 1988b). In the private sector, it denotes sluggish movement on the resource front. In the public sector, it refers to "stalled social structures" (Anheier & Romo, 1999, p. 241): "Decline as stagnation is evidenced by organizations that are bureaucratic, passive, and insensitive" (Weitzel & Jonsson, 1989, p. 93). Stagnant organizations become "bureaucratic and passive as evidenced by their insensitivity to new product developments, workers' interests, and customers' preferences" (Whetten, 1988b, p. 153).

Decline as cutback indicates a "reduction of internal resources" (Cameron, Sutton, & Whetten, 1988, p. 9), the "subtract[ion] of levels of resources at one point in time from levels at a later point in time" (p. 8). It refers to "decreasing internal resource munificence over time with respect to two critical resources: financial and human resources" (D'Aveni, 1989, p. 578). "Financial deterioration" (Renn & Kirk, 1993, p. 14), in turn, has been operationalized in an assortment of ways: declines in revenues (Cameron, Kim, & Whetten, 1988; Cameron, Whetten, & Kim, 1987) and/or sales (Grinyer, Mayes, & McKiernan, 1988); downward turns on "return on equity" (Lubatkin & Chung, 1985, p. 27) or "return on total assets" (Lohrke & Bedeian, 1998, p. 8) or "invested capital" (Barker & Duhaime, 1997, p. 21); "deteriorating profits" (Bibeault, 1982, p. 10); reductions in "net income" (O'Neill, 1981, p. 1); and "decreases in budget" (Whetten, 1988a, p. 33). Without delving into specific measures, it is clear that financial distress means a "substantial negative slope in a resource curve over a specified period of time, not just a slight depression" (Cameron, Kim, & Whetten, 1988, p. 209). Resource decline is also associated with "decreases in the number of organizational personnel" (Ford, 1980, p. 590). Or as Greenhalgh (1983) observes, workforce size is a "leading candidate to operationalize decline" (p. 266).

The second meaning of decline highlights "reduced adaptation to the organization's environment" (Greenhalgh, 1983, p. 267; also Sutton, 1990): "In this definition, decline is defined as the opposite of successful adaptation" (Weitzel & Jonsson, 1989, p. 92). That is, "decline occurs when an organization becomes less adapted to its environment" (Barker & Patterson, 1996, p. 2), is "out of step with its environment" (Sutton, Eisenhardt, & Jucker, 1986, p. 28), and is "unable to adjust to environmental changes" (Cameron & Whetten, 1988, p. 46). Greenhalgh (1983) provides the following synopsis of the environmental adaptation definition of decline:

> Organizational decline is viewed as deterioration in the organization's adaptation to its environment. Decline occurs when the organization fails to maintain the adaptiveness of its response to a stable environment, or when it fails to either broaden or increase its domination of a niche which has diminishing carrying capacity. (p. 232)

These organizations "become incapable of maintaining resiliency" (Cameron & Whetten, 1988, p. 46). They "are unable to compete successfully for a shrinking resource base" (Whetten, 1988a, p. 34) as the environmental niche contracts, or they "fail to shift into new activities" (p. 34) in a redefined niche.

Scholars of turnarounds also establish the boundaries of decline as a concept by attempting to separate it from related concepts. For example, Cameron, Sutton, and Whetten (1988) posit that "decline can be distinguished from . . . retrenchment" (p. 8). D'Aveni (1989) also shows that decline is not a synonym for "downsizing organizational operations" (p. 578). Relatedly, and as we discuss in more detail below, analysts reveal that decline is a relative term. For example, moving downward in absolute terms while holding one's place (e.g., in terms of market share) in a declining industry does not register as decline for a specific firm. Finally, Cameron, Sutton, and Whetten (1988) assert that "decline can be distinguished from turbulence, scarcity, and organizational ineffectiveness" (p. 8).

Before drilling more deeply into the literature on decline, a few notes are in order to set up our discussion of failing schools in the last part of the book. First, for organizations, "decline can be based in an industry contraction or be grounded in firm-specific problems. Industry contraction-anchored decline occurs when a firm's industry shrinks in size or munificence. . . . Firm-based decline usually occurs when a firm exists in a stable or growing industry but is maladapted, performing worse than the average for the industry" (Barker & Duhaime, 1997, p. 18). Second, periods of significant change and evolution, for example, the shift from an industrial to a postindustrial world, "impose greater risks of decline than periods of stability" (Bibeault, 1982, p. 22). Third, public organizations are less subject to the dynamics of decline than are private firms, especially large public organizations (Cameron, Whetten, & Kim, 1987): "Organizational dysfunctions of decline appear to be greater in privately controlled organizations" (p. 136). Fourth, at its core, decline is linked to managerial action or inaction. That is, "decline begins when an organization fails to anticipate or recognize and respond to any deterioration of organizational performance that threatens long-term survival" (Weitzel & Jonsson, 1989, p. 94).

Because decline and failure are "very relative term[s] and do not exist in the abstract" (Goldstein, 1988, p. 7), analysts contextualize definitions through presentations of measures of decline. For example, Cummings (1988) proposes that "decline can be defined as [an] aspirational comparative" (p. 418). Here the metric is how well the organization performs relative to how well the organization should perform.

Also, as noted above, decline can be assessed by the place a firm enjoys vis-à-vis other firms in the same industry (Grinyer, Mayes, & McKiernan, 1988; O'Neill, 1981), "competitive decline" (Pearce & Robbins, 1993, p. 616), or "declines relative to industry performance" (Pearce & Robbins, 1994b, p. 410). For example, in his study of turnarounds in the banking industry, O'Neill (1981) reported that "when a bank's net income increased at a lesser rate than industry net income, the bank's performance for that year [was] recorded as a decline" (pp. 1–2). Cameron, Sutton, and Whetten (1988) come at the industry performance issue from a slightly different angle. They assert that "if an organization is part of an industry characterized by shrinking consumer demand, it cannot be described as 'declining' if it is maintaining sales by increasing its market share" (p. 7).

Less comprehensively, "decline can be conceived relative to other organizations . . . that fall within a set of relevant comparisons" (Cummings, 1988, p. 418). Finally, and as a special case of judging decline against one's own performance, there is the concept of "decline as stagnation" (Cameron, Whetten, & Kim, 1987, p. 135) and "decline as stalemate" (Anheier & Romo, 1999, p. 242). Based on research by Whetten and Cameron and other colleagues who find that "the negative attributes . . . associated with decline are actually characteristics of both stable and declining organizations" (Cameron, Whetten, & Kim, 1987, p. 135), analysts sometimes hold that decline can be conceptualized as plateaued performance.

Turnaround analysts also address the issues of decline speed and stages of decline. On the topic of rate of decline, or what Cameron and Zammuto (1988) describe as "the continuity with which decline occurs" (p. 120), reviewers report the presence of both "gradual decline and sudden decline" (D'Aveni, 1989, p. 579): "That is, a decline in the availability of resources can occur suddenly or there can be a sustained, continuous decline in resource availability" (Cameron & Zammuto, 1988, p. 120). Reviewers also suggest that "while failures can be abrupt and sudden [see Figure 1.1] . . . they typically involve a drawn out process characterized by various attempts to rescue the organization" (Anheier & Moulton, 1999b, p. 277) and they follow a "long downward path" (Argenti, 1976, p. 149)—although there are hints in the literature that the speed with which organizations may be hitting the skids may be on the rise (Goldstein, 1988).

Scholars of decline and failure—disintegration in Figure 1.1— depict the phenomena as phased or staged, in terms of distinct periods in the march to finding oneself in a turnaround situation (Castrogiovanni, Bahga, & Kidwell, 1992; Shuchman & White, 1995; Weitzel & Jonsson, 1989). They also make the point that interventions in the earlier stages are easier to engage and, if done well, more likely to be efficacious than if applied when the downward spiral has gained momentum (Hegde, 1982; Lorange & Nelson, 1987): "As with cancer, the earlier the recognition, the higher the probability of survival. Early recognition is critical because, without it, a company may survive but never flourish again" (Bibeault, 1982, p. 82)— "the earlier the stage that the turnaround symptoms are properly diagnosed, the better the probability of achieving a successful prognosis" (Sloma, 1985, p. 34). In a related vein, scholars maintain that a sharp decline leading to crisis is more likely to trigger turnaround efforts than will slow stagnation (Schendel & Patton, 1976; Zimmerman, 1991).

Sutton (1990) and his colleagues (Cameron, Sutton, & Whetten, 1988) model a two-step process of organizational decline, one "first characterized by deterioration of adaptation to the microniche, and then followed by reduction of resources in the organization" (p. 208). Castrogiovanni, Bahga, and Kidwell (1992) present a five-stage model of decline:

> The "blinded" stage (stage 1) is the time when the weaknesses start to surface, although their effects on profits are not yet felt. In the "inaction" stage (stage 2), these problems persist and initial declines in profits occur. During the "faulty action" stage (stage 3), both weaknesses and profit declines continue, and the duration and severity of these problems make it clear to most observers that the business is in trouble. Eventually, problem severity may increase to a "crisis" stage (stage 4) of decline, and finally to a "dissolution" stage (stage 5). (p. 28)

Goldstein's (1988) model posits decline (and failure) unfolding through four phases:

> Companies, then, move through several stages on their way to failure. The first stage encompasses faulty management decisions

or failure to respond to change that weakens its strategic position. [In] the second stage of decline, operational and financial symptoms become clearer. Sales slip further as more customers are lost; advertising, promotion, and new product development may be cut back; morale within the organization dips, and the financially weak company begins to experience more chronic economic difficulties. This second stage is best characterized by a shift from positive, long-term thinking to a preoccupation with short-term operational problems. As the company advances to the third stage, it shifts to a defensive position. Losses mount, inventories dwindle, credit is curtailed, and cash flow becomes increasingly scarce. Finally, the company enters the fourth and terminal stage—a point from which few recover. (p. 34)

Failure

We begin our short discussion of failure with the same caveat we surfaced when examining decline, that is, "failure is a relative term" (Richards, cited in O'Neill, 1981, p. 20):

No two people think of "failure" in precisely the same terms. A firm can be characterized as a managerial failure, financial failure, or legal failure. Although these terms are sometimes used interchangeably, they have distinctively different meanings. A company can be a managerial failure long before it is a financial failure. And it can linger as a financial failure without ever becoming a legal failure. (Goldstein, 1988, p. 4)

We also observe that "any definition of corporate failure rests on expectations about the future" (Reich & Donohue, 1985, p. 53). Starting there, in this text, and in Figure 1.1, we use failure in two ways. First, failure means "failing," the reality that the enterprise has crossed some organizational performance line in the sand and that unless conditions change fairly dramatically, the firm will cease to function. Failure here "means protracted periods of poor profits and eroding market share" (Miller, 1977, p. 43); it "represents a situation where the realized rate of return on invested capital is significantly and continually lower than prevailing rates on similar investments" (Bibeault, 1982, p. 9), a situation "when the company does not earn an adequate return on risk capital" (Argenti, 1976, p. 49). It includes what Goldstein (1988) identifies as "managerial failure, . . . when the company fails to live up to its own potential" (p. 6) as well as "financial failure, . . . when the enterprise has chronic and serious losses or when the organization becomes insolvent with liabilities disproportionate to the assets" (p. 6). This is what we label in Figure 1.1 as a "turnaround situation."

Second, failure means "failed" and usually implies "the death of the organization" (Zammuto & Cameron, 1985, p. 236). In Figure 1.1, this is the end result of an unsuccessful turnaround effort. Here we "refer to a company whose performance is so poor that sooner or later it is bound to have to call in the receiver or cease to trade or go into voluntary liquidation" (Argenti, 1976, p. 6).

Meyer (1999) reminds us that there are at least three "dimensions of organizational failure" (p. 40): "(1) *technical* failure, or the inability to achieve and maintain economic efficiency in required transactions; (2) *political* failure, or the inability to achieve and maintain legitimacy among strategic constituencies; and (3) *cultural* failure, or the inability to achieve and maintain ideological bases" (p. 210). Thus failure can be a "matter of economic efficiency, . . . or low organizational performance on goal attainment" (Anheier & Moulton, 1999b, p. 279), or political dynamics. In a similar vein, Anheier and Moulton (1999b) maintain there are

> . . . four relatively distinct approaches to the study of failure. The first approach, *organizational* studies, looks at creation, growth, decline, and death as part of the organizational life cycle and emphasize the "fit" between organizational management and performance on the one hand and environmental conditions and changes on the other. According to the *political* perspective, organizations are seen as primarily political, rather than economic, entities that compete for advantages within a larger political economy inhabited by different institutions and constituencies. Legitimacy serves as the major explanatory variable in understanding organizational failures. In the *cognitive* approach, we emphasize aspects of definitions and perception of failure and focus on cultural blueprints and dispositions for declaring and managing breakdowns and other organizational catastrophes. Finally, the *structural* approach locates failures in the social fabric or relational patterns of organizations and institutions and stresses the combinatorial logic underlying different failure tendencies. (p. 273)

Miles (1980), in turn, argues that "we can think of failure with respect to a number of referents: (1) the organization's *form,* (2) the organization's *goals,* and (3) the organization's external *environment*" (p. 441). And finally, according to Arogyaswamy, Barker, and Yasai-Ardekani (1995),

> Decline, if unabated, leads to three consequences: (1) the continual erosion of external stakeholder support, (2) growing internal inefficiencies, and (3) deteriorating internal firm climate and decision processes. A declining firm fails when the combination of these consequences both exhausts the firm's financial resources and causes creditors to withdraw support from the firm. (p. 498)

Scholars of turnaround also shed light on the extent of organizational failure in both of the ways the term is employed herein. They declare (1) that "most organizations, at some time in their lives" (O'Neill, 1981, p. 17) "experience downturns in performance" (Ford, 1985, p. 770); (2) that success is often "fleeting, . . . that success and failure are terms distanced only by time" (Goldstein, 1988, p. 2); (3) that there are many "businesses with 'glass jaws'" (Goldstein, 1988, p. 4)—"that failures are quite common" (Khandwalla, 1983–1984, p. 6), "that failure is more common than success" (O'Neill, 1981, p. 17), and "that business failure and near failure are frequent occurrences" (Miller, 1977, p. 43); (4) that organizational failures are on the rise (Shuchman & White, 1995; Silver, 1992); (5) that new organizations (e.g., charter schools) are particularly receptive to the failure virus; indeed, "well over half of all failures are companies that are less than five years old" (Argenti, 1976, p. 50), and "about 90% of new businesses formed in a given year will fail within five years" (O'Neill, 1981, p. 17); (6) that, not surprisingly, failure is "greatest in periods of recession and slow economic growth" (Slatter, 1984, p. 18); and (7) that within certain industries "corporate casualties can often be found in stunning numbers" (Goldstein, 1988, p. 2). In summary, "the grim reaper of business is alive and well . . . [and] the corporate half-life is becoming shorter" (p. 1).

We close with perhaps an obvious point but one that needs to be underscored nonetheless. That is, there are real costs and "tragic consequences" (Khandwalla, 1983–1984, p. 7) associated with these "poignant business dramas" (Bibeault, 1982, p. 9), costs most visible in terms of "human suffering" (p. 8).

Turnaround

The economic and social costs of such failures warrants [sic] an explanation of how such losses may be prevented and how declining firms may be made healthy again—in other words, how declining firms may be turned around. (Arogyaswamy & Yasai-Ardekani, 1997, p. 3)

In today's environment of technological change, shifting economies, and increased competition, many firms encounter performance declines that can eventually lead to failure and dissolution. Therefore, developing an understanding of how some firms recover from declining performance is an important task for researchers interested in improving organizational effectiveness. (Arogyaswamy, Barker, & Yasai-Ardekani, 1995, p. 493)

Turnarounds exist in an infinite variety of shades and hues. (Sloma, 1985, p. 13)

In this section, we surface the turnaround concept while reminding the reader that the balance of the book is devoted to a comprehensive exploration of this phenomenon. After a few introductory notes, we furnish a three-part framework to help the reader understand turnarounds. We then turn the spotlight on two key dimensions of turnarounds—performance measures and processes.

Notes

We begin by positioning the reader in the model presented in Figure 1.1. That is, at this point in the narrative, decline has led to the emergence of a "failing company" (Slatter, 1984, p. 13), one usually confronted by a fairly severe crisis. The message here is that "an earnings crises" (Schendel, Patton, & Riggs, 1976, p. 8) or "a severe performance failure is first necessary to motivate turnaround action" (Schendel & Patton, 1976, p. 237) and that "recovery is about the management of firms in crisis" (Slatter, 1984, p. 13). We then layer in the knowledge that this state is actually fairly "widespread" (Schendel, Patton, & Riggs, 1976, p. 4). Or as Chan (1993) asserts, "failing corporations are as much a fact of life as death and taxes" (p. 29), and "the turnaround opportunity should be recognized as a normal part of everyday business life" (Goodman, 1982, p. 9).

Zeroing in on individual organizations, scholars report that "exogenous events cause performance to deteriorate . . . sooner or later in almost all organizations" (Meyer & Zucker, 1989, p. 23): "Most companies during their lifetimes are likely to confront disaster in the absence of willed change. That is, they need a turnaround" (O'Shaughnessy, 1995, p. 3). Scanning across organizations, analysts maintain that each year a good percentage of firms "must perform an organizational turnaround" (McDaniel & Walls, 1998, p. 132). Bibeault (1982) and Boyle and Desai (1991) peg that percentage in the 20 to 30 range, while Goodman (1982) and Schendel and his colleagues (1976) insinuate that it could be even higher.

Consistent with what we reported in our treatments of empirical work on disintegration in general and on decline in particular, we discover that the research base on turnarounds is informative, or "illustrative" (Reich & Donahue, 1985, p. 9), but not deeply developed (Silver, 1992). In particular, given the long-term nature of the turnaround process (discussed below), the infrequent use of longitudinal investigations is troublesome. So too is the regular use of study designs that examine turnarounds "without regard to the causes of the decline" (Barker & Duhaime, 1997, p. 17). Also problematic is a focus on turnaround success "without a sample of turnaround failures for comparison purposes" (Khandwalla, 1983–1984, p. 37). The summative theme here reads as follows: "Despite nearly two decades of turnaround research" (Arogyaswamy, Barker, & Yasai-Ardekani, 1995, p. 493), "there have been few systematic studies on turnaround" (O'Neill, 1986a, p. 167). Thus "the literature offers little in the way of a framework for orchestrating a business turnaround" (Robbins & Pearce, 1992, p. 288) or "mechanics for turning around sick complex organizations" (Khandwalla, 1983–1984, p. 8). As a consequence, "there are many unanswered questions about what characteristics set turnaround firms apart from firms which continue to decline and eventually fail" (Arogyaswamy, Barker, & Yasai-Ardekani, 1995, p. 493) and an inadequate understanding of "the distinct means by which a firm might turn around" (O'Neill, 1986a, p. 167).

Framework

Turnaround as condition. Academics and practitioners help us see that turnaround can be conceptualized in three somewhat overlapping ways. To begin with, turnarounds are often depicted as a "condition" (Armenakis, Fredenberger, Cherones, & Field, 1995, p. 231) or "situation" (Shuchman & White, 1995, p. 17). Second, turnaround is portrayed "as a process" (Short, Palmer, & Stimpert, 1998, p. 155) of returning a troubled firm to health or "attempt[ing] to reverse declining performance" (Barker & Patterson, 1996, p. 306). Finally, turnarounds are pictured as "a consequence, or end state, of successful strategic actions" (Short, Palmer, & Stimpert, 1998, p. 155), as pictures of "firms that have reversed their decline" (Oviatt & Bruton, 1994, p. 130).

Much of the literature addresses turnaround as a condition or situation. Here, turnaround defines "firms in decline" (Oviatt & Bruton, 1994, p. 130) and companies facing a "crisis requiring action" (Kierulff, 1981, p. 490)—those with records of "poor performance" (Hambrick & Schecter, 1983, p. 234), "declining profitability" (Bibeault, 1982, p. 81) or "poor profit pictures" (Slatter, 1984, p. 15), financial troubles (Kierulff, 1981; Silver, 1992; Sloma, 1985), or "hardships" (Chan, 1993, p. 29), "a deteriorating strategic position" (Oviatt & Bruton, 1994, p. 130), "a lost sense of direction" (Crandall, 1995, p. 9), plummeting sales (Goldston, 1992), "excessive liquidation problems" (Bibeault, 1982, p. 2), or "loss of legitimacy" (McDaniel & Walls, 1998, p. 146). Of special significance in this volume is this last point; that is, for professional organizations, "indicators of a need for a turnaround are likely to be indicators of the status of the profession or the professional organization with respect to its legitimacy" (p. 146).

Turnaround as situation "involves a number of negative forces, a general lack of resources, and exceptional time pressures" (Bibeault, 1982, p. 3). There is also a "threat for survival" (Arogyaswamy, Barker, & Yasai-Ardekani, 1995, p. 497): "Survival as a major participant in the industry [is] at stake" (Zimmerman, 1991, p. 23), "the very existence of the company is threatened" (p. 19). Indeed, "in most turnaround strategies . . . the time criticality of the firm's situation is quite severe. There is some imminent danger to survival" (Hofer, 1980, p. 21). Thus in a turnaround situation, "there is no alternative but for the firm to take major measures to alter the long-run potential of the company" (Grinyer, Mayes, & McKiernan, 1988, pp. 130–131).

Historically, "turnaround situations have been discussed either in terms of the areas of organizational performance to be improved or the time criticality of the turnaround situation" (Hofer, 1980,

p. 20). According to Zimmerman (1991), the following criteria "establish a company as a turnaround candidate" (p. 23):

1. *Profitability has declined* from the previous four-year average for a period of at least one year and profitability should not only be low but slipping.

2. *Profitability is either negative or significantly below the industry average* and there are instances when other competitors are clearly able to achieve higher profit rates selling similar products.

3. *Real revenue levels (revenue levels adjusted for inflation) have declined.*

4. *Market position is deteriorating* as represented by a loss in market share, a decline in the number of key distributors or dealers, or price erosion in the company's products.

5. *Investors, board members, or managers* express concerns regarding the condition of the company, and initiate actions in response to these concerns. These concerns commonly coincide with a deterioration in the company's cash position to the point that satisfaction of cash obligations is difficult. (pp. 23–24)

In addition, the following representative definitions of this first conception of turnaround (i.e., condition or situation) have been furnished over the last quarter century:

We use the term here to refer to those firms or operating units . . . whose financial performance indicates that the firm will fail in the foreseeable future unless short-term corrective action is taken. (Slatter, 1984, pp. 13–14)

A turnaround situation is defined as one in which business performance is persistently below some minimally acceptable level. (Hambrick, 1985, p. 10-2)

A turnaround candidate could be defined as a company or business entity faced with a period of crisis sufficiently serious to require a radical improvement in order to remain a significant participant in its major industry. (Zimmerman, 1991, p. 23)

Businesses whose sales and profits have fallen off precipitously and who are considered to be less of a factor in their primary business than they were five years ago [are] true turnaround candidates. (Goldstein, 1988, pp. ix–x)

A turnaround situation exists when a firm encounters multiple years of declining financial performance subsequent to a period of prosperity. (Pearce & Robbins, 1993, p. 623)

We define a turnaround situation as one where a firm suffers declining economic performance for an extended period of time and the actual level of firm performance is low enough that the survival of the firm would be threatened without performance improvement. Thus, by definition, firms in turnaround situations are sustaining resource losses that will cause the firm to fail if unabated. (Arogyaswamy, Barker, & Yasai-Ardekani, 1995, p. 497)

A business turnaround is a situation in which the organization's performance is deemed unacceptable and organizational change is initiated in order to produce improvement quickly. (Armenakis et al., 1995, p. 231)

A turnaround situation is characterized by financial failure and the imminent collapse of a company. (Boyne, 2004, p. 98)

Turnaround as process and consequence. Turnaround is also discussed in terms of "strategic change" and "a new strategic era" (O'Neill, 1986b, p. 87). It is represented as the process of moving from a troubled state to organizational stabilization, the "journey" (Stewart, 1984, p. ix) of the "survival of a troubled company" (Finkin, 1987, p. 57), or, as Barker and Mone (1998) report, "a concerted and organized effort . . . to respond to the firm's performance problems" (p. 1239), to their "firm-threatening performance declines" (Barker & Duhaime, 1997, p. 13). In this context, turnaround refers to "action taken to prevent the occurrence of . . . financial disaster" (Sloma, 1985, p. 11), to "a situation being changed" (Goodman,

1982, p. xix), and to "processes that move the organization from an unacceptably low level of performance to an acceptable level of performance" (McDaniel & Walls, 1998, p. 145).

Finally, turnaround is rendered as an end state, as "recovery" (Schendel, Patton, & Riggs, 1976, p. 3) or as "dramatic performance improvement" (Hegde, 1982, p. 292)—as "a substantial and sustained positive change in the performance of a business," a "regain[ing] of financial strength" (Stewart, 1984, p. 19), and as "sustainable recovery" (Slatter, 1984, p. 118) or the state of being able to make "above average profits in the long term" (p. 118). According to this third perspective (i.e., turnaround as consequence or outcome), a turnaround is "achieved" (Goodman, 1982, p. 110) when "objective indicators of decline [are] arrested" (Henderson, 1993, p. 331) so that "indicators of health predominate over indicators of disease" (Khandwalla, 1983–1984, p. 8). It occurs when "the once-threatened firm's economic performance returns to a profitable level that is . . . sustained over a long period" (Arogyaswamy, Barker, & Yasai-Ardekani, 1995, p. 497) and the institution is revitalized or "restored to a former vitality or brought to new life" (Crandall, 1995, p. 9). Turnaround here is seen "as the art of the possible" (Goodman, 1982, p. 20): "It means to produce a noticeable and durable improvement in performance, to turn around the trend of results from down to up, from not good enough to clearly better, from underachieving to acceptable, from losing to winning" (Goodman, 1982, p. 4). It occurs "when a firm that has experienced sustained performance deterioration is not only able to arrest further decline and avert failure, but is also able to rejuvenate and become healthy again (Arogyaswamy & Yasai-Ardekani, 1997, p. 3) and "sustain that high relative performance over a reasonable period of time so that [it] is now regarded as outstanding in its industries" (Grinyer, Mayes, & McKiernan, 1988, p. 2).

Measures

Since turnarounds "must be judged by improvement in hard performance indicators" (Khandwalla, 1983–1984, p. 39), measurement is an important dimension of attempts to stabilize a failing organization. While handicapped by the knowledge "that organizational performance lies largely ahead" (Meyer, 1999, p. 198), by the fact that analysts "differ with respect to the way they define performance" (O'Neill, 1986a, p. 167), and by the realization "that there exists no universal performance measure or threshold level" (Hambrick & Schecter, 1983, p. 235), measurement nonetheless is at the heart of turnarounds (Contino & Lorusso, 1982).

One aspect of the measurement algorithm is *"what* gets counted." Many analysts maintain that managers should employ "a broad array of measures" (Renn & Kirk, 1993, p. 25) "against a broad array of industry and business developments and trends" (Short, Palmer, & Stimpert, 1998, p. 172); that is, they should privilege "a multidimensional view of performance" (Hambrick & Schecter, 1983, p. 247). A review of the turnaround literature reveals the prevalence of an assortment of high-profile measures. Specifically, Chowdhury and Lang (1993) underscore that "return on investment has been the primary performance variable in most strategy research on decline and turnaround" (p. 11; also Hofer, 1980). Other well-known measures include "change in net income" (Schendel & Patton, 1976, p. 236), "return on invested capital" (Arogyaswamy & Yasai-Ardekani, 1997, p. 5), "return on assets" (Barker, Mone, Mueller, & Freeman, 1998, p. 65), "market share" (Hambrick & Schecter, 1983, p. 238), "stock market price" (O'Neill, 1986a, p. 167), "sales growth" (Schendel & Patton, 1976, p. 237), and "survival" (O'Neill, 1986a, p. 167).

Some examples of efforts to operationalize these measures follow. Barker and his team (1998) identified turnaround manufacturing firms based on the following dynamics:

1. Three consecutive years of declining return on assets (ROA). This declining performance also occurred after a base year (year before the decline) when the firm's ROA was above its industry's average.

2. During this three-year decline, the firm's performance had to become low enough to cause losses (i.e., negative ROA).

3. The three decline years were followed by three years of increasing ROA with performance in the best year (Year 6) being profitable (i.e., positive ROA). (p. 65)

Schendel and his colleagues (1976) employed the following rubric:

Downturn Phase: Four years of uninterrupted decline in net income as normalized by Gross National Product (GNP) growth.

Upturn Phase: Four years of increase in net income with allowance for a two-year deviation between the downturn and upturn phase. Again, net income was normalized by GNP growth. (p. 3)

Slatter (1984) operationalized turnaround

as a firm whose "real" profit before tax (measured in 1970 prices) had declined for three or more successive years; and a successful turnaround was defined as a firm whose real profits before tax increased in four out of the following six years. (p. 19)

Robbins and Pearce (1992), in turn, provide this understanding:

Two successive years of increasing ROI and ROS followed by: absolute, simultaneous declines in ROI and ROS for a minimum of two years, and (2) a rate of decline in ROI and ROS greater than industry average over this two-year period. (p. 295)

And the following formula for the downturn phase of the turnaround is offered by Shuchman and White (1995):

- Two or more years of substandard ROI
- Three or more years of sub-GNP growth in income
- Two or more years of 10% or more decline in net profit
- Performance in earnings consistently below the industry standard and regularly below 10% (p. 17)

Another dimension of measurement, and one visible in the operationalizations just reviewed, is the issue of "*how*" the "what" (e.g., profits) gets assessed, or what Short, Palmer, and Stimpert (1998) label measurement "referents on standards of comparison" (p. 154). According to the Short (1998) team, "referents are especially key to the turnaround process because they generate discussion frames that set the stage for strategic action" (p. 154). Common referents include comparisons to (1) a firm's own goals (p. 158) or "historical record" (O'Neill, 1986a, p. 168), (2) to the "performance of competitors" (Short, Palmer, & Stimpert, 1998, p. 154), or to (3) industry norms (O'Neill, 1986a; Robbins & Pearce, 1992), "standards," (O'Neill, 1986a, p. 168), or "averages" (Robbins &

Pearce, 1992, p. 293)—"factors specific to a particular industry" (Short, Palmer, & Stimpert, 1998, p. 159) or "strategic rival groups (p. 158). Our review here directs us to the following conclusion: "Both internal and external referents may be important in interpreting performance outcomes" (p. 157).

The final elements in the measurement equation address the *criteria* to be attached to the referent, whether absolute or relative standards are engaged and how much counts for success—or failure. Absolute standards specify set levels of outcomes, while relative standards define success in "terms of improvement" (Khandwalla, 1983–1984, p. 11). In their investigation, Hambrick and Schecter (1983) characterized a turnaround as successful if it "achieved an average ending return on investment (in years three and four) of at least 20 percent. An unsuccessful turnaround was defined as a business whose ending ROI [return on investment] was still less than 10 percent (even though it might have improved significantly" (p. 238). Thus they employed an absolute criterion and set the bar (i.e., the how much is needed) at 20 percent.

Process

Stages and time. In later chapters, we devote considerable space to exploring the process of turning around failing organizations in general and failing schools in particular. Here we foreshadow that analysis. We start by noting that a number of leading turnaround analysts conceptualize turnaround in terms of stages or "sequences of moves" (Hambrick & Schecter, 1983, p. 235). For example, Bibeault (1982) concludes that turnarounds flow across five stages: "the management change stage, the evaluation stage, the emergency stage, the stabilization stage, [and] the return-to-normal-growth stage" (p. 92). Sloma (1985) depicts four stages in the turnaround process: cash crunch, cash shortfall, quantity of profit, and quality of profit. Building from the work on turnaround stages, we employ a two-phase model of turnaround in this book: retrenchment and recovery (see Figure 1.1).

Researchers also have discovered (1) that "the amount of time required for a turnaround is of interest [for] its practical significance" (Hambrick & Schecter, 1983, p. 235) and (2) "that turnarounds go on for very long periods" (Zimmerman, 1991, p. 191), although "smaller companies usually do not take as long to turn around" (Dewitt, Harrigan, & Newman, 1998, p. 24). Therefore, while acknowledging the need to address pressing problems, turnaround managers need to "adopt a long term focus" (O'Neill, 1986b, p. 87). For example, in the study by Schendel and his colleagues (1976), "the average length of the downturn phase was 5.2 years [and] the average length of the upturn was 7.7 years" (p. 4), for a total of nearly 13 years. In his investigation, Bibeault (1982) discovered that the average period of decline was 3.7 years and that the average length of the upturn recovery period was 4.1 years, a total of nearly 8 years for the turnaround process. Pearce and Robbins (1994a) uncovered a peak-to-peak cycle of 10 years with an average recovery phase or "average turnaround timetable [of] three to four years" (p. 96). O'Neill (1986a) found a peak-to-peak cycle of seven years in the banking industry, while Zimmerman (1991) pegged the upturn recovery phase at "about 4 years" (p. 191) and Hofer (1980) placed it in the three-year range. The summative statement on this issue has been nicely laid out by Goodman (1982): "Because the remedies needed in a turnaround usually involve conditions that have existed for years, all concerned must recognize that a successful and durable turnaround takes time" (p. 113).

Strategy. Strategy in turnarounds is the "what" in "what is happening in the organizations as they experience and react between Time 1 and Time 2" (Whetten, 1988b, p. 157). It is the unfolding of "the fundamentals of crisis management" (Silver, 1992, p. 6). Strategy almost always includes "a number of responses" (Grinyer, Mayes, & McKiernan, 1988, p. 65) in an effort "to put the organization on a new growth plan" (Taylor, 1982–1983, p. 12). According to scholars in this area (Ackley, 1989; Khandwalla, 1983–1984), "there are two broad types of turnaround strategies . . . strategic and operating" (Hofer, 1980, p. 20) (see Figure 1.1):

> Strategic turnarounds can be divided into those that involve a change in the organization's strategy for competing. Operating turnarounds are usually of four types, none of which require changing the firm's business-level strategy. These emphasize increasing revenues, decreasing costs, decreasing assets, or a combination effort. (p. 20)

Inside this framework, we learn that "turnarounds are usually about cutting direct costs, reducing overload, fixing quality and customer service problems, and pricing and marketing strategically" (Finkin, 1987, pp. 8–9).

As we will see in great detail in later chapters, this differentiation of turnaround into phases "is useful because . . . it suggests that differing and different management actions are appropriate to each" (Sloma, 1985, p. 34). Exploration of these stages assists us in three ways: (1) it helps to identify which "responses to failure differentiate between the turnarounds and the non-turnaround firms" (Boyne, 2004, p. 98), (2) it aids us in patching together "a process for saving [a] troubled company" (Silver, 1992, p. 92), and (3) it informs management of the knowledge needed to conduct turnarounds (Bibeault, 1982).

Success. We open here with an important restatement of the obvious for turnarounds: "Where specific corrective action is taken by management, the outcome can be either successful or unsuccessful. Where recovery is accomplished, the firm is described as a successful turnaround. Attempts at recovery may, however, be unsuccessful" (Slatter, 1984, p. 15). Also, we remind the reader that "successful adaptation . . . can be known only retrospectively, not prospectively" (Ford & Baucus, 1987, p. 377).

On the downside, unsuccessful attempts at turnaround can lead to "corporate collapse" (Argenti, 1976, p. 2) or organizational "death" (Hager et al., 1999, p. 52). It can also result, surprisingly perhaps, in what Meyer and Zucker (1989) call "permanent failure—the combination of high persistence and low performance" (p. 22). This condition, which we suggest has relevance for the schooling industry, occurs when "performance is subordinated" (p. 19) to other matters or, we argue, performance becomes defined in less than standard ways. The point here is that "some declines are permanent" (Levine, 1978, p. 323) and that "organizational failure does not always equal organizational death" (Anheier & Moulton, 1999b, p. 278).

On the upside, since "the goal of turnaround is to restore financial health" (Sloma, 1985, p. xiii), "a turnaround begin[s] at that point when management's actions start to improve the financial performance of the firm" (Slatter, 1984, p. 74). According to Zimmerman (1991), the following "two attributes are crucial to turnaround success: low-cost production and product differentiation" (p. 251). In particular, "increased acceptance in the marketplace" (Barker et al., 1998, p. 62) is a hallmark of "most turnarounds" (p. 62). To these attributes, Stewart (1984) adds "improved return on investment" (p. 19). In addition, for many organizations, especially public institutions, "survival depends upon achieving social legitimacy or credibility" (Chaffee, 1983, p. 11). And, as Zimmerman (1991) reminds us, to count, recovery must be "a lasting event" (p. 26).

Somewhat more concretely, analysts and managers provide the following definitions and portraits of successful turnaround. According to Zimmerman (1991),

[W]hether the turnaround [is] successful center[s] around three necessary conditions: a return to profitability, a substantial improvement in profitability, and an overall improvement in market positions—all lasting at least several years and resulting in a measurably better situation for the company with respect to these criteria. More specifically, a turnaround was classed as successful if the following were achieved:

1. *Profitability improved from the levels of the period of crisis for a period of at least several years.*

2. *Profitability was positive.*

3. *Market position was significantly strengthened* either by increasing market share or by successfully concentrating on an important subset of the market. (pp. 30–31)

From Slatter (1984),

. . . sustainable recovery involves achieving a viable and defensible business strategy, supported by an adequate organization and control structure. It means that the firm has fully recovered, is making "good" profits and is unlikely to face another crisis in the foreseeable future. (p. 15)

Barker and Duhaime (1997),

. . . define a successful turnaround to be when a firm undergoes a survival-threatening performance decline over a period of years but is able to reverse the performance decline, end the threat to firm survival and achieve sustained profitability. (p. 18)

For Anheier and Moulton (1999b), success can "be defined as the ability of a social structure to keep relational elements indicative of failure at random levels" (p. 286). And returning to Zimmerman (1991),

> The general proposition advanced here is that a successful business turnaround involves improving the company's position as a low-cost provider of increasingly differentiated products and services, along with the nurturing of an appropriate turnaround organization which is competent, possesses industry-oriented technical expertise, and employs a general sense of fair play in dealing with employees, creditors, suppliers, shareholders, and customers. (pp. 11–12)

THEMES

In these final pages of our introduction to turnarounds, we overview an assortment of themes and findings that we deepen throughout the book. It is important to acknowledge at the start that while there is evidence that "it is possible for troubled companies to turn around" (Zimmerman, 1991, p. 11), we know that these "changes do not happen automatically" (Thurow, 2003, p. 250) and that "not all turnaround situations are recoverable" (Slatter, 1984, p. 115; also Lubatkin & Chung, 1985). Neither is it appropriate to assume that turnaround efforts are in the best interest of all troubled organizations. Sometimes "those with a stake in the organization [would be] better served" (Hofer, 1980, p. 31) if the organization were allowed to die.

There is also considerable support for the claim that "turnarounds may vary in nature" (Khandwalla, 1983–1984, p. 8) and that "no two [turnaround] firms are alike" (Grinyer, Mayes, & McKiernan, 1988, p. 129; also Baehr, 1993). Because firms "decline in many ways" (Harrigan, 1988, p. 130) and because "the particular mix of causes of the relative decline are different" (Grinyer, Mayes, & McKiernan, 1988, p. 63), "no two turnaround situations are ever exactly alike" (Finkin, 1985, p. 24)—"there are different ways to respond" (Harrigan, 1988, p. 130), and "no precise pattern of approach is satisfactorily applicable to every case" (Finkin, 1985, p. 24). Indeed, Hegde (1982) reminds us that turnaround actions tend to be multi-dimensional, multi-pronged efforts; and turnaround strategy tends to be built around eliminating the cause of sickness. There may be no one best turnaround strategy for it may, at least in part, have to be tailor-made to each specific situation. (p. 302)

There "is no universal panacea for all organizational ills; each turnaround strategy has to be tailored to a unique company situation" (Chan, 1993, p. 29): "There [is] no single road to success" (Harrigan, 1988, p. 131), and "many innovative ways of retrieving the value of a firm's assets [have been] found" (p. 131). Each "firm seeking to reverse a decline in performance faces several alternatives" (Lohrke & Bedeian, 1998, p. 4).

Successful turnaround treatment is a tailored, customized restorative program. While some symptoms may be shared by different stages of turnarounds, effective treatment is dependent upon accurate differentiation and selection of only those that are relevant to our specific patient. (Sloma, 1985, p. xiii)

Thus "there are different types of turnaround efforts" (O'Neill, 1986a, p. 168) and "multiple turnaround strategies" (Khandwalla, 1983–1984, p. 12).

Concomitantly, we are discovering that there are "some common features" (Grinyer, Mayes, & McKiernan, 1988, p. 129) and "some common elements that are present in successful turnaround strategies" (Chan, 1993, p. 29). "General patterns" (Harrigan, 1988, p. 131) are discernible, and there is some evidence that these commonalities extend across industries and sectors of the economy (e.g., service and manufacturing). We are also learning that some responses, although contextually dependent, "are more (or less) successful than other responses" (Harrigan, 1988, p. 130).

We also know that there is only a small window of opportunity available to firms in turnaround situations (Sloma, 1985), and "time is of the essence" (Hambrick, 1985, p. 10-3). Relatedly, by the turnaround point in the game, "turnaround managers basically get one round of moves. . . . There is no slack; there is no organizational resilience" (Hambrick, 1985, p. 10-3): "Successful turnarounds involve making bold moves in short times" (Rindler, 1987, p. 171).

If there is anything close to a law in the literature on turnarounds, it is that context is critical to recovery efforts. Age of the firm, size, type of industry, history, and a dozen other issues shape decline and turnaround (Oviatt & Bruton, 1994; Zimmerman, 1991). For example, on one of these context dimensions, Sloma (1985) informs us that "a relationship exists between the stage of the severity of the turnaround and the scope, timing, and nature of the remedial action that can (should) be taken" (p. 34). As with all the topics in this section, we explore the topic of context in greater detail in later chapters.

Somewhat unexpectedly, but consistent with the school improvement literature, successful turnarounds often look worse than unsuccessful ones in the early stages of the recovery process. As Zimmerman (1991) discovered, "during the principal periods of crisis, the best companies quite often looked worse, and the worst companies quite often looked better. It was only after several years that the superior effort of the successful firms enabled them to look better statistically" (p. 280).

On the management side of the story, we know that the leader's "response . . . is often the decisive factor in determining whether a firm dies early or goes on" (Bibeault, 1982, p. 17). There is also evidence that "turnarounds call for a different way of thinking and different types of action than do other strategic situations" (Hambrick, 1985, p. 10-2). Information is also emerging that because "a turnaround situation is an abnormal period in any company's history" (Bibeault, 1982, p. 1), "new and different problems must be surmounted in order to turn around a declining organization, . . . that coping with decline generally requires solutions not contained in organization's repertoires, and that managers' instinctive responses may exacerbate problems" (Meyer, 1988, p. 412): "In a state of crisis, the usual adaptive responses are inadequate to achieve balance" (Silver, 1992, p. 35) and "business as usual does not suffice" (Finkin, 1985, p. 14). "Management approaches [that are] unique and distinctly different" (Bibeault, 1982, p. 1) are called for—"the mode of operation in a recovering situation is often quite different from that described in the standard management textbooks" (Slatter, 1984, p. 13).

The literature also illustrates that this is arduous work, that a turnaround "is difficult to undertake" (Grinyer, Mayes, & McKiernan, 1988, p. 128): "Under conditions and assumptions of decline, the ponderables, puzzles, and paradoxes of organizational management take on new complexities" (Levine, 1978, p. 317). Turnaround work is "a complex task involving many characteristics and the balancing of competing claims. There are no single easily attainable recipes" (Grinyer, Mayes, & McKiernan, 1988, p. 128). Indeed, there is general acknowledgment that "successful turnaround performance requires technical management knowledge and human energy of a higher order" (Bibeault, 1982, p. 3) and that "of all the challenges confronting top managers, achieving a successful turnaround is surely one of the most difficult" (Short, Palmer, & Stimpert, 1998, p. 154): "Trying to make substantial improvements in a troubled company [is] . . . a trying test for management" (Bibeault, 1982, p. 2). Stress and strain are commonplace, and "management by 'thrashabout' [can] become the order of the day" (Sloma, 1985, p. 28): "Too often managers are under pressure to do something— anything quickly. The hazard . . . is that the pressure to find an attractive redirection, a plausible answer is accepted as the plan instead of the 'best' solution" (Dewitt, Harrigan, & Newman, 1998, p. 23). And as Sloma (1985) reminds us, "getting a turnaround program underway is far less important than getting the *right* turnaround program started" (p. 27). Clear focus, "ruthless adherence to objectives" (Bibeault, 1982, p. 3), alignment of efforts (Hofer, 1980), and high-quality implementation (Slatter, 1984) are the keys for turnaround managers.

Three additional insights (themes) from the turnaround literature merit notice. First, as should be clear from our analysis of turnaround measures, "losses [are] not required to be a turnaround candidate" (Oviatt & Bruton, 1994, p. 130). Deterioration and stagnation of results are the real "distinguishing characteristics of a turnaround candidate" (p. 130). Second, there are real costs to the organization in turnaround work, or as Grinyer, Mayes, and McKiernan (1988) inform us, "most sharpbends . . . have a harsh side to them" (p. 132)—lines of activity are dropped, resources are reallocated, and jobs are lost. Third, while we discuss successful turnaround as an end state, it is instructive to remember that (1) it is difficult to mark "when a full recovery has occurred" (Fredenberger, Lipp, & Watson, 1997, p. 169) and (2) end states begin to unravel as soon as they are created. Environments continually evolve, and internal dynamics are in constant flow. Therefore, there is no guarantee that adjustments today "will solve the company's problems thereafter" (Grinyer, Mayes, & McKiernan, 1988, p. 134): "Turnarounds are never permanent. Constant vigilance is required to remain competitive" (Zimmerman, 1991, p. 263).

PART II
Decline and Failure

CHAPTER TWO

Symptoms of Decline

Organizational decline is commonly preceded by early warning signals. (Zimmerman, 1991, p. 21)

Very few companies fail without adequate warning. For the most part the company in decline throws out a wide range of operational and financial signals. Symptoms give clues as to what might be wrong with the firm. (Chakraborty & Dixit, 1992, 346)

The true art of management is in reading the symptoms of a company heading for trouble and taking the appropriate steps to fend off disaster. (Goldston, 1992, p. 3)

In the turnaround model introduced in Chapter 1 (see Figure 1.1), we saw that symptoms act as "early-warning signals" (Arogyaswamy, Barker, & Yasai-Ardekani, 1995, p. 519) that an organization is entering a state of disintegration, that is, is on the path to decline and failure. Symptoms also are visible as the decline process matures. In this chapter, we unpack the scholarship on turnarounds to develop an understanding of these indicators of organizational trouble. In the first part of the chapter, we complete two assignments. We explore some general themes in the literature. We also expose the various ways that theorists and practitioners conceptualize these warning signals, beginning with listings of symptoms and moving to taxonomies. Based on this work, in the second half of the chapter we craft and populate a conceptual design of "the symptoms of decline" (Slatter, 1984, p. 55).

SETTING THE STAGE

A number of factors point to signs of prospective business failure. (Siegel, 1981, p. 10)

For both business and societal reasons, it is worthwhile to understand the early signs of decline. (Zimmerman, 1991, p. 19)

General Notes

There is a fair degree of agreement about the adverse trend signals in a declining company. (Bibeault, 1982, p. 661)

We open with a caveat, one that we offer in regard to many of the elements in the turnaround equation: "Relatively little empirical research has examined the antecedents of decline in organizations" (Whetten, 1988a, p. 33)—"the study of the symptoms of company failure has been a most neglected area of management" (Argenti, 1976, p. 57). The literature also helps us see that (1) warning signals, (2) symptoms of disease, (3) causes of decline, and (4) consequences of failing are interrelated. In fact, because "organizational failure resembles organic illness" (Goldstein, 1988, p. 15), "the causes of failure and its symptoms can be so intertwined that it is difficult to tell one from the other" (p. 33), although there is some evidence that "the symptoms of decline are easier to detect than the causes of decline" (Slatter, 1984, p. 55).

The research on turnarounds also illuminates the importance of time in the narrative of symptoms of organizational troubles. Analysts disclose that "a considerable time lag may occur between the first 'weak signals' and the ultimate decline in measurable business performance" (Lorange & Nelson, 1987, p. 43), that at least "some symptoms" (Argenti, 1976, p. 45) "of failure are observable for some years before the failure actually occurs" (p. 39). Ironically, they also document that even when visible, these early warning signs are often not read accurately, are "not recognized as symptoms of failure at the time" (p. 35). In particular, reviewers reveal that managers often look in the wrong place for signals of concern. That is, "the majority of managers mistakenly believe that the first signs of failure will appear in the financial statements. But the earliest and clearest signs are not financial, they are managerial and they can be seen long before—perhaps years before—the company's financial position begins to deteriorate" (Goldstein, 1988, pp. 32–33; also Oviatt & Bruton, 1994, p. 131). Finally, scholars confirm that the faint signals at the onset of decline become "more entrenched" (Lorange & Nelson, 1987, p. 43) and more pronounced and more visible "as time passes" (p. 43): "As a company gets close to the point of failure, a lot of other signals surface, but these are the final warning signals" (Bibeault, 1982, p. 71).

What turnaround analysts are discovering is that because symptoms provide early notice of trouble and because "it is generally difficult to discern and diagnose company problems before they threaten the progress or the very existence of an enterprise" (Bibeault, 1982, p. 61), management needs to be diligent in scanning for early signs of trouble in the organization: "For the most part, business warning signals don't jump up and demand to be heeded; they need to be sought out" (p. 61). These symptoms expose not only "trouble brewing" (Goldstein, 1988, p. 32) but reveal the contours of a "window of opportunity" (p. 32) for organizations to take corrective action, to examine these "clues as to what might be wrong with the firm" (Chakraborty & Dixit, 1992, p. 346). Thus, "if a firm's managers . . . are vigilant in scanning the organization for such signals, decline can be more easily detected and, if not avoided, at least responded to more quickly" (Arogyaswamy, Barker, & Yasai-Ardekani, 1995, p. 519).

Unfortunately, these same reviewers disclose "that powerful decision makers are not responsive to warnings" (Ford, 1985, p. 781), "that early-warning signals of decline are not acted upon" (Bibeault, 1982, p. 61). Indeed, usually "all the signs are there . . . but very few people . . . recognize them for what they are" (Argenti, 1976, p. 145). For a considerable variety of reasons that we review in detail in the next chapter on the causes of organizational decline, even though there are a well-known number of signals and a "few distinct failure syndromes" (Miller, 1977, p. 43), managers' ability to see and respond to "adverse trend signals" (Bibeault, 1982, p. 62)—and causes of decline—leaves a good deal to be desired. And this "refusal or inability to see problems" (Lorange & Nelson, 1987, p. 42) and "insufficient actions" (Zimmerman, 1991, p. 22) or "poor reaction[s] to the early warning signals" (Goldstein, 1988, p. 31) often mean that "problem situations fester and worsen before responsible members of management . . . initiate corrective action" (Zimmerman,

1991, p. 21). The consequence is that many organizations "wait until there is a crisis" (Bibeault, 1982, p. 61) before leaders begin to act. That is, examining Figure 1.1, rather than attacking problems at or near their onset, these enterprises wait until they are in a turnaround situation to act, a time when addressing problems successfully is considerably more difficult and "more painful and disruptive" (Lorange & Nelson, 1987, p. 43).

Taxonomies and Frameworks

Lists

Through studies of turnaround firms, we are able to compile an increasingly refined picture of the symptoms that can be seen in organizations (1) on the doorstep of disintegration and (2) on the downward pathway of decline. To provide a flavor for this work, in the following few pages we offer a representative sample of lists of warning signals generated by leading investigators of turnaround organizations—keeping in mind our earlier caveat about the difficulty of disentangling the symptoms and causes of decline and failure.

Armenakis and Fredenberger (1998) unearth the following warning signals: "decreases in product quality, market share, and profitability, or increases in employee absenteeism, turnover, and grievances" (pp. 40–42). Miller (cited in Siegel, 1981) "points to the [following] warning signs of business failure" (p. 11):

- Poor managerial planning
- Overambitious expectations
- Rigidness of financial management in terms of product line, geographic markets, and channels of distribution
- Vacuum in leadership
- A domineering president
- Insufficient financial and operating resources
- Inexperienced management team
- A lack of communication and cohesiveness among divisions (p. 11)

Lorange and Nelson (1987) posit that the following "nine characteristics in particular can give useful early warnings" (p. 43):

- Excess personnel
- Cumbersome administrative procedures
- Tolerance of incompetence
- Replacement of substance with form
- Disproportionate staff power
- Scarcity of clear goals and decision benchmarks
- Fear of embarrassment and conflict
- Loss of effective communication
- Outdated organizational structure (pp. 43–45)

Goldston's (1992) work turns up 11 symptoms or warning signals of organizational trouble:

- The firm is losing money from an operating profit standpoint.
- Market share has declined steadily or precipitously over a 12- to 24-month period.
- Quality mangers are departing from the firm with a degree of regularity.
- Company pride is greatly diminished, and individual initiative seems to be at lower levels, resulting in problems relating to idea generation and information flow.
- The company facilities appear to be run down. Overall cleanliness and quality standards seem greatly diminished, and manufacturing equipment is only repaired after breakdown.
- The company is having a hard time generating cash or is eating it.
- On-hand inventory levels exceed the normal three- to four-month supply level and more importantly do not accurately reflect the mix of the product line at retail.
- Expense reductions have resulted in a marked decrease in research and development and in advertising and promotional spending.
- In the case of a consumer product, the item is no longer the "brand of choice."
- New products/items appear to be cannibalizing existing items from both a retailer and consumer purchase standpoint.
- The company's manufacturing facilities are operating at less than 60 percent of capacity, and future projected increases in the unit volume base are less than 10 percent of the current year volume. (pp. 7–27)

Siegel (1981), in turn, highlights the following indicators of firms on the threshold of disintegration:

- Poor management quality
- Inept financial policies
- Weak financial reporting system
- Unprofitable business diversification
- Ease of entry into industry
- Failure to adjust on a timely basis to change
- Instability in profitability and cash flow
- Political, social, and economic difficulties (p. 12)

For Goldstein (1988), early warnings "can take several forms":

- New and more formidable competitors
- A shrinking market or decreased market share
- Legislation that could jeopardize the entity's ability to profitably operate
- Dependence on one product or too narrow a product line with weakening demand
- Dependence on, or loss of, a key franchise, principal customer, or principal supplier (p. 33)

Miller (1977) describes 12 signals of institutions on the path to failure:

- Power-hoarding chief executive
- Overly ambitious growth strategy
- Overextension of financial resources because of excessive leverage and bank debt
- Top managers' decisions that reflect ignorance of what is going on in the field
- Lack of strategic planning
- Overcommitment to old products, markets, and ways of doing things
- Elaborate standard operating procedures and extensively documented formal policies
- Leadership vacuum
- Decisions in one part of the firm that conflict with those in other parts
- Serious shortage of financial, managerial, or material resources

- A relatively new and inexperienced team of managers
- Turnaround work that is taxing the firm's resources (pp. 51–53)

Sloma (1985), in his comprehensive examination, uncovers 28 indicators of decline:

- Inability to pay debt service
- Inability to pay "taxes"
- Inability to pay contractual obligations
- Inability to pay accounts payable
- Inability to pay salaries, wages, commissions
- Inability to pay fringes, pensions, and so on
- Inability to pay purchase commitments
- Excessive debt/equity ratio
- Flat, falling sales
- Eroding gross margin
- Increasing unit labor cost
- Increasing unit material cost
- Increasing burden: people-related variable expense
- Increasing burden: people-related fixed expenses
- Increasing burden: plant-related variable expense
- Increasing burden: plant-related fixed expense
- Increasing sales/marketing expense
- Increasing finance/administration expense
- Increasing engineering in-house people-related expense
- Increasing engineering contract people-related expense
- Increasing engineering in-house product-related expense
- Increasing engineering contract product-related expense
- Inconsistent valuation of inventory input/output
- Increasing warranty expense
- Decreasing capacity utilization
- Decreasing product line profitability
- Decreasing unit sales
- Decreasing customer profitability (pp. 42–46)

And in addition to specified financial ratios, Bibeault (1982) underscores the importance of five "other early-warning signals" (p. 66):

- Declining margins
- Declining market share

- Rapidly increasing debt
- Declining working capital
- Management turnover (p. 67)

In his research on turnarounds in the hospital industry, Rindler (1987) uncovered eight "warning signs . . . of trouble" (p. 1):

- Loss on operations for two or more consecutive years
- Activity trends significantly worse than those in competing institutions
- Trustees holding private meetings to discuss concerns
- Declining market share for two or more consecutive years
- Always responding to marketing initiatives of competitors
- Weak board and management
- Offers to buy or merge from competing enterprises
- Concern among financial backers (pp. 1–2)

And in his work on small church turnarounds, Crandall (1995) lists the following warning signals and causes of decline:

- Low self-esteem of organization
- Fear of change and taking risks
- Lack of vision for the future
- Internal discord
- Presence of power cliques
- Lack of finances
- Lack of stewardship
- Apathy and burnout
- Lack of leadership
- A closed mentality
- Lack of hard work (p. 61)

Frameworks

Scholars of turnaround organizations also provide us with taxonomies and frameworks that allow us to organize a good deal of the information on symptoms contained in the various lists provided above. D'Aveni (1989, p. 578) and Oviatt and Bruton (1994, p. 131), for example, cluster symptoms into two categories, declining financial resources and declining managerial resources. Rindler (1987) employs similar groupings, citing activity trends and financial trends.

Arogyaswamy and Yasai-Ardekani (1997) organize warning signals into two bins, operations and human resources. Siegel (1981) bundles clues of "future distress" (p. 9) into three buckets: "financial ratios, financial characteristics, and operating characteristics" (p. 9). Similarly, Renn and Kirk (1993) feature internal operations and financial performance, but they add a third category, environmental factors (p. 43). Sloma (1985) highlights four categories of symptoms, those "revelatory of cash crunch, cash shortfall, quantity of profit, and quality of profit" (p. 39). And Zimmerman (1991) defines "seven basic families of problems" (p. 20) into which warning signals can be grouped: "liquidity problems, collection problems, profit problems, quality problems, employee problems, organizational problems, and ethical problems" (p. 20). Using a larger backdrop, Greenhalgh (1983) and Miller (1977) both help us understand that symptoms are likely to be visible in the following areas: organizational environment, or in the "relationships between the organization and important elements of the environment" (Greenhalgh, 1983, p. 235), organizational structure, the nature of a firm's strategy-making behavior, leadership, innovation, organizational slack, and workforce composition (Greenhalgh, 1983, p. 235; Miller, 1977, p. 44).

UNPACKING THE FRAMEWORK

The most commonly used symptoms indicating that a firm is in need of a turnaround are financial indicators, although many experienced banks, receivers and consultants have a number of non-financial factors which they also take into account. (Slatter, 1984, p. 55)

Measures of productivity and efficiency often illuminate the underlying causes of unfavorable . . . performance. (Renn & Kirk, 1993, p. 35)

Building on the foundational taxonomies and listings above, in this section we present a three-part framework to probe more deeply into the nature and texture of the early warning signals that often signify the onslaught of organizational decline. Specifically, we explore environmental, operational, and financial indicators, acknowledging at the outset that the financial signs are less applicable to turnarounds in public institutions such as schools.

Environmental Symptoms

An organization exists in a broader environment and is dependent on certain stakeholders in that environment. (Hambrick, 1985, p. 10-3)

Warning signals of distress can come from changes in the demographic characteristics of and economic conditions in an [institution's] local service area. (Renn & Kirk, 1993, p. 32)

One of the themes that ribbons the literature on turnarounds is that organizational environments change and managers in about-to-be-troubled enterprises are unable or unwilling to see important environmental shifts or to respond to them appropriately. Thus "deteioration in environmental support" (Sutton, 1990, p. 211) often provides a clue that an institution is heading into troubled waters. One pattern in this warning mosaic is a neglect of exchange or slowdown in "interactions with constituencies outside the institution" (Cameron, 1983, p. 367). Another is an inability to "perceive[d] shifts in the economic and political environment" (Siegel, 1981, p. 10) or failure to bring the institution back into equilibrium with a changing world. For example, Renn and Kirk (1993) and Siegel (1981) document how shifts in the geography and demographic characteristics of an organization's environment can provide markers of concern for a firm. Likewise, certain movements in the political environment and the "regulatory environment" (Renn & Kirk, 1993, p. 31) can cause alarm bells to ring for organizations. Either declining support from government sponsors or expanding "governmental regulations" (Siegel, 1981, p. 11) can clue leaders that they may be entering the pathway to decline.

Another environmental symptom of decline is loss of connectedness to one's customers. According to this line of analysis, "major market shifts" (Yates, 1983, p. 116), "declining market share" (Argenti, 1976, p. 145), and "changing customer preferences [should provide] early warning signals" (Weitzel & Jonsson, 1989, p. 99) to managers. So too should "increased customer complaints" (Castrogiovanni, Bahga, & Kidwell, 1992, p. 35; also Argenti, 1976). As Yates (1983) illustrates in the automobile industry and Slater (1999) reveals in the technology industry, decline often takes root when managers ignore or misread these symptoms of potential trouble. For example, Yates (1983) conveys quite dramatically that by assuming that the world will return to an existing equilibrium—or "return to spin in its accustomed orbit" (p. 118)—managers allow small symptoms to mushroom into large and often catastrophic problems. In a similar vein, deteriorating relations with other environmental actors such as dealers and suppliers and increasing "social risk," or a growing negative perception by society at large, can act as signals of impending organizational decline (Shook, 1990). What all this work conveys is that "reputation is a very perishable product" (Shook, 1990, p. 13), and, not surprisingly, a weakening of and later "stigmatization of a firm's reputation" (Barker & Duhaime, 1997, p. 20) is regularly uncovered as a telltale sign of danger in firms that entered a turnaround situation (Sutton, 1990).

Organizational Warning Signals

The factors responsible for the greatest risk of distress are a result of internal and operational problems. (Renn & Kirk, 1993, p. 34)

There is an emerging consensus that a variety of dysfunctional organizational attributes are associated with conditions of decline. (Cameron, Whetten, & Kim, 1987, p. 126)

Another tip-off is the rapid turnover of people. (Bibeault, 1982, p. 68)

Organizational symptoms of decline can be organized into the three somewhat distinct clusters or bins of people, product, and systems.

People

Clues that an organization may be a candidate for a turnaround situation are often visible as one looks at the human resources in the enterprise, at both the condition of individuals and the state of group relations (Cameron, Kim, & Whetten, 1988). One of the most prevalent warning signals in the turnaround literature is "the continuity" (Renn & Kirk, 1993, p. 37) of staff or, more directly, the "turnover of talented employees" (Barker & Duhaime, 1997, p. 20), especially the departure of "senior staff" (Gainer, 1999, p. 17) and "senior management" (Renn & Kirk, 1993, p. 37): "The workforce . . . undergoes qualitative shifts during decline such that the employees most crucial to organizational adaptation are likely the first to leave a declining organization" (Greenhalgh, 1983, p. 239)—"the most creative and most innovative individuals are frequently the first to leave an organization when decline occurs" (Cameron, 1983, p. 365). According to turnaround scholars, managers are often the first to discern signs of weakening in the organization. They also possess unique insights into the effectiveness—or ineffectiveness—of early efforts to steer the enterprise back on course. If they observe that those initiatives are missing the mark, they often become "disenchanted" (Gainer, 1999, p. 17), and those with opportunities to relocate elsewhere often do so (Kanter, 2003; Slatter, 1984).

On the flip side, less "talented" and less "aggressive" (Hambrick, 1985, p. 10-2) staff are more likely to remain. Often, as Sloma (1985) reminds us, "deadwood" (p. 146) begins to accumulate in firms ripe for decline and failure. On a related front, troubled firms often are characterized by "high staffing levels" (Renn & Kirk, 1993, p. 36) and a need to reduce personnel. Or, as Sutton and his colleagues (1986) find, "the need for workforce reduction [is] a symptom of decline" (p. 28). So too is the unwillingness of management to address the problem of overstaffing.

Scholars of turnarounds also unearth a cluster of human warning indicators focused on the morale and satisfaction of employees and on the dynamics of interpersonal and group relations. For example, Rindler (1987) features "unhappiness of staff" as a mark of organizational trouble. Goldstein (1988) and Shook (1990) highlight "decreasing morale" (Goldstein, 1988, p. 42). Shook (1990) and Starbuck, Greve, and Hedberg (1978) surface declining trust. Crandall (1995) exposes plummeting "self esteem" (p. 64) and growing "apathy" (p. 61). And Kanter (2003) zeroes in on increased "passivity and helplessness" (p. 61).

On the relationship front, Kanter (2003) reveals that an assortment of "organizational pathologies" (p. 60) often signal an organization in trouble, what Khandwalla (1983–1984) calls "overt symptoms of disease" (p. 20) and Greenhalgh (1983) describes as an erosion of "the social fabric of the organization" (p. 239). In the turnaround literature, we learn that deteriorating employee relations is often another "sign of debility" (Argenti, 1976, p. 21). The growth of a toxic climate or "ailing organizational culture" (Kanter, 2003, p. 61), one marked by "mutual distrust and hostility" (Khandwalla,

1983–1984, p. 20), is often an indication that decline and failure may loom on the horizon. In an unhealthy environment, "alienation, apathy, conflict, buck-passing" (Khandwalla, 1983–1984, p. 35) and "self-centeredness and sense of insecurity" (p. 23) are defining elements. So too are "secrecy and denial, blame and score, [and] avoidance and turf protection" (Kanter, 2003, p. 61); "conflict, resistance, and reluctance" (Cameron, Kim, & Whetten, 1988, p. 219); a decline in "energy and enthusiasm" (Starbuck, Greve, & Hedberg, 1978, p. 125) to engage new activities; an increase in "divisive organizational politics" (Greenhalgh, 1983, p. 239); and the "formation of cliques" (Khandwalla, 1983–1984, p. 20): "When an organization is sick, employees tend to feel insecure and think first of protecting themselves rather than worry about the health and well-being of the whole organization" (p. 23). Concomitantly, employees will often experience "less generous treatment" (Argenti, 1976, p. 145; Bibeault, 1982, p. 71) from the firm.

Product

Adverse signals or clues of organizational problems are also visible when the analytic spotlight is focused on an organization's products. Argenti (1976), one of the pioneers in the study of turnarounds, directed attention (1) to the issues of "ageing" (p. 21) or "outdated product" and "rising stock" (p. 40), (2) to declining "quality of service" (p. 145), and, as we discuss in detail below under financial warning signs, (3) to "declining market share" (p. 145). The scholarship of more contemporary analysts generally confirms the significance of these warning signals in the area of "product" (see, e.g., Gerstner, 2002, Shook, 1990, and Slater, 1999). Analysts also underscore the "elimination of services" (Renn & Kirk, 1993, p. 20), lack of innovation or "low product-market innovation" (Miller, 1977, p. 48), and "loss of technological leadership" (Lorange & Nelson, 1987, p. 41) as potential indicators of trouble.

Systems

Finally, in the area of organizational dynamics, turning the analytic prism to operational systems and strategies reveals another cluster of symptoms for organizations on the doorstep of decline and potential failure. That is, a "general consensus exists in the literature that declining organizations are characterized by a wide range of organizational processes" (Cameron, Kim, & Whetten, 1988, p. 209) that can expose the seeds of decline for managers. To begin with, a deterioration of "interpersonal and interdepartmental coordination and collaboration" (Khandwalla, 1983–1984, p. 32) often acts as an adverse warning signal (Starbuck, Greve, & Hedberg, 1978). For example, Kanter (2003) found that for the troubled firms in her study, "groups knew less about what was going on in other parts of the organization. . . . Various efforts were duplicated; each group felt it was easier to perform tasks itself than coordinate its actions with others" (pp. 60–61).

Observation of communication and information systems can also help managers see incipient signs of organizational trouble. Bibeault (1982), for example, asserts that "poor communication is the most important adverse behavioral signal" (p. 68) of organizational decline. Goodman (1982), in turn, highlights "poor flow of communications" (p. 25) and the presence of "little constructive communication" (p. 25) among organizational members as significant potential signals of decline. Fredenberger, Lipp, and Watson (1997) also help us see that the "neglect of information systems" (p. 170) can alert reviewers to the presence of decline, as this is often associated with an absence of "accurate, timely, and useful information" (p. 171) needed to lead an enterprise.

Scholars of decline and failure generally conclude that "most firms in need of turnaround are characterized by a noticeable lack of strategic thinking" (Slatter, 1984, p. 57): "There are no clear plans or strategies" (Miller, 1977, p. 48) and "no firm plans for corrective action" (Zimmerman, 1991, p. 21). Thus, "another warning signal is the absence or lack of use of strategic plans . . . and long-range plans" (Renn & Kirk, 1993, p. 37). "Lack of bold action" (Goodman, 1982, p. 27) and a general listlessness on the part of the organization and its leaders—a stance of "timidity" (Kanter, 2003, p. 62)—are also symptoms of declining organizations. "Playing it safe" (Cameron, 1983, p. 365)—or "cautious[ness] and fear of change" (Goodman, 1982, p. 27)—is a symptom that is often linked to the causes of organizational decline (Cameron, 1983). Troubled companies are want to replace strategy and action with (1) increased bureaucracy and centralization (Shook, 1990)—with "greater emphasis on standardization and routinization" (Cameron, Kim, & Whetten, 1988, p. 210), a disregard for and skepticism about the importance of delegation (Goodman, 1982), and a decrease in open communications (Kanter,

2003)—and (2) an unhealthy admiration for the status quo (Slater, 1999; Yates, 1983)—a penchant for "operating the same way as in the past" (Zimmerman, 1991, p. 21).

Not surprisingly, given the dynamics just presented, one often observes a decrease in accountability in turnaround organizations (Kanter, 2003), with "a tendency to pass the buck" (Khandwalla, 1983–1984, p. 33) and a habit of blaming others for problems acting as symptoms of decline. A reduction in self-reflection and self-criticism (Goodman, 1982) and the "prevalence of a defensive posture in the top management" (p. 24) are also symptoms of early stages of organizational problems. A final warning signal in the domain of accountability is the introduction of "creative accounting" (Fredenberger, Lipp, & Watson, 1997, p. 170). Indeed, according to Argenti (1976), the use of this "smokescreen" (p. 45) in lieu of accepting responsibility for the firm is "one of the most useful symptoms of impending failure" (p. 142).

Financial Symptoms

In some instances, there are unmistakable apparent signs that a [firm] is in financial stress. (Renn & Kirk, 1993, p. 20)

Low or declining income and cash flow were the most frequently mentioned signs of turnaround candidacy. (Oviatt & Bruton, 1994, p. 131)

The most common signals of early decline include a shortage of cash for meeting current obligations, increases in the aging of accounts payable and accounts receivable, lack of sales growth, several quarters of losses, as well as late financial information. (Fredenberger, Lipp, & Watson, 1997, p. 169)

In addition to environmental and organizational warning signs, turnaround analysts consistently find that "financial indicators" (Oviatt & Bruton, 1994, p. 131; Renn & Kirk, 1993, p. 38) such as dropping "total sales, profitability, [and] market share . . . all indicate deterioration" (Lorange & Nelson, 1987, p. 4) and a "worsening financial condition" (Rindler, 1987, p. 10) that are linked to the causes of decline and failure. The most cited and most significant "financial condition" (Rindler, 1987, p. 3) is profitability, the capacity "to generate an excess of revenue over expenses" (Renn & Kirk, 1993, p. 38), or more specifically, "decreasing profitability" (Slatter, 1984, p. 55) or "declining profit margins" (Bibeault, 1982, p. 66). One way to look at this topic, or "an important measure of profitability" (Renn & Kirk, 1993, p. 39), is to examine "return on net worth" (Shook, 1990, p. 11) or "return on capital" (Argenti, 1976, p. 36). Other methods include reviewing "operating profit margin and total profit margin" (p. 39) and "profitability as a percentage of sales" (Slatter, 1984, p. 55).

The turnaround literature also highlights the market position of the firm (Gainer, 1999), exposing the fact that "market-based distress signals should begin with an assessment of the structure of the [organization's] market" (Renn & Kirk, 1993, p. 27). Analysts regularly report that "declining business" (Rindler, 1987, p. 4) or "deterioration of a [firm's] position in its market is one of the earliest warning signals of financial distress" (Renn & Kirk, 1993, p. 26). Indeed, Bibeault (1982) maintains that "declining market share [is] the second most important early warning signal" (p. 67), next to profitability. "Market share analysis" (Slatter, 1984, p. 56) requires a company to measure "its performance with that of its major competitors" (p. 56). For example, Shook (1990) does a marvelous job of showing how this line of analysis in the late 1970s provided early clues of an emerging turnaround situation at Ford.

Still another financial symptom linked to the causes of organizational decline is "increasing debt" (Bibeault, 1982, p. 68; also Altman, 1983) or "high debt levels" (Hambrick, 1985, p. 10-2). Thus, "an increase in the firm's gearing, its debt-to-equity ratio, is a widely accepted indicator of impending trouble" (Slatter, 1984, p. 56), and "excessive financial leverage in the capital structure indicates high default risk" (Siegel, 1981, p. 10). Again, Shook (1990) explains how a spike in the debt-to-equity ratio at Ford in the early 1980s provided clues to the firm's leaders about the causes of decline.

Liquidity is a measure of a firm's "ability to meet its current obligations" (Renn & Kirk, 1993, p. 39), and "measures of liquidity are critical indicators of short-term financial health, as well as useful predictors of long-term solvency" (p. 39). In particular, a "decrease in liquidity" (Slatter, 1984, p. 56) should signal potential trouble, for as Greenhalgh (1983) has demonstrated, "slack resources disappear with the onset of decline" (p. 239): "Slack working capital becomes scarce while human resources and less liquid assets tend to become excessive" (p. 238). Thus "a deteriorating cash position" (Green & Hanson, 1993, p. 187) and a "general air of financial stringency" (Argenti, 1976, p. 145) provide clues about potential problems. A particularly salient clue, or what Bibeault (1982) labels "the earliest warning signal of decline" (p. 68), is the "rate of reinvestment" (p. 68) back into the firm.

In this same general domain, we learn that costs provide a window onto organizational problems (Renn & Kirk, 1993) and that "an understanding of cash flow is vital" (Argenti, 1976, p. 21). Specifically, analysts convey that "inability to control operating costs" (Siegel, 1981, p. 11) and "costs increasing faster than revenue" (Zimmerman, 1991, p. 227) provide additional "telltale signs" (p. 227) of possible decline. Relatedly, Argenti (1976) and Goldstein (1988) hold that taking longer to pay bills is "an important warning signal" (Goldstein, 1988, p. 37), as is a growing inability to secure new funds (Siegel, 1981). So too reviewers find that the presence of "deficient budgeting control system[s]" (Goldstein, 1988, p. 36) and the emergence of "creative accounting" (Argenti, 1976, p. 45) are symptoms that are often linked to the causes of decline: "The failed company will most likely suffer from the lack of accurate information in three critical areas: profits, costs, and cash position" (Goldstein, 1988, p. 36).

CHAPTER THREE

Causes of
Organizational Failure

Before we can start to talk sensibly about turnaround strategies, we need to have a good understanding of just how and why firms find themselves in a crisis situation. (Slatter, 1984, p. 24)

The first step which should be taken is an analysis of the cause of the turnaround. (O'Neill, 1986b, p. 87)

An argument can be made that declines are owed finally to: (1) inefficient conduct of an otherwise suitable corporate strategy, (2) a strategy no longer well-adapted to the environment. (Schendel, Patton, & Riggs, 1976, p. 11)

In this chapter, we examine the theoretical and empirical literature on the causes of organizational decline and failure. We underscore that cluster of conditions that set the stage for organizational disintegration and declining performance; that is, the variables at the lower left-hand position in Figure 1.1. The analysis unfolds in two parts. In the first half of the chapter, we offer a general discussion of the causes of organizational decline as seen in the turnaround literature on hospitals, government entities, churches, corporate firms, and so forth. We also provide a snapshot of some of the better-known frameworks and lists of causal factors in the turnaround literature. The second section opens with a discussion of the "external" reasons often offered to explain decline. We attend specifically to the negative conditions that confront organizations when there are unhealthy shifts in the political, legal, economic, and social environments in which these institutions are nested. We then review the internal causes linked to organizational disintegration, focusing heavily on the issue of institutional management.

UNDERSTANDING CAUSALITY

> *The causes of decline are set in motion long before their outward manifestation.* (Bibeault, 1982, p. 74)

The Nature of Causes

> *When analysing a firm's decline, the reader should be careful to distinguish between causes and symptoms of failure.* (Slatter, 1984, p. 24)

> *Combinations or compounding events and actions lies behind decline.* (Schendel, Patton, & Riggs, 1976, p. 7)

Earlier we observed that the first point of action in turnaround situations is the ability to discern symptoms of decline and disintegration. Here we argue that the second point of management in a turnaround situation is the capacity to identify the causes of poor performance: "What is important—if we are to help the sick firm to recover—is to find out the basic causes of the firm's problem" (Slatter, 1984, p. 24). Or, as O'Neill (1986b) maintains, "successful planning of a turnaround is critically dependent on the manager's ability to correctly diagnose the cause of the decline" (p. 86).

Goldston (1992), Miller (1977), Silver (1992), and others provide an important guiding principle in turnarounds: "the need to distinguish between cause and symptoms" (Argenti, 1976, p. 9). The latter "are merely 'tell-tale signs'—danger signals . . . that [provide] clues as to what might be wrong . . . , but they do not provide a guideline for management action" (Slatter, 1984, p. 24): "The symptoms of the troubled company . . . must not be confused with the causes of the company's predicament any more than the thermometer is making the room hot. What we are looking for as the underlying cause is the thing that, if it were removed, would cure the problem" (Goodman, 1982, p. 46). At best, symptoms "illuminate the underlying causes" (Renn & Kirk, 1993, p. 21).

The literature on turnarounds from the organizational sciences also teaches us that "there is no single reliable indicator for predicting failure" (Argenti, 1976, p. 124): "A variety of causes can force a company into a troubled period" (Shuchman & White, 1995, p. 8). It also informs us that "it is rare that one factor by itself will precipitate the need for recovery action" (Slatter 1984, p. 59), that "companies rarely fail because of any one single cause" (Zimmerman, 1991, p. 6; also Kanter, 2003; Schendel, Patton, & Riggs, 1976). Usually, "a combination of events and actions is required to cause severe decline" (Schendel, Patton, & Riggs, 1976, p. 7), what Anheier and Moulton (1999b) refer to as "a complex genesis of factors" (p. 276). Rather, "a chain of interrelated causal factors and multiple causes can be identified in most situations" (Slatter, 1984, p. 25; also Ford, 1985; Grinyer & McKiernan, 1990). Indeed, "organizational problems have many roots [and] crises almost always can be traced to a multitude of factors" (Miller, 1977, p. 50) and "an accumulation of decisions" (Kanter, 2003, p. 61). Generally, "one is central, the others contributory" (Smith, 1963, p. 15). Not surprisingly, "because combinations or compounding of events and actions lies behind declines" (Schendel, Patton, & Riggs, 1976, p. 7), most turnaround stories feature a "considerable amount of subjective judgment" (Slatter, 1984, p. 25) or "attributions" (Ford, 1985, p. 781), and most turnaround situations require "a multipronged attack" (Miller, 1977, p. 50).

Causal Domains and Concepts

Empirical literature suggests a host of reasons why organizations close. . . . The causes can be roughly divided into internal and environmental (external) factors, depending on whether the cause stems from the organization itself or from the environment in which it is embedded. (Hager, Galaskiewicz, Bielefeld, & Pins, 1999, pp. 53–54)

The significance of locus of causality is that it "tells" decision makers the source of a cause and where to apply corrective action. (Ford, 1985, p. 773)

Analysts who investigate turnaround companies offer various causal classification systems at the macro level. For example, they maintain that the problems that lead institutions into turnaround situations can be specific to a given firm, that is, "differ from one company to the next" (Silver, 1992, p. 69) or part of larger industry dynamics (Barker & Patterson, 1996; Krantz, 1985). In a related vein, researchers document that problems can be linked to certain sectors of the economy, such as the service area or the manufacturing sector (Silver, 1992). Problems can also be described as unique or "traced to cyclical patterns" (O'Neill, 1986b, p. 86).

Ford (1985), building on the work of Weiner, holds that individual causes "can be categorized along three dimensions: locus of causality, degree of stability, and controllability" (p. 773). According to Ford, "controllability is a continuum that reflects decision makers' perceptions of their ability to influence directly a cause of performance downturn" (p. 773). For example, chance actions (e.g., a natural disaster) or the actions of powerful others (e.g., the federal government's decision to close a military base) reflect a situation of low controllability. Stability, in turn, is a "continuum ranging from temporary to permanent that indicates the relative duration that decision makers attach to a cause" (p. 773). While assessments of controllability influence efficacy, evaluations of stability influence motivation. Locus of causality attends to the "origins" (Pearce & Robbins, 1994a, p. 94) of problems, specifically to "the external and internal attributions of causality" (McKelvey, 1988, p. 408). Locus of causality "research either (a) highlights failure as a consequence of external factors . . . or (b) exposes failure as a consequence of internal factors" (Anheier & Moulton, 1999a, p. 4). Thus according to Starbuck, Greve, and Hedberg (1978), organizational crises can "originate as threatening events in the organization's environment . . . [or] from defects within organizations themselves" (p. 112; also Finkin, 1985; Ford, 1983).

While "placing the blame for failure and decline in proper perspective is an age-old debate" (Bibeault, 1982, p. 23), with some scholars suggesting that causes are primarily "internally generated" (p. 23) while others see "changes in the external environment as the precursor to decline" (Cameron & Zammuto, 1988, p. 118), especially for the public sector (Whetten, 1988b), most scholars of practice and theorists who study the origins of organizational decline, crises, and failure conclude that "performance declines are usually the result of a combination of external and internal causes" (Barker & Patterson, 1996, p. 5; also Chan, 1993): "Sustained decline is likely to be due to a combination of both internal and external causes" (Arogyaswamy & Yasai-Ardekani, 1997, p. 10). These analysts emphasize that "crisis is precipitated by an organizational-environment (O-E) mismatch" (Milburn, Schuler, & Watman, 1983a, p. 1147). They document that "most of the organizations that die are done in by the interaction of two factors. One is incessant change, the turbulence of the environment. The other is the difficulty in adjusting to this volatility" (Kaufman, 1991, p. 35). In particular, they stress inability of internal management to anticipate and/or adjust to shifts in the environment, arguing that "an interaction of poor managerial decisions . . . coupled with or in response to unfavourable environmental events lies behind most of the cases" (Schendel, Patton, & Riggs, 1976, p. 7) of organizational decline.

Causes can be characterized along other dimensions as well. For example, severity and "critical mass" (Miller, 1977, p. 51) are sometimes highlighted in the literature (Hofer, 1980; Pearce & Robbins, 1993; Robbins & Pearce, 1992). We find, for example, that at times "one large [severe] error in judgment or a wrong critical decision" (Shuchman & White, 1995, p. 11) or one significant environmental crisis (Pincus & Acharya, 1988) creates a pathway to failure. At other times, a number of less dramatic problems accumulate to form a crisis that pushes an organization into a turnaround situation. Here, as Miller (1977) reveals, "weaknesses have a multiplicative effect" (p. 51). Speed of action and directness of impact also are concepts that are used to understand causes of organizational decline. For example, some causes can provide a rather direct and quick spur to action, or death, while others slowly and inexorably push an organization into a cycle of crisis and decline (Hambrick & D'Aveni, 1988).

Finally, "since the definition of a problem influences the solutions considered" (Whetten, 1988b, p. 162), analysts from all sectors of the turnaround literature "stress the importance of properly assessing the cause of the turnaround situation" (Pearce & Robbins, 1993, p. 620) and draw connections between analysis of the causes of crisis and the appropriate management response (Pearce & Robbins, 1994a; Schendel, Patton, & Riggs, 1976; Stopford & Baden-Fuller, 1990). They report that there is a "strong association between the cause of the turnaround situation and the direction of functional emphasis" (Pearce & Robbins, 1994a, p. 102), that "the cause of the decline is an important determinant of the turnaround strategy" (O'Neill, 1986b, p. 86). More specifically, to foreshadow material to follow in later chapters, firms that attribute turnaround status to external problems "tend to adopt entrepreneurial turnaround strategies" (Robbins & Pearce, 1992, p. 301), while organizations "that perceive their problems to be primarily internal in origin adopt efficiency turnaround strategies" (p. 301). In a similar fashion, researchers link severity of cause and change turnaround actions, arguing that "more severe problems require more drastic solutions" (Pearce & Robbins, 1993, p. 620).

Causal Frameworks

Developing a suitable system to classify factors causing decline is not as easy as it may seem at first glance. (Slatter, 1984, p. 24)

Over the years, investigators in the area of turnaround management have employed two overlapping strategies to frame the causes for organizational disintegration. The first approach is to provide lists of reasons for decline. While these lists are "an inadequate weapon in the prediction of failure" (Argenti, 1976, p. 152), they do provide a good picture of the landscape of causes for decline. The second approach is to develop concepts from the empirical and theoretical literature on turnarounds and then to weave these ideas together in conceptual maps. To provide a flavor of this work, below we outline examples from both methods.

Lists of Causes

From his analysis of troubled firms, Silver (1992) lists 10 of what he finds as "the most typical" (p. 69) causes for organizational decline:

- Product obsolescence
- Regional recession
- Key customers go out of business
- Aggressive price competition
- Industrywide recession
- Key suppliers go out of business
- Aggressive foreign competition

- Faulty production leading to cost overruns and shipping delays
- High overheads
- Ineffectual middle management (pp. 69–70)

He also furnishes 10 "primary reasons" (p. 3) that firms enter turnaround situations:

1. Managers are unprepared for trouble.

2. Managers tiptoe around stressors until they become crises.

3. Managers do not know where and how to slash expenses and raise cash.

4. Many of today's managers never have lived through seriously troubled times.

5. Managers think sales growth can disguise problems within their organizations.

6. Companies are undercapitalized.

7. Managers fail to respond to the market by continually reviewing products or services.

8. Managers fail to stay in contact with customers and to continually ask what they want.

9. There are not enough talented people in middle management.

10. Owners and managers become emotionally involved with their companies. (p. 3)

In his book *Corporate Collapse,* Argenti (cited in Zimmerman, 1991) explores 12 major causes of organizational failure in the private sector:

1. Poor management, including one-man rule, a nonparticipative board of directors, an unbalanced top team, and lack of management depth

2. Defective accounting information, including erroneous cash flow forecasts, costing systems, and asset valuations

3. Exposure to change, including competitive, economic, social, and technological change

4. Externally induced constraints, including governmental, union, public opinion, and consumer constraints

5. Overtrading, involving expansion that is faster than cash flow or profits will permit

6. The big project in which cost and time are underestimated and revenue is overstated

7. Excessive gearing up, in which the company borrows more money than the volume of business can reasonably support

8. Bad financial ratios, which, with traditional financial analysis, indicate slippage in the firm's competitive position

9. Creative accounting, involving the delayed publication of financial information, capitalized research and development costs, payment of dividends from borrowed money, reduction of maintenance on capital equipment, treatment of extraordinary income as ordinary income, and incorrect valuation of assets

10. Normal business hazards, involving strikes by suppliers and fires or other disasters for which the firm is unprepared

11. Nonfinancial symbols of decline, including low morale, poor maintenance, poor housekeeping, and slippage in quality of service

12. "Last few months" indicators, including low stock prices, management's denial of circumstance, and callous disregard for customers (pp. 20–21)

Slatter (1984), in turn, in his volume *Corporate Recovery,* outlines 11 "factors determining decline" (p. 26):

1. Lack of financial control

2. Inadequate management

3. Competition

4. High cost structure relative to competitors

5. Changes in market demand

6. Adverse movement in commodity markets (including interest rates)

7. Operating marketing problems

8. Big projects

9. Acquisitions

10. Financial policy

11. Overtrading (p. 26)

Looking specifically at small firms, Boyle and Desai (1991) record 24 "causes of failure" (p. 35):

1. Failure to carefully analyze financial statements

2. Inadequately managed capital requirements

3. Improper management of accounts receivable

4. Underutilization of assets

5. Declining margins of profit

6. Accepting contracts below standard price, and/or granting large discounts for early payment, in order to generate cash

7. Sudden or large increases in debt

8. Maintaining raw materials, work in process, and overly large finished goods inventories

9. Spending excessively as earnings begin to rise

10. Failure to manage success (e.g., production backlogs and incomplete orders as sales grow)

11. Unwillingness of an owner to delegate responsibility, especially as a business expands

12. Inability to successfully transcend stress points (e.g., $1 million in sales, $5 million in sales, $25 million in sales, $50 million in sales)

13. Key employee quits

14. Inability of an owner to perform both planning and administrative functions

15. Lack of product and/or market knowledge on the part of the owner

16. Declining market shares

17. Sudden drop in the number of prospects or inquiries

18. Losing the biggest account(s)

19. Excessive optimism in planning

20. Lack of comprehensive strategic planning

21. Lack of in-depth market information prior to start-up and/or ignoring negative market information

22. Company's product or service injures someone

23. Owner or principal manager is injured or becomes ill

24. National, regional, or industrial economic downturns (p. 35)

Ford (1983), in a more parsimonious classification, supplies "four primary characteristics which contribute to organizational crises" (p. 11):

1. Failure to identify variable relationships

2. Groupthink

3. Distribution and distortion of information

4. Misplaced optimism (p. 11)

As a final example, Lorange and Nelson (cited in Weitzel & Jonsson, 1989) offer nine causes of organizational decline:

1. Excessive personnel

2. Tolerance of incompetence

3. Cumbersome administrative procedures

4. Disproportionate staff power

5. Replacement of substance with form

6. Scarcity of clear goals and decision benchmarks

7. Fear of embarrassment and conflict

8. Loss of effective communication

9. Outdated structure (pp. 97–98)

Conceptual Designs

As we noted above, and return to in considerable detail in the second half of the chapter, the most prevalent conceptual design "classifies causes of turnaround situations as internal and external" (Pearce & Robbins, 1994a, p. 94), that is, a framework that holds that the "causes of decline occur in the internal and/or external environments of the organization" (Armenakis & Fredenberger, 1998, p. 40). All of the models below incorporate this central explanatory dimension in their designs.

Ford (1985) provides the following framework:

- External attributions
  - autonomy
  - competitors' actions
  - governments' actions
  - raw material shortages or costs
  - technological changes
  - consumer action groups
  - demographic shifts
  - weather

- Internal attributions
  - strategy
  - sales efforts
  - product or process development
  - quality control
  - production efficiency
  - management expertise
  - workforce skill (p. 773)

Levine (1978) has crafted a "four-cell typology of causes of public organization decline":

- Organizational atrophy
- Vulnerability

- Loss of legitimacy
- Environmental entropy (p. 318)

Tushman, Newman, and Romanelli (1988) use a three-dimensional model to analyze factors explaining organizational disintegration:

- Industry discontinuities
- Product life cycle shifts
- Internal dynamics (pp. 68–69)

Hambrick and D'Aveni (1988), in turn, employ a framework of four major constructs to explain decline:

- The firm's domain (product/market) initiatives
- The firm's environment's carrying capacity
- The firm's slack
- The firm's profitability (p. 2)

Boyle and Desai (1991) cluster empirical data on the causes of organizational decline into four conceptual buckets:

- Internal-administrative
- Internal-strategic
- External-administrative
- External-strategic (p. 35)

Meyer (1988) arranges three concepts in his map of "alternative causes of organizational failures":

- Declining industries
- Impoverished [environmental] niches
- Outmoded strategies (p. 412)

Argenti (1976) clusters his findings into a six-part framework:

- Top management
- Accounting information
- Change
- Accounting manipulations
- Rapid expansion
- Economic cycle (pp. 26–27)

Harrigan (1988) employs a three-dimensional causal map:

- Technological obsolescence
- Sociological or demographic changes
- Changing fashion (p. 131)

Hegde's (1982) analysis produces a map with seven categories of "causes of [organizational] sickness":

- Root cause
- External cause
- General management
- Finance and control
- R&D
- Operations
- Personnel (p. 292)

Another grouping of designs, while attending to internal and external causes of organizational failure, features a different conceptual scaffolding, one that underscores efficiency and strategic causes of decline. The scholarship of Schendel and his team (Schendel & Patton, 1976; Schendel, Patton, & Riggs, 1976) and Pearce and Robbins (1993, 1994a, 1994b; Robbins & Pearce, 1992) is instructive here. The design logic is that "both strategic and operational factors must be considered in any search for a better understanding of what caused failure in the first place" (Stopford & Baden-Fuller, 1990, p. 402). Pearce and Robbins's (1994a) framework is representative of work here:

- Strategic
  - decreased profit margins
  - increased wages
  - increased competition
  - raw materials shortages
  - management difficulties

- Operating
  - depressed price levels
  - recessions
  - labor problems
  - excess plant capacity (p. 94)

ANALYZING CAUSES OF FAILURE

Both strategic and organizational factors must be considered in any search for a better understanding of what caused failure in the first place. From our evidence the two seem to be intertwined. (Stopford & Baden-Fuller, 1990, p. 402)

Poor management and external environmental factors are the reasons that most businesses start to get in trouble. (Chan, 1993, p. 30)

External Causes

If you are looking for a way to predict failure, it is not enough to look at the firm itself. There are powerful external forces acting from outside the firm. (Bibeault, 1982, p. 29)

It is not always true that managerial incompetencies are rampant throughout the troubled organization. Economic and market conditions also stress corporate resources. (Zimmerman, 1991, p. 22)

We can differentiate four broad environmental influences on organizational survival. (a) Ecological theory highlights the importance of competition and the carrying capacity of resource environment. (b) Market theory focuses on the demand for organizations' goods and services. (c) Resource-dependency theory examines how well organizations maintain contacts with key funders, interlock with competitors, share information, and stay connected to developments in the community and in professional associations. Finally, (d) institutional theory points to the importance of a positive image and legitimacy and the dangers of becoming too vulnerable to outside normative controls. (Hager et al., 1999, pp. 56–57)

Organizational scholars (Allmendinger & Hackman, 1996; Amburgey, Kelly, & Barnett, 1993; Meyer, 1982; Miles, Snow, & Meyer, 1978; Staw, Sanderlands, & Dutton, 1981; Thompson, 1967) and turnaround analysts "agree that the environment plays a major role affecting the fate of firms" (Hambrick & D'Aveni, 1988, p. 3), in particular "that organizational malfunctioning may be induced by events in the external environment" (Khandwalla, 1983–1984, p. 6)— both external changes and external constraints (Bibeault, 1982). According to these analysts, "powerful external forces from outside the firm" (Argenti, 1976, p. 54) in a variety of domains and "abrupt environmental change" (Bennis & Nanus, 1985, p. 157) can "strike at the core of a company's business" (Bibeault, 1982, p. 27; also Hall, 1980) by reducing the amount of resources available and by forcing "structural and context shifts that impinge on the organization" (McKelvey, 1988, p. 404). Because these environments have potential to be "irregular, nonrecurring, irrational, and unpredictable" (Bennis & Nanus, 1985, p. 157), organizations often are able to exercise only weak control over them (Milburn, Schuler, & Watman, 1983a, p. 1156). The logic in the turnaround literature holds that changes in external conditions, or environmental decline (Hambrick, 1985), act as "triggering devices" (Austin, 1998, p. 88) "that suddenly make things that formerly worked no longer work" (Bibeault, 1982, p. 25; also Smith, 1963). In effect, these external changes create the "conditions of decline that require a new set of administrative and organizational responses" (Cameron, 1983, p. 359).

Probing a bit more deeply, the literature posits that when the organization's environment is benign and when the organization is in alignment with the environment, "even a weak organization can survive" (Hambrick & D'Aveni, 1988, p. 17). However, changes in the environment reset the rules. These changes are of two major varieties: (1) changed demands—"shifts in the requirements that it [the environment] places on organizations" (Hambrick & D'Aveni, 1988, p. 17) and (2) "deterioration of environmental support for the organization" (Sutton, 1990, p. 209) or "environmental entropy" (Whetten, 1988b, p. 161)—changes in "the capacity of the environment to support the . . . organization at prevailing levels of activity" (Levine, 1978, p. 318).

Researchers also discuss deteriorating environmental "carrying capacity" (Hambrick & D'Aveni, 1988, p. 17) in terms of changes in the size and shape of an organization's "environmental niche" (Cameron & Zammuto, 1988, p. 120). Changes in environmental carrying capacity in turn can also represent "dramatic shifts" (Haveman, 1992, p. 49) in the form of (1) exogenous shocks (Tushman & Romanelli, 1985), "revolutionary or discontinuous events" (Ford & Baucus, 1987, p. 369), or "environmental jolts" (Meyer, 1982,

p. 515) that throw the organization into an immediate turnaround situation (e.g., the destruction of a school in a fire) (Haveman, 1992; Shook, 1990; Slatter, 1984) or (2) slow erosions of environmental conditions (e.g., the bleeding of the major cities in the Midwest as key industries atrophied) (Austin, 1998; Whetten, 1988b; Zammuto & Cameron, 1985).

As we discuss more fully below, changing demands and environmental entropy change markets for organizations and entire industries (Hager et al., 1999; Miller, 1977). They can also produce a "loss of legitimacy" (Whetten, 1988b, p. 161) and a "tainted organizational image" (Sutton, 1990, p. 211), an especially "salient [variable] in the public sector" (Whetten, 1988b, p. 161). Also, as we explore below in our analysis of the internal causes of organizational decline and failure, a critical issue is how well managers anticipate, adapt, and respond to these changing environmental conditions. Or as Weitzel and Jonsson (1989) capture it, "decline occurs if the organization lacks sensitivity and fails to anticipate and respond to unfavorable conditions" (p. 96).

Examining external decline from a different viewpoint, and at a more concrete level, we uncover additional frameworks that have been created to portray causes of organizational decline. O'Shaughnessy (1995) describes four dimensions of environmental decline: "economic slowdown, increasing competition, social change, and technological change" (p. 3). Focusing specifically on nonprofit organizations, Hager and his colleagues (1999) identify five external factors responsible for organizational failure: "decreased donor demand, decreased consumer demand, isolation, crisis of legitimacy, and external normative control" (p. 65). Argenti (1976) and Bibeault (1982) each outline five key environments that influence organizational disintegration: competitive, political, social, economic, and technological. Tushman and Romanelli (1985) describe a similar framework but add "legal conditions" (p. 178) to forces that can make strategic orientations "no longer effective" (p. 178). Milburn and his team (1983a, 1983b), in turn, highlight seven "components of the external environment [that] represent important potential antecedents of organizational crisis" (1983a, p. 1150): "competitors, suppliers, customers/clients, regulation, society, owners/board of directors, and natural disasters" (1983a, pp. 1148–1149). And in his research, Mayntz (1999) distinguishes "four major types of environmental threats: resource scarcity, task obsolescence, positional challenges, and imposed structural change" (p. 72).

Blending all of this work, we forge a six-cell typology for examining external causes for organizational decline: economic slowdown, competition, technology, legal and political issues, social change, and political vulnerability. To start, we acknowledge that "economic turndown" (Argenti, 1976, p. 136) is one of the two "classic nutcrackers of failure" (p. 136), that there is a clear link between decline and the national business cycle (O'Neill, 1986a). According to Argenti (1976), three factors in particular are relevant in explaining *economic slowdown*: changes in GNP, stock market performance, and money supply. Altman (1983), in turn, describes five "categories of aggregate economic behavior" (p. 85) that are "potentially revealing indicators of business failure: economic growth activity, credit availability or money market activity, capital market activity, business population characteristics, and price level changes" (p. 85).

An assortment of analysts have shown how "competition can cause decline" (Bibeault, 1982, p. 30), both *competition* resulting from the evolution to a global economy (Slatter, 1984; Thurow, 2003) and ongoing competitive pressures within industries (Finkin, 1985; Grzymala-Busse, 2002). "Both price competition and product competition are common causes of decline" (Slatter, 1984, p. 32) in the saga of organizational failure (Bibeault, 1982). Brinkley (2003), Reich and Donahue (1985), Shook (1990), and Yates (1983), for example, all document at great length the role of global product and price competition as the catalysts in the decline of the U.S. automobile industry. The "theory of action" presented by organizational scholars here is quite simple: "As population fields become more crowded, the increased competition results in organizations' dying" (Hager et al., 1999, p. 55).

Argenti (1976) reports that a third major cause of decline "is failure to keep up with change in technology" (p. 30), including "new management techniques" (Yates, 1983, p. 120), or what Khandwalla (1983–1984) calls "technological turbulence" (p. 7; see also Sutton, Eisenhardt, & Jucker, 1986). *Technological change* provides a good example of the way external and internal causes of failure are yoked, for, as a number of turnaround analysts explain, the technology change is only the triggering event. Equally salient is "lack of foresight" (Bibeault, 1982, p. 32) by executives, or what Argenti (1976) in a less charitable turn of a phrase calls "rank bad management" (p. 47)—a story line laid out nicely by Slater (1999) in dissecting the near collapse of IBM in the late 1980s due to its failure "to adapt to the next big change in the world of information technology" (p. 6) and by Reich and Donahue (1985) in unpacking the spiraling decline of the U.S. automotive industry in the face of ungarnered technological advances.

Legal and government constraints have also been found to be key elements in the algorithm of organizational decline and failure (Bibeault, 1982), what some analysts label "interference by government in business decisions" (Argenti, 1976, p. 40). In his work, for example, Chan (1993) links "government funding cuts and changes in governmental regulations" (p. 30) to organizational decline. So too, Hager and his colleagues (1999) have associated "increased regulation by government" (p. 66) to decline. Bennis and Nanus (1985) have explored the role of government regulation in the demise of AT&T, and Argenti (1976) reveals how "Penn Central's failure . . . was substantially due to the operation of [government] constraints" (p. 131). As with earlier causes (e.g., economic slowdown), these constraints operate at both the macro level (e.g., exchange rates, monetary policy) (Altman, 1983; Argenti, 1976; Slatter, 1984) and the micro level (e.g., pollution control requirements) (Slatter, 1984). The constraint drivetrain is generally described in fairly straightforward terms: either external "constraints prevent . . . managers from making the responses they wish to make" (Argenti, 1976, p. 122) or they "force organizations to adopt forms that conform to external expectations but that are highly inefficient for the organization" (Hager et al., 1999, p. 56).

External decline can also be traced to the doorstep of organizations' failure "to see or react to such social trends as changes in lifestyles, in composition by age or colour of a given population, . . . and so on" (Argenti, 1976, p. 130). At times, these can be *changes in the larger socioeconomic and "sociopolitical environment"* (Mayntz, 1999, p. 76) (e.g., the importance of fundamentalism in the United States). For example, Benjaminson (1984) reveals how economic and social "changes in American society" (p. viii) helped kill an American institution—the afternoon newspaper. Ross and Kami (1973) document how A&P's inability to discern and respond to major sociocultural changes led to the decline of the largest grocery chain in America. And Reich and Donohue (1985) and Yates (1983) explain how Ford's and Chrysler's inability to detect social changes (e.g., the shift from an infatuation with styling to a concern for performance) pulled the U.S. automobile industry into a downward spiral of decline.

The pathway to failure here might best be labeled "demand declines" (Schendel, Patton, & Riggs, 1976, p. 6). "The demand for goods and services can change over time" (Hager et al., 1999, p. 55), and a "reduction in the demand for a product or service, or a change in the pattern of demand, to which the firm does not respond can be important causal factors in a firm's decline" (Slatter, 1984, p. 40). Another way to describe the result of the social change is in terms of "acceptance of organizational outputs" (Cameron & Zammuto, 1988, p. 119), especially in terms of "perceived value" (Yates, 1983, p. 286). Again, spotlighting the automobile industry, Yates (1983) exposes how the big American car "became extinct in the face of a radically changing [cultural and social] environment" (p. 93).

Finally, looking through a political lens (Anheier & Moulton, 1999b), organizations, especially public ones, decline because of *"political vulnerability"* (Levine, 1978, p. 319; Whetten, 1988b, p. 160). According to organizational theorists in general and turnaround scholars in particular, for nonprofit and government entities "survival largely depends on a positive image and a viable public mission" (Hager et al., 1999, p. 66; also Baum & Oliver, 1991; Meyer & Rowan, 1977). Scholars and analysts maintain that a stock of social capital and external legitimacy are essential to organizational well-being (Hager et al., 1999) and that causes of failure "ultimately . . . relate to the question of legitimacy" (Anheier & Moulton, 1999b, p. 280). Researchers here also point out that decline is linked as much to the inability of leaders to manage impressions as it is about the catalytic environmental events themselves (Anheier & Moulton, 1999a, 1999b).

Internal Causes

The internal environment is crucial in explaining the development of organizational crises. One could argue that unless the external environment is completely uncontrolled and its effects unpredictable, it is the internal environment that is often the culprit in an organization's crisis even if the culprit appears to be the external environment. (Milburn, Schuler, & Watman, 1983a, p. 1150)

Our firms were failing because their structures and systems had become ossified, making them incapable of responding adequately to the changing environment. (Stopford & Baden-Fuller, 1990, p. 402)

"While attributing failure to . . . predominantly external causes is popular" (Miller, 1977, p. 43), most analysts who study turnarounds conclude that decline is generally caused by internal factors. For example, Bibeault (1982), from his work on turnarounds, posits that decline is caused internally about eighty percent of the time. Boyle and Desai (1991) reach a similar conclusion. The logic is laid out nicely by Argenti (1976): "Obviously, however potent are the factors influencing failure that lie outside the firm, those within the firm must be paramount for otherwise all firms would fail whenever economic conditions turned sour!" (pp. 54–55). This is the case on the one hand because while there is little doubt that environmental factors, especially jolts that few could have anticipated, can cause organizational failure, and most environmental conditions are mediated by internal actions and structures. It is what the organization does in response to the environmental threat or change that determines whether the organization slides into a pattern of decline. It is true on the other hand because internal problems alone can push organizations into turnaround situations.

Scholars who study turnaround institutions—both those that fail and those that recover—have developed key explanatory variables and frameworks for specifying internal causes of decline. On the variable front, Boyle and Desai (1991) assert that "lack of control over operations" (p. 39) may be the key internal cause of failure, at least in the small firms they investigated. In a similar vein, Slatter (1984) illuminates key pillars in the architecture of organizational failure. To wit, "lack of financial control and inadequate top management at the level of the chief executive are clearly the major sources of decline and occur almost twice as frequently as any other single factor" (p. 54). Ford (1983), in turn, holds that decline can be traced back to the organization's "failure to understand its own internal dynamics" (p. 19), what he describes as "the failure to understand adequately both subtleties and complexities of the relationship among relevant variables" (p. 11).

Moving outward to the broader issue of frameworks, Smith (1963) posits that corporate crises often "arise from the faulty application of a structural, organizational, or managerial concept" (p. 22). Weitzel and Jonsson (1989) have "crises of leadership, autonomy, control, and bureaucratic red tape; . . . lack of attention to efficient management of basic operations; . . . and lack of regard for constituency satisfaction" (p. 96) in their framework. Milburn and his colleagues (1983a) group internal causes "into four classes: executive characteristics, experience and history, demographics, and attributes" (p. 1150). Finally, Hager and his colleagues (1999) list the following "organizational characteristics that might contribute to the demise of an organization: size, age, financial condition, personal capabilities, staff conflict, power struggles, clarity of mission, personnel loss and turnover, [and] change in goals" (p. 59). They cluster these characteristics in six bins:

1. Size (organization too small, organization too large)

2. Age (organization too young)

3. Instability (personnel loss and turnover, goal changes)

4. Managerial expertise (financial difficulties, personnel capabilities, conflict among staff, power struggles, unclear mission)

5. Success (organization completed its mission)

6. Other (p. 62)

Bad Management

Internally caused decline generally arises either (1) from conscious attempts by managers to adapt an organization to changing external conditions or (2) from the systematic loss of survival competence, that is, the loss of those knowledge and skill elements necessary both for responding to environmental change and for survival under new circumstances. (McKelvey, 1988, p. 405)

The main internal cause may be management's inability to manage large, complex structures, and tasks, shifts in the environment, and/or growth strategy. (Khandwalla, 1983–1984, pp. 19–20)

In investigating inadequate management as a cause of organizational decline, we are guided by the following road map. We commence with an examination of the power of bad management in the narrative of organizational failure, allowing leading scholars to speak in their own voices. We then explore three key aspects of poor management linked to institutional disintegration: poor environmental scanning, inaction, and maladaptation.

Bad management: A cardinal condition. We know from a plethora of studies that leadership is a keystone variable in the health of organizations (Yukl, 2002), or as Argenti (1976) captures it, "one might go so far as to say that the nature of the top management team in a company is of greater significance for success or failure than any of the company's products or skills or physical assets" (p. 37). We also understand that the saliency of management is enhanced in difficult circumstances (Baehr, 1993). Indeed, in most cases "an appropriate management response in a hostile environment [can] . . . prevent sickness" (Hegde, 1982, p. 296): "The more crises one examines, the clearer it is that many of them might have been avoided if management had just done the things that could reasonably have been expected of it" (Smith, 1963, p. 26). And while acknowledging that "the process of naming management as a scapegoat can hide the true value of potential causes of decline" (O'Neill, 1986b, p. 86) and can "locate the blame for a firm's decline without providing those charged with the recovery task with any useful information" (Slatter, 1984, p. 24), all the reviewers of organizational turnarounds conclude that a majority of businesses "fail because of internal factors affected by managerial action and discipline" (Boyle & Desai, 1991, p. 33): "The real problem lay in management" (Ross & Kami, 1973, p. 73). For example, focusing on *decline,* leading analysts conclude

Management problems are the principal reason for corporate decline. (Bibeault, 1982, p. 141)

Inadequate top management is the single most important factor leading to decline and stagnation. (Slatter, 1984, p. 178)

Mostly, however, it [decline] may be attributable to management failure of one kind or another. (Khandwalla, 1983–1984, p. 6)

Management problems are the root cause of most organizational decline. (Oviatt & Bruton, 1994, p. 131)

Management failure, directly or indirectly, by commission and omission, [is] a significant factor in decline. (Schendel, Patton, & Riggs, 1976, p. 7)

The cause of decline might be traced to administrative factors within the firm. (O'Neill, 1986b, p. 86)

Businesses do not decline on their own; they are managed into and through the process. (Goldston, 1992, p. 14)

Almost without exception, turnaround situations arise because of management's incompetence. (Sloma, 1985, p. 13)

On the topic of *organizational illness,* reviewers hold

In the majority of cases, sickness was caused mainly by inappropriate management. (Hegde, 1982, p. 292)

There are usually definitive reasons why companies find themselves in unhealthy situations. A common reason is poor management. (Chan, 1993, p. 29)

There is no way of getting around the fact that the major cause of continued malfunction in a business is management inadequacy. (Goodman, 1982, p. 45)

Turning to *failure,* analysts find

Management caused more than 80 percent of business failures. (Fredenberger, Lipp, & Watson, 1997, p. 169)

Dunn & Bradstreet's analysis of business failure from 1980 to 1990 shows that 62 percent of business failures are caused by various management shortcomings. (Shuchman & White, 1995, p. 12)

The overwhelming cause of individual firm failure is managerial incompetence. (Altman, 1983, p. 40)

Corporate calamities are calamities created by men (Argenti, 1976, p. 15) and bad management is the prime cause of failure. (p. 3)

And finally on the topic of *crisis,* scholars find

> Top managers are often the villains of crises. They are the real villains insofar as they steer their organizations into crises and insofar as they intensify crises by delaying actions or taking inappropriate actions. (Starbuck, Greve, & Hedberg, 1978, p. 132)

Scholars of turnaround organizations also expose "management patterns in the failure process" (O'Neill, 1981, p. 21). For example, Hegde (cited in Khandwalla, 1983–1984) in his studies has uncovered four types of deficient management—autocratic, conservative, reckless, and complacent—"as the chief causes of malfunctioning of Western companies" (p. 7). Bibeault (1982) outlines seven types of bad management, or seven symptoms:

> (1) One-man rule, (2) lack of management depth, (3) management succession problems, (4) inbred bureaucratic management, (5) a weak financial executive, (6) an unbalanced top management team, and finally, (7) a nonparticipative board. (p. 38)

Argenti (1976), in turn, describes six related dangers:

> One-man rule, non-participating board, unbalanced top team, lack of management depth, weak finance function, and combined chairman-chief executive. (p. 123)

To these elements, Slatter (1984) adds "management neglect of the core business" (p. 29), Miller (1977) adds "domination by a power-hoarding chief executive" (p. 45), and Bibeault (1982) adds "narrow vision" (p. 37).

Unpacking bad management. According to turnaround analysts such as Silver (1992), "businesses fail simply because their owners or managers are unprepared for crises. They either cannot see the stressors that precede the crisis, or they detour around the stressors, or they see the stressors but work on solutions in the wrong areas" (p. 5). They "fail to see the onslaught before it [is] too late . . . or take timid or retrograde steps" (Benjaminson, 1984, p. 189). Thus bad management is at its core about a combination of two factors: "environmental scanning and strategic action" (Hager et al., 1999, p. 55)—what managers see and "the type of change firms undertake" (Haveman, 1992, p. 53), or more accurately "inaction" (Sloma, 1985, p. 13) on the first factor and "imprudent action" (p. 13) on the latter. "Dramatic external changes that ruin [environmental] fit set up conditions for failure. Whether failure occurs or not depends on the organizational response to changing conditions" (Anheier & Moulton, 1999b, p. 277; also Sutton, Eisenhardt, & Jucker, 1986): "Change, or failure to respond to change, is a major cause of collapse. . . . The company either does not notice the change or does not respond correctly" (Argenti, 1976, p. 130), that is, it (1) displays "inertia" (Hambrick & D'Aveni, 1988, p. 2) or responds in a "sluggish" (p. 2) fashion or (2) selects "inappropriate 'recipes' or implements them ineffectively or inconsistently over time" (Stopford & Baden-Fuller, 1990, p. 402; also Milburn, Schuler, & Watman, 1983b).

According to this line of investigation, "an unfavorable external environment may be a precipitating factor of disease, but its effect may be greatly magnified by the difficulties caused by management" (Khandwalla, 1983–1984, p. 35): "External threats and managerial coping decisions work in consort to bring about organizational success or failure" (Anheier & Moulton, 1999b, p. 277).

> The evidence suggests that it takes unfavourable changes in the environment *coupled* with either, 1) inefficient operations under an existing corporate strategy, or 2) a strategy no longer suited to its competition, markets, or the economy, to cause sustained decline. (Schendel, Patton, & Riggs, 1976, p. 10)

Or, as Meyer (1988) explains it, "it is reasonable to conceptualize organizational decline as maladaptation" (p. 414). The leaders of failing "firms either do not see the need for reorientation or they are unable to carry through the necessary frame-breaking changes" (Tushman, Newman, & Romanelli, 1988, p. 63). Poor sight and delusion (Goldstein, 1988)—"failure to adjust" (Kaufman, 1991, p. 49)—and timid responses or over-the-top actions—"inadequate response to change" (Argenti, 1976, p. 178)—are at the heart of poor management. Argenti's (1976) antidote is quite explicit: "(1) Watch out for the symptoms of failure. (2) If you see them, act" (p. 69).

As noted earlier, "failure to scan the environment" (Weitzel & Jonsson, 1989, p. 98), that is, *"poor forecasting"* (Schendel, Patton, & Riggs, 1976, p. 7) of an organization's "environment, its changing nature, and its impact" (p. 8) is a central theme in the story of organizational decline and failure. Or as Goldstein (1988) explains, "most businesses fail not because they cannot solve their problems but because they cannot see their problems" (p. 30). And, "by implication, active organizations that search the environment for strategic information are more likely to survive" (Anheier & Moulton, 1999b, p. 276)—or "environmental monitoring is required to help avoid downturn" (Schendel, Patton, & Riggs, 1976, p. 11). Thus according to this line of thought, managers leading organizations into decline "neglect to read the signs of change" (Argenti, 1976, p. 34; Ross & Kami, 1973). Either they "cannot see" (Goldstein, 1988, p. 32) or they refuse to see (Slater, 1999; Sloma, 1985), a type of "myopia" (Yates, 1993, p. 140) that results in "managers' failure to monitor critical information" (Fredenberger, Lipp, & Watson, 1997, p. 174). And, of course, absent sight, it is almost impossible for managers to "react appropriately" (p. 174) to changing environmental conditions.

There is also considerable evidence "that organizations fail because of "inertia" (Hambrick & D'Aveni, 1988, p. 15) or *"inaction"* (Schendel, Patton, & Riggs, 1976, p. 10), that "organizational inertia [is] one of the main causes of failure in declining organizations" (Barker & Mone, 1998, p. 1246). Or as Smith (1963) concludes, "corporate difficulties are . . . often the result of inaction in the face of dangerous change" (p. 19), that is, a "lack of reaction to change" (Ross & Kami, 1973, p. 26) or an "inability or unwillingness to adjust to change" (Smith, 1963, p. 20; also Sloma, 1985), a "passive approach to the actual cause of the situation" (Milburn, Schuler, & Watman, 1983a, p. 1151). The macro-level theme here is as follows: "Deceptive reasoning shapes a firm's response to external change more than any other factor" (Bibeault, 1982, p. 50).

The turnaround literature allows us to craft a taxonomy of incarnations of inertia and inaction. Denial, the "ostrich-like mentality" (Sloma, 1985, p. 23) of "trying to hide the truth" (Argenti, 1976, p. 41) from oneself, fills one cell in the inaction framework. Sloughing off "nascent problems or trends [as] superfluous activities" (Miller, 1977, p. 47) fits here, as does "holding out the hope that external forces that [are] giving the company problems [will] simply go away" (Bibeault, 1982, p. 133; also Argenti, 1976; Goldstein, 1988). Also finding a home here is the practice of degrading unwanted knowledge. For example, Ford (1983) shows that in declining firms, information that "is contrary to accepted culture" (p. 13) is likely to be "ignored or discounted" (p. 13; also Whetten, 1988b). In particular, under the "degrading" scenario, "indicators of decline, often obvious to the objective observer, are discounted by responsible top managers" (Lorange & Nelson, 1987, p. 42; also Sloma, 1985). "False encouragement" (Hambrick & D'Aveni, 1988, p. 19), "self-deception" (Lorange & Nelson, 1987, p. 47), rationalization (Goldstein, 1988; Goldston, 1992), the search for confirming, optimistic evidence in a sea of disquiet, and "hubris and arrogance" (Slater, 1999, p. 20) help "decision makers delude themselves into believing that a problem does not exist or that it is not serious" (Hambrick & D'Aveni, 1988, p. 16) or "delude themselves into believing the convenient explanation" (Goldston, 1992, p. 18). Specifically, managers sometimes "tend to underestimate or minimize dangers" (Ford, 1983, p. 14) or underplay "how serious their company's situation is" (Argenti, 1976, p. 67). What we see here is a condition in which managers confronted by changing and dangerous environments are "unwilling to recognize symptoms" (Sloma, 1985, pp. 22–23) and simply "refuse to face the facts" (Argenti, 1976, p. 33).

Scholars of turnaround situations also reveal that inaction is linked to paralysis and withdrawal. Here managers see and acknowledge environmental problems but are overwhelmed by what confronts them and develop a "defensive posture" (Milburn, Schuler, & Watman, 1983a, p. 1151) or withdraw to avoid dealing with problems (Hambrick & D'Aveni, 1988). In a similar vein, inaction can be linked to victimization, scapegoating, "resistance to change" (Slater, 1999, p. 29), and "rationalization of performance failure by blaming the victim" (Levine, 1978, p. 319). In the first case, managers "delude themselves into believing [a] circumstantial action" (Goldston, 1992, p. 7) is responsible for their problems and develop "victim excuses" (p. 8). "Blaming the system" (Milburn, Schuler, & Watman, 1983a, p. 1151) and providing excuses for uncontrollable conditions then substitute for turnaround work, for as a wise philosopher has noted, nothing so economizes effort and energy as the knowledge that nothing can be done. What energy is generated may be directed to "face-saving strategies" (p. 1151).

Scapegoating occurs as managers, rather than deal with external threats, simply "strive to shift the blame" (Cummings, 1988, p. 423) to others. "Aversion to change" (Miller, 1977, p. 47), especially in ultraconservative cultures (Slater, 1999) and in organizations that historically have been highly successful (Lorange & Nelson, 1987, Starbuck, Greve, & Hedberg, 1978; Whetten, 1988b), manifests itself in misread environmental patterns and/or an unfounded sense of organizational well-being (Sloma, 1985). Under this scenario, managers often refuse to engage in actions that may be needed but that run counter to deeply prevailing norms (Miller, 1977).

Relatedly, inaction and inertia can result from active defense of the status quo (Lorange & Nelson, 1987). For example, there is considerable evidence that because change resets the system of managerial winners and losers in the organization, "the threat of innovation arouses defense of things as they are" (Kaufman, 1991, p. 53). Indeed, Starbuck and his colleagues (1978) reveal how oftentimes "prescriptions advocating different methods are received as advocating poorer methods, and prescriptions of different strategies are received as recommending less sound strategies" (p. 122).

Although it does not receive an abundance of attention, it is important to acknowledge that inaction is sometimes linked to three additional factors. First, "management is not always able to deal with outside forces even when they can see them gathering" (Bibeault, 1982, p. 23), especially in the public sector. Thus legitimate constraints sometimes prevent action. Second, management at times simply does "not know what needs to be done [or] . . . how to do what is needed" (Zimmerman, 1991, p. 266). Finally, managers sometimes display "complacency" (Hambrick & D'Aveni, 1988, p. 5; Lorange & Nelson, 1987, p. 42), "overconfidence" (Cummings, 1988, p. 421), or "misplaced optimism" (Ford, 1983, p. 13)—a sense of "invulnerability" (Ford, 1983, p. 13), "unassailability" (Benjaminson, 1984, p. x), or "invincibility" (Slater, 1999, p. 18)—in their organizations' ability to address external threats with existing routines and procedures. The "same strategic and organizational factors which were so effective" (Tushman, Newman, & Romanelli, 1988, p. 63) in the past can become "the seeds of complacency and decline" (p. 63), "mak[ing] them [managers] slow to respond to early indicators of serious external problems" (Cummings, 1988, p. 421) and consequently leading them to lose touch with clients and markets (Slater, 1999; Yates, 1983; Zimmerman, 1991)—with "consumer attitudes" (Yates, 1983, p. 9) and with "market needs and changes" (Khandwalla, 1983–1984, p. 7; Sloma, 1985, p. 15)—thereby "setting organizational decline in motion" (Lorange & Nelson, 1987, p. 421).

If some organizational decline can be traced to lack of effective scanning and forecasting and some can be linked to an unwillingness or inability to act on environmental information, other firms fail because of *poor adaptation* to environmental changes, problems, and challenges. According to Castrogiovanni, Bahga, and Kidwell (1992), "maladaption results from invoking perspectives and recipes that are increasingly invalid given the environment confronting the organization" (p. 34). One source of maladaptation that ribbons the literature on turnaround organizations is "the vicious circle of bureaucracy" (Cameron, Sutton, & Whetten, 1988, p. 10). Or as Ford (1983) describes it, yet another "factor which contributes to distortion is the existence of standard operating procedures" (p. 13), "bureaucratic management" (Bibeault, 1982, p. 42), and "bureaucratic hierarchy and orientation" (Lorange & Nelson, 1987, p. 42; Miller, 1977, p. 51). Turnaround analysts, for example, show how these conditions lead to the development of rigid structures and adherence to well-established methods of operation or "work response patterns" (Bibeault, 1982, p. 50), structures, and operations that may not serve firms well as they address environmental changes (Bibeault, 1982; Ford, 1983; Sutton, Eisenhardt, & Jucker, 1986).

These reviewers place the inability of managers to exercise moves beyond well-grooved routines on center stage in the maladaptation play (Sloma, 1985). Specifically, they discuss three problems: (1) the "applying [of] old cures to new problems" (McKelvey, 1988, p. 407), a tendency "to rely on well-rehearsed responses" (Sutton, Eisenhardt, & Jucker, 1986, p. 28)—what Khandwalla (1983–1984) calls "management overlearning, that is indiscriminate application in the present of a management formula that brought success in the past" (p. 7) but that fails in the current crisis; (2) too much focus on the "short term" (Wilson, Hickson, & Miller, 1999, p. 49)—what Goldston (1992) calls "'quarteritis,' a disease that causes management to mortgage the future of the business" (p. 20); and (3) "the use of decision criteria based primarily on the perceived desires and politics of the organization hierarchy, rather than on basic business demands" (Lorange & Nelson, 1987, p. 42).

Maladaptation also includes (1) actions that move the firm "away from the core business" (Oviatt & Bruton, 1994, p. 133) and into "nonviable venture[s]" (p. 133); (2) "action[s] that lead to deterioration of [the organization's] environmental resource base"

(Sutton, 1990, p. 210) or that result in the overresourcing of "poorly planned new ventures" (Zimmerman, 1991, p. 267); (3) "strategic vacillation" (Hambrick & D'Aveni, 1988, p. 16)—what O'Neill (1981) refers to as a focus on extremes or "an inability to preserve proper balance" (Smith, 1963, p. 22). According to Miller (1977), disintegration can be the outcome of three types of extremes—"too much product-market innovation or too little, too much emphasis on controls or too few controls, and an overly powerful chief executive or one who is a mere figurehead" (p. 57); (4) "displacement activity" (Bibeault, 1982, p. 37) in which managers focus on things they enjoy doing rather than the activities they "should do" (p. 37); (5) "hyperactivity" (Hambrick & D'Aveni, 1988, p. 3) or attempting to engage in too much reorientation work at one time—what Smith (1963) refers to as "going overboard" (p. 23); and (6) "decision overreach" (Wilson, Hickson, & Miller, 1999, p. 45), or more colloquially, "biting off more than one can chew" (Argenti, 1976, p. 34), which encourages managers to "overlook or insufficiently consider vital information" (Wilson, Hickson, & Miller, 1999, p. 45), or to "overtrade" (Argenti, 1976, p. 27), in which case they are "heavily dependent upon everything going right" (Argenti, 1976, p. 38), or to overtax organizational resources and thus to narrow options for recovery" (Anheier & Moulton, 1999b, p. 277)—and therefore through "disproportionality and irreversibility" (Wilson, Hickson, & Miller, 1999, p. 42) to "jeopardize survival" (p. 41). Examples of decision overreach in the literature include acquisitions that are too large and too complex (Smith, 1963); overtrading, "the process by which a firm's sales grow at a faster rate than the firm is able to finance from internally generated cash flow and bank borrowings" (Slatter, 1984, p. 52); and undertaking "big projects" (Argenti, 1976, p. 134) or "excessive or inappropriate expansions" (Weitzel & Jonsson, 1989, p. 95) that spiral out of control.

The turnaround literature also suggests that maladaptation can result from a host of problems that emerge from the work of attempting to bring the organization into alignment with shifts in the environment, including "bad communications" (Argenti, 1976, p. 30), "organizational atrophy" (Levine, 1978, p. 319), and "lack of a marketing effort" (Slatter, 1984, p. 43; also Schendel, Patton, & Riggs, 1976). Finally, the inability to manage the special problems associated with "newness and smallness" (D'Aveni, 1989, p. 585) seems to be an especially potent cause of decline and failure in organizations (Baum & Oliver, 1991; Hager et al., 1999). That is, "two of the most salient explanations of organizational closure are youth and small size" (Anheier & Moulton, 1999b, pp. 278–279). Or in a more active form, smallness and newness "increase [organizational] vulnerability to mortality" (Baum & Oliver, 1991, p. 190). In particular, "the risk of failure is strongly age-dependent and . . . acts as a powerful moderator of the relationship between organizational change and failure" (Amburgey, Kelly, & Barnett, 1993, p. 69).

Lack of Operating Controls and Operating Efficiencies

In addition to bad management, scholars who study turnaround situations regularly conclude that "an almost universal feature of troubled companies is the absence of a basic control system" (Bibeault, 1982, pp. 50–51; also Argenti, 1976): "If the firm faces a turn-around situation, there is probably a glaring lack of effective planning and control procedures" (Sloma, 1985, p. 14), in particular "a lack of adequate financial control" (Slatter, 1984, p. 30). They also find that companies can spiral downward when they ignore data from the internal information systems that they do have (Bibeault, 1982). According to scholars in this area, turnaround action is either not forthcoming or not pursued effectively because companies "do not know where they are and do not know that they are failing" (Argenti, 1976, p. 128) or "because the company's affairs become too complex for the information system to cope with" (Bibeault, 1982, p. 35; also Slatter, 1984). According to Slatter (1984), "the problem is more typically one of inadequate systems rather than no systems at all" (p. 30) and poor use of "management information" (p. 31).

"Lack of financial controls" (Slatter, 1984, p. 30), "cost controls" (Ross & Kami, 1973, p. 23), and "budgeting controls" (Argenti, 1976, p. 126)—a "weak finance function" (p. 125) over-all—in particular help account for organizational failures (O'Shaughnessy, 1995). Specifically, "it appears that in companies that fail no costing figures of any sort are produced, or they are manifestly inadequate or misleading or inaccurate" (Argenti, 1976, p. 127). Various types of financial policy, such as "the use of inappropriate financing sources" (Slatter, 1984, p. 51) are also linked to organizational failure.

Finally, from the portfolio of possible causes of decline and failure, analysts regularly conclude that "operating inefficiency is a major cause of corporate decline" (Slatter, 1984, p. 39) and that "operating inefficiencies are due largely to poor management" (p. 39), are visible long before decline sets in (Hambrick & D'Aveni, 1988), and often "affect all elements of the cost structure" (Slatter, 1984, p. 39).

CHAPTER FOUR

Crisis, Consequences, and Dysfunctional Reactions

I n this chapter, we take three more steps in our turnaround journey. Specifically, we examine the meaning of crisis, we explore the consequences of crisis for the organization, and we investigate how organizations often respond in inappropriate ways to crisis situations.

CRISIS

One of the most significant influences on an organization and its members is an organizational crisis. Its significance derives from its impact on the most vital aspects of the organization, with implications for its very life. (Milburn, Shuler, & Watman, 1983a, p. 1142)

The crisis stage. It is here that the organization reaches the critical point in its history, during which it must undergo major reorientation and revitalization or suffer certain failure. (Weitzel & Jonsson, 1989, p. 104)

A declining company seems at first to need a crisis, and until it reaches the crisis stage poor performance is readily tolerated. (Goldstein, 1988, p. 30)

We start here by placing ourselves in the larger turnaround narrative. As we see in Figure 1.1, Time Period 1 is an era of decline and failing performance, one marked by a series of warning signals or symptoms, fueled by an array of causes, and producing an assortment of problems for the organization and its employees. Based on these dynamics, in Time Period 2 we observe the emergence of crisis and the movement into a turnaround state. In this section, we briefly examine the literature on crisis as it is understood in the context of organizational turnarounds. In the following sections, we turn our attention to the consequences of crisis and dysfunctional organizational responses to crisis.

As outlined in Figure 1.1, crises can materialize in two ways. A sudden performance drop or the emergence of a cataclysmic event can trigger an organizational crisis (see dotted line in lower left-hand section of Figure 1.1) (Grinyer & McKiernan, 1990): "Organizational crises can be situations having been precipitated quickly or suddenly" (Milburn, Schuler, & Watman, 1983a, p. 1144). Generally, however, crises arise from the slower deterioration of a firm's performance, the decline → failure → crisis path we have traced to this point in the narrative: "The nature of corporate crises is that they seldom occur with the abruptness of a thunderclap, they just seem to" (Smith, 1963, p. 15). It is more often the case that a "series of failures ha[s] led to a climax which requires near term action to avert collapse" (Wyckoff, cited in Kierulff, 1981, p. 484). Regardless of how they develop, "crises are dangerous, by definition. After crises have fully developed, organizations face serious risks of failure" (Starbuck, Greve, & Hedberg, 1978, p. 122): "Organizational survival is, and is perceived to be, at stake" (Milburn, Schuler, & Watman, 1983b, p. 1161).

Milburn and his colleagues (1983a) explain that there are a variety of "types of crises distinguished by the three dimensions: The degree of the organization's control over the external environment . . . . whether the crisis situation is perceived as positive or negative . . . [and] the degree of the organization's susceptibility such that the organization is more likely to have crisis situations and less likely to initially respond to them effectively" (p. 1156). We also know that crisis is defined by turnaround analysts in a variety of generally overlapping ways and includes a core set of elements. On the definitional issue, Fink, Beak, and Taddoo (1971) characterize crisis as "a threat to survival" (p. 17). Staying at this broad level, Smith (1963) maintains that a "working definition of corporate crisis comes down simply to Big Trouble, not necessarily fatal, but always making for profound changes. . . . It oftentimes imperils the entire enterprise or at very least makes Draconian demands on the energies, ingenuity, and time of top management" (p. 14).

According to these scholars, a crisis is "'a major turning point' that can affect 'all future events'" (Lesly, cited in Pincus & Acharya, 1988, p. 183). Fink and his colleagues (1971) hold that a firm is "in a state of crisis when its repertoire of coping responses is inadequate to bring about the resolution of a problem which poses a threat to the system" (pp. 16–17). Or, from Hamblin (1958), a crisis is "an urgent situation in which all group members face a common threat" (p. 322). As we have already documented, at a more concrete level, crisis is always defined "compared to some standard of how things should be" (Billings, Milburn, & Schaalman, 1980, p. 312). More specifically, "a turnaround situation represents absolute and relative-to-industry declining performance" (Pearce & Robbins, 1993, p. 625) of great significance. And even more to the point, in corporations the major metric is profitability (Kierulff, 1981), while in schools it is student achievement results.

Turning to the strands embedded in the construct of crisis, Billings and his colleagues (1980), referencing the work of Herman, isolate three central elements: threat, decision time, and surprise (p. 301). Over the last quarter century, many other reviewers have also highlighted these patterns in the crisis mosaic (e.g., Slatter, 1984). The threat variable is often partitioned into two dimensions: serious-ness of the events—or "the value of possible losses" (Billings, Milburn, & Schaalman, 1980, p. 308) or the "magnitude" (Pearce & Robbins, 1993, p. 625) of the situation—and the likelihood of catas-trophe. Or, per Ford (1983), "threat encompasses both the magnitude or value of potential loss, as well as the probability of realizing that loss" (p. 10). In a crisis situation, Ford (1983) asserts, the magnitude of the problem "is so great that it has profound implications both for the immediate organization and its environment" (p. 10). Magnitude is also captured in terms of "deprivations of essential ingredients" (Kaufman, 1991, p. 27) needed to keep the organization alive. It refers to a situation in which the institution has "no choice but to make drastic changes" (Grinyer, Mayes, & McKiernan, 1988, p. 51). Likelihood, in turn, is generally cast in terms of the "perceived prob-ability of loss" (Billings, Milburn, & Schaalman, 1980, p. 308).

Turnaround analysts also help us see that "time pressure—the perception by the participants in the crisis of the amount of time they have to search, deliberate, and take action" (Ford, 1983, pp. 10–11)—is a hallmark dimension of threat (Kierulff, 1981). For, as Billings and his colleagues (1980) inform us, "perceived time pressure is necessary for the perception of crisis; without time pressure a problem will be left to the future and systematically misperceived" (p. 305). And finally, Milburn and his associates (1983a) teach us that the degree of "uncertainty about resolving a situation" (p. 1146) is also part of the definition of crisis, or at least part of "the severity of the crisis" (p. 1146).

Almost everyone agrees that a crisis is needed to focus turn-around work (Barker & Mone, 1998; Slater, 1999), "to focus everyone's attention on survival and thus energiz[e] the organization" (Meyer, 1988, p. 414)—that a stagnating or declining company seems to need a threat to galvanize it into action (O'Neill, 1981). This "crisis as catalyst" proposition has been laid out by Schendel & Patton (1976) and by Bibeault (1982).

> The scenario that emerges from this exploratory research is that a stagnating or declining company seems to first need a deepened threat or shock to spur it to action. Steadily poor performance so long as it does not develop a crisis seems to be tolerated. Once a crisis arrives, the firm can move into action. (Schendel & Patton, 1976, p. 240)

> This seems to occur most frequently in privately held companies where there is no public, or its representatives, to answer to. (Bibeault, 1982, p. 74)

It is at this point in the story line "that distressed managers begin to recognize that the company will not turn itself around and that a drastic reorganization effort is needed if the company is to have hope for long-term survival" (Goldstein, 1988, p. 34). Thus, "the prescription for recovery from the chaos [crisis] is to initiate a major reorganization and turnaround" (Weitzel & Jonsson, 1989, p. 105).

CONSEQUENCES

General consensus exists in the literature that declining organizations are characterized by a wide range of organizational processes that erode organizational effectiveness and undermine member satisfaction and commitment. (Cameron, Kim, & Whetten, 1988, p. 209)

Consequences of decline present several problems that threaten the viability of a declining firm. (Arogyaswamy, Barker, & Yasai-Ardekani, 1995, pp. 500–501)

In Chapters 2 and 3, we spent considerable space reviewing an assortment of factors that both reveal signs of decline and cause organizations to enter turnaround situations. We reported in both chapters that variables in these two sets overlap and wrap around each other. A signal in one case may be a cause in another and vice versa. And the same variable may be both a warning sign and a cause of decline. Here we introduce a third overlapping strand in our analytic coil, consequences of decline and crisis, and we reinforce the conclusion just developed; that is, consequences of decline are intertwined with symptoms and causes. We also note that there is a relatively large body of literature on the consequences of organizational decline and failure (Barker & Duhaime, 1997), and while almost all of these efforts are cast in terms of pathologies, this need not always be the case (Staw, Sanderlands, & Dutton, 1981). Nonetheless, decline consequences generally exert significant additional downward momentum into the organization (Starbuck, Greve, & Hedberg, 1978) and often contribute to firms' in turnaround situations "inability to initiate or implement a successful turnaround" (D'Aveni, 1989, p. 580). The consequences of decline have important implications for recovery efforts and for the long-term health of the organization (Greenhalgh, 1983), and "successful turnaround attempts must . . . manage the organizational dysfunctions caused by decline" (Barker & Patterson, 1996, p. 306).

As was the case with constructs treated in earlier chapters, scholars of turnaround organizations (1) have developed a variety of listings and frameworks to corral the consequences of organizational crises and (2) have described in some detail the dysfunctionalities of these consequences for turnaround efforts. For example, in terms of lists, Cameron, Whetten, and Kim (1987) "have linked at least 12 dysfunctional attributes to decline in organizations" (p. 127): "centralization, no long-term planning, no innovation, scapegoating, resistance to change, turnover, low morale, no slack, fragmented pluralism, loss of credibility, nonprioritized cuts, [and] conflict" (Cameron, Kim, & Whetten, 1988, p. 211). On the framework dimension, Arogyaswamy and his colleagues (1995) provide a portrait that shows "that declining firms are beset by three related consequences that, if unchecked, can cause the firm to fail or dissolve" (p. 499): "erosion of stakeholder support, loss of efficiency, and deterioration of internal climate and decision processes" (pp. 499–500). Because of the overlap among warning signals, causes, and consequences of decline and crisis, we have already explored the first two dimensions of the Arogyaswamy and colleagues (1995) framework in considerable detail. We do not repeat that analysis here. Rather, we concentrate on the set of internal climate variables that has not received much attention to this point in the narrative. First, we investigate the consequences of crisis for the members of organizations, both as individuals and in terms of group dynamics. We also highlight the resultant responses people often make in the face of these unhealthy conditions. Second, we examine consequences in terms of dysfunctional organizational processes.

Human Consequences

Decline and its antecedent conditions can affect an organization's relationships with its workers. (Greenhalgh, 1983, p. 244)

Organizational decline researchers have consistently argued that the deterioration of a firm's internal climate and decision processes are problems that plague declining firms, contributing to their eventual failure. (Arogyaswamy, Barker, & Yasai-Ardekani, 1995, p. 516)

Indeed, across a wide variety of situations, in banking, consumer products, retail, industrial products, software, education, and media in North America and Europe, I've found the same pattern. Organizational pathologies—secrecy, blame, isolation, avoidance, passivity, and feelings of helplessness—arise during a difficult time for the company and reinforce one another in such a way that the company enters a kind of death spiral. (Kanter, 2003, p. 60)

Changing the Workforce

Arogyaswamy and his colleagues (1995) remind us that "the most widely discussed consequence of decline is the deterioration of a firm's internal climate and decision making processes" (p. 500). In particular, they conclude that "the deterioration of a firm's internal climate creates a work environment that restricts the ability to use the firm's repertoires of skills and assets to compete effectively with rivals" (p. 501). One potential consequence in the "human dimension" under review here is a change in "workforce composition" (Greenhalgh, 1983, p. 243). Part 1 of this change is the "systematic loss of competent people" (McKelvey, 1988, p. 408), either through forced workforce reductions (Sutton, 1990) or through voluntary departures of the most committed and most effective workers. Greenhalgh (1983) explains the dynamics behind voluntary departure as follows:

> A passage from the state of adaptive growth or at least stability to decline and shrinkage would represent a breach of the implicit employment contract. That is, workers exchange their labor not only for accrued wages, but also for a stream of future opportunities. The resulting positive involvement takes the form of a general commitment to the organization and its mission. It induces the worker to exert more than the minimum necessary to "work to rule." The onset of decline and shrinkage curtails the perceived stream of future benefits. The effect is a shift from positive involvement to neutral or negative involvement. The shift changes the quality of involvement from more committed toward more calculative or alienated; the power typically exerted on the organization's members from more moral and social toward remunerative and possibly coercive; and the organizational type away from normative. . . . The onset of decline . . . threatens the continued availability of inducements and thereby abrogates the existing psychological contract. The perceived discontinuity in the psychological contract alters organizational participants' relationships to the organization. The affected variables include job security [and] propensity to leave. (pp. 246, 250)

The flip side, of course, "is that the proportion of relatively incompetent employees grows, so that the chance the organization will suffer from the efforts of incompetence grows" (McKelvey, 1988, p. 408). And as this consequential spiral accelerates, so too does the outflow of "talented employees" (p. 408) and the "average level of ability falls" (Starbuck, Greve, &

Hedberg, 1978, p. 120): "Voluntary turnover of all employees increases with the onset of decline, and it is usually the most valuable workers who leave first. The residual pool of poorer-quality workers will at best inhibit recovery, and at worst, accelerate decline" (Greenhalgh, 1983, p. 243).

Psychological and Social Characteristics

A second consequence of crisis is the growth of a deleterious climate that hinders productive work. Consequences here are visible at the individual and group levels. Scholars consistently find that "organizational crisis directly threatens the well-being—on a personal level—of the individuals who comprise an organization" (Pincus & Acharya, 1988, p. 185) and that "decline has a great effect on the relationship between the organization and its participants [and that] much of this effect takes the form of individuals' reactions to their perceptions of changes" (Greenhalgh, 1983, p. 245). To begin with, the literature confirms that "crises bring emotional trauma" (Pincus & Acharya, 1988, p. 195). In general, under conditions of crisis, "organization-member responses are characterized by significantly more . . . resistance to change, low morale, [and] . . . conflict" (Cameron, Kim, & Whetten, 1988, p. 217). Research reveals that because (1) "crises are situations high in anxiety-producing signals" (Pincus & Acharya, 1988, p. 185), (2) organizations respond to crises in stress-inducing ways (Mohrman & Mohrman, 1983), and (3) employees generally see crises in "personal terms" (Pincus & Acharya, 1988, p. 190) organizational decline "provokes anxiety . . . among members" (Sutton, 1990, p. 223) of the organization (Mohrman & Mohrman, 1983).

The research also substantiates that because anxiety is often "a precursor to severe stress" (Pincus & Acharya, 1988, p. 190) and "decline increases stress" (Greenhalgh, 1983, p. 260), "a common side effect of decline is personal stress" (Cameron, 1983, p. 263): "As employees perceive their organizations entering a crisis, fear followed by panic, both of which create severe stress, may grip—or even paralyze—their cognitive, emotional, and decision making abilities" (Pincus & Acharya, 1988, p. 188)—"conditions of uncertainty combine with feelings of lack of control to create an extremely stressful situation for individuals" (Mohrman & Mohrman, 1983, p. 453).

Anxiety and stress are often bedfellows with "decreasing morale within the organization" (Goldstein, 1988, p. 42) and diminished sense of efficacy. In declining organizations, morale becomes "fragile" (Hardy, 1990, p. 6) and often "sags" (Cameron & Zammuto, 1988, p. 122). "Working under the worst conditions and with too many pressures" (Goldstein, 1988, p. 49), employees are often "demoralized" (p. 111). There is "a general lack of excitement about future opportunities" (Mohrman & Mohrman, 1983, p. 452): "Everyone associated with the company believes the company will fail, often a self-fulfilling prophecy" (Goldstein, 1988, p. 49). Concomitantly, employees often experience a "diminishing . . . sense of control over their lives" (Pincus & Acharya, 1988, p. 185) and a "decline in self-esteem" (p. 188). They often become discontented (Cameron, Kim, & Whetten, 1988), "disenchanted" (Goldstein, 1988, p. 49), "discouraged" (Finkin, 1987, p. 12), "frustrated" (Goldstein, 1988, p. 35), "disheartened" (Finkin, 1987, p. 41), and "alienated" (Greenhalgh, 1983, p. 263). They often feel "threatened" (Sutton, 1990, p. 223). In turn, "commitments to organizational goals fade" (Starbuck, Greve, & Hedberg, 1978, p. 120; also Cameron, Kim, & Whetten, 1988).

At the collective level, "conflict . . . and scapegoating" (Cameron, Kim, & Whetten, 1988, p. 210) often "increase in an organization that is experiencing decline" (Mohrman & Mohrman, 1983, p. 459). In particular, "decline frequently triggers strong intra-organizational conflict" (Rosenblatt, Rogers, & Nord, 1993, p. 84) and "competition" (D'Aunno & Sutton, 1992, p. 121) and often "strain[s] inter-departmental relations badly" (Mohrman & Mohrman, 1983, p. 460). "Intergroup conflict" (p. 460) is also often "accentuated by decline" (p. 460). Blame and mistrust (Kanter, 2003) often occupy the high ground in firms in turnaround situations. Because "decline helps to transform an organization into a 'political arena' where conflict and political forces dominate" (Rosenblatt, Rogers, & Nord, 1993, p. 79), so too does "organizational politics" (Goldstein, 1988, p. 79): "The organization's political system [is] probably quite responsive to . . . decline. . . . Issues [will] probably crystallize almost instantaneously around partisan interests. Coalitions [will] close ranks and the parties [will] begin manipulating perceptions to protect their interests . . . thus polarizing their positions" (Greenhalgh, 1983, pp. 245–246).

Dysfunctional Responses

We know from the research on turnarounds that the psychological and social consequences of decline and failure often, in turn, trigger dysfunctional personal behaviors that harm recovery efforts, that is, in "behaviors dysfunctional for the organization" (Cameron, Kim, & Whetten, 1988, p. 218). Specifically, "in this stress-charged atmosphere, employees' judgment, decision-making, and information-processing abilities may be distorted or neutralized" (Pincus & Acharya, 1988, p. 182). To begin with, "decline engenders psychological withdrawal" (Greenhalgh, 1983, p. 260); "individuals become withdrawn and preoccupied with their own problems" (Pincus & Acharya, 1988, p. 188). They reduce both their commitment to the enterprise and "their willingness to continue participation" (Greenhalgh, 1983, p. 261). They are likely to actively "resist change" (p. 260) and to demonstrate "task avoidance" (Pincus & Acharya, 1988, p. 188), to "misdirect . . . attention away from the task at hand" (p. 188). When actions are taken, they are likely to be "self-protective" (Mohrman & Mohrman, 1983, p. 459). Decline often "compels individuals to engage in conservative and self-protective behavior" (Cameron, 1983, p. 363). This often means behaving in the service of "personal needs and ignoring the organization's needs" (Pincus & Acharya, 1988, p. 189). Employees are often "no longer primarily concerned with their work but with their own security" (Goldstein, 1988, p. 111). It is also visible in the growth of opportunistic behavior (Starbuck, Greve, & Hedberg, 1978) and "calculative involvement" (Greenhalgh, 1983, p. 263): "Actors frame their situations and responses in the most favorable light for self-protection" (p. 242).

As we discuss below, when anxious and stressed actors do engage in the vortex of crisis, they often demonstrate "impaired thinking ability" (Pincus & Acharya, 1988, p. 187) and select less adaptive moves. As Mohrman and Mohrman (1983) found, "the crisis of decline brings out the survival instincts of the participants [and] the survival behaviors of all are based on past, proven approaches, despite the likelihood that these approaches may have contributed to the decline" (p. 461): "Decline increases stress, which in turn makes organizational actors less adaptive, relying doggedly on standard operating procedures" (Greenhalgh, 1983, p. 260) and "cling[ing] to well-learned responses" (Sutton, 1990, p. 224) "when the organization most needs to change them" (Greenhalgh, 1983, p. 260).

Finally, we know that member behavior in the information arena in periods of crisis is often nonproductive (Sutton, 1990). Because "stress reduces significantly an individual's ability to handle complex information" (Pincus & Acharya, 1988, p. 187), the capacity of employees in turnaround situations "to process information about the crisis will be impeded, distorted, or paralyzed" (p. 188). "The information flow is almost always constricted" (Cameron & Zammuto, 1988, p. 122)—there is generally "a decrease in openness of communication flow" (Mohrman & Mohrman, 1983, p. 458). And communication is often deliberately distorted as it moves through the system. In particular, Pincus and Acharya (1988) find that anxious, stressful, and disenchanted employees often "deny, misinterpret, selectively perceive, or tune out information from management about the crisis situation" (p. 189).

Organizational Consequences

Decline engenders tunnel vision, . . . authoritarianism, failure to involve others in decision making, and expediency at the expense of creativity. (Greenhalgh, 1983, p. 263)

Staying in the information arena, but shifting from the responses of individuals to information systems, a plethora of researchers corroborate that these operations and mechanisms often hold up poorly in times of organizational decline and failure. Fredenberger, Lipp, and Watson (1997) convey in their review, for example, that turnarounds are marked by a wide array of "problems associated with information" (p. 171). We also learn that oftentimes environmental scanning procedures are not available or not used well in failing organizations. There is a "tendency to focus inward" (Sutton, 1990, p. 224). There is also some consistency in the finding that turnarounds accentuate rigidity in organizational structures (Sutton, 1990). Reduced experimentation and risk aversion often characterize firms in the midst of turnaround efforts (Greenhalgh, 1983). Coordination systems are often underutilized (Khandwalla, 1983–1984).

Mohrman and Mohrman (1983) find that in crisis situations, organizations often concentrate on "short-term solutions and goals" (p. 458). There is also a narrowing of concentration so that "under conditions of decline, institutions seem to de-emphasize activities that [are] thought to be nonessential or auxiliary to the main concerns" (Cameron, 1983, p. 367)—Greenhalgh's (1983) "tunnel vision" (p. 263). Consistent with these findings, researchers regularly report that crisis leads to the privileging of mechanistic responses and the standardization and routinization of operational systems (D'Aunno & Sutton, 1992; Staw, Sanderlands, & Dutton, 1981). For example,

Arogyaswamy and his colleagues (1995) substantiate that internal changes that unfold in turnaround organizations make decision processes more mechanistic. Greenhalgh (1983) draws a parallel with leadership, and Sutton (1990) finds support for mechanistic shifts in job structures in the turnaround firms included in his review of the literature. This increased "use of rigid procedures" (p. 224) correlates highly with both "less long-term planning" (p. 224) and less use of innovative procedures and processes. Indeed, Greenhalgh (1983) establishes that "there is a general inverse relationship between decline and innovation" (p. 241). Decline gives momentum "to forces that inhibit even the normal level of innovation, so that the organization becomes less and less adapted to its environment" (p. 264).

Reviewers also routinely discover that decline and crises are associated with "additional centralized control" (Starbuck, Greve, & Hedberg, 1978, p. 121) and the "constriction of control" (Sutton, 1990, p. 230) already in play (D'Aveni, 1989). In terms of operations, this "tendency toward centralization" (p. 225) unfolds in two ways: (1) a tendency "to seek less input" (Greenhalgh, 1983, p. 239) and "counsel" (Mohrman & Mohrman, 1983, p. 459) from subordinates, to "reduce the number of people involved in the decision process" (Sutton, 1990, p. 225) and to "decrease the delegation of authority" (p. 225) and (2) the practice of increasing "subordinate job standardization" (p. 224), the redesign of jobs "so that employees have less control over work methods and pace as well as "less skill variety and less task identity" (p. 226).

DYSFUNCTIONAL ORGANIZATIONAL REACTIONS

Crises are times of danger, times when some actions lead toward organizational failures. (Starbuck, Greve, & Hedberg, 1978, p. 112)

Organizations affected by decline respond in a number of ways, some functional, others dysfunctional. (Cameron, Sutton, & Whetten, 1988, p. 7)

Organizational success or failure is the result of coping attempts taking place at several organizational levels at the same time. (Mayntz, 1999, p. 87)

Introduction

The point of departure in reacting to crisis and its consequences is acknowledgment, understanding that "an entity's tendency toward business failure must be . . . recognized" (Siegel, 1981, p. 13) if action, good or bad, is to materialize, for, as Milburn and his colleagues (1983a) affirm, "organizations do not have a crisis until it is perceived" (p. 1144). At the same time, we learn that "change requires not just recognition of the problem but recognition of a suitable solution, and the drive and willingness to try to carry it out" (Grinyer, Mayes, & McKiernan, 1988, p. 58) and that "more accurate . . . perception of crisis" (Billings, Milburn, & Schaalman, 1980, p. 315) is connected to more productive response moves.

The turnaround literature establishes that there is a wide assortment of reactions to crisis and that they sort into the two central categories of "coping and avoiding" (Pincus & Acharya, 1988, p. 193). We also discover that these "coping strategies seek either to influence the environment such as to eliminate a threat or to adapt to the changed external circumstances in such a way as to ensure the persistence of the organization as a functioning whole" (Mayntz, 1999, p. 72).

One cluster of coping reactions that we do not address in this volume is illegal responses, for example, "buying political influence" (Whetten, 1988b, p. 165). Productive strategies to attack crisis comprise a second cluster of responses. It is these operations that we examine in later chapters. Here we highlight a third bundle of reaction moves, dysfunctional organizational responses to crisis. These, in turn, are of two varieties, failures to act—or "passive responses" (Ford & Baucus, 1987, p. 373—and inappropriate responses: "Inaction can be described as failure to admit the organization is deteriorating, thus eliciting well-rehearsed responses and self-deception. . . . Faulty action can be described as ill-conceived corrective action" (Armenakis & Fredenberger, 1998, p. 42). The remainder of the chapter is devoted to exploring these two categories of dysfunctional reactions. Before we begin that analysis, however, a few comments are in order.

As we have reported throughout the text, the model in Figure 1.1 makes the turnaround story line appear more linear than it really is. That is also the case at this point in our framework because reactions overlap with elements of the developing crisis and emerging consequences of failure, as well as with a host of contextual variables.

In short, "response choices are not separate stages in a linear process" (Ford & Baucus, 1981, p. 372). In addition, the dysfunctional responses we review here are often not the final moves in the face of crisis. Organizations in trouble often progress through phases of reactions (Fink, Beak, & Taddoo, 1971; Ford, 1985) in which earlier dysfunctional responses (e.g., blaming, self-justification) give way to more productive actions. We also know that specific coping strategies matter (Cameron & Zammuto, 1988; Ford & Baucus, 1987), that "the choice of coping strategies to deal with different kinds of threat at the different organizational levels is an important determinant of the final outcome of the transformation" (Mayntz, 1999, p. 82): "Different kinds of responses have disparate implications for organizational effectiveness and survival" (Milburn, Schuler, & Watman, 1983b, p. 1161).

Turnaround analysts also affirm that response choices in crisis conditions are contingent on a variety of overlapping factors. The scholarship of Ford (1983, 1985), in particular, establishes that reaction moves owe much to the meaning given to the turnaround by key leaders: "The entire adaptation process is one of interpretation" (Ford & Baucus, 1987, p. 377) and "is based on the collectively shared interpretations of top decision makers established through social interaction" (p. 369). Thus, leaders' "interpretations of performance downturns strongly influence the extent and kind of . . . symbolic and substantive responses" (Sutton, 1990, p. 226). Response actions also "reflect organizational structure" (Ford & Baucus, 1987, p. 373), organizational culture and values, and "decision makers' assessments of organizational strategy and strategic capabilities" (p. 373).

Furthermore, responses are linked to the consequences of crisis we discussed above. In particular, "how an organization responds to a crisis depends on how individuals respond to the stress from the crisis" (Milburn, Schuler, & Watman, 1983b, p. 1162). Barker and Patterson (1996) find that "a firm's responses to declining performance are influenced by the factors that the firm's top managers blame for decline" (p. 304). Milburn and his associates (1983a) conclude that management style, especially "degree of detachment" (p. 1152) from the crisis, shapes response moves. And Mayntz (1999) demonstrates that "external conditions affect the choice of coping strategies" (p. 72). "Characteristics of the external environment play a dominant role" (Cameron & Zammuto, 1988, p. 118) in the selection and effectiveness of coping actions.

Analysts have also forged taxonomies of inappropriate responses to turnaround situations, categorizations that we rely on to construct the framework we present below. Sutton (1990) and Pincus and Acharya (1988) delineate four responses to crisis: "concealing, . . . acknowledging the situation without admitting any damage, . . . denying responsibility, . . . and withdrawing" (p. 191). Ford and Baucus (1987) also depict four inappropriate reactions: "anger, denial, alter importance, [and] resignation" (p. 368). So too do Weitzel and Jonsson (1989): "denial, avoidance, resistance, [and] procrastination" (p. 100).

Robust analysis confirms that these dysfunctional reactions to crisis often share a lethal set of complex and often contradictory identifying markers. There is often a strange feeling of complacency mixed with a sense of uncertainty (Milburn, Schuler, & Watman, 1983a). There is a noticeable tendency to "fight reality" (Bibeault, 1982, p. 75; Goldstein, 1988, p. 31). Inappropriate reactions are often defined by rigidity (D'Aunno & Sutton, 1992) and an unhealthy focus on saving face (Goldstein, 1988). "Avoidance defense" (Whetten, 1988b, p. 163) thinking often dominates planning. Defense responses all share a patina of primitiveness (Krantz, 1985). They are often marked by a shocking willingness "to pursue the failing cause" (Caldwell & O'Reilly, 1982, p. 133) and thus by inactivity (Weitzel & Jonsson, 1989). All in all, "the propensity to prolong . . . , to fail to take action, to tone down measures and to compromise is enormous. Excellent reasons can always be addressed for cautious inactivity" (Grinyer, Mayes, & McKiernan, 1988, p. 134).

Passive Responses

Passive responses do not attempt to connect or compensate for downturns and are evidenced where decision makers ignore, become angered, deny or create illusions about downturns, change the levels of importance attached to performances, or resign themselves to the situation. (Ford & Baucus, 1987, pp. 371–372)

We expect that, when firms decline, their top managers will display a tendency to cognitively distance themselves from the decline by attributing it to factors that preserve their self esteem . . . to factors such as economic cycles that are external to the firm, beyond management's control, and will go away with time. (Barker & Patterson, 1996, p. 307)

Not acting, however, means certain failure. (Weitzel & Jonsson, 1989, p. 105)

While it may seem obvious, "the very first step in a turnaround situation is for management to realize that their business strategies and plans have to be changed [and] that if they do not change . . . the probability of the company going under will increase greatly" (Chan, 1993, p. 30): "For declining performance to stimulate . . . search and higher order organizational learning, managers must recognize *and* correctly interpret 'bad news'" (Short, Palmer, & Stimpert, 1998, p. 156); that is, "recognition by management is . . . a trigger for change" (Grinyer, Mayes, & McKiernan, 1988, p. 61). Thus the first passive response to crisis is, not surprisingly, *failure to recognize the problem,* a type of managerial blindness to the troubles confronting the enterprise.

Even when "a problem may be recognized it does not imply that it will necessarily be acted upon" (Grinyer, Mayes, & McKiernan, 1988, p. 57), which opens the door to an assortment of overlapping passive responses or forms of "inaction" (Billings, Milburn, Schaalman, 1980, p. 305) in the face of a turnaround situation. One such passive reaction is simply *ignoring the problem* (Shook, 1998), a type of "organizational inertia" (Barker & Mone, 1998, p. 1230). For example, Short and his associates (1998) report that "research has shown that new information is frequently ignored because it does not coincide with management's a priori cognitive maps" (p. 156). Arogyaswamy and his colleagues (1995) also expose that problems are ignored because of managers' "misdiagnosis of the sources of the firm's decline" (p. 510), the misattribution of problems. Researchers describe, in particular, a tendency for managers to "look for environmental factors" (Shook, 1998, p. 276) that legitimize inaction, especially "to attribute the firm's decline to causes indicative of temporary industry-contraction-based decline" (Arogyaswamy, Barker, & Yasai-Ardekani, 1995, p. 505).

Relatedly, Cummings (1988) claims that *denial* is "one of the most thoroughly documented reactions to decline and the threat of failure" (p. 422). That is, managers in turnaround situations have been known "to deny that a crisis exists" (Whetten, 1988b, p. 162;

also Ford, 1983; Krantz, 1985), to express skepticism about the seriousness of the problem (Reisner, 2002), and to simply maintain that problems are not really problems (Whetten, 1988b)—they exhibit a "tendency to deny unpleasant realities" (Boulding, 1975, p. 9) and they are "unwilling and/or psychologically unable to admit that something [is] wrong" (Kierulff, 1981, p. 491). According to Starbuck and his colleagues (1978), "it is a normal human characteristic to adhere to one's prior beliefs in spite of evidence that they are incorrect" (p. 119), but, nonetheless, this is a response that has high costs for the organization (Slatter, 1984). Ford (1983) sums up the denial reaction nicely as follows:

> In many cases, the initial response to a crisis is denial. Based on the assumption that the problem(s) confronting the organization is (are) transitory (for example, increased competition, economic recession, currency devaluation), managers underestimate the need to make any changes. This assumption stems from the belief that crises result from changes external to the organization, not from organizational deficiencies, and is fostered by groupthink and the insistence of those who made the decisions and policies which contribute to the crisis that the decisions and policies are sound if only given time to work. (p. 14)

Turning the analytic prism 180 degrees, we find that *withdrawal* is yet another passive response to crisis (Pincus & Acharya, 1988; Sutton, 1990). Here, according to O'Neill (1981), leaders recognize and acknowledge the crisis but "accept the decline as inevitable" (p. 21). Managers interpret the crisis as so severe that they "simply withdraw" (Hamblin, 1958, p. 327) from it. Or, as Johnson (cited in Stopford & Baden-Fuller, 1990) commented in his research, "when the going got tough the managers would return to the 'foetal position'" (p. 404).

Inaction in the face of crisis can also be supported by a penchant to *blame* and to "scapegoat" (Rosenblatt, Rogers, & Nord, 1993, p. 77) others for troubles (Armenakis & Fredenberger, 1998). Blaming shifts the nature of work from "diagnosing the problem" (Cummings, 1988, p. 422) and developing a reorientation strategy to identifying an enemy. Failure is attributable to "unstable factors" (Barker & Patterson, 1996, p. 310) that are "beyond [managers'] control" (p. 310) and that "will go away in time" (p. 310). Slater

(1999) does a marvelous job of exposing how IBM at its moment of crisis in the 1990s responded with blame rather than reorientation: "Akers and his team, ignoring the realities, pointed the finger of blame at anyone and anything but IBM. It was the fault of the American economy, or the turmoil in Europe. It was never IBM's fault. It simply could not be" (p. 30). And Yates (1983) and Reich and Donahue (1985) provide a similar chronicle in the automobile industry in the 1970s where crisis was attributed to the U.S. government, wars, and oil embargoes rather than problems internal to the car companies themselves. Ford (1985) and others also explain how blaming can turn into an especially hostile activity.

Other dysfunctional passive responses include "retrospective reinterpretation" (Cummings, 1988, p. 419), lowering expectations (Short, Palmer, & Stimpert, 1998), and holding out for a miracle. In the *miracle* scenario, rather than attacking the crisis, leaders cling to the belief that solutions will be delivered forthwith by someone else or by the convergence of a hard-to-fathom set of fortunate circumstances that reside just over the organizational horizon. In the *lowered expectation* scenario, as Grinyer and colleagues (1988) have documented, firms avoid proactive work by "adjust[ing] downwards their expectations of what constitutes a satisfactory performance" (p. 45), thus eliminating or postponing the need to respond. And in the "*retrospective reinterpretation*" scenario, organizations react to crisis by creating "an alternative 'sense' of history" (Cummings, 1988, p. 419) that permits them to define their way out of crisis, of acknowledging the trouble but arguing that "it is misunderstood and not really discrediting" (Sutton, 1990, p. 213). In effect, the crisis is "explained away" (Slatter, 1984, p. 69).

Central to the passive and "self defeating" (Rosenblatt, Rogers, & Nord, 1993, p. 77) responses are efforts to *defend* the current state of affairs, crisis notwithstanding (Pincus & Acharya, 1988; Starbuck, Greve, & Hedberg, 1978). We observed this element in some of the reactions above (e.g., blaming), and we will see more of it in some of the responses below (e.g., self-justification). According to turnaround analysts, rather than trigger reorientation moves, crises sometimes lead managers to assume a "fortress mentality" (Short, Palmer, & Stimpert, 1998, p. 168) or a "'wait out the storm' mentality" (Lohrke & Bedeian, 1998, p. 12), to hunker down and wait for the storm clouds to pass. This "defensive attitude" (Short, Palmer, & Stimpert, 1998, p. 169) seems to be an especially prevalent reaction in organizations with a long history of success (Weitzel & Jonsson, 1989), "in highly bureaucratic settings or in ideologically based institutions" (Whetten, 1988b, p. 163), and in firms with large numbers of "longer-tenured executives" (Barker & Patterson, 1996, p. 306). Defensive action is almost always associated with "conservatism" (Rosenblatt, Rogers, & Nord, 1993, p. 77) and an unhealthy commitment to (1) the "status quo" (Barker & Patterson, 1996, p. 306), (2) "business-as-usual" (Weitzel & Jonsson, 1989, p. 102), and (3) the current "failing course of action" (Caldwell & O'Reilly, 1982, p. 132) as, again, leaders work to "absolve themselves of responsibility for the firm's decline" (Barker & Patterson, 1996, p. 306) and "to retain power and status" (Starbuck, Greve, & Hedberg, 1978, p. 118). Indeed, "the realities of the organization, the face-saving concerns, the political model of organizations, and the momentum of stability weigh heavily against top management throwing out the old assumptions" (Milburn, Schuler, & Watman, 1983a, p. 1153). Defense of current arrangements appears reasonable to managers in the face of these "inertial forces" (Arogyaswamy, Barker, & Yasai-Ardekani, 1995, p. 511) that block more active recovery efforts. Thus, according to Weitzel and Jonsson (1989)

> One of the factors contributing to organizational inaction is the tendency for leaders to increase commitment to the present course of action. This is especially true if they were involved in its formulation. Past successes are used to justify present policies and procedures. These factors, along with the need to maintain predictability within the organization, predispose organizations toward conservative actions. (p. 100)

A particularly well-documented passive strategy with roots in both denial and defense is "justification" (Seibel, 1999, p. 196)—or "*self justification*" (Caldwell & O'Reilly, 1982, p. 122) or "collective rationalization" (Armenakis & Fredenberger, 1998, p. 42). Here we find that "once the signs of crisis become visible . . . management begins to look for reasons to 'explain the crisis away'" (Slatter, 1984, p. 69; also O'Shaughnessy, 1995). To "avoid or mitigate cognitive dissonances" (Seibel, 1999, p. 96), managers "rationalize" (Cummings, 1988, p. 421) away the problem and create "social defenses" (Krantz, 1985, p. 11): "When a company is not doing well its executives may refuse to admit it and may put forth impressive arguments to justify their poor showing" (Bibeault, 1982, p. 74). They respond with a type of "learned helplessness" (Mohrman & Mohrman, 1983, p. 451). There is a "continued commitment to the failing strategy" (Caldwell & O'Reilly, 1982, p. 121). And it is "the ability of top decision makers to provide plausible and viable inter-pretations" (Ford & Baucus, 1987, p. 376) that "do not challenge existing interpretations" (p. 375)—to engage in "impression man-agement" (Caldwell & O'Reilly, 1982, p. 134)—that promotes the continuation of current activities and their own exercise of power (Ford & Baucus, 1987; Starbuck, Greve, & Hedberg, 1978), the cri-sis notwithstanding. As is the case with denial, two propositions form the core of justification:

> First, the signs of crisis are attributed to the firm's effort to change (e.g., new products, new capital investment, etc.) and it is only a matter of time before performance will improve. The second argument is that poor performance results from short-term envi-ronmental pressures beyond the control of the firm (e.g., exchange-rate fluctuations, economic recession, etc.). Both these arguments support the view that no management action is necessary to avert the impending crisis. (Slatter, 1984, pp. 69–70)

The theme here is that decision makers facing crisis conditions "may manage information to justify their failure" (Caldwell & O'Reilly, 1982, p. 134), a kind of "dodging the truth" (Bibeault, 1982, p. 74):

> Decision makers, when confronted with evidence that they are responsible for a failure, will attempt to justify their decision by managing the information made available to others. This process may include the highlighting of favorable information and the suppression of unfavorable items. (Caldwell & O'Reilly, 1982, p. 134)

As just noted, a recurring aspect of self-justification is the *"selective use of information* to construct arguments in support of committed behaviors" (Caldwell & O'Reilly, 1982, p. 124), that is, in support of the current state of affairs. Here Cummings (1988) observes, leaders "focus attention on comparisons that place the organization's performance (and their contribution to it) in the most favorable light" (p. 419), including "filtering" (Caldwell & O'Reilly, 1982, p. 124), "manipulating" (p. 133), selectively interpreting, distort[ing] (Ford, 1983, p. 14), and "discounting or even ignoring unfavorable performance data" (Short, Palmer, & Stimpert, 1998, p. 166). For example, in their review of the literature, Short and his associates (1998) conclude that managers of turnaround organizations "are likely to rely on those performance referents which cast their firms most favorably" (p. 163). Consistent with the central theme of this entire section on dysfunctional reactions to crisis, the Short team also affirms that "this self-serving approach to information interpretation is . . . exactly the opposite of what is needed by most firms facing turnaround" (p. 163).

Still another common dysfunctional passive response is to "*delay* taking corrective action" (Weitzel & Jonsson, 1989, p. 100), for as Slatter (1984) has deduced, "delaying action in a crisis situation rarely, if ever, produces improvement" (p. 70). Taking a "'wait-and-see' approach" (Mohrman & Mohrman, 1983, p. 451), "weather[ing] the storm" (Ford, 1985, p. 781), or waiting for the "problems [to] blow over" (Finkin, 1987, p. 12) is not an efficacious move in a period of organizational crisis: "Those situations for which delays produce improvements are not crises. In fact, situations are not crises if normal behaviors produce improvements. Crises are dangerous, in part, because normal behaviors make them worse" (Starbuck, Greve, & Hedberg, 1978, p. 119). Delay, as is the case with denial, self-justification, and other passive responses, is often grounded in a belief that problems are due to short-term malaise in the industry (e.g., unnaturally high oil prices in the automobile industry) (Hambrick & Schecter, 1983). Here, as there, "the organization takes no action and waits to see if the crisis will go away" (Ford, 1983, p. 14), which, as we have reported, it almost never does (Bibeault, 1982; O'Neill, 1986b): "Patience and perseverance by the firm are rarely sufficient to produce profitable performance" (Pearce & Robbins, 1993, p. 615).

Finally, turnaround reviewers observe that leaders sometimes respond to crisis with attempts to "*conceal* their difficulties" (Goldstein, 1988, p. 39). In this case, we find that leaders may engage in "activities to persuade constituents that all is well" (Weitzel & Jonsson, 1989, p. 101). In particular, turnaround analysts suggest that some organizations confronting crisis "resort to creative accounting to disguise pathetic performance" (Goldstein, 1988, p. 36). Or, as Whetten

(1988b) captures it, "'creative accounting' is a related defense mechanism identified in several case studies of business failure" (p. 162). So too is "creative reporting" (Weitzel & Jonsson, 1989, p. 101) of information.

Faulty Responses

After managers have acknowledged that a crisis situation exists and have constructed a causal map for making sense out of it, a response is formulated. (Whetten, 1988b, p. 162)

Failure to turn around can be traced to several sources. The strategy choice could be the wrong choice. (O'Neill, 1981, p. 22)

To this point in the narrative, we have investigated multiple forms of inaction in the face of crisis. Here we reveal that "eventually a company that is sliding downhill has to admit the seriousness of the situation. The time is at hand when the leaders begin seeking answers to their problems and can no longer be satisfied with excuses" (Bibeault, 1982, p. 76). Equally important, however, we also show that proactive moves can be dysfunctional, that when confronting crisis, organizations can "choose the wrong strategy or implement the correct strategy poorly" (Cameron, Sutton, & Whetten, 1988, p. 8). We examine what Staw and his colleagues (1981) call "maladaptive tendenc[ies] in reacting to adversity" (p. 501) and Weitzel and Jonsson (1989) refer to as "maladaptive decisions" (p. 103), the engagement of "change actions that do little or nothing to correct the problems" (p. 102) and a willingness to work on some issues but not "the real problems" (Bibeault, 1982, p. 74) at the heart of the crisis—all the result of the fact that "most managers are not prepared to face the many negative forces at work when the company reaches its crisis point" (p. 76). We cluster these "faulty responses" into three highly interrelated categories: responses that match poorly with problems, rigidity of response, and adherence to old scripts or longstanding ways of doing business.

Poor Matches With Problems

The first domain of dysfunctional proactive responses is the forging of reactions that align poorly with the problems at hand. We begin with the scholarship of Arogyaswamy and his associates (1995) that concludes that "recovery strategies need to match the causes of a firm's decline . . . and the firm's competitive positioning in order to be effective" (p. 511). We discover that one way things go awry here is when "those in charge look for problem causes . . . in the wrong places" (Armenakis & Fredenberger, 1998, p. 42) and when they "misdiagnose the causes of their firm's problems" (Arogyaswamy, Barker, & Yasai-Ardekani, 1995, p. 511). Misdiagnosis, it turns out, has a good deal to do with the facts (1) that "formal adaptive responses are predicated on decision makers' collectively shared interpretations" (Ford & Baucus, 1987, p. 372) and (2) that those interpretations often do not align well with the realities of the crisis situation.

One dimension of the "match" problem can be labeled "problemistic search" (Cyert and March, cited in Whetten, 1988b, p. 164) behavior, when conditions in a crisis "conspire to prevent managers from engaging in problematic search or even questioning the beliefs and understandings held in their mental models" (Short, Palmer, & Stimpert, 1998, p. 173). Problematic search also occurs when leaders in crisis times "search for solutions in the area closest to the problem" (Whetten, 1988b, p. 164). Another aspect of this dysfunctional reaction category is failing to acknowledge the multidimensional nature of crisis and "considering only one set of factors in diagnosing and responding to it" (Cameron & Zammuto, 1988, p. 127). A third component of the match problem is "the common mistake of solving the wrong problem, . . . exemplified by the tendency to solve symptoms rather than underlying problems" (Whetten, 1988b, p. 164). A fourth strand of the match flaw is "the common error of attaching the wrong solution to the right problem in managing . . . crisis" (p. 164).

In particular, part of the "match" problem, as we discuss in more detail below, is that leaders in crisis situations are prone to "emphasize exploitation of the known or low-level learning" (Short, Palmer, & Stimpert, 1998, p. 156) when new strategies to attack the crisis are demanded (Staw, Sanderlands, & Dutton, 1981): "Leaders will attend to efficiency issues about which they are very familiar rather than making critical decisions about actions affecting the future" (Weitzel & Jonsson, 1989, p. 101; also McKinley, 1993)—an undue focus on incremental decision making and the proposal of "incremental solutions for quantum problems" (Whetten, 1988b, p. 164): "So the inhabitants' first reactions to crisis are to maintain their palaces intact—they shore up shaky foundations, strengthen points of stress, and patch up cracks—and their palaces remain sitting beautifully on eroding mountaintops" (Starbuck, Greve, & Hedberg, 1978, p. 120).

Rigid Responses

Relatedly, there is considerable but not unanimous agreement (see Ashmos & Duchon, 1998; Barker & Mone, 1998) in the turn-around literature that crises "lead to rigid responses" (D'Aunno & Sutton, 1992, p. 117) and "mechanistic shifts" (Barker & Mone, 1998, p. 1232) by organizations—and consistent with the theme of this section that these "threat rigidity effects can be maladaptive" (Staw, Sanderlands, & Dutton, 1981, p. 502), that they can exacerbate rather than alleviate organizational troubles. Not unexpectedly, according to Cummings (1988), "the greater the perceived organizational threat, the more likely the rigidity" (p. 419), although as we show in the next chapter, context plays an important role in the rigidity equation. According to analysts of this dysfunctional response to crisis, there are two types of threat rigidity effects:

> First, a threat may result in restriction of information processing, such as a narrowing in the field of attention, a simplification in information codes, or a reduction in the number of channels used. Second, when a threat occurs, there may be a constriction in control, such that power and influence can become more concentrated or placed in higher levels of a hierarchy. (Staw, Sanderlands, & Dutton, 1981, p. 502)

Crises, in turn, are often linked to "four classes of rigidities in organizations: (a) restriction in information processing (rigid use of existing organizational procedures), (b) constriction of control (less participative decision making), (c) conservation of resources (work force reduction), and (d) competition among members" (D'Aunno & Sutton, 1992, p. 117; also Fink, Beak, & Taddoo, 1971).

Scholars regularly assert that these "effects" lead to certain patterns of management behavior in the domains of information systems and control processes (Staw, Sanderlands, & Dutton, 1981). Leaders often "become more closed and rigid . . . and turf conscious" (Cameron & Zammuto, 1988, p. 122). Their behavior becomes "less varied or flexible" (Staw, Sanderlands, & Dutton, 1981, p. 502), more "autocratic" (Slatter, 1984, p. 64), and more controlling (Barker &

Duhaime, 1997). They demonstrate "a cognitive rigidity that severely impairs decision-making" (Chowdhury & Lang, 1993, p. 9). Leaders often "restrict information processing, centralize control, and conserve resources" (McKinley, 1993, p. 3). Proactiveness is generally "dampened and an aversion to risk takes over" (Cameron & Zammuto, 1988, p. 122). Managers who "fall victim to threat rigidity effects" (Short, Palmer, & Stimpert, 1998, p. 160) "focus on efficiency" (McKinley, 1993, pp. 3–4) and "internal operations" and [display] a decreased awareness of peripheral clues" (p. 160).

The same analysts also conclude that these behavior patterns in crisis situations are "unsuited" (Slatter, 1984, p. 64) to resolving the organization's deep-rooted problems, that they "propel failure" (Chowdhury & Lang, 1993, p. 9). Or, as Cummings (1988) cautions, "rigidity of response . . . is destructive to the organization" (p. 419). The autocratic organization that results "is usually too rigid to adapt to a declining environment" (Slatter, 1984, p. 64), to permit "strategic reorientation" (Barker & Mone, 1997, p. 1228).

Overreliance on Established Procedures

The turnaround literature affirms that a special aspect of the dysfunctional proactive responses examined above is the tendency for managers to employ "established procedures" (Milburn, Schuler, & Watman, 1983a, p. 1154) or old scripts to handle crises, existing operations that often do not align well with the organization's troubles. According to Staw and his associates (1981), there is a proclivity in organizations for "decision makers to rely heavily on past experience or prior knowledge" (p. 512)—to "restrict . . . actions to previous strategies" (Shook, 1998, p. 276) and to employ "the same structures, processes, and personnel" (Weitzel & Jonsson, 1989, p. 103)—"to rely on well proven techniques" (Mohrman & Mohrman, 1983, p. 454), "routine solutions" (Billings, Milburn, & Schaalman, 1980, p. 305), "existing procedures" (D'Aunno & Sutton, 1997, p. 128), "well-tried strateg[ies]" (Grinyer, Mayes, & McKiernan, 1988, p. 45), "'tried and true' arrangements" (Fink, Beak, & Taddoo, 1971, p. 23), "well-developed technologies" (Bozeman & Slusher, 1979, p. 343), and "prior commitments and responses" (Ford & Baucus, 1987, p. 375). All of this results in an "insensitivity to the uniqueness of new problems [, an] unwillingness to cast aside old assumptions" (Milburn, Schuler, & Watman, 1983a, pp. 1151, 1156), and an "inhibition of response creativity" (Ford & Baucus, 1987, p. 37). It leads to the exhibition of "habitual response[s]" (Bozeman & Slusher, 1979, p. 343; also Fink, Beak, & Taddoo, 1971), the "rigid use of existing procedures" (D'Aunno & Sutton, 1992, p. 119), and "'off the shelf' responses" (Ford & Baucus, 1987, p. 371).

Thus, because managers "have learned to trust the mythologies of past successes and efficiency of institutionalized practices, decision makers' dependencies on these and the likelihood of using them in downturns increases" (Ford & Baucus, 1987, p. 374). They "cling to well-learned" (D'Aunno & Sutton, 1992, p. 120) or "dominant" (Staw, Sanderlands, & Dutton, 1981, p. 502) responses and "replicate what once worked" (Reich & Donahue, 1985, p. 87): many leaders "respond to mounting difficulties by implementing well-tried strategy more vigorously and by trying harder rather than making fundamental changes to meet changed environmental and market conditions" (Grinyer, Mayes, & McKiernan, 1988, p. 45). As a consequence, "the way crises were handled before will be how they will be handled in the future" (Milburn, Schuler, & Watman, 1983a, p. 1154). In short, decision makers "try to make it through the bad times by continuing the same actions as in the past" (Billings, Milburn, & Schaalman, 1980, p. 304), with "habituation to old programs" (Milburn, Schuler, & Watman, 1983a, p. 1151).

According to the analysts referenced above, because "current methodologies are not adequate" (Mohrman & Mohrman, 1983, p. 451) to the task at hand, this reliance on well-developed and well-used scripts to solve crises range from generally dysfunctional to "grossly inappropriate" (Staw, Sanderlands, & Dutton, 1981, p. 502). Choice is constrained (Bozeman & Slusher, 1979), and "forces may be set in motion that make it difficult for an organization to adapt to its environment" (McKinley, 1993, p. 4) and to address the crisis situation: "The results are often low performance and organizational failure" (Shook, 1998, p. 276).

CHAPTER FIVE

Context and Analytic Frames for Turnarounds

Effective turnaround strategy evolves from and is unique to the institution. (Chaffee, 1983, p. 29)

Performance decline is framed as a strategic decision problem to be solved by a turnaround strategy. (Barker & Duhaime, 1997, p. 14)

To this point in the analysis, we have examined the path of organizational decline from warning signals of impending difficulties through inappropriate and unproductive institutional responses to crisis. In Parts III and IV, we will investigate recovery using the definition of turnaround as process and consequence introduced in Chapter 1, that is, the movement away from crisis and toward organizational health: "Once-successful firms that experience severely declining performance for a protracted period of time overcome their troubles and return to match or exceed their most prosperous periods of pre-downturn performance" (Robbins & Pearce, 1992, p. 307). In this final chapter in Part II, we anchor our analysis of recovery (Part III and Part IV) in two important ways. We explicitly underscore the centrality of context in the struggle for the reintegration of any troubled enterprise. We also overview the ways scholars have portrayed turnaround work to provide a backdrop for the categories we employ to guide our analysis in later chapters.

Context

The selection of a turnaround strategy should depend on the situation. (Hambrick & Schecter, 1983, p. 234)

The particular turnaround strategy chosen by an organization may depend partly on contingency factors. (Khandwalla, 1983–1984, p. 12)

Because turnaround investment strategies are likely to vary in effectiveness according to a firm's individual circumstances, a consideration of critical contingencies is required. (Lohrke & Bedeian, 1998, p. 13)

In Chapter 1, we posited that if there is anything close to a law in the turnaround literature, it is that context is critical. In Chapter 3, we then discussed the significance of context in relation to the causes of organizational decline and failure. Here we revisit context and the important role it plays in turning around declining enterprises (Shook, 1998), acknowledging at the outset that "accounting for these contingencies will help determine the efficacy of particular [recovery] strategies in specific situations" (Lohrke & Bedeian, 1998, p. 17): "The success of a type of turnaround effort is related to contextual factors" (O'Neill, 1986a, p. 168). Or, stated in the obverse, "a simplified view of the strategies appropriate for declining industries is inadequate for the needs of managers running . . . businesses because [of] differences in industry structures, in the reasons for such declines, and in the expectations regarding future demand" (Harrigan, 1988, p. 148). Scholars and practitioners have identified an assortment of contingencies that can influence turnaround work—both turnaround moves engaged and the likelihood of success of these actions (see Figure 1.1). Below, we cluster these variables into three broad domains, industry and environmental context factors, organizational contingencies, and context conditions associated with the nature of decline.

Industry and Environmental Contingencies

It [was] found that appropriateness of particular strategies for dealing with decline depended upon the characteristics of the industry. (Harrigan, 1988, p. 130)

While the case is less than definitive (Oviatt & Bruton, 1994), there is some agreement that the *sector* a business occupies tells us something about needed recovery strategies (Hambrick & Schecter, 1983; Robbins & Pearce, 1992). For example, it is sometimes suggested that efficacious recovery initiatives for industrial companies may be different from actions that might advantage public sector organizations. In similar fashion, *"the nature of the industry"* (Hambrick, 1985, p. 10-4) or "the structure of the industry" (Harrigan, 1988, p. 131) merits analysis. In particular, "industry differences" (Oviatt & Bruton, 1994, p. 139) provide important contextual variations that impact turnaround efforts (Barker & Duhaime, 1997; Siegel, 1981). Arogyaswamy and colleagues (1995), Harrigan (1988), Oviatt and Bruton (1994), and Siegel (1981) also explain how the environments of specific industries assume significance in shaping turnaround actions. For example, Hambrick and Schecter (1983) maintain that in some instances negative industry dynamics negate the ability of individual firms to engage recovery efforts successfully. Or as Slatter (1984) and Arogyaswamy and Yasai-Ardekani (1997) remind us, turnaround in an industry in recession or general cyclical downturn is different than turnaround in an industry characterized by growth: "Companies in weak market positions in growing markets can succeed by cutting back and restructuring. Companies in mature or declining sectors must focus on efficiency of operations . . . in order to survive" (Shuchman & White, 1995, pp. 17–18). Finally, "the general nature of the firm" (Miller, 1977, p. 50), including its history (Miles, 1980), exposes additional contingencies.

As touched upon above, the *general environment* is also an important context theme in the turnaround narrative; that is, there is a "relationship between environment and the strategies an organization is likely to pursue" (Smart & Vertinsky, 1984, p. 201), a "relationship between a firm's environment and certain attributes of crisis management strategies" (p. 211): "To develop meaningful recommendations for turnaround . . . it is important to understand the environment in which the firm is operating" (Chakraborty & Dixit, 1992, p. 347). Of special interest here is the economic environment confronting firms in trouble (Grinyer, Mayes, & McKiernan, 1988). For as Lohrke and Bedeian (1998) reveal, "the appropriateness of specific turnaround investment strategies can be tied directly to industry resource and growth rate (i.e., environmental munificence)" (p. 13). Strategies likely to work in highly munificent environments may prove to be much less efficacious in less generous environments, and vice versa (Lohrke & Bedeian, 1998). The same logic holds when it comes to environmental complexity and certainty (Khandwalla, 1983–1984):

> Environments that are highly complex and turbulent are perceived to be very uncertain. Such environments encourage retrenchment and adaptive responses to discontinuities. . . . In contrast, simple environments, which tend to foster a strong belief in the ability to control events, promote an entrepreneurial response to crisis. (Smart & Vertinsky, 1984, p. 211)

Organizational Contingencies

> *Organizational context also affects management's choice of referents.* (Short, Palmer, & Stimpert, 1998, p. 160)

> *Organizational factors may directly and indirectly affect the extent of strategic reorientation enacted during turnaround attempts.* (Barker & Mone, 1998, pp. 1232–1233)

> *It was theorized that the choice of a particular turnaround strategy would be a function of the business's situation, particularly its market share and its capacity utilization.* (Hambrick & Schecter, 1983, p. 244)

Scholars of turnarounds expose a variety of organizational contingencies that influence which recovery strategies are played (Hambrick, 1985; Slatter, 1984). These context issues fit into one of two overlapping groupings, conditions of the organization writ large and management characteristics. In the first domain, there is evidence that "corporate *age*" (Honig, 1987, p. 4) interacts with recovery strategies: "Thus, how an organization responds to decline may be influenced by its state of development (age)" (Ford, 1980, p. 594). In particular, researchers inform us that not only is "organizational age . . . directly related to organizational survival" (Hager et al., 1999, p. 54) and business failures" (Honig, 1987, p. 4), but that turnaround moves for newer businesses generally need to be different than recovery steps for more "mature" (Hambrick & Schecter, 1983, p. 231) companies (Boyle & Desai, 1991; Oviatt & Bruton, 1994).

In parallel fashion, we know "that *size* . . . is directly related to organizational survival" (Hager et al., 1999, p. 54; also Barker & Mone, 1998) and that recovery for "large, established corporations" (Lorange & Nelson, 1987, p. 41) is built from different strategies and constructed using different tools than those required in smaller organizations. Newness means both more "vulnerability" (Kierulff, 1981, p. 493) and fewer opportunities for missteps in the turnaround phase (Chowdhury & Lang, 1993).

In the organizational domain, analysts also place special emphasis on *organizational slack* (Barker & Mone, 1998), or as Arogyaswamy and colleagues (1995) conclude, one of the most "important contingencies influence[ing] the extent to which managers at turnaround firms apply decline-stemming strategies [is] the level of organizational slack at the time of the turnaround attempt" (p. 504). The research here finds that firms with sufficient slack have the luxury of "adopt[ing] a 'wait and see' attitude" (Ford, 1985, p. 777). Limited slack pushes firms to gravitate toward the use of operating or efficiency turnaround strategies where the focus is "on short term revenue enhancement, cost cutting, and asset sales" (Oviatt & Bruton, 1994, p. 128), while firms with sufficient slack can emphasize strategic approaches or turnaround actions that attend to "achieving long-term competitive advantage" (p. 128).

"*Capacity utilization* . . . [and] *market shares* of the enterprise . . . at the time of the malfunctioning" (Khandwalla, 1983–1984, p. 39) also help direct the selection of turnaround steps: "It appears that businesses do select a turnaround strategy partly on the basis of their market share and capacity utilization" (Hambrick & Schecter, 1983, p. 245). As was the case with organizational slack, greater market share permits firms to adopt less draconian measures and to power turnarounds through strategic as opposed to efficiency plans (Hambrick & Schecter, 1983). Relatedly, researchers have found that "strategic and tactical health" (Khandwalla, 1983–1984, p. 14) or strategic capability of firms—organizations' "power and their abilities to engage successfully in action, [their] ability to affect their long term growth and development" (Ford, 1985, pp. 775–776)—shapes turnaround actions. Specifically, enhanced strategic capability permits the use of strategic turnaround moves: "If strategic health is poor, . . . strategic turnaround action involving diversification, niche hunting, acquisitions, or updating of competitive strength is called for. If tactical strength is weak, cost reduction, sales improvements, asset disposal, etc., strategies are required" (Khandwalla, 1983–1984, p. 14).

The *degree of bureaucratization* is another organizational context condition of importance in the literature on turning around failing enterprises (Oviatt & Bruton, 1994), with entrenched hierarchy acting as a shackle on turnaround vigor. In a similar vein, *"managerial discretion"* (Lohrke & Bedeian, 1998, p. 14), a measure of "the degree of decision latitude present in an industry" (p. 14) or firm, is still another context variable of interest, one that crosses the environmental-organizational contingency divide. For example, from their research, Lohrke and Bedeian (1998) conclude that "a firm facing low managerial discretion [will] often be limited to implementing turnaround strategies within its present domain" (p. 14). Finally, *distance to the break-even point* is known to help direct the selection of turnaround moves; that is, which tactical turnaround strategy is needed "will depend upon how far below the break-even point the firm is operating" (Khandwalla, 1983–1984, p. 14).

Turning to management characteristics, we know that choice of turnaround moves is shaped by *management's view of the crisis,* specifically whether they consider the crisis to be merely "transient or . . . indicative of a more chronic worsening of the organization's operations" (Khandwalla, 1983–1984, p. 12). Turnaround actions are also contingent on management structure, or as Chowdhury and Lang (1993) discovered in their study of small firms, "a significant part of the exploration of how small firms respond to either crisis or decline situations seems to be in the management structures that characterize them" (p. 9). So too, "leadership ability" (McKinley, 1993, p. 5) inside the organization "moderate[s] the direction of the decline-adaptation relationship" (p. 5). Another "critical contingency" (Lohrke & Bedeian, 1998, p. 15) that influences turnaround plans and ultimately turnaround success is "the *nature of a firm's top management group"* (p. 15). Research has shown, for example, that the top management group "plays a central role in determining goals and services to emphasize, markets to penetrate, opportunities to develop, and leadership to exploit" (p. 15) in a turnaround situation:

> TMGs with dominant backgrounds in internally-oriented functional areas (e.g., production) have been found to effectively implement domain-defense strategies. Similarly, TMGs with dominant backgrounds in externally-oriented functional areas (e.g.,

sales) have been found to effectively implement domain-offense strategies. Finally, TMGs with dominant backgrounds in support functions (e.g., finance or law) have been found to effectively implement domain-creation strategies. (Lohrke & Bedeian, 1998, pp. 15–16)

Previous experience with downturns appears to guide the ways that organizational leaders think about decline as well as the tools they select to right the enterprise (Ford, 1985). Finally, "*decision maker characteristics*" (Ford, 1985, p. 777), their "perceptions and interpretations" (McKinley, 1993, p. 5), ego involvement, and commitments (Ford, 1985), "determine responses to organizational decline" (McKinley, 1993, p. 5) in terms of turnaround steps selected (Ford & Baucus, 1987; Slatter, 1984).

Decline Contingencies

There are some indications . . . that other factors affect the turnaround process. These factors are the timing of the strategy and the nature of the decline. (O'Neill, 1981, p. 89)

In Chapter 3, we devoted considerable space to examining the causes of organizational decline. Here we report that "the origin of the business trouble" (Hambrick & Schecter, 1983, p. 240) and turnaround actions are linked (Ford, 1985, 2001; Hegde, 1982), that "causality is a prime determinant of response strategy" (Shuchman & White, 1995, p. 18). "A deep understanding of the *causes of decline*" (Chakraborty & Dixit, 1992, p. 345) is a critical element in the selection of appropriate turnaround moves (Barker & Duhaime, 1997), or as Khandwalla (1983–1984) argues, "turnaround steps differ depending on which management deficiency was the primary cause of the malfunctioning" (p. 15). Specifically, we learn that to be successful, "turnaround attempts must address the source of the problem" (Hambrick & Schecter, 1983, p. 247) and that the nature of the problem suggests which recovery strategies are more likely to be effective (Chakraborty & Dixit, 1992): "If the problems are internal to the business, then solutions tend to be focused on efficiency and management styles, while externally caused problems are responded to by entrepreneurially driven reconfiguration of the remaining assets" (Shuchman & White, 1995, p. 18). Turnaround plans "tend to reflect an attempt to remedy the cause of the sickness" (Hedge, 1983, p. 302)—or "turnaround strategies are likely to be strongly influenced by the causes of sickness" (p. 292): "If sickness has been due to stagnation in the firm's industry, diversification may be the cornerstone of a turnaround strategy; if mismanagement has been the cause, its change and revitalization may be the cornerstone" (p. 292).

Responses to downturn and appropriate paths to health also depend on interpretations of the *stability and controllability of decline* (Ford, 1985). So also, *the state of decline* is another important context variable in the turnaround algorithm (Chan, 1993; Dewitt, Harrigan, & Newman, 1998). Bibeault (1982), for example, asserts that "troubled companies fall into three general levels of seriousness" (p. 203) and that reform moves should vary depending on the stage of decline a firm finds itself in.

In parallel fashion, the *slope of decline* is a contingency variable that shapes turnaround work (Chowdhury & Lang, 1993)—or in some cases explains the absence of turnaround strategies (Hambrick & D'Aveni, 1988). Researchers in this area conclude that "the severity of the situation" (Hambrick, 1985, p. 10-4) or "the *severity of decline*" (Lohrke & Bedeian, 1998, p. 13) influences the selection and employment of turnaround tactics (Arogyaswamy, Barker, & Yasai-Ardekani, 1995; Robbins & Pearce, 1992): "The process of responding to the various problems is affected by . . . the severity of decline" (Shuchman & White, 1995, p. 17). For example, less severe problems are often "responded to by cutbacks and overall cost reductions. Severe problems are responded to by drastic cost reductions as well as asset reductions and dispositions" (p. 17):

> In low severity situations . . . a firm may have the resources to implement a domain-offense or domain-creation strategy. . . . Alternatively, the firm facing low severity may have the resources necessary to implement a domain-creation strategy and move into more promising industries. In high severity situations . . . more drastic action may be required. A firm may find it necessary to implement domain-defense actions. (Lohrke & Bedeian, 1998, p. 14)

ANALYTIC FRAMEWORKS

A successful turnaround is a divine experience but it is difficult to achieve. (Silver, 1992, p. 160)

There is a process and methodology for the logical salvation of the business and procedures for its eventual resurrection. (Shuchman & White, 1995, p. 16)

Any turnaround attempt requires attention on several components of the business simultaneously. (O'Neill, 1981, p. 90)

Scholars who describe organizational turnarounds generally employ overlapping approaches, they (1) chronicle stories of the recovery process; (2) distill elements, characteristics, ingredients, and principles of successful transformation; (3) discuss turnaround actions, approaches, and strategies; (4) delineate phases, steps, or stages of turnarounds, and (5) display explanatory models of how organizations move from sickness to health. For example, on the *narrative* front Bratton and Knobler (1998) relate the story of the turnaround of the New York City Police Department in the mid-1990s; Crandall (1995) outlines turnaround stories of a number of small churches; Rindler (1987) and Green and Hanson (1993) detail the revitalization of an individual and multihospital system, respectively; Mirvis, Ayas, and Roth (2003) describe the turnaround of the Dutch company Unilever in the late 1990s; Reich and Donahue (1985) unpack the story of Chrysler's turnaround in the early 1980s, while Shook (1990) provides a parallel analysis for the Ford Motor Company; Slater (1999) and Gerstner (2002) narrate the turnaround of a very troubled IBM corporation in the 1990s; Trompenaars and Hampden-Turner (2002a) explore the story of turnaround at Club Med in the late 1990s; and Grzymala-Busse (2002) chronicles the transformation of anemic communist parties in East Central Europe at the end of the cold war era.

Turnaround analysts also describe organizational recovery in terms of key *ingredients or elements*—or characteristics, factors, principles, and capacities. For example, Krantz (1985) lists "capacity for flexibility" (p. 5) as a key element of successful turnarounds. Bibeault (1982) suggests that "human understanding and energy" is "the key ingredient to turnaround success" (p. 89). Ross and Kami (1973) reveal a number of guiding principles for turnarounds, such as the following:

- The board must actively participate.
- Avoid one-man rule.
- The customer is king. (p. 13)

So too does Argenti (1976). For example,

- Avoid working with people with the same knowledge as yourself.
- Avoid overtrading. (pp. 179, 181)

Goodman (1982) underscores "sixteen key principles with a history of success" (p. 36) in turnarounds, including the following:

- Begin with a clear picture of the customer.
- Develop industrywide yardsticks for appraising people.
- Focus on growth.
- Be results oriented.
- Build in margins of safety.
- Delegate but don't abdicate. (pp. 37–41)

Crandall (1995) outlines an assortment of "keys to building a viable renewal strategy in local churches" (p. 18), and Bratton and Knobler (1998) distill essential ingredients of turnarounds based on the recovery of the New York City Police Department, including the following:

- Focus on the customer.
- Set ambitious improvement goals.
- Engage in "relentless follow-up and assessment." (p. 224)

Shook (1990), Gerstner (2002), Kanter (2003), and Jackson (2001) reinforce the principle of customer focus and add another on the need to continually challenge the status quo in organizational operations. Shuchman and White (1995) distill 20 rules to follow in managing turnarounds, including the following three examples:

- First assumptions are usually incorrect.
- There are no fixed expenses.
- Even when managing . . . under fire, the standard rules of good management still apply. (pp. 39–40)

Slater (1999) provides three elements of successful turnarounds based on his analysis of IBM:

- Focus on performance, not activity.
- Align the system.
- Ensure accountability.

Zimmerman (1991) exposes the following key ingredients of turnarounds:

- Stamina
- Integrity
- Discipline
- Prudence
- Sacrifice

Rindler (1987) and Chaffee (1983) report that strong trustees or strong boards are a key ingredient of successful turnarounds. And an assortment of turnaround analysts are convinced that "one common characteristic of all successful turnarounds is a leader—someone who can energize the organization, overcome the obstacles, and head the company toward a new beginning" (Goldstein, 1988, p. 43; also Bibeault, 1982; Breault, 1993; Crandall, 1995; Finkin, 1987; Kramer, 1987; McArthur, 1993; Rindler, 1987; Shelley & Jones, 1993; Shook, 1990; Short, Palmer, & Stimpert, 1998; Stephens, 1988; Tushaman & Romanelli, 1985).

Portraits of turnarounds captured in terms of key *actions and strategies* include those provided by Goldstein (1988):

- Cost-cutting actions
- Revenue-generating actions
- Asset-reduction actions (p. 7)

By Slatter (1984):

- Change of management
- Strong central financial control
- Organizational change and decentralization
- Product-market reorientation
- Improved marketing
- Growth via acquisitions
- Asset reduction

- Cost reduction
- Investment
- Debt restructuring and other financial strategies (p. 78)

By Grinyer and colleagues (1988):

- Major changes in management
- Stronger financial controls
- New product market focus
- Diversified
- Entered export market vigorously
- Improved quality and service
- Improved marketing
- Intensive effort to reduce production costs
- Acquisitions
- Reduced debt
- Windfalls (p. 64)

By Khandwalla (1983–1984):

- One or more powerful change agents committed to turning the organization around
- Fairly dramatic credibility-building actions by the change agent
- Mobilization of the organization for turnaround by emphasis on organizationwide missions and goals, concretization of goals and problems, and the involvement of personnel in the turnaround
- Quick payoff action to generate badly needed cash and provide an experience of success for cynical rank-and-file
- Reprieve from external pressures by the management's seeking rapport with key outside pressure groups and negotiating temporary relief from pressure with them
- Opportunistic harnessing of the external environment by identifying and seizing the opportunities it provides
- Management's selective strengthening of some of the mechanisms for influencing the external environment of the organization
- Selective changes in the organization's product mix
- Selective professionalization of management systems
- Motivational strategy

- Coordination strategy
- Performance control strategy
- Institutionalization of the appropriate style of management (p. 19)

By Schendel and colleagues (1976):

- Organization and management changes
- Marketing programme changes
- Major plant expenditure
- Diversification—product
- Diversification—geographic
- Efficiency increases
- Divestiture
- Vertical integration (p. 8)

By Hofer (1980):

- Revenue generation
- Product/market refocusing
- Cost cutting
- Asset reduction (p. 25)

By Shelley and Jones (1993):

- Creating an organizational vision
- Identifying organizational values
- Defining a culture
- Redefining policies, procedures, and practices
- Structuring the organization (p. 69)

By Ford (1985):

- Internal actions
  - operative change
  - administrative changes

- External actions
  - domain defense responses
  - domain offense responses

   o domain abandonment responses
   o domain creation responses (p. 772)

By Fredenberger, Lipp, and Watson (1997):

- Financial actions
- Operational actions
- Strategic actions (p. 171)

And by Shuchman and White (1995):

- Cutbacks
- Restructuring
- Management
- Growth

Staged lenses for understanding turnarounds include those provided by Bibeault (1982):

- The management change stage
- The evaluation stage
- The emergency stage
- The stabilization stage
- The return-to-normal stage (p. 92)

By Chan (1993):

- Realize need for turnaround.
- Replace CEO.
- Cut costs.
- Refocus and reinvest. (p. 32)

By Hambrick (1985):

- Crisis
- Stabilization
- Rebuilding (pp. 10–13)

By Goldston (1992):

- Stop the bleeding.
- Adopt a cash management policy.

- Accumulate data.
- Determine who is going to play.
- Assess manufacturing capabilities.
- Create the playbook.
- Set realistic goals.
- Create an idea-generating process.
- Create a war chest.
- Show demonstrable progress. (p. 55)

And by Khandwalla (1983–1984):

- A dynamic change agent (or a team of change agents); preferably from "outside," with high position authority and with a strong sense of mission, is recruited.

- The change agent seeks credibility-building opportunities, such as by standing up to blackmail, resolving a deadlocked issue or a long-standing grievance, or through some outstanding performance.

- The change agent mobilizes the rank-and-file by getting them to focus on the organization's mission, concrete goals, and problems and by involving them in the turnaround.

- The organization undertakes a series of projects that can yield quick payoffs with reasonable certainty.

- The organization gets reprieve from serious external pressures, particularly with respect to industrial relations, finance, key inputs, and interference of owners.

- The organization mobilizes external resources and seizes environmental opportunities.

- The organization strengthens mechanisms for influencing the environment, such as marketing and public relations.

- The organization makes selective changes in the product mix, dropping the low-payoff products and taking on high-payoff products. It avoids taking on very unfamiliar products.

- Management functions and system are selectively strengthened, beginning with the areas of great weakness. A good financial control system is often a high priority.

- Managers are motivated by means of challenging tasks, a sense of participation, operating autonomy coupled with clear accountability for performance, peer group pressure for excellence, competition for excellence, example set by change agent, and so on.

- Coordination is induced by regular performance review meetings of managers, formation of coordinating committees, and an emphasis on direct face-to-face, nonhierarchical settlement of disputes.

- Performance control is secured by some form of MBO, that is, by the setting of concrete targets by managers, with the help of their bosses, with provision for a fairly hard-nosed review periodically, and by the creation of a number of responsibility centers (including profit-and-cost centers).

- A progressive, open, participative, results-oriented, risk-taking, innovation and professional management-oriented style is institutionalized through the above steps. (p. 36)

By Pearce and Robbins (1994b; Robbins & Pearce, 1992):

- Retrenchment
- Recovery (p. 411)

By Zimmerman (1991):

- Preturnaround situation
- Period of crisis
- Period of recovery (p. 24)

By Shuchman and White (1995):

- Survival
- Resurrection (p. 19)

By Fredenberger and colleagues (1997):

- Crisis
- Stabilization
- Recovery (p. 171)

By Kierulff (1981):

- Assessing the situation
- Developing a turnaround plan
- Implementing the plan (p. 494)

By Arogyaswamy and colleagues (1995):

- Decline-stemming strategies
- Recovery strategies (p. 493)

By Silver (1992):

- Diagnosing the crisis
- Mitigating the crisis
- Generating cash
- Preparing a turnaround plan\negotiating the plan
- Implementing the plan (pp. 7–9)

And by Slatter (1984):

- Analysis phase
- Emergency phase
- Strategic change phase
- Growth phase (p. 122)

Finally, carefully delineated *models* to capture turnarounds have been crafted by many leading organizational scholars. For example, see Armenakis and Fredenberger (1998, p. 41); Arogyaswamy and colleagues (1995, p. 498); Ford and Baucus (1987, p. 368); Hambrick (1985, p. 10-1); Hambrick and D'Aveni (1988, p. 14); Hegde (1982, p. 301); and Shook (1998, p. 269).

In the chapters that follow, we capture material from all five ways of unpacking turnarounds presented above. Specifically, we blend researching findings into broad categories that slot into the most powerful and parsimonious model of turnaround stages, the two-step design of retrenchment and recovery discussed by Arogyaswamy and associates (1995), Hofer (1980), Pearce and Robbins (1994b), and Schendel and his colleagues (1976). We develop categories that both honor the research on turnarounds and that fit the special context of government-funded organizations such as public schools. We begin in Chapters 6 and 7 by examining the dimensions of the retrenchment phase of the turnaround process.

PART III

Retrenchment

Retrenchment is the key to survival. (Hardy, 1990, p. 6)

There is growing evidence to suggest that a basic set of activities are prevalent among successful turnaround firms. . . . These activities are best known as retrenchment. (Robbins & Pearce, 1992, p. 287)

Research results provide evidence of a common strategic action among firms that have successfully confronted decline. This action, referred to as retrenchment, entails deliberate reductions in costs, assets, product lines and overhead. In short, research to date suggests that for firms facing declining financial performance, the key to successful turnaround initially rests in the effective and efficient management of the retrenchment activities. (Pearce & Robbins, 1993, p. 614)

CHAPTER SIX

Getting the Right Leadership

There can be no doubt as to the key role of new chief executives in the process of fundamental change. (Grinyer & McKiernan, 1990, p. 141)

The key is to have a specifically designed turnaround program . . . that is led by a strong, experienced individual at the top. (Finkin, 1987, p. 25)

Turnarounds appear due much more to management actions than to favorable environmental events. (Schendel, Patton, & Riggs, 1976, p. 10)

A s reported in Chapter 5 and seen in Figure 1.1, the first half of a turnaround is a series of actions collectively described in the research literature as retrenchment. While the primary focus of retrenchment in the corporate world (i.e., cost reductions and efficiency) is different than in the public sector, the broad phases of retrenchment culled from the literature hold up well for nonprofit and government enterprises as well as firms. These general stages include getting the right leadership, diagnosing the problem, and taking emergency action. We explore the leadership issue in this chapter and diagnosis and emergency action in Chapter 7.

In nearly all situations, leadership is seen as a central variable in the equation of organizational success. Even in routine times, "a business short on leadership has little chance for survival" (Bennis & Nanus, 1985, p. 20). In times of significant change and in periods of crisis, the saliency of leadership is dramatically increased (Crandall, 1995; Rindler, 1987; Shook, 1990): "Turnarounds are when leadership matters most" (Kanter, 2003, p. 67); "when adversity obscures prospects of success and organizational morale falters, dynamic and articulate leadership . . . can make the difference between success and failure" (Bibeault, 1982, p. 189). Such "strong leadership can create order out of chaos and excellence out of mediocrity" (Rindler, 1987, p. 219). Indeed, as Shelley and Jones (1993) conclude, "only strong leaders can guide their organizations through troubled times" (p. 71). Here we examine leadership in four ways. We review the literature that documents the power of leadership in times of crisis. We explore the importance of changing leadership in troubled organizations. We present the rationale for management change at the apex of the organization. And we portray the characteristics commonly associated with effective turnaround leaders.

LEADERSHIP AS A KEY TO REINTEGRATION

Leadership . . . emerges, then, as being crucial to effective turnaround. (O'Shaughnessy, 1995, p. 5)

Management is the principal catalyst and the root of ultimate responsibility in the revival of troubled firms. (Zimmerman, 1991, p. 6)

One might go so far as to say that the nature of the top management team in a company is of greater significance for success or failure than any of the company's products or skills or physical assets. (Argenti, 1976, p. 37)

It is impossible to miss the most pervasive pattern in the reintegration mosaic crafted by turnaround artists: "For most writers, the 'key' is leadership. The effective leader not only triggers change, he changes the climate of the company, its vision, and gives it new direction" (Grinyer, Mayes, & McKiernan, 1988, p. 59). Indeed, in the turnaround literature "the importance of finding a good manager or management team cannot be overstated" (McArthur, 1993, p. 228; also Starbuck, Greve, & Hedberg, 1978). Reviewers consistently conclude that "in all turnarounds leadership [is] needed" (Finkin, 1987, p. 18), "executive action is required for strategic reorientation" (Tushman & Romanelli, 1985, p. 204; also Stephens, 1988), and "leadership is the most important element in institutional transformation" (Gerstner, 2002, p. 235).

The logic here is that almost all other elements of the turnarounds are dependent upon and "inexorably linked with management cognition and interpretation" (Short, Palmer, & Stimpert, 1998, p. 154), that "though many variables are involved in turnaround success or failure, competent management can impact most of them" (Zimmerman, 1991, p. 6). In particular, as Stopford and Baden-Fuller (1990) find, the role of the chief executive is "critically important both in triggering the initial change and in acting as teacher during the ensuing steps" (p. 412). In organizational turnarounds, it is leadership that provides "a sense of direction by setting priorities and short-term goals; establish[es] a sense of urgency; define[s] responsibilities; resolve[s] conflict; convey[s] enthusiasm and dedication; and give[s] credit where it is due and reward[s] it accordingly (Slatter, 1984, p. 148).

CHANGING LEADERSHIP

One nearly universal generalization must be made. A precondition for almost all successful turnarounds is the replacement of the current top management of the business in question. (Hofer, 1980, p. 25)

It is usually a foregone conclusion that the CEO will change in a turnaround. (Rindler, 1987, p. 12)

Replacing top leaders can often be an essential first step in turning around declining organizations. (Meyer, 1988, p. 413)

The first step or first priority in a turnaround is "to address leadership" (Breault, 1993, p. 203), "to see that proper management is in place" (Schendel, Patton, & Riggs, 1976, p. 10): "The first step in a turnaround, without which everything else is apt to fail, is the firm recognition that management must be strengthened" (Goodman, 1982, p. 47)—more specifically, the recognition that new management can make the difference (Arogyaswamy, Barker, & Yasai-Ardekani, 1995; Barker & Mone, 1998).

According to Bibeault (1982), leadership change can unfold in a number of ways. It "can mean either changing management or changing its approach" (p. 141), although most turnaround analysts are quick to point out the difficulty of pursuing the latter approach, a difficulty that we explore in considerable detail shortly. On the former front, changing management can entail securing a new CEO or management team or bringing in "outside help" (Breault, 1993, p. 206), often in the form of turnaround consultants (Kierulff, 1981).

> At this stage, it is obvious that some change is needed in management. If no change is made, the organization will ultimately reach the failure stage and will be dissolved. However, if a change is made, it may take either of two forms. One is to change the management practices by following the advice of consultants. The other is to replace the top manager. (Armenakis & Fredenberger, 1998, p. 42)

While acknowledging this dual approach, it is important to point out that management change is a core element and a dominant theme in the turnaround literature, "that recovery from decline is often facilitated by replacing the CEO and other top executives" (Barker & Duhaime, 1997, p. 20): "One of the most unanimous assertions of past researchers is that a declining firm's chief executive officer or top managers will usually be removed to initiate the turnaround process" (Arogyaswamy, Barker, & Yasai-Ardekani, 1995, p. 505; also Grinyer & Spender, 1979; Slater, 1999)—"the evidence suggests more often than not management should be changed" (O'Neill, 1986b, p. 87). Visible in the literature is a clear message that, in general, there is a "need for an infusion of new top managerial blood to revitalize the company and direct the turnaround" (Modiano, 1987, p. 174), a sense that "a firm in need of a turnaround almost surely needs to replace some key people" (Stewart, 1984, p. xii), that turnarounds often "require substantial changes in the management team" (O'Neill, 1981, p. 21), a need for executive replacement" (Milburn, Schuler, & Watman, 1983b, p. 1171) and usually "new executives from outside the organization" (Tushman, Newman, & Romanelli, 1988, p. 73). These "outsiders are believed to be an essential ingredient for firms to turnaround successfully" (Lubatkin & Chung, 1985, p. 26). Over 70 percent of the companies in the study by Schendel and colleagues (1976) made major changes in management, while all the firms in the O'Neill (1986a) study did so.

As a prelude to the following section, we note that the logic for management change has been nicely formulated by Brenneman (1998): "The same team that leads a company into a crisis is rarely able to get it back on track. The hard news about a turnaround is that you have no choice but to sweep out the old to make way for the new" (p. 166). Or, alternatively from Finkin (1987): "It is almost impossible for a cultural change to be made without an agent for change who is not beholden to company tradition—a new top manager. This is one of the reasons a company usually requires a change in top management" (p. 52). "It is almost axiomatic that if management is the key cause of the decline, then changing management will go a long way toward correcting the problem" (Bibeault, 1982, p. 113). The literature generally posits that turnarounds require the appointment of "chief executives who are outsiders and unfettered by allegiances to organizational traditions or precedents and untarnished by past disasters" (Khandwalla, 1983–1984, p. 20).

The "rule" of CEO change in turnarounds requires more fine-grained analysis, however. In short, some caveats are in order (Barker & Mone, 1998). To begin with, the "conventional wisdom" (Castrogiovanni, Bahga, & Kidwell, 1992, p. 38) of CEO change is often just that, and not an ironclad law. As Grinyer and McKiernan (1990) correctly infer, "we should not assume, however, that a new chief executive is either necessary or sufficient to effect radical change" (p. 141): "Not all turnarounds require a change in top management" (O'Neill, 1986b, p. 82). It is also instructive to remember that nonsuccessful turnaround firms are also likely to change top managers (Castrogiovanni, Bahga, & Kidwell, 1992) and that research on the issue, outside of case studies, is not as robust as often portrayed. As Arogyaswamy and his colleagues (1995) indicate

> Despite the central role that top management change assumes in many descriptions of the turnaround process, there is little empirical evidence from large sample studies that changing top managers is associated with a recovery of performance. (p. 496)

Thus, while changing the chief executive is a way of achieving sharp improvement in performance, it is by no means a guarantee (Grinyer, Mayes, & McKiernan, 1988; Lubatkin & Chung, 1985), at best necessary in many situations but insufficient in most cases.

Relatedly, other options on the management front merit attention, including the engagement of "internal mavericks" (Castrogiovanni, Bahga, & Kidwell, 1992, p. 37). In addition, obviously the "benefits of CEO change depend on the quality of the selection decision" (p. 27) and "the presence of needed strengths and the absence of certain weaknesses in the person pick[ed]" (Bibeault, 1982, p. 113). Benefits also are influenced by whether a "charter to take drastic action" (p. 113) and to engage in frame-breaking work (Bratton & Knobler, 1998; Tushman & Romanelli, 1985) is provided. Similarly, gains depend on (1) whether the change occurs early enough in the turnaround process so that sufficient degrees of freedom remain for action (Castrogiovanni, Bahga, & Kidwell, 1992)—that changes not occur "too late even for a highly experienced new management team to make the organization effective once again" (Milburn, Schuler, & Watman, 1983b, p. 1172)—and (2) the extent that change agents who are adept at reform not remain too long on the job, into the period when "the emphasis is on building the organization for the long term" (Slatter, 1984, p. 83).

A variety of turnaround analysts also confirm that there are often real costs associated with management changes and that these costs need to be surfaced and weighed in the decision process (Barker & Mone, 1998; Castrogiovanni, Bahga, & Kidwell, 1982). For instance, Arogyaswamy and his colleagues (1995) maintain that "in certain decline situations the benefits of changing CEOs may be outweighed by the costs. . . . Actions by the board of directors to remove the CEO may actually exacerbate the firm's decline" (p. 518). Concomitantly, the "view that managerial action is the source of turnaround behavior must be tempered by recognizing that management variables are not solely responsible for strategic actions" (D'Aveni, 1989, p. 600).

There is also evidence here, as nearly everywhere in this volume, that context cannot be ignored. Castrogiovanni and his team (1982) argue that executive change moves need to be linked to "assessments of what caused the performance decline" (p. 31). Arogyaswamy and his colleagues (1995), in turn, deduce from their analyses that "type of decline" (p. 518) should be used "as a moderator when examining . . . top management changes" (p. 518). Relatedly, management change is moderated, it is held, by the type of industry (Oviatt & Bruton, 1994). For example, Arogyaswamy and his associates (1995) posit a "positive relationship between top management team changes and turnaround attempt success in stable or growing industries but possibly a negative relationship in cyclical or declining industries" (p. 518). Likewise, Grinyer and his team (1988) hold that the introduction of new executives is especially significant when turnaround involves "a re-orientation of the business and giving up long established activities" (p. 106). Finally, according to Castrogiovanni and colleagues (1992), "the desirability of CEO change varies by decline stage" (p. 28). According to these scholars, there is a correct period in the decline-failure-recovery story line for the emergence of new leadership. Changes made before or after that time, they aver, can be nonproductive. While in general "the costs of CEO change diminish as business performance declines" (p. 29), the objective is to make the switch at the point when "the potential benefits of CEO change" (p. 30) are highest and the "cost of changing" (p. 30) are lowest.

We close our exploration of the caveats around CEO change with two insights. First, the essence of the change activity is the ability to secure executives with the appropriate skills, and there is disagreement on the issue of what is featured in that skill set. What appears most appropriate is that the change agent has a combination of general turnaround expertise and industry-specific knowledge (Bibeault, 1982; Slatter, 1984; Zimmerman, 1991). More specifically, "selection should be based on matching the individual's specific capabilities . . . with the type of adaptation problem facing the business" (Castrogiovanni, Bahga, & Kidwell, 1992, p. 27): "The answer depends on the characteristics of the turnaround firm" (Slatter, 1984, p. 79).

Second, the desirability of changing the entire senior team of executives is contested. Indeed, "views vary enormously among turnaround experts as to the need for major changes at the level below that of the chief executive" (Slatter, 1984, p. 83). Some analysts consider this as an important aspect of recovery (Starbuck, Greve, & Hedberg, 1978)—"replacements of one or two managers at a time are not enough" (p. 125)—while others express little support for this approach (Khandwalla, 1983–1984). All of these cautions help us understand "that CEO change, rather than being a panacea, may be a valuable tool in a turnaround effort" (Castrogiovanni, Bahga, & Kidwell, 1992, p. 38).

RATIONALE FOR CHANGE

It is unlikely that the existing management of a firm can implement a turnaround successfully after the crisis and denial stage has been in existence for any period of time. (Slatter, 1984, p. 74)

In more than seven out of ten cases, management has to be replaced because they either cannot cope with the problem or they, themselves (or at least the CEO), are the problem. (Bibeault, 1982, p. 141)

The rationale is that the present manager has already demonstrated ineptness by allowing the business to deteriorate; he or she is psychologically wedded to the present way of doing things and, because of his or her close ties to subordinates, customers, and other parties, he or she could not make the hard decisions that must be made in a turnaround situation. (Hambrick, 1985, p. 10-27)

As we documented above, while management change is not the answer in every turnaround, it nonetheless appears to be justified in many cases and in nearly all those situations that have progressed to the crisis phase. Bibeault (1982), as seen in the introductory quote above, proffers two reasons for leadership change: either current managers caused the problem (or they are the problem) or they cannot cope with the crisis. In addition, Khandwalla (1983–1984) observes that firing existing managers can signal the importance of change to internal and external stakeholders. He also holds that removing managers may "facilitate experimentation and the search for fresh options" (p. 13) and the rejection of "assumptions that have underlain the previous disastrous strategy" (p. 13). Building from these and related analyses, below we review four reasons for terminating the current CEO and perhaps others from the top management team: manager as the problem, management adherence to dysfunctional norms, managerial inability to act, and replacement as signaling.

Managers as Cause of the Problem

Present management is most unlikely to accomplish a success-
ful turnaround for two reasons: First, they got the company into
its present difficulties. (Bibeault, 1982, pp. 44–45)

To begin with, as we reported in Chapter 3, leaders are often "a contributing source of decline" (Arogyaswamy, Barker, & Yasai-Ardekani, 1995, p. 506). Or, as Goldstein (1988) argues, "most managers must bear in mind the painful reality that they got their business in trouble in the first place" (p. 58), either actively or passively: "The current CEO may have implemented a poor strategy or failed to implement necessary strategic changes which ultimately placed the organization in a turnaround situation" (Chan, 1993, p. 30). Executives, according to this line of analysis, either directly caused the problems at the heart of crisis, failed to "recognize the problems early enough" (Bibeault, 1982, p. 94), or "didn't want to do anything about them" (p. 94): "If they had been sufficiently competent to get the needed results, they would have taken action earlier in the first place, and thereby, precluded the need for turnaround action" (Sloma, 1985, p. 24). Thus, because current managers "got the company into its present difficulties" (Bibeault, 1982, p. 145), "the declining firm's top managers are stigmatized and lose credibility with external stakeholders and firm employees" (Arogyaswamy, Barker, & Yasai-Ardekani, 1995, p. 502).

The summative logic here has been nicely laid out by Kanter (2003)—"if the old CEO had wrong ideas in the past, why should people believe that he or she has the right idea now" (p. 64)—and by Whetten (1988a)—"problem causers have little credibility as problem solvers" (p. 37). In this case, "new leaders . . . who are perceived as both unconnected to previous firm problems and skilled enough to stem decline may have a greater ability to stabilize the firm's internal climate" (Arogyaswamy, Barker, & Yasai-Ardekani, 1995, p. 506).

Managers Restrained by Existing Culture

The current management . . . usually has a strongly held set of
beliefs about running the business, and it is this belief structure
that has led to the trouble. (Kierulff, 1981, p. 488)

Organizations in crisis must often remove top managers so that
obsolete dominating ideas and standard operating procedures
can be unlearned. (Cameron, Sutton, & Whetten, 1988, p. 11)

Even when the current leader is not viewed as the cause of the organizational crisis, she or he may be so enmeshed in the current culture as to make change, especially needed frame-breaking change, difficult or impossible (Goldstein, 1988; Short, Palmer, & Stimpert, 1998; Slater, 1999), thus necessitating replacement. As discussed in earlier chapters, this especially appears to be the case when "the CEO has had considerable success with [the firm] in the past" (Castrogiovanni, Bahga, & Kidwell, 1992, p. 34). It also seems to occur when the CEO or management team has been on the job for an extended period of time, because longer-tenured managers are more likely to attribute failure to noncontrollable (external) causes (Barker & Patterson, 1996).

What seems to be the theme here is that "obsolete dominating ideas and standard operating procedures" (Cameron, Sutton, & Whetten, 1988, p. 11) and existing structures, goals, and norms at the core of the organization are often taken as fixed by current leaders (Barker & Mone, 1998; Slatter, 1984). They tend to be committed to these "policies and practices" (Barker & Duhaime, 1997, p. 20) and to "business as usual" (Ford & Baucus, 1987, p. 375): they "are often locked into a particular perspective yielding specific recipes for running the business. This perspective can be so strong . . . that CEOs fail to see the need for change and, therefore, fail to change perspective as performance problems mount" (Castrogiovanni, Bahga, & Kidwell, 1992, pp. 28–29). In particular, "old management may be wedded to solutions which have failed but which it continues to apply because it has made a public commitment to them" (O'Shaughnessy, 1995, p. 5).

On the other hand, it is argued, "declining organizations need to abandon old priorities" (Sutton, Eisenhardt, & Jucker, 1986, p. 19). And replacement, logic holds, introduces new decision makers who

because they are unencumbered by prior involvements and commitments to current organizational characteristics, and because
they have different interpretive schemes derived from different
experience histories, are less influenced by existing organizational characteristics and, therefore, are likely to create different
interpretations. (Ford & Baucus, 1987, p. 375)

Analysts here maintain that new leaders "are better able to disentangle system dynamics because they are not caught up in them" (Kanter, 2003, p. 64): "The new executive team is unfettered by prior commitments linked to the status quo. . . . They bring different skills and a fresh perspective" (Tushman, Newman, & Romanelli, 1985, p. 72), a "fresh perspective on the business's problems" (Castrogiovanni, Bahga, & Kidwell, 1992, p. 28), and a "fresh viewpoint on the business position" (Chan, 1993, p. 30): "Hence both the very presence of new leadership and its freedom from association with the difficulties of the past will facilitate the fundamental changes in attitudes and behaviour" (Grinyer, Mayes, & McKiernan, 1988, p. 132) and will promote "new knowledge, beliefs, and assumptions" (Castrogiovanni, Bahga, & Kidwell, 1992, p. 34). Because "they are less committed to the organization's past strategies and values . . . and to current management" (Lubatkin & Chung, 1985, p. 26), they are "expected to shift priorities or emphasize new goals" (McNeil & Thompson, 1971, p. 633), "to alter the mission, objectives and strategies of the organization" (Lubatkin & Chung, 1985, p. 26). They are believed to have "the advantage of objectivity in evaluating the situation" (Bibeault, 1982, p. 95) as well as to be "more capable of taking drastic measures" (p. 95).

Inability to Perform

Present management is often emotionally inhibited and cannot apply the necessary remedies. (Bibeault, 1982, p. 145)

In a parallel vein, there is a considerable body of literature that reveals that managers in failing firms often lack the ability to lead their organization successfully through a turnaround, that "they cannot get the business out of trouble on their own" (Goldstein, 1988, p. 58). Scholars report that these leaders often lack "the mindset and skills needed to support" (Mirvis, Ayas, & Roth, 2003, p. 25) reorientation.

On the one hand, current executives are often unable to "cope with the problem" (Bibeault, 1982, p. 94), that for a variety of reasons they have a difficult time "facing up to and articulating a turnaround need" (Goodman, 1982, p. 3). In short, they lack the *mind-set* for change, they "shy away from turnaround thinking in [their] own situations" (p. 4): "Their management philosophy is presumed to be defective" (Kierulff, 1981, p. 490). It is sometimes seen that "CEOs of failing organizations . . . tend to let their egos get in the way" (Chan, 1993, p. 30) of needed turnaround work, often providing "self-serving attributions for the cause of decline" (Barker & Patterson, 1996, p. 18). It has also been shown that sometimes management is so emotionally attached to current systems that they cannot "apply the necessary remedies" (Bibeault, 1982, p. 145). The theme here is that "the workout business requires an entirely different mind-set" (Silver, 1992, pp. 94–95), one that managers in troubled organizations are unable to cultivate.

On the other hand, "proponents of the competence argument claim that even if CEOs desire to shift perspectives and strategies, they may not possess the *skills* needed to deal with decline" (Castrogiovanni, Bahga, & Kidwell, 1992, p. 29). This appears to be the case, scholars often posit, because turnarounds call for frame-breaking change leadership (Schendel, Patton, & Riggs, 1976) and a recognition that turnarounds represent in fundamental ways a different type of business than the normal business that one is in: "The manager of a crisis-riven company must recognize from the outset that he or she is no longer in the widget business, but is now in the workout business" (Silver, 1992, p. 90). As a consequence

> an executive with industry experience who has been "successful" in the industry but does not have experience in managing a turnaround situation may not be as good as an experienced turnaround man with no relevant industry experience. (Slatter, 1984, p. 80)

It is also the case because "the skills to manage adversity are not entirely commonplace" (Zimmerman, 1991, p. 10). The skills and "business knowledge" (Mirvis, Ayas, & Roth, 2003, p. 25) required "to turn business performance around differ from those needed to maintain performance levels both before decline sets in and after turnaround is accomplished" (Castrogiovanni, Bahga, & Kidwell, 1992, p. 29; see Mirvis, Ayas, & Roth, 2003). The turnaround manager "needs to have special characteristics and skills that may be different from those in a healthy firm" (Slatter, 1984, p. 82): "Managers accustomed to more 'normal' business conditions usually lack an adequate understanding of the special techniques" (Finkin, 1985, p. 2) and "requisite skills" (Kierulff, 1981, p. 488) "necessary to accomplish a turnaround" (Finkin, 1985, p. 14); they "are poorly educated to cope with decline" (Sutton, Eisenhardt, & Jucker, 1986, p. 18). Thus, the case is made that old managers, even "CEOs who have good records as 'custodial managers' . . . may not be good change agents or turnaround managers" (Castrogiovanni, Bahga, & Kidwell, 1992, p. 29) and, therefore, (1) efforts to right declining organizations often fail (Finkin, 1985) and (2) the replacement of these executives with leaders possessing appropriate managerial competencies (Castrogiovanni, Bahga, & Kidwell, 1992) is necessary to restore organizations to positions of strength.

Replacement as Signaling

The appointment of new top managers can be an important signal that a failing organization is serious about recovery. (Boyne, 2004, p. 99)

The appointment of a new chief executive to begin the turnaround is, in some senses, a symbolic act which marks the end of the disintegration and the beginning of the recovery. It is an important step in initiating the turnaround process. (Slatter, 1984, p. 74)

Proponents of the signaling argument focus on the symbolic aspects of CEO change, claiming that replacement of the CEO is the most dramatic way that a business can signal to stakeholders a willingness to change and a commitment to new ways of doing things. Noting that poor business performance results in a CEO's loss of credibility in the eyes of key stakeholders, proponents argue that turnaround is unlikely unless stakeholder confidence is restored. Only by replacing the CEO can an appropriate signal be sent that motivates the various stakeholders to contribute the effort and resources necessary for turnaround. (Castrogiovanni, Bahga, & Kidwell, 1992, p. 29)

Finally, numerous turnaround analysts explore the symbolic importance of changing leaders in declining organizations, the highly visible demonstration of "the end of disintegration and the beginning of regeneration" (Starbuck, Greve, & Hedberg, 1978, p. 175). This "positive signaling to concerned . . . stakeholders" (Castrogiovanni, Bahga, & Kidwell, 1992, p. 28) changes the psychology of the situation" (Finkin, 1987, p. 2), removing some of the distrust and suspicions likely held by internal and external constituents. Thus, according to Weitzel and Jonsson (1989), CEO replacement "has the additional benefit of serving as a symbol of the need for major change and provides [a] 'scapegoat' to relieve tension" (p. 105; see also Slatter, 1984; Starbuck, Greve, & Hedberg, 1978): "It appears that the change in management represents a clear signal to all interested parties that the firm is serious about its attempt to turnaround" (O'Neill, 1986b, p. 87), and this seems to be the case whether existing managers "created the mess" (Goldstein, 1988, p. 45) or not or whether the new manager knows what to do or not (Finkin, 1987).

CHARACTERISTICS OF TURNAROUND LEADERS

Perhaps it would be more accurate to say that a turnaround depends more on a leader with certain personality traits than with certain managerial skills. (Goldstein, 1988, p. 55)

The traumatic circumstances of a turnaround require the presence of certain character traits. (Zimmerman, 1991, p. 189)

Several leadership qualities are critical to successful turnaround. (Shelley & Jones, 1993, p. 71)

In this final section of getting the right leadership, the introductory phase of retrenchment, we examine the characteristics and traits of turnaround leaders. We start with two introductory notes. First, while traits in general can be culled from the recovery literature, "the specific managerial strengths that are most in need will depend on the organization and its own unique problems and opportunities" (Goldstein, 1988, p. 44). That is, "various styles are used by turnaround leaders depending on the situation at hand" (Bibeault, 1982, p. 168), and selecting "the most appropriate type of turnaround manager" (Hambrick, 1985, p. 10-28) requires a good deal of knowledge about the organization in question.

Second, the spotlight here is on personality or traits. Actions and behaviors are examined primarily in the context of the retrenchment and recovery work, that is, in the balance of the book. Notwithstanding, we do list here the presence of three broad frames of action that often define successful turnaround executives. These women and men tend to be transformational leaders (Goldstein, 1988; Grinyer, Mayes, & McKiernan, 1988). They also are often marked by an "entrepreneurial instinct" (Bibeault, 1982, p. 153). Finally, they are leaders of change (Barker & Patterson, 1996; Shelley & Jones, 1993). Collectively, the "accent is on action, on bold decisive moves" (Bibeault, 1982, p. 160) and risk taking (Crandall, 1995; Rindler, 1987). They are "very much opportunity-oriented, not problem-oriented" (Goldstein, 1988, p. 48); they are "opportunistic and exploitive" (p. 56) and proactive (Goodman, 1992):

> First and foremost the turnaround leader is the architect of change. He or she must shape the organization from what it is to what it can or must become. As architect, the leader must clearly and objectively assess the present condition of the company, create a realistic vision of its future, and develop the game plan for getting it there. (Goldstein, 1988, p. 48)

Turning to the traits themselves, Silver (1992) reminds us of their importance when he reports that "it takes certain kinds of people to pursue a survival plan and to thrive amidst the chaos" (p. 102). We learn from nearly every chronicle of recovery that "turnarounds are not executives with faint hearts and weak stomachs" (Rindler, 1987, p. 1). Turnaround managers tend to be remarkably *optimistic* leaders (Bratton & Knobler, 1998; Silver, 1992; Stewart, 1984), "committed and positive" (Grinyer, Mayes, & McKiernan, 1988, p. 66). In this mode, they radiate "a spirit of hope and endurance" (Crandall, 1995, p. 31): "They believe that anything is possible and that miracles can be achieved" (Rindler, 1987, p. 222). The turnaround leader has a "positive attitude and transmit[s] it to the rest of the organization" (Bibeault, 1982, p. 184). She or he has an "optimistic belief that goals can be met" (p. 195) and a deep faith in her or his "power to mold the organization to the vision of a reconstructed future" (Silver, 1992, p. 89). Indeed, as Mohrman and Mohrman (1983) affirm, no cases of recovery are likely to be found unless the CEO becomes "an active and enthusiastic proponent" (p. 463) of the change work.

Optimism, in turn, is based on enthusiasm and confidence (Goldstein, 1988; Slater, 1999; Stewart, 1984) and includes the ability to instill in others "the belief that they [can] accomplish almost anything" (Bibeault, 1982, p. 153). In fact, Bibeault (1982) goes so far as to suggest that "self-confidence in their own abilities is the key to turnaround leaders" (p. 156).

In addition, turnaround managers are often *"achievement oriented"* (Khandwalla, 1983–1984, p. 20) leaders. They tend to display an "action orientation" (Bibeault, 1982, p. 153) and a basis for action" (Grinyer, Mayes, & McKiernan, 1988, p. 66), are "hungry for achievement" (p. 153), and are moved primarily by a need to "achieve results" (p. 152). These leaders are "opportunistic" (Goldstein, 1988, p. 56). They gravitate toward new opportunities rather than problems (Sloma, 1985). They have "a passion for quality" (Rindler, 1987, p. 1) and a "commitment to excellence" (Bibeault, 1982, p. 191).

Sloma (1985) reminds us that turnaround management is "hard, oftentimes tedious work" (p. xii) often "requir[ing] twice the management effort as required by the more stable enterprise" (Goldstein, 1988, p. 55). It is not surprising, therefore, to discover that turnaround leaders are generally high-energy men and women (Grinyer, Mayes, & McKiernan, 1988) who *"relish hard work"* (Bibeault, 1982, p. 159). They tend to be "intense" (Goodman, 1982, p. 48), "no-nonsense executives" (Bibeault, 1982, p. 159) who have a "capacity for a great deal of hard work" (Goldstein, 1988, p. 55). Indeed, "hard work appears to be a common denominator for [their] success" (Bibeault, 1982, p. 159) and the success of the recovery effort (Bibeault, 1982; Bratton & Knobler, 1998).

Effective turnaround managers are likely to be "hands-on" (Bibeault, 1982, p. 159) leaders. Because of the arduous situations with which they deal, turnaround managers often are defined by a "toughness and competitiveness" (p. 151): "The turnaround leader must be a *tough-minded* manager with an equally 'thick skin' because the decisions he or she makes are usually painful" (Goldstein, 1988, p. 52). Not unexpectedly, these executives generally have a high presence in the organization (Grinyer, Mayes, & McKiernan, 1988) and are more "authoritarian" (Bibeault, 1982, p. 168) and "self-reliant" (p. 156) than the average manager (Bratton & Knobler, 1998; Rindler, 1987; Slater, 1999).

At the same time, they *lead by example* and by modeling (Crandall, 1995; Zimmerman, 1991): "They practice leadership by example, providing a model for others" (Kramer, 1987, p. 91); "a turnaround leader sets up the example himself and throws up a challenge that effective people will accept" (Bibeault, 1982, p. 191). As a consequence, productive turnaround executives are known for their "trustworthiness" (Zimmerman, 1991, p. 193) and "credibility" (Kanter, 2003, p. 65): "Successful turnaround agents exhibit honesty and trustworthiness" (Zimmerman, 1991, p. 233); they "exhibit character traits involving old-fashioned honesty, morality, and hard work" (p. 237). Partly as a result of this, they are often portrayed as highly persuasive leaders (Mohrman & Mohrman, 1983; Stopford & Baden-Fuller, 1990). They are adept at convincing others that their "views of the future will become reality" (Silver, 1992, p. 89).

Finally, there is abundant evidence that turnaround CEOs are often *courageous and persistent* leaders (Austin, 1998; Gerstner, 2002; Silver, 1992) and somewhat "fearless" (Silver, 1992, p. 89), with a penchant for boldness (Bratton & Knobler, 1998). Because recoveries "call for a speed of decision and ruthlessness in decision making: a willingness to take unpleasant decisions and to face criticism" (Taylor, 1982–1983, p. 6), turnaround executives "tend to make bold, decisive moves quickly" (Bibeault, 1982, p. 16). Concomitantly, because "turnaround efforts are long and arduous" (Zimmerman, 1991, p. 190), "perseverance is [an] . . . essential attribute" (Goldstein, 1988, p. 56) of turnaround executives. "The ability to handle failure" (Goodman, 1982, p. 48) on the path to recovery is of special significance.

Studies confirm that courageous perseverance includes a heavy dose of flexibility (Crandall, 1995; Rindler, 1987). While effective turnaround leaders display a remarkable assiduousness in their pursuit of goals, they are also "flexible and adaptable, ready to . . . drop one activity for another with greater promise (Goldstein, 1988, p. 56): "They consistently are dogged in their pursuit of objectives and the accomplishment of goals, while maintaining the flexibility to change intermediate goals as the situation develops" (Bibeault, 1982, p. 150). In addition, "their leadership is flexible, not a single style or predefined role or function that will remain the same while everything else around it changes" (Crandall, 1995, p. 108).

CHAPTER SEVEN

Diagnosing the Situation and Taking Emergency Action

The first step in a turnaround . . . is a recognition that change is needed. (Rindler, 1987, p. 219)

Turnaround management must simultaneously evaluate the condition of the company, formulate a strategy for recovery from the crisis, and deal with the financial emergency to address the crisis. (Fredenberger, Lipp, & Watson, 1997, p. 170)

As reported earlier, Part II of the book attends to the stabilization of the crippled organization—the so-called retrenchment phase of turnaround. In Chapter 6, we detailed the importance of changing leadership. Here, we discuss the other two pieces of retrenchment: diagnosing the condition of the troubled firm and taking emergency action, especially in the area of costs and cash flows.

DIAGNOSING THE SITUATION

The evaluation stage of a turnaround entails making a viability analysis of the business and preparing an action plan to solve the problems of the company in the short run. (Bibeault, 1982, p. 203)

A Starting Point

The turnaround manager's first task is to gather and analyze facts about the firm's situation. (Hambrick, 1985, p. 10-5)

A business turnaround must start with a sound assessment of present conditions. (Stewart, 1984, p. 18)

The first step in a sharpbend is clearly to undertake ... an appraisal. This should tackle first those areas of the business which are undermining performance. (Grinyer, Mayes, & McKiernan, 1988, p. 147)

In his investigation of recovery of small churches, Crandall (1995) observed that the leader needs to form a sound understanding of where a "congregation is in relation to where it has been and where it is going" (p. 38). According to nearly every analyst in the turnaround game, this means that after "having made the key decision that strengthening management is the vehicle to take you to your turnaround [see Chapter 6], the next step is an accurate evaluation" (Goodman, 1982, p. 50) of the organization, developing a sound understanding of the jumping-off point or "a sense of the start" (Umbreit, 1996, p. 3). Thus, "the crisis manager first learns as much as possible about the nature and extent of the company's crisis" (Silver, 1992, p. 7)—about "the extent of the crisis, the urgency of the situation, and how drastic the corrective action must be" (Goldstein, 1988, p. 73). According to Armenakis and Fredenberger (1998), "diagnosis consists of gathering and analyzing information and planning and implementing corrective actions" (p. 44). The evaluation stage of retrenchment "focuses on the viability of the company and the preparation of a survival and/or turnaround plan" (Bibeault, 1982, p. 95):

> The analysis needed to begin implementing a recovery strategy may take any time from two to three days for a small firm, to six months for a large firm. Analysis involves problem identification, deciding the appropriate mix of turnaround strategies needed for short-term survival, and developing a detailed action plan. The action plan may include the need for additional analysis prior to making decisions about the strategic change and growth phases of the recovery. The actual time available for

analysis is obviously determined by the severity of the crisis and the size and complexity of the business. (Slatter, 1984, p. 122)

At the beginning, the spotlight is on gathering and/or producing data "with no attempt to generate any solution to identified problems" (Umbreit, 1996, p. 3). Later on in the process, it will be "time to make some judgments about what caused the . . . decline and what steps would be necessary for recovery" (Rindler, 1987, p. 91).

Turnaround authors refer to this "analysis phase" (Slatter, 1984, p. 122) or diagnostic function as a "viability analysis" (Bibeault, 1982, p. 205). And while there are fundamental differences between this assessment work in private firms and public institutions such as schools—for example (1) the variables of primary interest in corporations are nearly all financial in nature (Hambrick, 1985) (e.g., cash flow) and the diagnostic tools are, perforce, monetarily grounded (e.g., breakeven analysis) (Slatter, 1984) and (2) there are profound differences in available solution strategies (e.g., eliminating unprofitable customers and selling part of the firm are common recovery actions in the corporate world that are not possible in schools) (Kramer, 1987; Slatter, 1984)—the logic and framework of diagnosis are quite applicable in the education sector. The trick is to search for appropriate analyses. Bibeault (1982) informs us that a viability analysis is comprised of two major elements.

First, a preliminary analysis is done that goes beyond a turnaround leader's initial feel but falls short of a detailed, segmented analysis. This preliminary viability analysis focuses on the company's management strategies and tactics which have led to the current state of affairs. By balancing company strengths and weaknesses this analysis weighs the company's ability to survive. This analysis usually takes only a very few days, regardless of the size of the company. The second type of viability analysis is more nitty-gritty and is more detailed in its segmentation of problems. It goes well beyond published information and normal top-level reports. It usually involves a lot of face-to-face, on-the-spot evaluation. It utilizes special reports rather than the standard fare. (p. 205)

As we detail below, the key action here is securing the right information in the most efficacious ways.

Goals and Rules

The functional audit provides a necessary foundation for the turnaround. (Stewart, 1984, p. 34)

Goals

On a grand scale, diagnosis of a turnaround organization's condition can provide the "strong and well-engineered foundation" (Stewart, 1984, p. 109) required to support recovery. It permits leaders to "gain a sufficient understanding of the situation to determine where to concentrate efforts so as to get the greatest leverage in the shortest period of time" (Bibeault, 1982, p. 96). Diagnostic work can help break the spiral of failure described by Stewart (1984) in which troubled organizations simply do more of the same or pursue random silver-bullet solutions:

> Very often these companies continue to follow the same practices that caused the original failures. They leap without looking onto one panacean bandwagon after another, with no comprehensive evaluations of their real weaknesses. As these firms devote the majority of their time and effort to each newfound cure-all, less and less time becomes available to correct their basic weakness(es). Thus further deterioration occurs. (p. 110)

Specifically, assessments can "provide measurable insight into the severity, intensity, pervasiveness, regularity (or lack of it), and the characteristics of symptoms" (Sloma, 1985, p. 70) and problems (Bibeault, 1982) and causes (Goldstein, 1988): "When taken in their entirety, the various input gathering sources enable the [organization] to create a comprehensive listing of . . . threats" (Rindler, 1987, p. 96); they "focus the attention of the turnaround manager on the key problems and issues" (Slatter, 1984, p. 144). They provide "a 'reality-based' picture" (Mirvis, Ayas, & Roth, 2003, p. 41) of the organization and its circumstances on a function-by-function and unit-by-unit basis (Stewart, 1984), an "organized assessment of problems and opportunities" (Stewart, 1984, p. xi).

The diagnostic process also has a symbolic function (Mirvis, Ayas, & Roth, 2003). For example, Small (cited in Umbreit, 1996) discovered that well-conceived diagnostics at failing firms begin "to teach employees how to think in a different way" (p. 52). And, as

Rindler (1987) discovered in his study of a turnaround hospital, the diagnostics provided the goal "to think constructively about what to do next" (p. 67).

Diagnosis is centrally about shaping recovery work. On the one hand, assessment work can galvanize support for action (Mirvis, Ayas, & Roth, 2003). It can create a "sense of urgency" (Umbreit, 1996, p. 52). It can build ownership in the organization's recovery (Rindler, 1987), ownership that is often conspicuous by its absence in failing enterprises. On the other hand, the initial evaluation helps determine "if the business can be saved in its present form, if it should be liquidated, or if it should be 'right sized' into something smaller and more valid" (Silver, 1992, pp. 7–8). Diagnosis is also the basis for the development of short-range emergency planning and "comprehensive . . . long-range plan[s] (Stewart, 1984, p. 110). Thus, it establishes the foundation for turnaround work (Bibeault, 1982; Zimmerman, 1991).

Rules

Assume nothing and question everything. (Rindler, 1987, p. 34)

An examination of the turnaround literature uncovers a collection of guidelines about conducting diagnostic work that has considerable utility for educational leaders confronted with the task of recovering failing schools and failing school districts. To begin with, the diagnostic process requires commitment and "strong involvement" (Goodman, 1982, p. 52) from the leader himself or herself. There are times in organizations for delegation. This is not one of them. The leader needs to be at the center of the evaluation in the retrenchment phase (Bibeault, 1982; Schendel, Patton, & Riggs, 1976); if not, "the turnaround will have little chance of success" (Bibeault, 1982, p. 53). The leader's fingerprints need to be all over the diagnostic work; that is, involvement means hands-on work (Trompenaars & Hampden-Turner, 2002b): "No company can be precisely measured by sitting in an office. If the turnaround leader is from outside the organization he or she has to kick some tires" (Goldstein, 1988, p. 73).

Another set of diagnostic rules address time issues. Analysts consistently and poignantly conclude that "early recognition of the need for a turnaround posture" (Goodman, 1982, p. 12) is a key to recovery: "The longer a company waits to address its crisis the more desperate the situation becomes" (Silver, 1992, p. 63). These same authors also disclose that even under the time pressures associated with organizational crisis, leaders "should resist change which lacks evaluation" (Bibeault, 1982, p. 96; also Slatter, 1984). That course of action is generally a recipe for final collapse. One reality in failing organizations is that "time is more of a premium" (Sloma, 1985, p. 74), or as Goldstein (1988) remarks, "when the company is badly hemorrhaging, time becomes one precious commodity" (p. 71). Under this constraint, "seriously crippled corporations can hardly afford the luxury of crossing the 'Ts' on endless reports. Too many companies die on the operating table while their surgeons linger over the x-rays" (p. 71). Often, as we report below, "the art of approximation" (Sloma, 1985, p. 74) within limits must then be the rule. In short, "the emphasis in diagnosing the firm's problems and developing an appropriate recovery strategy must be speed" (Slatter, 1984, p. 141). Something in the 30- to 90-day range for schools seems reasonable.

Analysts also unveil guidelines around the collection and use of data. To restate the one from Rindler (1987) that opened this subsection, the leader should "assume nothing and question everything" (p. 34). The leader "must be skeptical of any numbers he is provided with and must dig to get facts" (Slatter, 1984, p. 144), as there are a variety of reasons that information in failing organizations is distorted or otherwise of little use, including the fact that organizations in turnaround situations "routinely fool themselves as to their strengths and weaknesses" (Hambrick, 1985, p. 10-10). Starting with this warning does not gainsay the fact that objective data are to be privileged over less reliable sources of information (Rindler, 1987) and that "hard data should be used whenever possible" (Hambrick, 1985, p. 10-10). And "if only subjective impressions are available, it is important to obtain such impressions from multiple sources" (p. 10-10).

The following data-gathering rule is especially important: "Having the right information is more important than having a lot of information" (Goldstein, 1988, p. 72); that is, collect "information about the critical problems that have turnaround leverage" (Bibeault, 1982, p. 97). Certain problems if addressed provide significantly more payout than others. Data collection should be directed here, focusing on a half dozen or so "absolutely essential figures" (Argenti, 1976, p. 30). Management should not fall into the trap of dealing "with the little problems it feels it can handle—simple areas, easily corrected—[that] lack turnaround leverage" (Bibeault, 1982, p. 97). It is also important to ground and contextualize data, starting with some "historical period and frequency" (Stewart, 1984, p. 20), and to establish benchmarks and indicators. There is widespread agreement in the turnaround literature that gathering "as much detailed information as possible about [one's] competitors' performance" (Goodman, 1982, p. 38) is an especially desirable strategy. So too, it is wise to accumulate answers about where one stands on a variety of measures on the "industry performance curve" (p. 33), measures that "assess the dimensions of key importance in the industry" (Hambrick, 1985, p. 10-3). In addition, the overall performance shortfall should be quantified so that the turnaround "begin[s] with a clear understanding on the part of all concerned of the distance between [the firm] and [its] objectives" (Goodman, 1982, p. 33). Finally, leaders need to attend to a "cardinal principle related to effective symptom identification and measurement" (Sloma, 1985): specifically, the measurements need to be unitized; "that is, when-ever practical and feasible, evaluate the data in terms of *each* unit of product or service" (p. 40).

We close our discussion of diagnostic rules with a few precepts on the process of evaluation in the emergency stage of recovery. The first is to be "realistic, not optimistic" (Slatter, 1984, p. 131). Conditions are always more problematic and troublesome in turn-arounds than one expects. Forecasts should anticipate this reality. In particular, it appears that "the ability to be realistically self-critical" (Grinyer, Mayes, & McKiernan, 1988, p. 135) is a hallmark of successful recoveries. The second is to be "conscious of the symbolic implications" (Chaffee, 1983, p. 28) of the diagnostic work. What gets evaluated, how, by whom, and what becomes of the data all con-vey powerful messages to the organization. Effective turnaround leaders attend to the "symbolic as well as the substantive" (p. 28) issues in diagnostic work. This is particularly important, the research shows, in getting "the management team . . . in the firm sharing [the] values and standards of the turnaround manager" (Slatter, 1984, p. 133). We also learn from the recovery research that the diagnostic process works best when it becomes layered into a longer-term, ongoing evaluation system (Goldstein, 1988). Finally, because indi-viduals in troubled organizations are often unaware of the real mean-ing of failure and have a penchant for shifting blame to others

(Rindler, 1987), it is important, as alluded to above in the discussion of "unitizing" data, that performance information uncovered in the diagnostic process be attached to specific people, with the following caveat: "Never judge people—only measure and evaluate results and performance" (Sloma, 1985, p. 203).

Gathering Diagnostic Information:
The What of the Evaluation Process

The turnaround leader must define clearly all the information needed for an appraisal and must understand the role and importance of each key indicator. Very often the company must produce data never before compiled and implement controls thought to be beyond its capabilities. (Goldstein, 1988, p. 72)

Obtaining information relevant to identifying the critical operating problems is much like turning over rocks, hoping to find something interesting under some of them. (Finkin, 1985, p. 18)

Reviewers of turnaround organizations provide a variety of useful frameworks for addressing what information should be collected in the emergency-phase diagnostic process. Five that have special applicability for public sector organizations are outlined below. One particularly helpful design has been crafted by Goldstein (1988), who maintains that "through the evaluation process management must integrate sufficient facts to resolve five issues" (p. 84):

1. How serious is the overall problem? Is the company in critical condition, or is it still relatively stable and in fair health?

2. What is the gravity of the downturn? If the company has a deteriorating financial condition, how rapid is the deterioration and with what speed must the turnaround be accomplished?

3. What are the causes of the downturn? Are the problems reoccurring, or are the causes of decline continuing? Can the causes be clearly defined? Is there more than one cause, and if so, what are the more significant causes?

4. Does the company primarily need a strategic turnaround (profit improvement) or financial restructuring (debt reduction)? If both are required, which should occur first?

5. What are the relative strengths and weaknesses of the firm? Is the company sufficiently strong to withstand a turnaround? Are any weaknesses likely to be fatal to the turnaround effort? (p. 84)

Grinyer and colleagues (1988) hold that "careful appraisal of the business" (p. 132) should be undertaken around seven factors:

1. The causes of relative decline

2. Product market potential

3. Sources of competitive advantage
   a. Quality of staff and their skills
   b. Sources of cost and price competitiveness
   c. Nonprice competitiveness, including particularly marketing and quality
   d. Goodwill associated with established products or services
   e. Market shares and existence of effective barriers to entry

4. Appropriate organizational structure

5. Methods of financial control and management information

6. A financial strategy and a time path for the achievement of change

7. The need for motivation and commitment (p. 133)

Bibeault (1982) furnishes a three-pronged evaluation design highlighting available resources and addressing "financial strength, market competitiveness, and people" (p. 209)—and including judgments about both operational health and strategic health. Finkin (1985) also outlines three domains in which diagnostic information must be collected: "cost areas, organizational strategies, and personnel problems" (p. 14). And Stewart (1984) suggests that the evaluation "consists of . . . five parts" (p. 18):

1. An inventory of current financial strengths, weaknesses, and trends

2. An audit of the performance level of each management function

3. An evaluation of each key employee in the organization

4. Input from each key employee on needs, problems, and opportunities

5. A preliminary listing of problems and opportunities to be attacked first on a short-range basis (p. 18)

Stewart also proposes that this approach to retrenchment assessment "list the key functions in [the] organization. Under each, note the elements most critical to the success of that function. Below each element jot down as many pertinent questions as you can" (p. 18).

Financial Data

The reason so many companies are in trouble is because they do not know where they are making or losing money and the reason they don't know is because they have poorly designed financial information systems. (Goldstein, 1988, p. 78)

The first step in assessing a firm's current operating health is to look at its current financial condition. (Hofer, 1980, p. 21)

From the frameworks outlined above, we examine the categories of financing, people, and products to develop the diagnostic snapshot. Because "the financial variable above all is critical to survival" (Bibeault, 1982, p. 212) in the corporate world, financial diagnosis dominates in the turnaround literature. Thus, analysts observe that a key "step in the evaluation process is to grasp the overall financial condition of the company" (Goldstein, 1988, p. 76). The logic here is that the financial review will uncover the nature of the problem— profitability or insolvency or both—which, in turn, will shape the recovery plan and the specific solution strategies. Central messages that the evaluation conveys are that (1) financial data in general are critical, (2) information on return on investment in particular is important, and (3) the leader is zeroed in on the essential aspects of the business.

As we discus in considerable detail below, assessment of the cash position of the firm is of special interest in the diagnostic work in the retrenchment period of a turnaround (Kramer, 1987), that is, analysis of "whether the company has the ability to stabilize itself and survive long enough for a long-term debt restructuring or strategic turnaround plan to take hold" (Goldstein, 1988, p. 74). And, as Bibeault (1982) informs us, while there are hundreds of volumes that examine financial diagnostics (see Stewart, 1984, for example), four "aspects of the financial analysis are important to the turnaround executive in the evaluation stage" (p. 213):

1. The state of the company's balance sheet and the ability of the company to finance the turnaround from internal sources

2. The difference between operating-statement profits and cash flow

3. The need for the turnaround leader to gain a personal knowledge of how money is made in the type of business he's in

4. The state of the company's information systems in the financial area (p. 213)

In short, what is required is a "financial inventory to identify the glaring and subtle financial strengths and weaknesses" (Stewart, 1984, p. 20), a diagnostic to answer the following:

- How probable is it that the firm may go bankrupt in the near future without changes in its strategy?
- How much time is available before it would go bankrupt?
- What is the magnitude of the turnaround needed to avoid bankruptcy?
- What financial resources could be raised short term to aid in the battle? (Hofer, 1980, p. 21)

Parallels between education and business emerge when we replace the outcome of importance in the corporate turnaround literature, that is, profits, with the core purpose of schooling, that is, student learning. Specifically, the financial story line presented above translates directly to education on the key variable in the diagnostic portfolio, return on investment, or return on assets. The diagnostic challenge for educators is to forge the correct measurement yardstick. Beyond that, not the logic but the particulars begin to break down, because education has not developed a parallel array of indicators and indices to dissect learning that the corporate world has crafted to diagnose the financial strength of a firm.

People

Many turnarounds are nothing more than a turnaround of the human resources. (Goldstein, 1988, p. 79)

People, both as individuals and in organized groups, have to be good if the organization is to perform. Many chief executives have difficulty in evaluating this area properly. (Bibeault, 1982, p. 223)

In many organizations, but especially in labor-intensive institutions such as schooling, assessment of employees must be at the heart of any diagnostic activity. As Stewart (1984) reminds us, "people are the key resource for any business. The right people, properly motivated, can make mediocre plans and systems succeed. The best plans and systems fail when used by mediocre people" (p. 61). Thus, "perhaps the harshest part of the initial inventory is taking a cold look at the human capital of the firm—the people working for it and their skills and abilities" (Grinyer, Mayes, & McKiernan, 1988, p. 138).

"One of the first and most important tasks to be conducted by the turnaround manager" (Hambrick, 1985, p. 10-22) in the people domain is the "evaluation of key managers" (p. 10-21), with a focus on five aspects of leadership: integrity, knowledge, aptitude, commitment, and attitude (Hambrick, 1985, p. 10-22; Stewart, 1984, p. 69). "Once the evaluation of the existing team is done with proper care and accuracy, it provides a basis for deciding what changes need to be made and where the opportunities are for strengthening the team" (Goodman, 1982, p. 54). And, as the literature reveals, "both judgement and courage are needed to select the key managers successfully and to dispense with the services of those who are not going to cope with the new focus of the firm" (Grinyer, Mayes, & McKiernan, 1988, p. 138).

Another essential diagnostic here is the department-by-department and function-by-function assessment (Slatter, 1984), "an objective assessment of each group's strengths and weaknesses" (Rindler, 1987, p. 69). Finally, a diagnostic needs to be conducted on each position (Rindler, 1987), employing the "industrywide yardstick" (Goodman, 1982, p. 37) we introduced above. And, while the manager is cautioned "not to be overenamored with axing people"

(Bibeault, 1982, p. 225) and to undertake as much of the assessment work himself or herself as possible—at least all the employees in a direct reporting relationship (Stewart, 1984)—in many cases cost savings needed for recovery can only be garnered through workforce reductions.

Product

After sizing up your financial strength, you should evaluate the fundamental competitiveness of the business. (Bibeault, 1982, p. 219)

Emergency diagnostics are also required to be run on the organization's products. When cast in terms of "market position [and] production capabilities" (Hofer, 1980, pp. 21–22), as is often the case in the turnaround literature, product assessment often takes on the overcoat of finance. For example, Sloma (1985) asserts that a cardinal analysis here is the "hard-copy listing in descending sequence of gross (or standard) margin percent of each product line" (p. 89). This arrangement will, he avers, permit the reader to "quickly . . . draw a line below which the margin percent becomes unacceptable" (p. 90). Here, as elsewhere, the metric of "competitiveness" (Bibeault, 1982, p. 231) is central to the evaluation.

Assessment in the product domain focuses on three issues:

1. The company's competitive strategy in the market segments in which it operates

2. The company's market position

3. The effectiveness of the company's marketing organization. (Bibeault, 1982, p. 220)

On the issue of market position, Hofer (1980) reports that

. . . two calculations are relevant. One is a comparison of the size of the business' current product/market segments versus its break-even points. The second is an assessment of the maximum sales that could be achieved from all other products that the firm has made and still has the capacity to make. (p. 21)

Stewart (1984) and other analysts also maintain that diagnostics should be run on the production function, especially on four factors related to outcomes: "delivery integrity; productivity; performance to a sound, formal strategic plan; and adequate production control reports" (p. 47). As we explained above in the financial assessment area, these measures clearly provide a better fit for private, for-profit firms than they do for schools. Nonetheless, they offer a framework from which analog measures can be created and employed to diagnose failing educational organizations.

Gathering Diagnostic Information: The Who and the How of the Evaluation Process

While [financial] analysis is crucial, it is just an adjunct to the data that the manager must gather from interaction with key managers, employees, customers, suppliers, and other sources. (Hambrick, 1985, p. 10–7)

Personal diagnostic practices are considerably more effective than impersonal practices. (Armenakis & Fredenberger, 1998, p. 51)

There is absolutely no substitute for hearing firsthand what customers think about a company's performance. (Bibeault, 1982, p. 223)

While diagnostic information about the health of the turnaround organization can come from a variety of actors in a multitude of roles, two groups are especially important, customers and employees. As a starting point, Goodman (1982) reminds turnaround managers that "high-performance companies like to let customers run their business. This means that they begin with a clear picture of the customer targeted, and then cultivate an intense awareness of how each customer feels about everything the company does" (pp. 36–37). Bibeault (1982) recommends two methods to gather diagnostic information, surveys and visits in the field, "to learn about [customer] attitudes toward the company and the reasons for these attitudes" (p. 224). It is especially important to discover how customers believe that the organization "got into trouble in the first place" (Rindler, 1987, p. 63) and how the organization stacks up against competitors

(Rindler, 1987). At the same time, turnaround scholars affirm that employees occupy a central niche in the emergency phase evaluation.

In their study of turnaround organizations, Armenakis and Fredenberger (1998) concluded that "personal and interactive" (p. 51) diagnostic practices are more effective than impersonal strategies that require no "real-time interaction" (p. 51). Finkin (1985) underscores the importance of this hands-on assessment when he observes that "the further removed one's source of information from the actual event, the less likely the information is to be currently correct" (p. 18). Not unexpectedly, he concluded that "there is no substitute for walking a plant" (p. 18), observing actions, and meeting "informally and spontaneously with managers and employees" (Armenakis & Fredenberger, 1998, p. 45). In addition to diagnosis by walking around, turnaround analysts make a strong case for using one-on-one meetings with important managers and other employees as a key assessment tool (Bratton & Knobler, 1998). Focus groups and other structured meetings with targeted groups of employees can also be important weapons in the diagnostic arsenal (Armenakis & Fredenberger, 1998). Of the noninteractive tools, there is some support for the use of professionally designed employee opinion surveys to collect diagnostic information on the conditions confronting the troubled organization as well as the reasons for the institution's decline (Goodman, 1982). While we do not take up the issue of the corrective plan that flows from the diagnostic work until later, it is important to set the stage here by acknowledging that (1) judgments must be made about the data collected and (2) data and judgments need to be lashed to a specific plan of action.

TAKING EMERGENCY ACTION

In the short run, survival is the most important thing. First find out what needs to be done to survive and do it. (Rindler, 1987, p. 102)

In the emergency stage a company does what is necessary to ensure survival. (Bibeault, 1982, p. 99)

Time and resources do not exist to improve everything at once. Those things that have the greatest impact on cash flow and profitability must be the center of attention. (Finkin, 1985, p. 24)

The emphasis is on cash flow and tight financial control. (Slatter, 1984, p. 122)

An interrogation of the literature on recovery in the noneducational sector reveals that emergency action is focused almost exclusively on improving the cash flow needed to keep the failing organization alive. The most common depiction is of a critically ill patient who is bleeding to death. The emergency response is to stanch the flow. Only then, it is held, can the leader begin to consider more fully actions needed for the firm to recover (Altman, 1983; Bibeault, 1982): "If you don't cure stage 1, there won't be a future" (Sloma, 1985, p. 169). Immediacy is the center of concern, and the relevant timeline is short, very short in severe cases. Given the differences between firms and public-sector organizations, much of the advice on managing the emergency phase does not apply directly or smoothly to the education sector. Nonetheless, a deeper and more nuanced reading does unearth important insights for leaders assigned the arduous task of turning around failing schools and school districts, especially if readers can recast "earnings" into value added in the area of student learning. We cluster these lessons into two categories: planning and strengthening cash flow.

Planning

But without compromising this essential long-range building program, management must, at the same time, do everything possible to improve current results. (Goodman, 1982, p. 110)

Grand, long-term strategies with long gestation periods may not be as useful during the early part of a turnaround as well-publicized, piecemeal, successful actions that build confidence, counteract skepticism, and generate cash. (Khandwalla, 1983–1984, p. 26)

The first rule of emergency planning is to move quickly: "The business needs a turnaround; the turnaround needs rapid energizing" (Stewart, 1984, p. 116). And while the organization may have a choice between using an ax or a knife during the emergency phase, there is almost never time for traditional planning work, with the following caveat. Leaders nonetheless need to be cognizant that they are "planting the seeds for the company's repositioning" (Goodman, 1982, p. 111). That is, they must stop the bleeding with one eye on the eventual recovery of the patient.

A second guideline is that the emergency plan itself should be "formulated from the information gathered during the evaluation stage" (Bibeault, 1982, p. 239), from the initial diagnosis of the troubled organization discussed above.

A third principle is to "focus on the short term" (Rindler, 1987, p. 221). The foundation of the plan is "the near term" (Breault, 1993, p. 203). There should be "a short-range action plan designed for immediate earnings improvement" (Stewart, 1984, p. 110). Finkin's (1987) perspective here is quite helpful:

> The management team organizing and implementing the turn-around of a troubled company needs strategic planning. But the perspectives of this planning will differ greatly from what one normally associates with the words "strategic planning." Instead of a three- to five-year time frame, the planning will deal with issues of today and coming months. Strategic planning in a turn-around must be accomplished quickly. (p. 59)

Specifically, the plan should be bounded. The emergency plan will typically feature work over the next 6 to 12 months (Slatter, 1984) and underscore "specific goals that can be accomplished in less than a year (preferably in six months)" (Stewart, 1984, p. 111).

This is, as Khandwalla (1983–1984) reminds us, the "time when organizational energies need to be strongly focused on urgent tasks" (p. 26). Therefore, the fourth guideline is that the plan should highlight "the critical problems that have turnaround leverage" (Bibeault, 1982, p. 239). Bibeault (1982) goes on to advise that "it's more important to solve 80 percent of the problems with imperfect solutions than to go after the last 20 percent, but in doing so take three times as long to produce results" (p. 239).

Five, the plan must be unequivocally goal-focused; a failing organization needs to "place increased emphasis on meeting its end goals" (Mohrman & Mohrman, 1983, p. 457), even at the expense of addressing mediating conditions. Stated alternatively, there needs to be a "spotlight on results" (Goodman, 1982, p. 38) and an orientation toward outcomes and standards of performance (Goodman, 1982).

Sixth, the plan should feature leadership from the top and a tightening of organizational operations and controls (Bratton & Knobler, 1998; Sloma, 1985; Taylor, 1982–1983). While there are appropriate times to underscore decentralization and distributed management, the emergency phase of a turnaround is not one of them. The turnaround leader needs to be the hands-on manager at the center of action (Sloma, 1985).

> If you establish a short-range program, even one with a perfect set of bells and whistles, and then turn your attention to something else while waiting for your subordinates to accomplish their goals, you might as well forget the turnaround. (Stewart, 1984, p. 141)

Controls, in turn, "should measure actual progress against planned progress and should prevent program slippage by raising early warning signals" (Stewart, 1984, p. 142).

Seventh, as we discuss in considerable detail in the next section, "the emergency plan centers on cost containment and cost reduction" (Bibeault, 1982, p. 247); "the core of the emergency plan focuses on cash flow improvements" (p. 242). Eight, because "the rapid attainment of short-term goals is an absolute necessity in a turnaround situation . . . it is extremely important to make a quick, significant score with the short-range program" (Stewart, 1984, pp. 139–140). And finally, we know from the research on recovery in general and improvement efforts in schools specifically that "things often get worse before they get better" (Goodman, 1982, p. 34); therefore, the plan should be scaffolded on possibilities, not hopes, and should build in a "substantial margin of safety" (p. 40).

Strengthening Cash Flow

During the emergency stage in the turnaround, cash is king and the cash flow statement becomes the road map to the kingdom. (Goldstein, 1988, p. 96)

If financial problems are not resolved early, there may be no organization left to turn around. Early emphasis should be on cost control. (Rindler, 1987, p. 220)

Firms achieving turnaround are those able to marshall financial support for the turnaround. (Chowdhury & Lang, 1993, p. 14)

Introduction

Cost reduction strategies are invariably a characteristic of successful turnaround situations. (Slatter, 1984, p. 168)

It is impossible to rehabilitate a company without locating free cash through a refinancing. (Silver, 1992, p. 8)

Reducible cost must be avoided, and successful turnaround efforts require a high degree of well-placed frugality. (Zimmerman, 1991, p. 38)

In the corporate turnaround world, "raising cash is critical to the successful workout" (Silver, 1992, p. 171), and, as noted above, successful turnaround firms are adept in strengthening their cash flows, while unsuccessful turnaround firms are not (Bibeault, 1982; Zimmerman, 1991). Thus, it is easy to discern why turnaround analysts assert that the turnaround leader's "mission is to raise cash" (Silver, 1992, p. 172) and that turnaround organizations "must be guided by a singular objective: to put the company in a positive cash position and to keep it there" (Goldstein, 1988, p. 95), not an especially easy task, as a failing organization is "usually missing several important skills needed to improve its effectiveness in . . . decreasing its costs of doing business" (Finkin, 1985, p. 22). Therefore, the "first phase of the recovery program involve[s] the commencement of an operating strategy aimed at cost reduction" (Ackley, 1989, p. 41; also Reich & Donahue, 1985): "The reduction of cost emerges as the appropriate short-term strategy" (Zimmerman, 1991, p. 45), and "the first task in stabilizing a financially troubled company is to stop the cash drain and replenish the corporate coffers with a reasonable cash cushion" (Goldstein, 1988, p. 85). This cash flow work has been nicely encapsulated by Bibeault (1982) as follows:

You must treat negative cash flow the way that you treat the human body that is bleeding. First you've got to control the bleeding by applying a tourniquet; then you must analyze the nature of the wound and perform the surgical procedure necessary to stop the bleeding on a permanent basis. Cash flow problems must be treated in much the same manner. (p. 269)

We are also able to cull important lessons from the research to inform the turnaround work here. First, in the emergency phase of recovery it is difficult to grow out of failure (Breault, 1993):

Revenue expansion is a risky strategy that may result in little profit improvement. The all-too-frequent pattern of expenses growing faster than revenue makes the revenue expansion strategy impractical for many turnaround situations unless it is preceded by major improvement in efficiency. (Zimmerman, 1991, p. 40)

Cost reduction holds center stage and "internal efficiency should be emphasized" (p. 45). Second, tight controls are needed in the emergency phase of the turnaround (Taylor, 1982–1983). Third, because "a division in trouble usually doesn't know its costs" (Finkin, 1985, p. 16), centralized control should be accompanied by well-crafted accounting systems that constantly allow managers to know where they are on the pathway to recovery (Sloma, 1985). These information systems should "provide a good understanding of one's own costs" (Finkin, 1985, p. 23), promote comparisons with the cost structures of competitors, and foster understanding and use of industry norms (Sumeren, 1993). Argenti (1976) and Silver (1992) encapsulate this line of thinking as follows:

The cash flow forecast is the one vital tool that managers must use. (Argenti, 1976, pp. 38–39)

The cash flow statement projection is the troubled company's road map out of the swamp. (Silver, 1992, p. 75)

In the next subsection, we explore the types of activities that for-profit enterprises undertake to meet the goal of stopping cash drains and rebuilding financial reserves. As we noted earlier, we recognize that differences between firms and public organizations make much of this chronicle directly applicable to schools in only limited ways. For example, factory cash discounts, bad debt expenses, and selling assets have very little meaning in schools. Neither can schools pursue such actions as eliminating high cost and unproductive customers. We also acknowledge that only a broad overview of the cash flow story is presented here. Much more detailed analyses are available in many of the turnaround volumes cited herein (see, for example, Argenti, 1976; Bibeault, 1982; Goldstein, 1988; Goodman, 1982; Silver, 1992; Slatter, 1984; Stewart, 1984; and Zimmerman, 1991).

At the same time, there are lessons here at three levels that schools would do well to consider in their turnaround work. First, analysis at the broadest level provides two critical insights that are generally ignored in the turnaround literature in education: (1) begin the recovery with efficiency/operational moves rather than with entrepreneurial/strategic moves and (2) start by amassing resources to engage the turnaround, focusing primarily on freeing up less productive assets for more productive use. Second, at the intermediate level, the cost-cutting categories identified in the literature provide a template for schools to employ when they weigh expense reductions. And third, at a more micro level, the analysis surfaces specific revenue accumulation tools that can be used in the organizational reconstruction work during the emergency phase of the turnaround.

Strategies and Areas of Emphasis

Unfortunately a good deal of surgery is often required and it is nearly always necessary to dismiss some employees and sell some assets before the profitable core of the business has been exposed. (Argenti, 1976, p. 35)

The crisis management approach is to sell assets, slash expenses and generate multiple cash flow channels to maximize liquidity and cash flow and build a pile of free cash to apply to flash points during the workout. (Silver, 1992, p. 109)

Operational costs are eliminated by divesting whole divisions or product lines, by shutting down operations, by significantly reducing manpower, by reducing inventory investments, by controlling purchasing, and by significantly increasing productivity. (Bibeault, 1982, p. 278)

Without attempting to develop a cost accounting manual and/or a comprehensive taxonomy of expenses, we are still able to isolate a broad array of actions that are featured in the cost-cutting portfolios of turnaround organizations. For example, Grinyer and colleagues (1988) discuss six measures:

Expenditure-reducing measures, putting off all non-essential purchases, centralization of spending to improve control, stopping expansion or job replacement, improved management of debtors and stock, and strict control of wastage. (p. 80)

Silver (1992) lists "slashing expenses, selling off unused assets, . . . [and] spin-offs of divisions" (p. 8; see also Bibeault, 1982; Sloma, 1985; Sumeren, 1993). Hofer (1980) highlights the following levers to enhance short-term cash flow:

Collecting receivables, cutting inventories, increasing prices when possible, focusing on high-margin products, stretching payables, decreasing wastage, and selling off surplus assets. (p. 28)

And Chan (1993) examines the following cost cuts: "cutting back the workforce, selling off certain businesses, abandoning bleak projects, reducing capital assets and reducing inventories" (p. 30). Our cross-section review of this literature produces the following broad categories: reducing material costs, eliminating services, renting/selling assets, centralizing operations, reducing the costs of products, borrowing, and reducing labor costs.

Slatter (1984) concludes from his research that "the major options open to management to *reduce material costs* are to improve buying [and] use less materials" (p. 168). On the "using fewer materials strategy," analysts maintain that a host of "general and administrative expenses [can] be lowered and, when possible, paid for over time" (Silver, 1992, p. 129). Altman (1983), Green and Hanson (1993), and others describe how this approach allows for the improvement of "efficiency within the existing scale of operations" (Slatter, 1984, p. 184). By focusing only on the most important purchases and by implementing personal oversight by the top management team—by "taking control of the cash flow pipeline" (Bibeault, 1982, p. 247)—these authors hold that significant cost savings can be garnered from the "cash avoidance and cost prevention" (p. 247) strategies and that the cash can be placed back into the organization. Shook (1990) and Reich and Donahue (1985) illustrate how this approach was featured in the successful turnarounds at Ford and Chrysler in the last quarter of the twentieth century. Gerstner (2002) paints a similar picture of the recovery of IBM in the 1990s as does Rindler (1987) for Beloit Memorial Hospital in the early 1970s. The core operating principle, which is provided by Silver (1992), is as follows: "No expense item is safe" (p. 16).

On the "improved buying" side of the ledger, one path forward entails paying less for the goods and services used to operate the enterprise. The performance principle here again has been penned by Silver: "You can always get something for less money and there is always a less expensive vendor" (p. 114). Savings are achieved here by (1) "negotiat[ing] lower prices with existing suppliers" (Slatter, 1984, p. 169), that is, "renegotiat[ing] vendor terms" (Sloma, 1985, p. 142)—through "the use of aggressive competitive bidding, common sense evaluation of alternatives and hardball negotiation strategies" (Rindler, 1987, p. 50)—and (2) "identifying alternative suppliers for each high expense item" (p. 50). Another approach to "buying more economically means taking maximum advantage of suppliers' terms of trade, such as quantity discount schedules and minimum order sizes" (Slatter, 1984, p. 171).

Eliminating lines of work and/or products and services is a second cost-cutting tool stressed in the recovery literature (Finkin, 1985; Hegde, 1982). Unlike in the approach above, the focus here is not on "improving efficiency in the existing scale of operations [but on] a reduction in the scale of operations by the complete elimination of a part of the manufacturing process" (Slatter, 1984, p. 183), the "divesting of operating units" (Bibeault, 1982, p. 153), or what Sloma (1985) labels the elimination of "unprofitable channels" (p. 164) and "unprofitable regions" (p. 165). Under this strategy, as Chan (1993) remarks, "turnaround firms get out of businesses where they [do] not think they [can] be profitable and concentrate on those that [have] potential . . . [to] be competitive" (p. 131). In the recovery literature, this action is known as "product pruning" (Sloma, 1985, p. 162).

Selling fixed assets is a third widely discussed cost-cutting, cash-generating strategy for the emergency phase of an organizational recovery (Bibeault, 1982; Taylor, 1982–1983). Or as Slatter (1984) observes: "Most companies utilize asset-reduction strategies when in a recovery situation. These strategies comprise fixed-asset-reduction strategies and working-capital-reduction strategies" (p. 153). The guideline here has been captured by Goldstein (1988): "Survival under a turnaround means stripping the company of every item of unproductive equipment. From ceiling to floor, if it is not nailed down, it is a candidate for sale or a less costly replacement" (p. 94) and by Silver: "As a first step, take a personal inventory of your company's assets and sell everything that is not needed in the business" (p. 172). The rule in action is nicely illustrated by Clausen (1990) when he shows how $9.6 billion was garnered in the first 78 days of a turnaround at BankAmerica, by Gerstner (2002), who discusses how during the recovery at IBM in the mid-1990s the company sold off all "assets that [were] not essential to the company" (p. 66), and by Reich and Donahue (1985), who document the massive sale of assets that helped fuel the turnaround at Chrysler in the late 1970s.

The focus here is on the identification of assets that are "not being employed effectively—that is not earning money" (Altman, 1983, p. 200), or in the case of schools, not contributing to student learning. In the business sector, these assets can be inventory, "unused items of capital equipment" (Carrington & Aurelio, 1976, p. 15), and freed-up space (Silver, 1992; Sloma, 1985). And here, Slatter (1984) asserts, larger assets trump smaller ones.

A fourth method to reduce costs and raise cash is to *centralize operations.* That is, centralizing efforts are not only a critical element in a turnaround leader's portfolio of actions to gain control of a listing organizational ship, but they may help "avoid staff duplication . . . and . . . provide economies of scales in many areas" (Chan, 1993, p. 131).

Another, albeit longer-term strategy to raise cash is to *change the way the product is made* (Sloma, 1985), to get costs out of the product—to "increase level of productivity" (Slatter, 1984, p. 173) of labor to reduce material costs:

> There are only two principal approaches. First, change the way the product is made to wring out direct labor time. Second, *redesign* the product such that it takes less time than before to make each unit. (Sloma, 1985, p.174)

Although it is not a cost reduction maneuver, it is important to note that resources can be secured by *borrowing,* by convincing banks and other key actors (Carrington & Aurelio, 1976) to assist the troubled enterprise. In a similar vein, credit lines and debt services can be renegotiated (Sloma, 1985).

Finally, and "perhaps most obvious[ly]" (Silver, 1984, p. 179), and in many ways most important (Kierulff, 1981), cash can be raised by *reducing salaries* (Silver, 1992) and by *cutting jobs*—by "reduc[ing] people-related expenses" (Sloma, 1985, p. 145) or what Kierulff (1981) labels "changes in the organizational structure" (p. 489). The jumping-off point here is provided by nearly all the major turnaround analysts. For example,

> Almost always, in a turnaround situation, more people are employed than the company can afford. Choices must therefore be made regarding who goes and who stays. (Zimmerman, 1991, p. 190)

> The company in trouble is like an overloaded lifeboat: every third person has to get off or the boat will sink. (Bibeault, 1982, p. 248)

> The vast majority of companies are overstaffed. Frequently the company can cut payroll by 25–30 percent within the first 60 days and perhaps reduce payroll another 10–15 percent over the workout period. (Goldstein, 1988, p. 90)

And the literature on emergency action to save troubled firms is replete with examples of the application of the workforce reduction strategy (see, for example, Ackley, 1989; Clausen, 1990; Gerstner, 2002; Reich & Donahue, 1985; Rindler, 1987; Shook, 1990; and Trompenaars & Hampden-Turner, 2002a).

According to Sloma (1985), this is "the principal realm of action that has 'immediately' favorable effects on both cash and profits" (p. 145): "Manpower reductions are the biggest single component of operating improvements during the emergency stage" (Bibeault, 1982, p. 278). Action here includes hiring freezes, attrition, layoffs and terminations, and across-the-board pay cuts, and can, as we have seen in recent recovery efforts in the airline industry, include rene-gotiation of union contracts (Hegde, 1982; Sloma, 1985). According to Chan (1993), "the reduction of employees results in more than just payroll and fringe benefit expenses. Fewer employees would mean a reduction in equipment and space, travel expenses, telephone and utility bills" (p. 31).

While a full examination of workforce reduction moves is beyond the scope of our charge here, we would be remiss if we did not introduce the following points. First, most leaders "find this to be the toughest realm of action" (Sloma, 1985, p. 145) and a "challenging leadership problem"(Rindler, 1987, p. 291). Second, if personnel cuts "are mismanaged, severe harm can befall the prospects for turnaround success" (Sloma, 1985, p. 145): "While often necessary for the survival of the company, a redundancy programme that is implemented poorly can be extremely risky, and may even put the very survival of the company in jeopardy" (Slatter, 1984, p. 198). Third, since this is such a difficult assignment, turnaround authors supply a series of guidelines that leaders should follow in handling personnel reductions (see, for example, Argenti, 1976; Bibeault, 1982; Goldstein, 1988; Goodman, 1982; Slatter, 1984; and Sloma, 1985). For example, leaders are advised to

- Avoid layoffs in the first 60 days, if possible (Kierulff, 1981)
- Avoid the temptation to reduce personnel in a piecemeal fashion; that is, since a drawn-out process of continual terminations undercuts an organization, avoid waves of layoffs and terminations (Hambrick, 1985)
- Avoid "across-the-board percentage reductions for each department" (Rindler, 1987, p. 32); that is, base reductions on measures of productivity and quality whenever possible (Shook, 1990)
- "Spread layoffs throughout the organizational ranks" (Sutton, Eisenhardt, & Jucker, 1986, p. 21), beginning with management (Rindler, 1987)
- Attend to the needs of individual employees (Chan, 1993)

Crosscutting Lessons on Cash Flow

Cost reduction involves change: change in established methods of operation, change in the organization structure, change in the organization culture and, more importantly, change in the attitude of management and staff. (Slatter, 1984, p. 190)

Troubled organizations are generally in financial distress, and cutting expenses is a characteristic turnaround move. But how this is done has a big impact on whether the turnaround is a temporary fix or a path to sustainability. (Kanter, 2003, p. 67)

In a turnaround, speed is much more important than elegance. (Rindler, 1987, p. 31)

Truly significant results can almost always be achieved in cutting operational costs when the pressure is on. (Goldstein, 1988, p. 90)

In addition to the area-by-area guidelines detailed above, a careful review of the turnaround literature reveals a variety of macro-level, hard-learned lessons and caveats that need to be attended to in the emergency phase of reintegration. We list the most important of these principles here under the two headings of Focus and Caveats.

Focus

- Effective cost reduction work focuses on dollars not population (Sloma, 1985, p. 150).
- Personnel cuts should overemphasize nonproduction workers (Bibeault, 1982), people in the production equation "but not directly involved in production of product" (Sloma, 1985, p. 149).
- "Aggressive purchasing" (Rindler, 1987, p. 50) and negotiating merit much more attention than they usually receive.
- "Decrease or eliminate current expenditures that have no measurable current or future payout" (Bibeault, 1982, p. 292).
- "Effective turnaround leaders emphasize reductions in bureaucracy, that stifle initiative" (Kanter, 2003, p. 67).
- "When developing supply reduction strategies, go for the big dollars" (Rindler, 1987, p. 43).

Caveats

- "Another important lesson to remember when cutting costs is never to compromise on quality" (Rindler, 1987, p. 58).
- "A key consideration with respect to expense reduction must be the assurance that the firm's customers will be at least as well served after the elimination . . . as before (Sloma, 1985, p. 165);

"expense cutting concentrates on the elimination of waste and does not go beyond that to hurt quality of product, service to customers, or the long-range objectives of the company" (Goodman, 1982, p. 117).

- "The well-managed company prudently and carefully spends money designing, building, and nurturing the products and services it provides to customers. All these expenditures benefit customers. Unsuccessful companies spend money on overhead, offices, promotion, and executive compensation, and none of these benefit customers. This simple difference is often a crucial factor in turnaround success" (Zimmerman, 1991, p. 73).
- "Don't postpone expenses now if postponement will increase costs later" (Bibeault, 1982, p. 247).
- "Cost cutting is very important but should be done judiciously" (Chan, 1993, p. 31).
- "Identify the resources and skills that the business will need in order to implement its long-term strategy [and] protect [them] during the short-term action program" (Hofer, 1980, p. 26).
- "In a crisis it [is] even more important to retain [the] most promising people" (Gerstner, 2002, p. 99).
- "Because achieving short-term savings in a turnaround situation does not necessarily ensure long-term viability" (Sumeren, 1993, p. 111), sustainable cost reductions need to be featured (Slatter, 1984)—immediate gains cannot lead to higher costs downstream.

Protecting the Core

Retain and protect the core, the motherlode. (Bibeault, 1982, p. 249)

The identification of the core business, or "motherlode" as it is often called, is critical at the earliest stages of the turnaround because both short-term and long-term planning will revolve around the preservation of the viable core and the shedding of all extraneous activity. (Goldstein, 1988, p. 74)

Two hallmark lessons from the cost-cutting action in the emergency phase of recovery merit highlighting. The first focuses leaders on the importance of defining and protecting the viable core of the enterprise—"that nucleus of the activity that is both a cash generator and profit generator, and [that] can serve as the foundation for rebuilding the company" (Goldstein, 1988, p. 74). According to Bibeault (1982), "the emergency stage generally means shrinking back to those segments of a business which have achieved or can achieve good gross margins and can compete effectively in the marketplace" (p. 264). Basically, this means that one has "to move in and break the business down into segments, make value judgments on these segments, and divest the company of those segments that aren't contributing to cash flow" (p. 101). The goal is to "eliminate the losers and strengthen the winners" (Altman, 1983, pp. 201–202), to "shed all extraneous activity" (Goldstein, 1988, p. 74), and to "prune the product line" (Finkin, 1985, p. 20) "drastically" (Bibeault, 1982, p. 252): "Traditional product lines are heavily pruned; marginal businesses are closed; and distribution is rationalized to focus on a few big outlets" (Taylor, 1982–1983, p. 8; also Reich & Donahue, 1985). The "company ends up concentrating on the strong" (Bibeault, 1982, p. 324), the aspects of the business that produce real results:

> In serious cases, anything that cannot contribute positively to cash flow within a very short period of time must go. You must perform the surgery, divesting the company of the noncontributing segments of the business, then converting their assets to cash that can be used to reinforce your financial resources. (p. 264)

A subobjective is "to prevent directing management attention away from the main aspects of the business" (Finkin, 1985, p. 23). The approach is to examine closely the return on investment on the assets used in the production process—"profitability analysis" (Bibeault, 1982, p. 274).

A related lesson, and one ribboned throughout this chapter and underscored here, is that the focus must be primarily on efficiency: "For profitability to be improved, efficiency moves must precede strategic moves" (Zimmerman, 1991, p. 56). For as Zimmerman (1991) has observed: "Operational efficiency [is] a primary factor in every successful turnaround case and was absent in almost every unsuccessful case" (p. 42). Unlike successful turnaround organizations, failed firms often attended to growth first, on acquisitions and mergers.

Thus "efficiency must be asserted in every aspect of the organization in order to effect recovery" (p. 57). Zimmerman (1991) provides the following practical lessons on operating efficiency:

- Successful firms concentrate on efficiency first, products second, and then on marketing and sales. Revenue expansion based upon inefficient operations results in severe operating losses.

- Successful companies reduce costs to present revenue levels. Unsuccessful companies attempt to increase revenue to cover existing costs.

- Successful companies implement proven efficiencies immediately—but work through people.

- Successful firms achieve scale economies at the component or process level and not at the level of the overall business unit.

- Successful companies work productively with suppliers to reduce product cost.

- Successful managers make investments to sustain and improve efficiency—but understand processes well enough to know what really pays off. (p. 57)

PART IV

Recovery

In most case descriptions of turnaround, the retrenchment phase gradually yields to a second stage of the turnaround process, known as recovery. (Robbins & Pearce, 1992, p. 290)

Turnaround also requires the successful implementation of recovery strategies. Recovery strategies are management actions and policy changes that attempt to eliminate or cope with the causes of a firm's decline in order to raise firm performance to acceptable levels. (Arogyaswamy, Barker, & Yasai-Ardekani, 1995, p. 506)

CHAPTER EIGHT

Pathways to Recovery

Operational Vision, Efficiencies, and Organizational Processes

Organizations can benefit from crises if they can perceive their opportunities and can marshall the coverage and enthusiasm to pursue them. (Starbuck, Greve, & Hedberg, 1978, p. 135)

The lesson we learn from surviving companies is that the turnaround may be an opportunity in disguise to look at the continued quality of their products or services with the same objectivity customers will, and to gain the competitive edge with products of enhanced quality. (Goldstein, 1988, p. 120)

Turnaround efforts require a redefinition of the firm's business. (O'Neill, 1986b, p. 82)

In this part of the book, we turn our analytic lens onto the period of the turnaround process known as recovery, or what Stopford and Baden-Fuller (1990) refer to as "corporate rejuvenation" (p. 399). It "follow[s] the retrenchment phase as the second stage in the turnaround process" (Pearce & Robbins, 1994b, p. 417). The recovery dimension "extend[s] from the cessation of asset and cost reductions until the firm achieve[s] or fail[s] to achieve turnaround" (Robbins & Pearce, 1992, p. 296) (see Figure 1.1). It is dependent on successful retrenchment efforts, because as Grinyer and associates (1988)

187

inform us, "in the longer term if the initial steps to improve the company's position have not laid the foundation for continuing improvements, the recovery will tend to be short-lived" (p. 109).

During this period of the turnaround, "specific actions are put in motion to improve the health of the firm. The actions taken can be appropriate or inappropriate—effective or ineffective. The turnaround itself may be either successful or unsuccessful" (Zimmerman, 1991, p. 26). Recovery includes "the set of reactions designed to profitably reposition the firm that is experiencing a turnaround situation" (Pearce & Robbins, 1994b, p. 413). It encompasses "deliberate efforts . . . to address each of the pathologies" (Kanter, 2003, p. 60) of the troubled organization. It "is not a one-off set of measures which somehow enables the company to do better indefinitely. It is a change to a new form of behavior" (Grinyer, Mayes, & McKiernan, 1988, p. 109). Recovery attends to both "rectifying a lot of things which have been done wrongly" (p. 127) as well as "taking new measures correctly" (p. 127). As we discuss below, while retrenchment is "more concerned with efficiency . . . rejuvenation includes both efficiency and the building of effective systems and skills needed to create sustainable growth" (Stopford & Baden-Fuller, 1990, p. 401).

Throughout these chapters, we have demonstrated that a critical activity in portraying phases of the turnaround process is to unpack existing classification formats and to forge new taxonomies that permit evidence to be accumulated and dimensions of recovery to be described in meaningful ways. With this analytic strategy in mind, we proceed as follows. In the opening section, we review existing taxonomies and concept maps and introduce our composite framework. In later sections, we examine the first three pillars in that composite conceptual model: developing an operational vision, capturing efficiencies, and building more productive organizational processes and structures.

PATHWAYS TO RECOVERY

A theory of . . . turnaround should include the option of post-retrenchment recovery strategies that range from efficiency to entrepreneurial in orientation. (Pearce & Robbins, 1993, p. 621)

Successful turnarounds . . . will be based on combination efforts which include aspects of cost reduction and revenue generation. (O'Neill, 1986b, p. 171)

In this introductory section to organizational recovery, we provide an overview of frames that analysts have employed across the years to examine this phenomenon. One group of reviewers has applied general classification schemes from the business literature to organizational recovery. A second collection of analysts has crafted frames more inductively and more specific to turnaround work. Of particular importance to our understanding of recovery is the distinction between operational and strategic change tactics embedded in, or at the heart of, these various ways of portraying and investigating recovery. We explore each of these issues below and then introduce a composite framework based on that analysis. We turn first to an examination of the more general analytic architecture.

General Frames

Grinyer and his colleagues (1988) employ McKinsey's 7S framework in their investigation of sharpbends: structure, strategy, systems, skills, style, staff, and shared values (p. 131). Bozeman and Slushser (1979) explore recovery using a general framework of four strategy choices: domain, technology, structure, and processes (p. 337). Building on the scholarship of Hofer and Schendel, Lohrke and Bedeian (1998) reveal that an organization's recovery work "can be analyzed with regard to its competitive, political, and investment substrategies" (p. 5). A general, two-step design of corrective action and effective reorganization is outlined by Rosenblatt, Rogers, and Nord (1993, p. 87). Crandall (1995), in turn, links the Kouzes and Posner framework of exemplary leaders to recovery in troubled small churches: challenge the process, inspire a shared vision, enable others to act, model the way, and encourage the heart (p. 111). Cameron and her associates (1988) believe that structure, strategy, process, and leadership (p. 15) are key lenses to use in understanding organizational recovery.

Pearce and Robbins (1994a) report that recovery can be investigated productively using "five components of strategy: markets, products, manufacturing system, management and organization system, and distinctive competencies" (p. 97). Milburn and his team (1983a) also use five general "subsystems of the organization" (p. 1144) to illuminate organizational recovery: productive system, supportive system, maintenance system, adaptive system, and managerial system. And Finkin (1987) explores recovery in terms of methods of operating, products, and marketing (p. 37).

Turnaround-Specific Frames

While this first group of analysts applies existing managerial and organizational frameworks to recovery, a second group of turnaround scholars build their classification schemes and taxonomies using inductive molds. For example, based on their studies with small firms, Boyle and Desai (1991) provide a two-part system featuring administrative and strategic response categories: "Administrative factors include short-term operational activities, such as scheduling, procedures, managing employees, and analyzing reports. Strategic factors include long-term tasks such as planning" (p. 34). O'Neill (1986b), from his work on turnarounds in the banking industry, offers a framework of four recovery strategies: management, cutback, growth, and restructuring (p. 82):

> *Management strategies* are those actions which involve a change in top management personnel, or are enacted personally by the top management team. These include a switch in chief executives, the formation of new top management teams, and the building of morale among employees. . . .
> *Cutback strategies* are those actions which are taken to stem further decline (that is, closing the door after the horse has left). . . .
> *Growth strategies* are those which are designed to "boot" the firm ahead. This category includes such actions as entering a new product area, installing new product promotion methods and making some acquisitions.
> *Restructuring strategies* are those actions which involve redesigns in the central core of the business. These activities can be distinguished from strategies of the add-on variety (such as cutback and growth) in that they involve doing a particular task in a whole new way. These substrategies include adapting new manufacturing methods, establishing new distribution methods, and designing new organizational structures. (pp. 81–82)

Hegde (1982), in turn, highlights three broad sets of turnaround actions, "some organizational in character (such as change in top management or introduction of staff departments), some strategic (divestiture, diversification, joint ventures), and some operational (aggressive marketing, automation, retrenchment)" (pp. 300–302).

Grinyer and colleagues (1988) have unearthed six factors in sharpbend organizations: reductions in production costs, changes in management, windfalls, stronger financial controls, new product market focus, and improved marketing (p. 63). Schendel, Patton, and Riggs (cited in Weitzel & Jonsson, 1989), in turn, describe three strategies linked to reversing organizational decline: "the introduction of new leadership, diversification through product development and acquisition, and divestment of failing lines and divisions" (p. 104). In his work, Hambrick (1985) analyzes recovery using five frames: strategic, political, human, organizational, and symbolic (p. 10–32). Based on their grounded analysis in troubled firms, Grinyer and his team (1988) maintain that achieving a successful recovery entails four sets of actions: getting the right organization, developing good product focus, controlling costs, and energizing and unleashing the workforce (p. 146). Zammuto and Cameron (1985) furnish a two-part model of recovery featuring structural adjustments and strategic responses:

> Structural adjustments are internal changes that occur within an organization in response to environmental pressures. . . . Strategic responses focus externally on repositioning the organization in the changing environment by modifying the organization's domain. They differ from structural adjustments in that strategies are designed to affect the major domains within which organizations have selected to function. Structural adjustments affect the activities and methods used to function within those selected domains. (p. 245)

Looking specifically at recovery in churches, Snyder (cited in Crandall, 1995) outlines five dimensions of renewal: personal renewal, corporate renewal, conceptual renewal, structural renewal, and missiological renewal (p. 43). A four-cell matrix of strategic responses is provided by Smart and Vertinsky (1984): strategic, tactical, planning, and fire-fighting (p. 202), with the first two responses falling into the entrepreneurial bucket (i.e., attempts to modify the environment) and the second two falling into the adaptive bin (i.e., attempts to adapt to the environment) (p. 201).

Stopford and Baden-Fuller (1990) dissect recovery into five dimensions: structure, strategy, systems, technology, and individual behavior. Barker and his colleagues (1998) define recovery in terms of strategic reorientations, product introductions, and overhauls of organizational culture (p. 78). Looking specifically at recovery in the hospital industry, Shelley and Jones (1993) assert that there are five nonfinancial aspects of organizational recovery:

- Creating an organizational vision that transcends the initial cost-cutting measures
- Identifying organizational values that facilitate the turnaround process
- Defining a culture built on continuous improvement and efficiency
- Redefining policies, procedures, and practices to capitalize on the basic desire of people to do a good job
- Structuring the organization to perform more effectively. (p. 69)

Hofer (1980) lays out four pathways to recovery: revenue generation, product market refocusing, cost cutting, and asset reduction (p. 26). And a group of turnaround scholars describe recovery in terms of domain defensive and domain offensive strategies (see, for example, Cameron, 1983; Ford & Baucus, 1987; Lohrke & Bedeian, 1998; Zammuto & Cameron, 1985).

Domain defense is oriented towards preserving the legitimacy of the existing domain of activities and buffering the organization from hostile environmental conditions, possibly through the formation of coalitions with similar organizations. Domain offense focuses on expanding those activities that the organization already does well. (Whetten, 1988a, p. 37)

Operational (Efficiency) Versus Strategic (Entrepreneurial) Actions

The most dominant classification scheme in the organizational recovery literature "distinguish[es] between entrepreneurial, return-to-growth recovery strategies and efficiency, operating, recovery strategies" (Robbins & Pearce, 1992, p. 296). That is, "turnarounds can consist of both operating and strategic elements" (Pearce & Robbins, 1994b, p. 413)—"various management actions are modeled as either attempts to increase efficiency or changes in strategy"

(Arogyaswamy, Barker, & Yasai-Ardekani, 1995, p. 496; also Hofer, 1980; Schendel & Patton, 1976).

Strategic/Entrepreneurial Tactics

Strategic recovery moves emphasize "change[d] competitive strategy (Pearce & Robbins, 1994a, p. 93) and "product or market based activities" (Pearce & Robbins, 1993, p. 628) and underscore "growth and innovation" (Boyne, 2004, p. 99), "revenue-generat[ion]" (Pearce & Robbins, 1993, p. 620), and "new product lines, new competencies and new markets" (Ashmos & Duchon, 1998, p. 234). They focus on major organizational changes. Strategic moves are concerned with "doing different things" (Hambrick & Schecter, 1983, p. 232) rather than with "doing things differently" (p. 232).

"Entrepreneurial recovery strategies involve reformulation of a firm's products, services, markets, and principal technologies in ways that represent a new or radically altered competitive posture" (Pearce & Robbins, 1994a, p. 91). Entrepreneurial tactics are of two types, revenue-generation and product/market refocusing: "A revenue-generating strategy is an attempt to increase sales by some product (re-)introductions, increased advertising, increased selling effort and lower prices. A product/market refocusing strategy . . . involves a shifting of emphasis into defensible or lucrative niches" (Hambrick & Schecter, 1983, pp. 233–234). Specifically, "changing marketing processes, entering new businesses, integrating vertically, diversifying, divesting, and changing top management [are] considered strategic responses" (Shook, 1998, p. 264). So too are "repositioning the firm's product or service offering, its primary markets, principal technologies, distinctive competencies, competitive advantages, and strategic alliances" (Robbins & Pearce, 1992, p. 307).

Operational/Efficiency Tactics

Operational moves, on the other hand, "entail retaining the current competitive orientation" (Pearce & Robbins, 1994a, p. 93) and "product-market-technology orientation but on a smaller and more efficient scale" (p. 91). The spotlight is on "belt-tightening and streamlining of operations" (Pearce & Robbins, 1994a, p. 98) and "efficiency-oriented tactics" (Ashmos & Duchon, 1998, p. 224). The focus is on "the production and management systems" (Pearce

& Robbins, 1993, p. 628). Hambrick and Schecter (1983) outline two efficiency-based strategies: cost cutting and asset reduction.

> A *cost-cutting* strategy typically involves cutbacks in administrative, R&D, marketing, and other seemingly discretionary expenses. Improved management of receivables and inventories also could be considered within the spirit of a cost-cutting strategy. An *asset reduction* strategy involves disposal of assets— primarily fixed assets. (p. 234)

These operational tactics include activities designed to reduce "costs, assets, and plant expenditures, improving the operations of functional areas, and improving efficiency" (Shook, 1998, p. 264)— to "increase efficiency through cost cutting, cost improvements and containment, asset reduction programs" (Ford & Baucus, 1987, p. 372); ". . . changes in organizational design, information and intelligence systems, and performance requirements" (Shook, 1998, p. 264); and other "efficiency-oriented tactics" (Ashmos & Duchon, 1998, p. 224). Whereas with entrepreneurial tactics attention was devoted to doing different things, in the operational domain the focus is on doing the same things differently, more efficiently (Hofer, 1980; Schendel, Patton, & Riggs, 1976).

The question of which actions (efficiency or entrepreneurial) or combination of moves makes the most sense for recovering firms cannot be answered fully at this stage in our investigation. Nonetheless, some placeholders can be established. To begin with, it appears that oftentimes a combination of strategies from the two approaches is desirable (although "a difficult pairing to manage simultaneously" [Grinyer, Mayes, & McKiernan, 1988 p. 105]), especially in conjunction with appropriate turnaround leadership (Zimmerman, 1991). For example

> results show that turnarounds in banks are indeed fuelled by both revenue generation and cost control. . . . The results confirm that the successful turnaround bank exhibits elements of both selective product market pruning and piecemeal productivity. (O'Neill, 1986a, p. 180)

At the same time, there is a general consensus that this is a two-step process: "Successful turnarounds first achieve low-cost operation and then enhance product differentiation" (Zimmerman, 1991, p. 253). In short, it is difficult to simply grow one's way out of a turnaround situation, especially in mature industries; efficiency moves are essential (Bibeault, 1982; Barker et al., 1998; Hambrick & Schecter, 1983). Concomitantly, relying exclusively on operational tactics may be inappropriate. There is at least some concern expressed in the turnaround literature that a myopic focus on efficiency "may lead to stagnation and possible demise" (Cameron, 1983, p. 376), that including "entrepreneurial activities in the recovery response" (Boyne, 2004, p. 99) is generally a good idea (Austin, 1998; Cameron, 1983). Barker and his colleagues (1998) suggest that this may be the case because efficiencies are often a by-product of growth, that efficiencies garnered over time might better "be attributed to expanding sales than better utiliz[ation of] existing employees and other assets" (p. 75).

Second, as should be clear by this point in the narrative, the choice of broad strategy and specific tactics has a good deal to do with the cause of the turnaround (see Chapter 3) and the context of the recovery (see Chapter 5). For example, Hambrick and Schecter (1983) posit that "the appropriateness of a strategic or operating turnaround depends on whether the firm's 'illness' stems from poor strategy or poor operations" (p. 232). Similarly, Robbins and Pearce (1992) hold that "efficiency recovery responses are successful for firms whose performance problem is primarily attributable to internal causes [while] entrepreneurial recovery responses are successful for firms whose performance problem is primarily attributable to external causes" (p. 292).

Third, while the choice of turnaround strategy is important, "an equally or more important choice is *how* the strategy will be implemented" (Ashmos & Duchon, 1998, p. 234). Thus, "turnaround . . . requires two kinds of decisions: one about which path to take; and a second decision about *how* best to pursue the chosen path, that is, how best to self-organize in a manner which will prove to be a successful adaptation" (p. 227).

A Composite Frame

Drawing from these various taxonomies, models, and conceptualizations of how to portray the recovery phase of turnaround, we employ a five-part framework to capture empirical findings on organizational recovery: developing a focused operational vision, capturing operating efficiencies, revitalizing organizational processes, reconstructing the organizational work ethic, and improving products. In this chapter, we take up the first three phases of the recovery— operational vision, efficiencies, and organizational processes. In Chapter 9, we examine the final two dimensions of our framework— organizational work ethic and products.

OPERATIONAL VISION

When we closely examine successful turnarounds we find they each: (1) define clear objectives and a vision for the company [and] (2) develop the strategies needed to achieve the objectives. (Goldstein, 1988, p. 97)

In a turnaround situation, an effective strategic plan should include a mission statement and an organized listing of objectives . . . and strategies. (Stewart, 1984, p. 183)

Consistent with the extensive literature on organizational recovery, we partition operational vision into two clusters for analysis: mission, values, and guiding principles, and plan of action.

Mission, Values, and Guiding Principles

When an organization decides to pursue a turnaround strategy the organization is in critical need of conversation about the organization's values and vision. (Ashmos & Duchon, 1998, p. 233)

Companies in trouble must focus on what needs to be done. . . . This need to focus begins with company ideals. (Zimmerman, 1991, p. 209)

The processes of disintegration make shambles of the ideologies in crisis-ridden organizations, and the top managers confront the task of building new ideologies on these shambles. (Starbuck, Greve, & Hedberg, 1978, p. 134)

Unless the company has an objective, a corporate purpose, identity, and vision of what the organization should become, it will either remain adrift or be channeled in the wrong direction. (Goldstein, 1988, p. 98)

Troubled organizations are either locked into a downward spiral guided by an obsolete and nonfunctional mission (see Clausen, 1990; Gerstner, 2002; and Yates, 1983), or, more often, they have lost their way, both in terms of what to do and how to do it and who they are and what they stand for. "Causal maps and mental models" (Arogyaswamy, Barker, & Yasai-Ardekani, 1995, p. 510) used in the organization no longer work. The story of BankAmerica is typical of the first type of directional problem. In the words of its CEO

We faced the reality that what had been successful in the past was no longer working. As basic as this appears, it was essential to recognize this reality and to develop strategies to meet today's challenges, rather than continuing to operate as if yesterday's circumstances still prevailed. In essence, we restructured both the organization of the bank and our approach to banking. (Clausen, 1990, p. 33)

What William Bratton found when he assumed control of the Metropolitan Transit Authority in New York City is representative of the second type of dysfunction, the lost way: "When I arrived the Mets were a dispirited, reactive, day-to-day operation with no direction, goals, or vision for the future. . . . This was a department that was lying down dying" (Bratton & Knobler, 1998).

Turnaround literature teaches us that for recovery to work, as a starting point the people in the organization "need something to get excited about. They need ideals" (Zimmerman, 1991, p. 210). They require something to care about (Shook, 1998). And turnaround managers need to "concentrate their attention on ideological phenomena such as . . . beliefs, goals, values, and ideas" (Starbuck, Greve, & Hedberg, 1978, p. 133). They must attend to the "articulat[ion] of corporate philosophy in terms of policies and cultural values" (Finkin, 1987, p. 183): "Successful turnaround leaders clearly articulate ideals, purposes, and procedures" (Zimmerman, 1991, p. 193) and promote "the development of shared value systems"

(McDaniel & Walls, 1998, p. 47; also Grinyer, Mayes, & McKiernan, 1988; Rindler, 1987; Slater 1999).

The turnaround literature unearths two types of directional support on the pathway to recovery: objectives and strategies (which we examine in the next section) and ideas. Ideas, in turn, include statements of principles (Gerstner, 2002; Goodman, 1982), new (or reenergized) values (Stewart, 1984), and new assumptions (Milburn, Schuler, & Watman, 1983a, 1983b). Rejuvenated organizations tend to be principle-centered and value-based (Grinyer, Mayes, & McKiernan, 1988). These principles, values, and assumptions often find expression in new visions and new missions. Indeed, there is considerable evidence from various sectors of the economy (public agencies, nonprofit organizations, private firms) that turnaround leaders concentrate on "imparting a new vision" (Crandall, 1995, p. 68) in the organization. This aspect of recovery work is nicely illustrated in the New York City Police Department by Bratton and Knobler (1998), in small churches by Crandall (1995), at the Chrysler Corporation by Reich and Donahue (1985), at IBM by Gerstner (2002) and Slater (1999), at Beloit Hospital by Rindler (1987), at Uni-Lever by Mirvis and colleagues (2003), and at Fairmont Hotels by Umbreit (1996). The central message here is expressed by Crandall (1995):

Pastors who make a difference [in turning around failing small churches] have a dream and a vision of the way things can be (p. 114). Whatever else these pastors do, they bring with them and plant in the hearts and minds of their congregations a vision of what can be done. (p. 33)

We discover from the turnaround literature that "vision is foremost" (Shelley & Jones, 1993, p. 71): "In a turnaround situation a cogent vision of organizational effectiveness is particularly important" (p. 72), and "establishing such an operational vision can do more than anything else to ensure that improvements take place" (Modiano, 1987, p. 179): A "distinctive critical factor leading to sharpbending [is] . . . the ability to give vision and direction to the whole organization" (Grinyer, Mayes, & McKiernan, 1988, p. 143).

We also learn that successful turnaround leaders are especially adept at forging powerful visions of the future for troubled organizations and, as we explain below, making those visions come to fruition inside their institutions (Grinyer, Mayes, & McKiernan, 1988; Trompenaars & Hampden-Turner, 2002b). They are "vision-oriented" (Bennis & Nanus, 1985, p. 121) people (Yates, 1983).

In addition, the recovery literature helps us see that the vision provides the new way of doing business, that it is the exit ticket from turnaround status. A wonderful example of this can be seen in the New York City Police Department in the 1990s, where the vision of preventing crime as opposed to dealing with crime was infused throughout the police force (Bratton & Knobler, 1998). Another example in the 1990s took place at IBM, where a vision of service, solutions, and networks replaced the vision of IBM as a provider of computing hardware (Gerstner, 2002; Slater, 1999).

Finally, the turnaround literature illuminates the mechanism at the core of vision, the DNA of vision. The vision provides a "common destiny" (Devos & Hampden-Turner, 2002, p. 147). It "drives the company" (Grinyer, Mayes, & McKiernan, 1988, p. 68). It creates the "blueprint" (Kramer, 1987, p. 8) for the future. In short, "forward momentum is propelled by vision" (Austin, 1998, p. 103).

Closely related to and overlapping the topic of vision is the concept of organizational mission (Stewart, 1984). Mission is primarily about purpose—"a shared view of what the company is about" (Goldstein, 1988, p. 122), that is, "the nature of its business" (Goodman, 1982, p. 140). The research on organizational recovery is clear that "in turnaround work, it is especially important for members of the organization to understand the mission of the company and its reason for existence. . . . As a practical matter, when the difficulties of the organization are intense, members of the organization need an important, noble purpose in which to believe" (Zimmerman, 1991, p. 210; also Ackley, 1989; Hall, 1980): "The most important step in the success of this [recovery] process is clarifying the . . . purpose" (Crandall, 1995, p. 115); that is, "the most important factor for any sharpbend is for the firm to work out where it is trying to go" (Grinyer, Mayes, & McKiernan, 1988, p. 135):

> To develop and communicate a . . . *unified sense of direction* to which all members of the organization can relate, is probably the most important concept in management for top level consideration, and yet it is frequently overlooked. Unless the organization—its people and management—have an objective—a corporate identity—a philosophy of what you are in business for—and

some plans to achieve these objectives—then there is no unified direction that management can use to relate day to day directions. And to employees the company will become just a place to work. (Ross & Kami, 1973, p. 22)

And the research is also clear that leadership in the area of mission development is closely linked to successful recovery (Rindler, 1987; Shook, 1990; Yates, 1983).

Plan of Action

Especially in a turnaround situation, strategic planning is essential. (Goodman, 1982, p. 137)

The velocity, amplitude, and life span of [the] turnaround will depend more on the results of your strategic planning effort than on anything else. (Stewart, 1984, p. 180)

The point to be made here is that the incremental value of time invested in serious planning by far exceeds the incremental value of time invested in "taking action." (Sloma, 1985, p. 31)

The turnaround leader is the architect of the turnaround strategy. (Bibeault, 1982, p. 149)

Planning Work

Short and his team (1998) remind us that "once managers have determined that their firms are, in fact, in trouble, they must . . . formulate and implement appropriate strategies for achieving turnaround" (p. 154; also Finkin, 1987). And Goodman (1982), based on his analysis of organizational reintegration, informs us that "planning [is] a vital ingredient in turnaround" (p. 110): "For a turnaround company, . . . the first step is to realize that battles and wars are not won without battle plans" (p. 152). Goldstein (1988) reinforces this perspective when he explains that "seldom do companies 'stumble' into a new beginning. More often it is the result of an architect who kn[ows] how to take the corporate components and build a new house" (pp. 98–99). "Orchestrating a turnaround process . . . requires implementation of a comprehensive organizational strategy" (Shelley

& Jones, 1993, p. 80). Thus, "one of the most powerful lessons to be learned . . . is that however well equipped we may be for a course of action the end result will be closely tied to the skill and thoroughness of planning that went before" (Goodman, 1982, p. 103). And an assortment of reviewers expose the fact that the purpose-driven, value-based organizations we discussed above take shape "through some form of strategic planning" (Crandall, 1995, p. 112). They also illuminate the linkages between planning and organizational performance: "More and more, superior performance begins with superior planning. A durable turnaround cannot be achieved without a five-year road map to provide guidance for the management in its long and difficult mission" (Goodman, 1982, p. 38). Effective plans permit "leaders to control change and make it orderly" (Goldstein, 1988, p. 107).

According to Goldstein (1988), "a plan is a series of steps that provides the means for the [turnaround] firm to go 'from here to there.' 'Here' comprises one set of operating circumstances and 'there' constitutes a totally different set of circumstances" (p. 107). Goodman (1982) weighs in on the definition as follows:

> The planning function is management's way of anticipating the forces that will affect future performance and then developing programs for achieving desired results in the expected environment. The plan becomes the launching pad for successful action. (p. 104)

And Crandall (1985) characterizes planning as a way to "put flesh on the bones of dreams" (p. 116)—and values, principles, and mission. In less evocative form, Sloma (1985) defines turnaround planning as

> the process of deciding what to change today so that tomorrow will be significantly different from yesterday. Note that planning is a series of decisions about what *to do;* NOT the doing itself. Planning is an exercise in anticipation. It requires the ability to foresee likely consequences of prior, yet untaken action. It is the ability, too, to forge an inference chain backwards from a desired future result to the present set of circumstances. (p. 190)

In addition to examining definitions, it is instructive to expose the ingredients or components that form the structure of turnaround planning. According to Rindler (1987), the plan, or what he and his recovery team refer to as the "strategic slate" (p. 99), is

> . . . a limited set of measurable and prioritized objectives which need to be accomplished to ensure survival. The strategic state [provides] the focus necessary to concentrate on what [is] important, and [is] the planning vehicle for achieving a unified effort to save [the firm]. Lastly, the strategic slate [gives] management and board the end points which, when achieved, would be grounds for celebration. . . . It is a short list of measurable targets created by the people who have to achieve those targets. It is a page or two long that becomes smudged with finger prints and perhaps an occasional tear or two, because it is referred to so often. It is a concise document which focuses the management's efforts on those tasks which make the difference between the [organization's] life or death. And, it is a document with which the board can measure objectively the effectiveness of its management. (pp. 99–100)

Goldstein (1988), in turn, maintains that "a well-designed turnaround action plan includes [four components]: who is to do it, what is to be done, how is it to be accomplished, [and] when is it to be completed" (p. 104). Khandwalla (1983–1984) refers to planning in terms of "mobilization strategy" (p. 24), the main ingredients of which are "the primary goals and mission of the organization, . . . articulation of visible, concrete, and challenging tasks for the organization, and the involvement of the personnel in the turnaround" (p. 24).

Silver (1992) describes the turnaround plan as a "rehabilitation plan" (p. 9), a framework that includes "restructuring debt, negotiating new terms with suppliers, redeploying assets and personnel, and raising capital. Sloma (1985), in turn, tells us that a

> turnaround plan should be vibrant, dynamic, compelling, aggressive, attention-getting, even inspirational—but most important it must be do-able! The plan itself is the basic, fundamental motivational opportunity. It should not be a cold, dispassionate, esoteric collection of dry, sterile financial statements and exhibits. Rather, it should be challenging, personal, easy to comprehend and easy to monitor. It should pinpoint and spotlight personal assignments and commitments. People will react to, act on,

respond to and believe in only what they either fear or desire. The plan should encourage their desire for job security, career enhancement, and a brighter future. (p. 189)

He informs us that there are three sections to this type of document, the target forecast, the run-rate forecast, and the objective forecast.

The target forecast embodies the minimum financial performance levels of the firm that will sufficiently mollify the owners/ creditors. . . . The run-rate forecast is a projection of financial performance of the firm if *no* changes are implemented by operating management; essentially, it is a measure of the "do nothing new" alternative. The objective forecast, in effect, is the numerical difference between the earlier two forecasts. The objective forecast identifies the specific line-items on the P&L, balance sheet, and cash flow, and measurably defines the magnitudes of the changes in the firm's performance which the operating management must meet or exceed. (pp. 190–191)

Argenti (1976), in one of the earliest forays into corporate reintegration, outlines what he labels "a systematic corporate planning procedure" (p. 180). For him

this means identifying what the company's long-term objectives are. Then examine the company to list its major strengths and weaknesses—i.e., what it is really good at or bad at. Then forecast what trends and events in the future environment of the company are likely to be important. Then devise a long-term strategy which will carry the company forward in a shape and condition that allows it to take advantage of opportunities and avoid threats. Finally set up a long-term strategy monitoring system. (p. 180)

Finkin (1987) argues that turnaround plans include the following components:

- The major business assumptions concerning the external environment
- The intended scope of the business, including such matters as products, markets, manufacturing strategy, and geographical coverage—the company mission

- The resources and organizational arrangements needed to support the company mission
- The key indicators to signal whether or not the strategy is succeeding
- The elucidation of specific company objectives—the ambition toward which the management will work
- The specification of company goals—milestones along the path of achieving the company objectives (pp. 174–175)

And Slatter (1984) portrays four steps in planning for turnarounds:

(1) Identify and list the tasks needed to implement the recovery strategy. Go through each functional area or department to determine which tasks need to be undertaken; (2) assess the relative importance of the tasks, and rank in order of priority according to which has *greatest* impact on results; (3) for each task, develop practical action steps. Do not jump straight to the obvious. There is usually more than one way of tackling a task; (4) agree [on] short-term actions with subordinates. Decide what is to be done, by whom and when. Assign specific management responsibility and set up review dates. (pp. 145, 147)

These same scholars also present insights about the "how," or the process of turnaround planning, and proffer that "how the visioning process [is] carried out [is] as important as its content" (Austin, 1998, p. 103). Indeed, many troubled organizations "have found the strategic planning activity itself to be more beneficial than the plan they adopted" (Stewart, 1984, p. 181). They posit that

the ignition of creativity; the dependence on integrated teamwork; the information unearthed about customers and competitors, internal and external resources, and organizational relations; and an education in the techniques surrounding selection and implementation of alternative strategies could in the long run pay greater dividends than the choice of any one strategy. (p. 181)

Turnaround analysts suggest that the planning "process should be top down and bottom up" (Goodman, 1982, p. 123), should emphasize "open-end, conceptual thinking" (p. 139), and should ensure that the formal leaders of the organization are heavily invested in the work.

Performance objectives, it is held, are at the heart of the recovery plan (Contino & Lorusso, 1982; Slater, 1999). These objectives, in turn, promote the enumeration of specific goals "necessary to accomplish a stated mission" (Stewart, 1984, p. 184). And it is "these concrete goals [that] become the focus of rational end-means analysis throughout the organization, and are highly visible benchmarks against which progress can be measured" (Khandwalla, 1983–1984, p. 23):

> They define the specific performance, results, and standards that the realization efforts of the organization are designed to produce. Objectives are the milestones guiding the organization along the path toward the fulfillment of its corporate mission. They are the means for measuring group and individual performance and the means for measuring corporate recovery and growth. (Goldstein, 1988, p. 99)

According to Stewart (1984), objectives for a turnaround organization should

1. Be specific, measurable, and in written form

2. Clearly define the final results that are to be achieved

3. Be presented in order of their priority

4. Be challenging

5. Include a balanced menu of short-range, long-range, routine, problem-solving, innovative, and personal objectives

6. Be integrated with overall organizational needs, be consistent with corporate planning, and be established so that when achieved, they will support achievement of higher-level goals. For this reason, gaps and overlaps need to be avoided. The . . . goals structure should be established so that when all individual goals are achieved, the goals of the company will also be met

7. Be communicated to everyone involved in the program (pp. 127–128)

The critical nature of objectives and target goals to the voyage of organizational recovery is consistently illustrated in the turnaround literature. For an excellent example in the public sector (the New York City Police Department), see Bratton and Knobler (1998), and in the private sector (BankAmerica), see Clausen (1990).

Critical Elements

A review of the planning activity in various turnaround organizations allows us to tease out the critical elements of this strategic work. We learn that planning should be "bifocal" (Goodman, 1982, p. 111); that is, it should *attend to both long-run and short-run objectives* and work plans, with initial emphasis on establishing long-range specifications (Goldstein, 1988).

We are reminded that *simplicity* is an important element, especially early in the recovery process as it promotes understanding (Sloma; 1985; Zimmerman, 1991). Or as Stewart (1984) captures it, during planning

> it is imperative that the levels of comprehensiveness and sophistication remain well within the digestion limits of participants. Otherwise, the plan just won't work. (p. 183)

> A turnaround plan is too complex if it cannot be completely understood by key employees within a 15-minute meeting. (Goldstein, 1988, p. 100)

Planning should feature *"competitive positioning"* (Goodman, 1982, p. 141); that is, it should appraise "performance against leading competitors" (p. 141) using both backward- and forward-looking analysis.

While, as we noted earlier, time is often critical in the turnaround narrative, that is, there is a real sense of urgency (Finkin, 1987), it is nonetheless important that the planning work not be unduly hurried. *"Enough time* to do the job right" (Goodman, 1982, p. 138) must be provided: "Any attempt to squeeze the long-range planning process into strip-model proportions will undermine the quality of the plan, and the lesser amount of time used is apt to be wasted" (p. 138).

Also "of towering importance is the realization that the plan must be *tailored and customized* to the particular firm at a particular point in time" (Sloma, 1985, p. 35). General rules for planning are helpful; generic plans are not.

We have already addressed the essential nature of leadership at the top in organizational turnaround. Here we note that the *personal involvement of the CEO* in the planning process is critical to organizational recovery.

Turnaround plans, and the objectives, goals, and strategies that define them, should be *realistic yet stretch the organization* and its employees (Gerstner, 2002; Shelley & Jones, 1993). The institution must both set what Mirvis and his team (2003) call "stretch targets" (p. 126)—ones that "cannot be reached merely by adequate management" (Stewart, 1984, p. 165)—while "root[ing] out wishful, optimistic planning not supported by the facts" (Goodman, 1982, p. 123). Plans need to be "steeped in tough-minded analysis" (Gerstner, 2002, p. 225):

> A greater danger in setting turnaround objectives is that they may be unrealistic. Optimism is a valuable commodity in a turnaround situation but not when it encourages fantasy and delusions about what the company can soon become. The objectives must be achievable from both a financial and operational viewpoint, after realistic reflection of both the prior track record of the company and the resources now available to it. In short, the objectives represent a degree of "realistic corporate stretch." (Goldstein, 1988, p. 100)

Flexibility regularly appears in the catalogue of critical planning elements: "The plan must . . . leave the company enough back doors and circuit breakers to make alterations" (Silver, 1992, p. 9); "for turnaround strategies to work they have to be extremely flexible and adaptive. Strategies in a turnaround are often reactive" (Goldstein, 1988, p. 102).

The literature on reintegration reveals that the objectives and goals in the recovery plan should *promote incremental work* (Zimmerman, 1991) or, in Austin's (1998) terms, be "evolutionary" (p. 95): "To implement the turnaround then, it may be necessary to walk in small steps" (Goldstein, 1988, p. 106).

In addition, effective recovery plans *feature "specific strategies"* (Gerstner, 2002, p. 202) that "automatically allow people to properly set priorities" (Finkin, 1987, p. 52) and that can be "translated into day-to-day execution" (Gerstner, 2002, p. 222; also Bratton & Knobler, 1998). That is, recovery plans must be "*actionable*" (Gerstner, 2002, p. 225). They must pour energy into the objective of "achieving the main results of the plan" (Goodman, 1982, p. 143). One key aspect of actionability is budget. Specifically, as Stewart (1984) informs us, in effective recovery plans, budgets mirror needed turnaround work.

The use of *explicit benchmarks* generally surfaces in explorations of the critical elements of turnaround plans (Goldstein, 1988; Henderson, 1993). Turnaround analysts maintain that there should be clear understandings of what progress "should look like at reasonably spaced intervals along the way" (Goldstein, 1988, p. 108) to recovery. The plan should emphasize where the organization "will be at various milestones along the strategic route" (Stewart, 1984, p. 185).

> Once the plan is put into action, effective management control depends on being able to compare actual performance against planned results. A turnaround plan is worse than useless if actual performance progress cannot be tracked and its impact upon corporate recovery evaluated. (Goldstein, 1988, p. 107)

Concomitantly, and overlapping with our discussion of benchmarks, in good recovery plans the central elements are *measurable.*

> The organization is likely to adapt to change far slower than management would hope. The greater the measurable detail of each step, the easier are the managerial tasks to control organizational behavior and to exercise the organizational power needed to successfully execute the plan. (Goldstein, 1988, p. 106)

This means, of course, that the recovery activities to be taken "must be *quantified*" (Sloma, 1985, p. 7): "Good strategies are long on detail—they lay out multi-year plans in great quantitative detail" (Gerstner, 2002, p. 225).

And, finally, the *specification of responsibility* for engaging pieces of work and *specification of accountability* for achieving targets of performance are essential ingredients in effective recovery plans (Rindler, 1987): "Responsibility must be pinpointed if the turnaround plan is to work" (Goldstein, 1988, p. 105).

The Central Place of Focus

Lack of focus is the most common cause of corporate mediocrity.
(Gerstner, 2002, p. 219)

"Focus" is such a critical and multifaceted construct in the pathway to recovery narrative that it merits extended discussion. At the broadest level, focus is about establishing clear priorities about what is important (Austin, 1998; Motroni, 1992, Stopford & Baden-Fuller, 1990), of setting "definitive objectives among . . . conflicting objectives" (Modiano, 1987, p. 179), of "hav[ing] a clear understanding of the five or six central things" (Gerstner, 2002, p. 225) that need to be done "in the base business to be successful" (p. 225). Here focus means concentrating on "basic strengths" (Clausen, 1990, p. 100) and "on the key lines essential to rebuilding the company" (Goldstein, 1988, p. 120)—"to the basics of the business" (Shook, 1990, p. 67). Specific focusing advice on priorities is offered throughout the literature. For example

Of particular concern is the main core business of the company that must be protected, cultivated, and purified. It is the core that will finance the turnaround and provide a platform for the future. (Bibeault, 1982, p. 103)

Make sure that the heavy emphasis is on the few key factors that make the big difference in the company's performance. To scatter your shot over too may targets will mean more misses than hits. (Goodman, 1982, p. 106)

The answer to each of these problems lies in concentrating on a small number of issues that will produce the greatest cash flow and/or profit, then setting up good communications to ensure that everybody in the firm knows what these are. (Slatter, 1984, p. 145)

In terms of focus on key lines, Goldstein (1988) and other turnaround analysts suggest that "shrinking the product line is usually the surest route to higher profits and higher return on investment" (p. 120). "Successful turnaround agents focus attention on the basics" (Zimmerman, 1991, p. 208), "promoting a few basic improvements"

(Stewart, 1984, p. 183). Concentrating on key lines also means "preserv[ing] development resources only for things that need to be done" (Zimmerman, 1991, p. 127). Because "it is through the resource allocation process that strategic change is implemented" (Slatter, 1984, p. 235), this, in turn, necessitates linking resources to "the activities that really count" (p. 209), especially the willingness to "take resources away from some other activity in the company and reassigning them to the highest priority" (Gerstner, 2002, p. 226; also Bratton & Knobler, 1998). Attending to key lines also requires avoiding "acquisitions, divestitures, diversification schemes, and new ventures" (Zimmerman, 1991, p. 220) that pull the organization away from its core business and new vision and mission.

> The track record of turning around a company by entering a new field is very poor—particularly when the company shows no capacity to manage its old field. If we cannot keep our basic business healthy, what shred of evidence is there to suggest that we can manage something else? (p. 276)

Focus also means having the organization attend first and foremost to customers (Grinyer, Mayes, & McKiernan, 1988), of being customer driven rather than producer driven. (We add a good deal to this point below as well.) It means a willingness to pursue those activities "expected to bring the quickest results" (Goodman, 1982, p. 186)—to have an "immediate impact" (Clausen, 1990, p. 99). Focus tells recovery agents to concentrate on "the few essential performance barometers" (Goldstein, 1988, p. 108). According to academics and practitioners alike, "it is considerably better to constantly monitor the key indicators than to become immersed in extraneous detail that can only cloud matters" (p. 108). Finally, and in line with all previous analysis, focus means keeping "two key overall objectives . . . in mind at all times, . . . return on capital and growth" (Stewart, 1984, p. 190), or "rate of return on investment" (Silver, 1992, p. 198; also Slatter, 1984; Sloma, 1985).

ORGANIZATIONAL EFFICIENCIES

It was found that efficiency measures are major avenues toward improved profits. (Hambrick & Schecter, 1983, p. 246)

What may be crucial to turnarounds is improving efficiency. (Arogyaswamy & Yasai-Ardekani, 1997, p. 4)

In order to succeed, the first priority of the troubled firm should be to improve efficiency. (Zimmerman, 1991, p. 275)

Promoting and garnering efficiencies is the second pillar of recovery from organizational decline and failure. So far, we have already provided considerable space to this element of the recovery framework. Specifically, because capturing efficiencies during the recovery phase of turnaround is really an extension of the cost-savings work in the retrenchment phase (see Chapter 7), we have already introduced most of the foundational components of this second pillar. In addition, much of the discussion just completed on entrepreneurial versus efficiency recovery tactics fits here as well. Rather than revisiting all that analysis here, we limit our discussion to two points: the cardinal importance of efficiency during recovery and examples of ways to capture efficiencies in the service of recovery.

Importance

Increased efficiency is important for turnaround. (Arogyaswamy & Yasai-Ardekani, 1997, p. 9)

A key to the achievement of turnaround is for firms to meet financial or competitive adversity with carefully considered, and thoughtfully measured cost reductions. (Pearce & Robbins, 1993, p. 616)

Efficiency is used in the turnaround literature in two ways. Primarily it is about "measures to reduce costs and control them" (Grinyer, Mayes, & McKiernan, 1988, p. 80). Or, as Short and colleagues (1998) capture it, "an efficiency strategy aims to enhance performance through a relentless emphasis on cost cutting" (p. 161). On this first front then, efficiency is a matter of "cost reduction" (Barker & Duhaime, 1997, p. 34). It is also used less often but more accurately to capture the idea of "using fewer resources to obtain the same output" (Grinyer, Mayes, & McKiernan, 1988, p. 100) or to "get more output from the same resources" (p. 106).

Regardless of the perspective employed, the turnaround literature is fairly consistent on one central point. That is, there is widespread recognition from a variety of studies that "the adoption of efficiency-oriented recovery strategies" (Pearce & Robbins, 1994a, p. 92) and the realization of efficiency gains are absolutely essential to successful recovery. For example, in their work, Grinyer and colleagues (1988) discovered that sharpbenders differed from control companies in that "substantially more of them reduced their production costs" (p. 64). The primary concern of these recovered firms was "on improving cost competitiveness" (p. 64), and "they made major efforts to cut costs, particularly central overheads, and introduced strong controls to manage expenditure[s]" (p. 105). Thus, Zimmerman (1991) concludes that

> although it is difficult to isolate a single cause of turnaround success, modest overhead and high rates of inventory efficiency are commonly present among successful companies. These well-managed firms spend less money on general and administrative expenses, office buildings, purposeless travel, unnecessary selling expenses, and other items not related to products or customers. They employ frugality as an ongoing mode of operation. In addition, cost-reduction programs at the successful firms are longer lasting and more even-handed with respect to rank. When expenses must be cut, managers lead the way by cutting their own salaries first before implementing cost reductions elsewhere in the organization. When expenses need to be reduced, they are reduced. Unsuccessful firms apply token cost reductions and then permit expenses to rise before the firm's health is restored. Excessive costs impede efficient operations. (p. 86)

More firmly still, based on his conclusion that "successful [turnaround] companies [are] noticeably more efficient in operations than unsuccessful firms" (p. 257)—that is, a "significantly larger percentage of turnaround firms improved efficiency" (Arogyaswamy & Yasai-Ardekani, 1997, p. 8)—Zimmerman (1991) identifies "low cost operations" (p. 13) as one of the "three key factors in successful turnaround" (p. 13). That is, "for firms competing in declining industries, efficiency or operating recovery strategies offer the best prospects for successful turnaround" (Pearce & Robbins, 1993, p. 621). More aggressively, Arogyaswamy and his team (1995) report that "published large sample studies have failed to verify the effectiveness of any particular turnaround strategy other than those aimed at achieving firm efficiency" (p. 496): "Large sample studies comparing turnaround and non-turnaround firms' strategies have found that efficiency-oriented strategies, not strategic change, were the route to profit recovery" (p. 517). Barker and Duhaime (1997) raise a similar point when they note that "findings would seem to provide evidence discounting the assertion that strategic change is adaptive for declining firms" (p. 15).

Less clarity is discernible in the research about the efficacy of employing efficiency tactics in combination with entrepreneurial strategies. There is some evidence that combination strategies can be effective in promoting organizational recovery at least in some industries (see O'Neill, 1981, 1986a)—and perhaps, most important here, in nonprofit and government agencies (Cameron, Kim, & Whetten, 1988). There are also indications that efficiency moves may be the driver elements in successful recovery efforts featuring both types of improvement initiatives—that efficiency actions are critical to garnering the slack resources needed "to implement strategic change" (Barker & Duhaime, 1997, p. 20).

Efficiency Strategies

The successful companies spent less on selling, general and administrative expense, and other non-cost-of-sales expense. (Zimmerman, 1991, p. 258)

In a turnaround situation, it is often best to refocus R&D onto cost reductions. Figuring out how to more cheaply make one's current products has a faster payback than developing products for sale far into the future. (Finkin, 1985, p. 21)

As was the case with retrenchment (see Chapter 7), the literature is replete with rich examples of the cost reductions and efficiencies found in organizations that successfully recover from decline. To begin with, there are signs in cases of successful reintegration that the idea of efficiency becomes woven into the basic fabric of the organization (Gerstner, 2002): "Cost consciousness [is] more likely to be a cultural characteristic of successful [turnaround] firms than unsuccessful [turnaround] firms" (Zimmerman, 1991, p. 258). Zimmerman (1991) also informs us that in "successful turnaround cases . . . management often play[s] exemplary roles in cost reductions" (p. 238). Finally, he helps us see how "cost reduction programs in successful turnarounds [are] pragmatic, disciplined, and evenhanded" (p. 258).

To illustrate efficiency, we present two snapshots from the literature, one in narrative form and one in the form of a taxonomy. The story is provided by Arogyaswamy and Yasai-Ardekani (1997):

Hollaender Manufacturing Company, a maker of pipe fittings for handrails and other structural applications, was in financial trouble due to a slumping construction market, outmoded management structure, and low-priced competition from abroad. In an effort to improve efficiency, the company consolidated its product line to include segments that utilized 85% of capacity and accounted for 95% of sales. Instead of personnel cuts, the CEO took a pay cut of 25%. . . . Human resource training was undertaken for all employees. An analysis of the company's operations revealed that Hollaender's scrap and quality-related problems were costing it $1 million a year. Using a JIT inventory system, forming manufacturing cells, simplifying plant scheduling, optimizing plant layout, and increasing flexibility of the machines paid great dividends. (p. 8)

The taxonomy of cost ideas is taken from the work of Grinyer and his research team (1988):

1. Cost control over
   a. raw-material costs
   b. labour costs
   c. pilferage

2. Production engineering, work study, etc., used to minimize production costs

3. Technology regularly reviewed to see cost reductions

4. Productivity measured and reviewed regularly

5. Workforce consulted about improvements and their ideas sought

6. Marketing and distribution cost monitored and controlled
7. Firm makes good use of
   a. computers and office automation
   b. OR and O&M
   c. management training
   d. NEDO and DTI advice and support (p. 126)

Across the two snapshots, we see that cost reductions center around asset reductions (Hambrick & Schecter, 1983; Slater, 1999); shedding less-productive business units (Grinyer, Mayes, & McKiernan, 1988); "reducing contracts with more marginal customers" (Brightman, 1995, p. 46); dropping (or cutting back aggressively on) business functions (Pearce & Robbins, 1994a); slashing "operating and overhead costs" (O'Neill, 1986a, p. 182); downsizing the workforce (Dewitt, Harrigan, & Newman, 1998); "increas[ing] labor and managerial productivity . . . by improving current management and designing jobs for enhanced employee retention" (Pearce & Robbins, 1994a, p. 104); and by "reducing manufacturing cost through product design" (Zimmerman, 1991, p. 103)—"through the effective design of products and services" (p. 103).

ORGANIZATIONAL STRUCTURES AND PROCESSES

In a turnaround situation, organizational structure can be a key. (Hambrick, 1985, p. 10-24)

Firms in dramatically changing environments may be compelled to adjust their . . . structures in order to survive. (Haveman, 1992, p. 73)

The [turnaround] process must also involve fundamental organizational change . . . change in the policies, procedures, and structures that organize and deploy resources. (Shelley & Jones, 1993, p. 69)

The third pillar in our composite framework for recovery is the revitalization of organizational processes and structures. Turnaround scholars and turnaround specialists provide a variety of frames to explore this dimension of reintegration. Some, as we have seen, situate it within the larger conception of turnaround designs. For example, Grinyer and Spender (1979) posit that structural change is one of four key elements of turnaround work—structure, strategy, personnel, and ideology. Rosenblatt and her team (1993) view structure as one of three key components of recovery—structure, perceptions, and politics. Others unpack the construct. For example, Shelley and Jones (1993) dissect structure into procedural and structural dimensions.

These same analysts also provide insights about the central dynamics and elements of organizational structure in turnaround firms. They observe that cumbersome structures and "procedures tend to accumulate" (Goodman, 1982, p. 115) in failing organizations, that "decreases in structure occur at a slower rate during decline and in some cases may even increase" (Ford, 1980, p. 595). They confirm that the crisis management prevalent in the retrenchment phase of turnaround (see Chapters 6 and 7) needs to give way to efforts to revitalize "management practices and organizational structures" (Whitney, 1987, p. 55) during recovery. While not all aspects of the enterprise will benefit from "more appropriate structure" (Grinyer, Mayes, & McKiernan, 1988, p. 116), the message seems to be "to rationalize what is amenable to rationality" (Trompenaars & Hampden-Turner, 2002b, p. 136).

Most important for our purposes here, turnaround managers and analysts disclose the importance of changing organizational structures and processes in the service of organizational recovery. They affirm that the ways in which people and systems are organized in troubled organizations "can have a major impact on effectiveness" (Grinyer, Mayes, & McKiernan, 1988, p. 141). They reveal that failure often occurs because new strategies and goals are not accompanied by "the organizational changes needed to accomplish them" (Mirvis, Ayas, & Roth, 2003, p. 45). Reviewers document that in "unsuccessful turnarounds there is less attention to restructuring activities" (O'Neill, 1986b, p. 83). They conclude that new structures are required to accomplish new visions and missions and to effectively implement turnaround plans (Motroni, 1992), that "significant organizational changes" (Grzymala-Busse, 2002, p. 52) are often essential to make "programmatic transformation feasible, credible, and sustainable" (p. 52): "Significant organizational change may be necessary to ensure that refocusing actually occurs" (Slatter,

1984, p. 235). And there is a general consensus that "large payoffs" (Khandwalla, 1983–1984, p. 29) can result from thoughtful efforts to strengthen organizational processes and structures, especially in conjunction with the other pillars of recovery.

Surprisingly, reviewers are less helpful in uncovering patterns and themes that demarcate organizational restructuring for recovery, often providing what on the surface appears to be contradictory advice. The most useful work in this area is provided by Grinyer and his associates (1988), who, in their research on sharpbender firms, isolate "five general characteristics of appropriate organizational structure" (p. 116):

1. It should be as simple as possible.

2. The head office should be no larger than strictly necessary.

3. It is advantageous to have profit or cost centers with operating decisions delegated to them.

4. In large firms a fairly formal strategic planning approach is necessary, while the smaller organization needs regular but informal reviews.

5. A balance needs to be struck between giving divisions or subsidiaries the freedom and motivation to develop their sector on their own and making sure that they do what head office wants, particularly in regard to expenditure, costs, marketing, etc. (p. 116)

Other reviewers argue that organizational reintegration needs to be accompanied by change in policy (O'Neill, 1986b) and in patterns of managerial behavior (Khandwalla, 1983–1984; Zimmerman, 1991). Based on our examination of all the work on the structural pillar of recovery across multiple sectors of the economy (nonprofit, public, and corporate organizational forms), we highlight three major lessons for turnaround efforts below.

Backward Map Structures From the Customer

I came here with a view that you start the day with customers, that you start thinking about a company around its customers, and you organize around customers. (Gerstner, cited in Slater, 1999, p. 181)

In order to succeed, a company must establish a customer-first mentality and ingrain this mentality into the company's culture. (Motroni, 1992, p. 32)

One of the most important ingredients in successful [turnaround] planning is a deep understanding of customers. (Goodman, 1982, p. 106)

Perhaps nowhere is the literature on organizational recovery clearer than in the area of customer focus. While, as we have seen, trouble has many roots in turnaround organizations, the taproot is generally failure to stay close to customers and to organize the enterprise based on customer needs. In case after case—in churches, hospitals, political parties, universities, and in nearly every sector of private enterprise, both manufacturing and service—we see that decline can be traced to a disconnect from the customer (Finkin, 1987; Goldstein, 1988). We are exposed to an almost limitless supply of examples in which attending to internal dynamics (Goldstein, 1988; Rindler, 1987; Slater, 1999) "where work is determined by department requirements rather than customer requirements" (Shelley & Jones, 1993, p. 80), failure to know and understand customers (Bratton & Knobler, 1998, Yates, 1983), focusing primarily on "completing tasks and procedures" (Shelley & Jones, 1993, p. 79), and creating a producer-driver culture can cause organizations to derail.

On the flip side, we see repeatedly in every sector of the recovery literature that turnaround efforts that "look outside in" (Mirvis, Ayas, & Roth, 2003, p. 105) and that "build the [organization] from the customer back" (Gerstner, cited in Slater, 1999, p. 173)—that "put the customer first" (Slater, 1999, p. 177); that pay "continuous attention to the market and what the customers want" (Grinyer, Mayes, & McKiernan, 1988, p. 123); that make "listening and staying close to customers . . . part of the fabric of the organization" (Rindler, 1987, p. 135); and that create structures and processes predicated on customer needs—that, in short, provide the infrastructure for a "customer-driven" (Shook, 1990, p. 166) organization—offer real promise for "marked improvements in performance"

(p. 26; also Mirvis, Ayas, & Roth, 2003). "Healthy corporations are market-oriented; their managerial energy is directed to meeting customer needs" (Goldstein, 1988, p. 119). And this lesson holds quite generally whether we are talking about "pastoral visitations" (Crandall, 1995, p. 101) or meeting with clients and suppliers in the service (Motroni, 1992; Rindler, 1987; Slater, 1999; Trompenaars & Hampden-Turner, 2002b), in the manufacturing (Mirvis, Ayas, & Roth, 2003), and in the industrial (Reich & Donahue, 1985; Shook, 1990; Yates, 1983) sectors.

Focus on Results and Continuous Improvement

Results are all that count. (Goldstein, 1988, p. 28)

Gradual and consistent incremental improvement [is] the operative style in place during successful turnarounds. (Zimmerman, 1991, p. 214)

Fixing the accountability for performance . . . appears to be an important action in a turnaround. (Khandwalla, 1983–1984, p. 33)

Troubled organizations have a tendency to feature inappropriate measures of success (e.g., effort) and to rationalize unsatisfactory performance on outcome measures (Gerstner, 2002; Goodman, 1982). If the organization is to recover, this culture needs to change, and, more directly to the point here, the organizational structure and processes essential to scaffolding a reculturing need to be forged and put in place. Studies of successful turnarounds disclose that these organizations create a "performance loop" that grounds the restructuring work, a loop comprised of standards, assessment, continuous improvement, and accountability.

Standards

One strand of the performance loop is the establishment of high standards of performance (Khandwalla, 1983–1984), of challenging everyone in the organization to meet "very ambitious goals" (Slater, 1999, p. 134; also Bratton & Knobler, 1998), for, as Slatter (1984) reminds us, "the establishment of performance standards plays a key role in changing the . . . organization" (p. 149): "What it takes to set the stage for a turnaround are high standards [and] a freedom from self-delusion" (Goodman, 1982, p. 9). And a critical dimension of high standards and ambitious goals is an "orientation toward results" (Khandwalla, 1983–1984, p. 34)—or outcomes or achievement or productivity or profits, all expressed in terms of value added (Finkin, 1985, 1987; Goodman, 1982; Goldstein, 1988; Shook, 1990; Slater, 1999). On one hand, this requires the specific delineation of objectives and targets of performance (Argenti, 1976; Bibeault, 1982; Goldston, 1992). More deeply, it necessitates not thinking in terms of what is required to do the work but in terms of what can be done "significantly better to improve results" (Fine, cited in Goldstein, 1988, p. 79; also Gerstner, 2002).

Rigorous Monitoring and Assessment

The second link of the performance loop is the development of monitoring structures and procedures. We begin our analysis with two acknowledgments: (1) for the goals of the "performance standards to be effective they must be measured" (Slatter, 1984, p. 149) and (2) in "a turnaround company there is often a lack of the kind of management information needed to focus attention on results improvement" (Goodman, 1982, p. 243).

Rigorous monitoring and assessment starts with a *bias for information gathering and analysis* (Hambrick, 1985), with an understanding of the need for "massive amounts of quantitative analysis" (Gerstner, 2002, p. 223). That is, successful turnarounds are "analytically based" (Austin, 1998, p. 93). Or, obversely, "in a turnaround situation it is a good idea to develop a low tolerance for assumptions as a basis for action" (Goodman, 1982, p. 238).

A basis for information also is defined by proactiveness in the data-gathering process. For example, based on his research, Zimmerman (1991) maintains that unsuccessful turnaround organizations "frequently [have] significant gaps in their information flows and tend to make decisions mostly on what information [is] needed" (p. 214). There is also a perception in the literature that the existing data systems in many turnarounds have been created to do things other than address "decision support needs" (Sumeren, 1993, p. 113). Successful turnaround firms, on the other hand, "are more studious about obtaining the information necessary for good decisions"

(Zimmerman, 1991, p. 17). There is evidence in the turnaround literature that managers of effective recovery efforts carefully attend to data external to the organization as they work to monitor organizational progress (Lohrke & Bedeian, 1998; Zimmerman, 1991).

Also central to the second link in the performance loop is what Bratton and Knobler (1998) call *"relentless assessment"* (p. 231). We know, as reported above, that such a commitment to evaluation is low in troubled organizations (Bibeault, 1982; Mirvis, Ayas, & Roth, 2003). Concomitantly, we are aware that successful turnarounds move to forge structures and processes that allow them to "constantly check to ensure that products meet or exceed customer requirements. Unsuccessful [turnaround] companies presume that quality is high but do not check" (Zimmerman, 1991, p. 161). In successful turnaround organizations, there is "routine monitor[ing] and report[ing] on quantifiable quality objectives" (Green & Hanson, 1993, p. 193). "Active and timely intelligence" (Bratton & Knobler, 1998, p. 224) defines these organizations. There is a "meticulous monitor[ing] of quality" (Caldwell, cited in Shook, 1990, p. 79) "to see how the organization is progressing" (Khandwalla, 1983–1984, p. 33; also Stewart, 1984). Where recovery flourishes, special attention is provided to what Zimmerman (1991) calls "in process" (p. 14) assessment: "The emphasis on quality as an ongoing discipline is one factor which distinguish[es] the successful from the unsuccessful turnarounds" (p. 149)—"in process quality is the major emphasis at successful companies. At unsuccessful companies, more emphasis is on the end product" (p. 149; also Bibeault, 1982; Bratton & Knobler, 1998) only.

In addition, organizations that reverse the cycle of decline closely and regularly monitor costs. That is, they establish "effective budgeting system[s]" (Slatter, 1984, p. 150) and develop a "clear picture of the cost of things done as a basis for judging whether the result obtained justifies the cost" (Goodman, 1982, p. 183).

At the heart of the performance loop is a preoccupation with *"continuous improvement"* (Shook, 1990, p. 83)—the belief that products and services can regularly and consistently be made more effective (Mirvis, Ayas, & Roth, 2003) and that the "job of improvement is a never-ending one" (Bibeault, 1982, p. 314)—and a commitment by "management . . . to provide leadership to make possible meaningful change" (Shook, 1990, p. 84). In practice, this dedication is energized by the monitoring and assessment systems described above. Continuous improvement, in turn, gives meaning to data; it ensures that data are used in a results-oriented fashion.

Research on organizational recovery documents that in-process data are used to take immediate action on problems and in situations where results diverge from targets (Bratton & Knobler, 1998; Ross & Kami, 1973): "Quality is maintained because precision is expected at every link in the value chain; when quality is not forthcoming, changes are made. Unsuccessful [turnaround] companies lack discipline" (Zimmerman, 1991, p. 149). The essence of turnaround management is "the ability to spot and act on problems at the earliest possible stage" (Goldstein, 1988, p. 32; also O'Neill, 1981). Where recovery efforts fail, on the other hand, "known quality problems and product shortcomings remain in the product for years after they [are] discovered" (Zimmerman, 1991, p. 161).

The research also exposes a second dimension to continuous improvement, one less focused on immediate attention to correcting quality problems than on the constant strengthening of already good work and constant enhancement of already impressive results. In successful turnaround organizations, there is an emphasis on "constant meaningful change" (Shook, 1990, p. 84): "Gradual and consistent incremental improvement is the managerial style of successful turnarounds. . . . In contrast unsuccessful firms make abrupt, drastic changes" (Zimmerman, 1991, pp. 17–18).

Accountability

The final link of the performance loop, and again one linked tightly to recovery (Khandwalla, 1983–1984; Trompenaars & Hampden-Turner, 2002b), is the development of structures to ensure accountability and to acknowledge high performance (Austin, 1998; Crandall, 1995; Slatter, 1984). Or, as Gerstner and Clausen capture it based on their work in turning around IBM and BankAmerica, respectively: "Proper execution involves building measurable targets and holding people accountable for them" (Gerstner, 2002, p. 231) and "the final step is recognition and reward" (Clausen, 1990, p. 104). A key element is bringing personnel evaluation procedures in line with an orientation toward value-added outcomes (Bratton & Knobler, 1998). The connection here to lesson number one above on customer focus is provided by Shelley and Jones (1993): "To focus employees on satisfying customers, all those involved in service delivery must be held accountable for customer outcomes" (p. 80):

"Accountability must be demanded, and when it is not met, changes must be made" (Gerstner, 2002, p. 231). Concomitantly, reward structures need to be overhauled to better mesh with accomplishments: "You can't transform institutions if the incentive programs are not aligned with [the] new strategy" (p. 100). In addition to providing end-of-the run rewards, these new structures should provide acknowledgment for intermittent progress on the pathway to meeting performance targets.

Create Structures to Integrate Work

Successful, dynamic institutions typically have developed organizational structures that emphasize key business processes rather than occupational specialties and then align workers to satisfy customer requirements rather than departmental requirements. (Shelley & Jones, 1993, p. 78)

It is clear that improved . . . coordination among departments can positively affect quality and outcomes. (Musfeldt & Collier, 1993, p. 128)

Managers who are attempting turnarounds in professional organizations must promote interactions among professionals in order to generate shared meanings that will facilitate action. (McDaniel & Walls, 1998, p. 149)

The turnaround research, especially work on decline and crisis, illuminates the fact that recovery is often hindered because opportunities are constrained by an absence of integration throughout the troubled organization (Kanter, 2003), that is, "by insufficient interfunctional cooperation" (Modiano, 1987, p. 177). Prevalent conditions in declining firms include the separation of managers from workers (Mirvis, Ayas, & Roth, 2003)—the presence of "a notoriously aloof bureaucracy" (Bratton & Knobler, 1998, p. 257)—and the separation of functions into separate silos—the "tendency to work in chimneys rather than to work together" (Shook, 1990, p. 14) and to feature "a narrow functional focus" (Modiano, 1987, p. 176). The objective in these troubled organizations oftentimes is to "optimize individual return" rather than maximize outcomes for the organization.

On the other side of the equation, however, in successful turn-around organizations, there is an understanding that "problem solving requires collaboration across departments and divisions" (Kanter, 2003, p. 65) and "functional disciplines" (Modiano, 1987, p. 175), what Shelley and Jones (1993) refer to as "integrated customer service" (p. 78). That is, "coordinated activities" (Bratton & Knobler, 1998, p. 257) that bring together teams "of people of various ranks and responsibilities across the corporation" (Zimmerman, 1991, p. 186) are quite helpful to recovery efforts. The research also affirms that moving toward more integrative and coordinated activity in a troubled organization "will challenge traditional role definitions, reporting relationships, . . . and management of resources" (p. 79). The literature on recovery provides wonderful examples of how this integrative function focused on "improving coordination" (Khandwalla, 1983–1984, p. 32) can take structural form in organizations (see, for example, Bratton and Knobler, 1998, and Shook, 1990).

We know that the troubled firm struggling to recover is likely not to have the right "mix of people" (Finkin, 1987, p. 45). There is also evidence that in these organizations there will be some, perhaps significant, resistance to changes brought into play by creating coordinating structure (Starbuck, Greve, & Hedberg, 1978). Therefore, a key ingredient in the coordination agenda for recovery is getting the "right people" (Shook, 1990, p. 142) and then helping them "bring their expertise to the party" (p. 142). Thus, coordination is both about creating opportunities (Crandall, 1995) and linking the right people to those new opportunities, with "right" defined in terms of industry expertise (Goldstein, 1988; Zimmerman, 1991).

CHAPTER NINE

Organizational Work Ethic and Products

Sharpbends are based heavily on people. (Grinyer, Mayes, & McKiernan, 1988, p. 150)

People are the most important element in all turnarounds. (Finkin, 1987, p. 17)

Personnel is the most important element. (O'Shaughnessy, 1995, p. 4)

The difference is the human factor. (Yates, 1983, p. 239)

In this chapter, we discuss the final two dimensions of the recovery framework. We begin with an overview of building human capacity inside the organization and close with a brief analysis of the place of products and services in the organizational turnaround.

ORGANIZATIONAL WORK ETHIC

People are at the heart of a successful turnaround. This fact cannot be emphasized enough. (Finkin, 1987, p. 41)

Ultimately, management must develop a people-oriented philosophy if the turnaround is to succeed. (Goldstein, 1988, p. 109)

The first lesson about organizational work ethic in turnarounds is that people are the essential ingredient in recovery: "The key attribute to a successful turnaround . . . boils down to retaining the most honest people who want to work hard, who know something about the business they are in, and who want the company to succeed" (Zimmerman, 1991, p. 275). Thus, according to Shelley and Jones (1993), "the executive orchestrating a . . . turnaround must recognize that organizational dynamics—how people within the organization behave—is as important as organizational structure" (p. 70). Or, as Kanter (2003) discovered in her research, "successful corporate turnaround depends on relationships as well as information" (p. 64). Successful turnaround artists understand that "people are always the firm's most important and potent asset" (Sloma, 1985, p. 187). They practice the art of leadership through and with people (Grinyer, Mayes, & McKiernan, 1988), and they are committed to developing people in the organization (Mirvis, Ayas, & Roth, 2003).

Leaders who place their organizations on the path to reintegration are cognizant that "the way people feel on the job can make them perform like cripples or champions" (Goodman, 1982, p. 97): "The attitudes of the people within the organization are more critical in a turnaround situation than at any other time in a company's life" (Goldstein, 1988, pp. 110–111). They also understand that achieving a new vision and enhancing productivity are heavily dependent on the knowledge and skills possessed by the institution's employees—a topic that we return to in detail below.

As we explained in Chapter 4, the culture and norms in failing organizations are almost always unhealthy and often toxic. "Discouragement and disappointment" (Goodman, 1982, p. 210) abound, and "morale is usually rock-bottom" (Goldstein, 1988, p. 111). For recovery efforts to take root and grow, however, "the existing culture cannot be allowed to constitute a barrier" (Finkin, 1987, p. 48). Thus, reintegration work has a good deal to do with "turn[ing] people around" (Goldstein, 1988, p. 111), with helping "people move beyond assigning blame for problems" (Kanter, 2003, p. 64) and wallowing in a climate of despair: "Unless the basic motivation of the people in the company changes from that of a defeatist attitude . . . , it is doubtful that the company can stabilize its gains and return to healthy growth" (Bibeault, 1982, p. 181). Or, according to Kanter (2003), "all turnaround leaders share the overarching task of restoring confidence through empowerment—replacing denial with dialogue, blame with respect, isolation with collaboration, and helplessness with opportunities for initiative" (p. 67).

Recovery has much to do with "the emergence of new community norms and behaviors" (Austin, 1998, p. 101). Recovery inevitably can be linked to "the corporate climate created by the turnaround leader" (Goldstein, 1988, p. 109). At its core, it is about creating "a whole new approach to life in the company, involving everyone in a new way of approaching his job" (Goodman, 1982, p. 210). Indeed, as Bibeault (1982) observes, "it is very difficult for a company to sustain a turnaround unless it can turn its people around" (p. 181). Turnaround leadership "moves people toward respect" (Kanter, 2003, p. 64). It is about recognizing the talents and special gifts of employees as a "critical first ingredient in establishing a sense of hope and potential for a . . . future" (Crandall, 1995, p. 45). The new culture is characterized by an assumption of competence, a conviction that "the critical information that the organization needs to turn around successfully is . . . possessed by people throughout the organization" (Ashmos & Duchon, 1998, p. 231) and a belief in the importance of people (Crandall, 1995; Kanter, 2003).

An interrogation of the research on successful recovery exposes a shift in how these organizations think about employees, from "managing human resources [to] leveraging human assets" (Shelley & Jones, 1993, p. 76), a focus on building human capital. Successful turnaround organizations are "people-sensitive" (Goldstein, 1988, p. 114) places. And research on these institutions uncovers "an emphasis on 'people' within the firm [as a] key feature of sustained improved performance" (Grinyer, Mayes, & McKiernan, 1988, p. 128). Successful turnaround leaders display the "ability to pull together employees, solidifying relationships, and throw a cloak of support around the organization" (Goldstein, 1988, p. 110). They realize that a failing company "will not prosper in the middle and longer terms unless it motivates its employees" (Bibeault, 1982, p. 181). These women and men are skilled at fostering "relationship-building skills" (Shelley & Jones, 1993, p. 74), of "motivating . . . employees to attain a higher level of performance than they have in the past" (Modiano, 1987, p. 179). Turnaround leaders are effective in providing people "something to get excited about" (Zimmerman, 1991, p. 220). They understand "that employee productivity is an important variable in turnaround" (O'Neill, 1986a, p. 182), and they strive "to get better performance from the people than they themselves sometimes feel they can deliver" (Sloma, 1985, p. 201).

Rallying and Mobilizing People

A turnaround may be initiated by an individual or by a small group, but obviously cannot be accomplished by one or two people: it is necessary to mobilize a large proportion of the staff for the changes that have to be made. Mobilization means getting people to focus on the mission of the organization and the removable obstacles to that mission (Khandwalla, 1983–1984, pp. 22–23).

> One of the strongest themes to emerge from our study was the need to gain the commitment to motivate and to harness the energies of people at all levels within the company purposively. (Grinyer, Mayes, & McKiernan, 1988, p. 144)

Motivating People

The achievement of a sustained recovery requires that the organization be motivated towards this end: it is achievable through the leadership of the chief executive. (Slatter, 1984, p. 148)

The turnaround of a company requires many changes to be made in the way a business is run. These changes can best be accomplished by the people the company already has. In short, you must accept that demoralization has begun; that it can only be modified by gross attitudinal changes; that these can be effected only by strong leadership exhibited through positive communications efforts. To succeed, you must motivate the company's current employees to accept and advance change. (Finkin, 1987, p. 31)

According to turnaround analysts, "the rallying and mobilizing function" (Khandwalla, 1983–1984, p. 13) is a central element of rebuilding the work ethic in a troubled firm, especially given the trauma that accompanies failure and the types of reforms associated with the retrenchment phase of reintegration (Bibeault, 1982; Slatter, 1984). As explained above, a cardinal ingredient here is motivating employees, of "convinc[ing] people to do things that they never intended to do" (Silver, 1992, p. 89) or believed that they were capable of doing. As a general principle, therefore, turnaround artists hold that "a motivation climate must be set" (Ross & Kami, 1973, p. 30). They also maintain that "motivation cannot start until some level of achievement has been reached" (p. 188). Thus, while in the retrenchment phase "management relies on movement rather than motivation" (p. 188), motivation moves front and center during the recovery phase of turnaround—"it takes genuine motivation to sustain progress" (p. 187) in recovery. The underlying premise at the recovery stage of the turnaround is that poor performance is likely the "result of the corporate condition, [thus] indicating the need to motivate rather than terminate" (Goldstein, 1988, p. 80).

Studies of successful organizational recovery expose motivation as the engine to "get the necessary enthusiasm and commitment to make a difficult change" (Grinyer, Mayes, & McKiernan, 1988, p. 127) and to sustain reform (Bibeault, 1982)—to "restore the confidence of the employees that they can succeed in turning the company around" (Finkin, 1987, p. 29). Research has unearthed broad categories of motivation for turnaround firms as well as accompanying action strategies. For example, Bibeault (1982) provides the following three-part taxonomy:

- The motivators of growth and advancement are actuated by reestablishing a climate of success.
- The motivators of responsibility and work itself are actuated through participation.
- The motivators of recognition and a feeling of achievement are largely actuated through written and verbal communication. (pp. 188–189)

Goodman (1982), in turn, helps us see the importance of standards and performance targets. Khandwalla (1983–1984) documents an assortment of motivational mechanisms, including "greater challenge in the job, peer-group pressure, competition for excellence, a sense of participation, operating autonomy coupled with fairly clear responsibility for performance, example setting, and . . . nurturance" (pp. 30–31). Sloma (1985) adds the motivational strategy of team building, and Finkin (1985) describes the importance of inspiring people to contribute ideas and energy and creating a "sense of urgency" (p. 21) for the team. And Zimmerman (1991) touts the motivational value of generating "a genuine appreciation for others" (p. 281) throughout the organization.

Motivation is also about building understanding (Bratton & Knobler, 1998) and knowing others (Crandall, 1995). Arguing that "nothing a chief executive officer can say will speak as loudly as his or her personal involvement" (Musfeldt & Collier, 1993, p. 131), researchers draw connections between leader visibility, commitment, and involvement and motivation (Dewitt, Harrigan, & Newman, 1998; Kramer, 1987; Slater, 1999). Consequently, Bibeault (1982) and Shook (1990) hold that letting employees get to know the leader personally and having the leader in a troubled organization get to know employees is a robust motivational strategy. Obversely, "the tendency of top management to isolate itself from the front-line troops [is] fatal in bad times" (Goldstein, 1988, p. 116).

Building Morale

It is only the manager's personal leadership skills that will improve morale and motivate the organization to meet the longer-term goals (Slatter, 1984, p. 148).

The enthusiasm with which people try to implement any plan, the more likely that the execution will be better, more complete. The greater the enthusiasm (or morale, if you prefer), the more performance will reflect the spirit of the plan, and the less performance will be compliance only to the letter. (Sloma, 1985, p. 188)

Closely related to the task of motivating employees in a troubled firm is the work of building their morale (Khandwalla, 1983–1984). For morale in the ranks to grow, people in the organization "must see strength coming from the top" (Goldstein, 1988, p. 49): "The turnaround leader must believe in the future of the company and clearly and continuously convey that belief" (p. 113). Thus, "the turnaround leader must be a dealer in hope" (Mahoney, cited in Goldstein, 1988, p. 110). Morale increases when leaders build confidence, "a shared belief in the management mission and a growing conviction that the frustrations of the past are on the way out and a new period of success is on the way in" (Goodman, 1982, pp. 108–109). Turnaround leaders restore "people's confidence in one another. . . . They lead a psychological turnaround" (Kanter, 2003, p. 59). Morale deepens as a culture of positivism and a climate of success begin to spread (Grinyer, Mayes, & McKiernan, 1988).

More concretely, morale is enhanced when the negative effects of adverse personnel actions associated with retrenchment are minimized. Strategies for accomplishing this include "maintaining openness as much as possible, using realistic rather than optimistic projections, and assisting employees in seeing the best- and worst-case scenarios" (Weitzel & Jonsson, 1989, p. 104). We also observe here that "fair play in dealing with employees" (Zimmerman, 1991, p. 12), especially being "even-handed in implementing layoff policies" (Sutton, Eisenhardt, & Jucker, 1986, p. 19), contributes to morale (Kramer, 1987). So too does the willingness to address interpersonal conflicts in an equitable manner and to "reduce the tension of competing claims" (Crandall, 1995, p. 116). "Building management from within [also] . . . results in better morale" (Goodman, 1982, pp. 83–84), as does the regular acknowledgment and showcasing of "gains" (Goldstein, 1988, p. 115): "There is no surer boost to morale than tasting group success after failure" (Goodman, 1982, p. 47). And turnaround analysts assert that there is considerable opportunity to garner such successes and strengthen morale when new leadership is at the helm of recovery efforts.

Looking at the issue from a slightly different angle, research reveals that "for employees to end their demoralization, they must be informed about the status of business . . . and matters affecting the firm" (Finkin, 1987, p. 28). Transparency, "openness, frankness, and truthfulness" (p. 41) in the communication network are critical. And finally, in terms of fair play, recognition and appreciation for contributions have been connected to enhanced morale in organizational recovery (Zimmerman, 1991).

Relatedly, morale is associated with what Zimmerman (1991) identifies as "an atmosphere of justice" (p. 190). And there is some evidence to "suggest that successful turnaround companies embrace traditional concepts of morality and fairness" (p. 259).

In situation after situation, evidence suggests that adherence to concepts of basic fairness is as important to a successful turnaround as strategic direction, marketing experience, or other managerial attributes. Though fair play is a very difficult concept to measure, the proxy indicators available on the sample companies in this study suggest that successful turnaround agents are generally perceived as dealing fairly with employees, creditors, suppliers, and customers. The perception of fairness (or lack of it) influences the willingness of organization members to extend the extra effort necessary to mobilize a turnaround. (p. 233)

Scholars are also providing insights about some of the critical aspects of justice in turnaround organizations. One is a commitment on the part of leaders to disproportionately share the pain accompanying turnaround efforts (Goldstein, 1988), in terms of work undertaken, accountability for results, and financial hardships. A second ingredient is the willingness to share success as the organization emerges from the shadows of failure: "Turnaround leaders who are successful over the very long term share center stage and the credit of success with other members of the organization" (Zimmerman, 1991, p. 193).

"Recognition of achievement" (Zimmerman, 1991, p. 187) is also a discernible pattern in the morale mosaic of successful turnarounds. Here the literature underscores the provision by the organization and its leaders of recognition for those who carry the freight on the path to recovery (Rindler, 1987), "the acknowledgment [of] outstanding performance" (Bibeault, 1982, p. 188) and the allotment of "intangible rewards" (Hambrick, 1985, p. 10–23) as well as "incentives and [tangible] rewards for staying with the company through the hard times" (Goldstein, 1988, p. 49). Acknowledgment includes, according to turnaround analysts, the use of "compensation schemes that link rewards to accomplishments" (Kramer, 1987, p. 9; also Shook, 1990) and public ceremonies to reward employees (Armenakis et al., 1995; Bratton & Knobler, 1998; Kramer, 1987), a bundle of activities that fall into the broad category of "job recognition" (Goldstein, 1988, p. 213).

The broad principles here have been delineated by Crandall (1995) in his analysis of turning around small failing churches: "Learn to respect, affirm, encourage, and compliment everyone you can for anything you can" (p. 67) and "applaud areas of change and growth and then challenge the next step in the process" (p. 68). Here we also see the recognition that challenges and morale are connected (Bibeault, 1982; Zimmerman, 1991). "The point of all this is that management must create a culture . . . that both recognizes and rewards employees for their efforts in implementing strategies that produce desired results" (Clausen, 1990, p. 104) in the turnaround organization.

Finally, in terms of morale, it is important to underscore the finding that successful morale-building efforts during recovery rest on a foundation of trust (Austin, 1998) and credibility (Khandwalla, 1983–1984), a "climate of mutual cooperation and trust spanning all levels of the organization" (Contino & Lorusso, 1982, p. 71). As Shook (1998) notes based on his turnaround work: "There is no magic. It boils down to having people trust the company they work for; with trust they will do better work" (p. 208; also Finkin, 1987). "A cogent vision" (Shelley & Jones, 1993, p. 72) in a turnaround must be "built upon a 'trust culture'" (p. 72), and the presence or absence of a trust culture can be traced directly back to the leadership of the turnaround firm (Shook, 1990): "The trustworthiness of the top management team [is] a factor in rallying the troops to put forth the extra efforts needed for a turnaround" (Zimmerman, 1991, p. 184). And trustworthiness at the top has much to do with "concrete deeds and tangible activities" (Austin, 1998, p. 99) that match espoused values, a disposition to shoulder more than a fair share of the burden, and a willingness to "face up successfully and dramatically to [the] crisis" (Khandwalla, 1983–1984, p. 21).

Communicating Openly

The ability to communicate is essential if the [turnaround] leader is to motivate and activate. (Goldstein, 1988, p. 51)

The first task of a turnaround leader is to open channels of communication. (Kanter, 2003, p. 62)

People are at the heart of the majority of the company's problems. They are also at the heart of the solution to these problems. The way you influence people is through good communications. (Finkin, 1987, p. 27)

Systematic and aggressive communication is the third strand of the mobilizing and rallying strand of changing the organizational work ethic (Slatter, 1984). The research literature on organizational recovery paints a picture of communication as it exists in many troubled firms (see also Chapter 4), illustrates the need for and the importance of communication in recovering firms, underscores leadership as a critical variable in making quality communication come to life in turnaround organizations, and reveals important elements of communication in institutions that successfully address decline and failure.

On the first issue, we learn that in failing firms, "most managers are poor communicators and are reluctant to communicate because so much news [is] bad" (Goldstein, 1988, p. 52). We also discover that communication in many troubled organizations leaves a good deal to be desired in other ways as well. Secrecy and "hiding or minimizing negative information" (Finkin, 1987, p. 31) is commonplace. And, as Goldstein (1988) observes, "managers of the troubled company have a natural reluctance to come into contact with those viewed as hostile to the company, which may easily include just about everyone involved in the company" (p. 52).

On the second theme, "need," we know that failing organizations are institutions in turmoil. As such, "vast changes will be required and people's support needed in implementing these changes, rather than opposing them. Long-accepted norms and procedures will disappear. People will disappear. A cultural revolution will occur. Effective employee communication will be needed to accomplish this" (Finkin, 1987, p. 28). The research also confirms that "many turnarounds have failed only because the leader failed to build adequate communication within the company and with . . . customers and suppliers outside" (Goldstein, 1988, p. 51). What the organization's leaders "think is communication overkill will rarely be so in practice. The type of turnaround strategies adopted in a recovery situation and the speed with which they have to be implemented are often so alien . . . that effective communication is more important than ever" (Slatter, 1984, p. 149).

The above line of analysis leads directly to the category of "importance." Information in this bin affirms that "communication is an important part of holding a company together during the difficult period and of motivating people later as the company achieves success" (Bibeault, 1982, p. 198): "Effective employee communication will not solve all of a troubled company's problems, but it will solve a good many of them" (Finkin, 1987, p. 29). In building motivation in a failing company, a first prerequisite then, according to Goodman (1982) and others, "is for leadership to develop and apply communication skills with its people" (Shook, 1990, p. 190). Such open and credible communication is often linked to the emergence of a new organizational work ethic in general and to enhanced motivation and morale specifically (Clausen, 1990; Khandwalla, 1983–1984). Indeed, "honest, open, and frequent communication may be the cornerstone for creating this new corporate climate" (Goldstein, 1988, p. 115).

Consistent with a core theme of this book (see especially Chapter 6), turnaround research features the "centrality of top leadership" in the creation and employment of systems of communication. Or as Dewitt and colleagues (1998) posit, "leadership plays a critical role in keeping employees informed of why change is needed and what changes are required" (p. 30), that is, "the chief executive [in troubled firms] must be the chief communicator" (Slatter, 1984, p. 148). In particular, concerns and rumors "abound in troubled organizations and employees must hear the facts straight from the top" (Goldstein, 1988, p. 111).

Finally, scholarship on recovery throws the spotlight on "characteristics of communication systems" found in successful turnaround organizations. This work reveals that communication in firms on the path to recovery is direct (Kanter, 2003; Taylor, 1982–1983). Personal "face-to-face meetings" (Goldstein, 1988, p. 115) of various forms—individual and small and large groups—trump "paperwork systems" (Taylor, 1982–1983, p. 6). "Top management is highly visible" (Goldstein, 1988, p. 199) in the communication chain. Leaders listen (Goodman, 1982), tell stories (Mirvis, Ayas, & Roth, 2003), negotiate (Goldstein, 1988), and frame meaning (Ford, 1985; Starbuck, Greve, & Hedberg, 1978). Communication is "upward as well as downward" (Finkin, 1987, p. 29). Communication is not constrained by or confined to reporting relationships (Goodman, 1982). It extends to "all types of employees" (Finkin, 1987, p. 42)—"between all levels and among all units" (Kramer, 1987, p. 9). Finally, the communication system is generally well planned and comprehensive (Finkin, 1987). Things are not left to chance (Bratton & Knobler, 1998; Shook, 1990).

Growing People

All participants in the turnaround program must demonstrate close teamwork. (Stewart, 1984, p. 6)

Any strategic vision for a turnaround must therefore involve the concept of teamwork. (Shelley & Jones, 1993, p. 72)

We know from the literature on recovery that success depends on the ability of the organization "to grow its people" (Mirvis, Ayas, & Roth, 2003, p. 19). The research here also helps us see that growing people is comprised of three overlapping dimensions: empowering people, building teams, and training employees.

Empowering People

Participation of organizational members is an important key to any turnaround strategy. (Ashmos & Duchon, 1998, p. 224)

Recovery research affirms that "encourag[ing] employees to participate in the turnaround process" (Goldstein, 1988, p. 116) is an important plank in the task of organizational reintegration, that "participation . . . is of particular importance in times of organizational decline" (Ashmos & Duchon, 1998, p. 234), and that "involvement efforts are often an organizational attempt to reverse decline" (Mohrman & Mohrman, 1983, p. 449). Indeed, it is probably safe to conclude that empowering employees is a requirement for successful recovery (Contino & Lorusso, 1982; Goldston, 1992): "To truly energize the organization, employees must actively participate in the turnaround program" (Goldstein, 1988, p. 116)—"in the end, the only way a CEO can reverse a corporate decline is to change the momentum and empower people" (Kanter, 2003, p. 62). Finkin (1987) corrals this essential point when he reports that "companies in turnaround . . . need employee involvement in the need to make change—change needed to reduce cost and increase the ability of the company to survive" (p. 54). And Hamel and Prahalad (cited in Ashmos & Duchon, 1998) expose the heart of the matter when they assert that "it is not cash that fuels the journey to the future, but the emotional and intellectual energy of every employee" (p. 235).

A full treatment of the rationale and benefits of participative action in organizations is beyond the scope of our charge here. At the same time, it is worth exposing a few of the themes in the general literature that surface when studying organizational recovery. First, participation generates understanding (DeWitt, Harrigan, &

Newman, 1998): "better understanding of why new behaviors are required and why old behaviors are inappropriate" (p. 24). Second, because workers are at the front line, they often "know what the problems are [and they] can be a wealth of information about the true corporate condition" (Goldstein, 1988, p. 35). Third, concomitantly, they often have insights about appropriate solutions for the organization's problems (Mirvis, Ayas, & Roth, 2003; Shook, 1990). Fourth, participation and involvement often lead to ownership of problems (Hambrick, 1985), a critical ingredient in addressing the organization's troubles. Fifth, participation can promote efficiency, that is, "the best way to maximize human resources" (Shook, 1990, p. 87) in a failing firm is to involve employees (Zimmerman, 1991). Finally, and most important, participation is linked to enhanced organizational performance: "Over the long pull, given equal talent, participatively managed companies do better, handle management succession more smoothly, and retain their vitality longer (Goodman, 1982, p. 42).

It is also instructive to surface the key concepts that define participation in the recovery literature, the mechanisms "to channel real and active input from the entire work force into the decision-making arena" (Contino & Lorusso, 1982, p. 67). According to an assortment of scholars, empowerment is one important element (Kanter, 2003; Khandwalla, 1983–1984). Here we see that firms in the recovery phase of turnaround that are poised for success often "educate workers to make decisions rather than follow directions [and] grant authority based on the problems to be solved rather than the organizational hierarchy" (Shelley & Jones, 1993, p. 77). They give people meaningful authority and responsibility and hold them accountable for results (Bratton & Knobler, 1998).

Relatedly, the concepts of inclusion and involvement mark recovery efforts (Contino & Lorusso, 1982; Khandwalla, 1983–1984; Mohrman & Mohrman, 1983). So too do the strategies of decentralization (Kramer, 1987), shared governance (Rosenblatt, Rogers, & Nord, 1993), democracy (Starbuck, Greve, & Hedberg, 1978), and voice (Goodman, 1982; Mirvis, Ayas, & Roth, 2003). Finally, deepening leadership, that is, creating leadership-dense organizations, often helps define participation in recovery firms (Crandall, 1995). It is also important to note that in all cases in successful recovery, participation and its many components are supported by the creation of "new structures" (Taylor, 1982–1983, p. 9).

Building Teams

Teamwork among people [was] crucial for growth and success.
(Mirvis, Ayas, & Roth, 2003, p. 67)

Especially in a turnaround situation where the problems are deep-seated and the company is after a breakthrough into unaccustomed high performance, you need the best in teamwork to get the best in performance from your people. (Goodman, 1982, p. 97)

No corporate turnaround or restructuring is the result of one individual working alone. Success is the result of melding and motivating a team—diverse talents working together with a common purpose to achieve a desired goal. (Clausen, 1990, p. 103)

There is an extensive body of research and development work on the elements, importance, and effects of teams in organizations, especially on building highly effective work teams. It is not our intention to examine that full body of literature here. Rather, our objective is simply to link successful organizational recovery and the development and use of highly effective work teams, to reinforce the significance of this body of work for institutional reintegration, and to highlight elements of the research here that are especially relevant to turnaround situations.

We start with the most generalized conclusion of the turnaround literature in the team-building domain: "Teamwork provide[s] the launching pad for sustainable rejuvenation" (Stopford & Baden-Fuller, 1990, p. 408)—"a well-orchestrated corporate comeback requires a team of trained people" (Goldstein, 1988, p. 57). Because "teamwork is invaluable in a turnaround situation" (Shelley & Jones, 1993, p. 72), for an organization in a spiral of failure to rebound, members of the institution need to become especially effective in working together (Finkin, 1987; Stewart, 1984). We also know that bringing effective teams into existence in troubled enterprises is not a fortuitous event. Rather, as we see below, it is a consequence of team-building training (Mirvis, Ayas, & Roth, 2003) and the presence of effective team-building skills in the top cadre of managers (Goodman, 1982).

Turnaround research confirms that "the creation and coordination of an effective team" (O'Shaughnessy, 1995, p. 5) at the managerial level is a central dimension of organizational recovery (Rindler, 1987). Or, as Zimmerman (1991) observes, "successful turnarounds [have] deep managerial teams" (p. 270). Scholarship here also informs us that these teams are constructed around "clearly defined roles and functions" (Green & Hanson, 1993, p. 189; also Bibeault, 1982; Goodman, 1982) and include only those who are capable of repositioning the enterprise for success (Bratton & Knobler, 1998; Clausen, 1990).

Team building also entails forging functional teams deep in the organization, that is, below the level of top management (Bratton & Knobler, 1998; Shook, 1990). In particular, successful recovery efforts are often distinguished by "cascading teaming" (Mirvis, Ayas, & Roth, 2003, p. 83) in which team building flows downward throughout the organization. Teams in recovery firms often "slice through the organizational chart vertically, diagonally, and horizontally" (Kanter, 2003, p. 66). As we explore below, these teams are trained to demonstrate "the characteristics of good teamwork" (Goodman, 1982, p. 98; Zimmerman, 1991) and the elements of "highly effective teams" (Mirvis, Ayas, & Roth, 2003, p. 95). It is also clear that in organizations on the pathway to reintegration, teamwork is turned in the service of promoting reintegration. Teamwork here leads to "a sense of personal involvement and urgency" (Finkin, 1987, p. 4) in completing work, the creation of an "intentional agenda" (Crandall, 1995, p. 125), a redefinition of relationships and a development of an understanding of the entire enterprise (Mirvis, Ayas, & Roth, 2003), and enhanced productivity (Gerstner, 2002; Stephens, 1988).

Training and Development of People

A troubled organization is usually missing important skills of all types . . . needed for the company to improve its effectiveness in carrying on its business. (Finkin, 1987, p. 46)

Turnarounds progress because the entire organization learns new tasks and how to do old tasks better. (Zimmerman, 1991, p. 80)

There are confirming data in the turnaround research that the pathway to recovery includes a considerable amount of education and development of employees, that in regeneration work "continuing education . . . is the best investment you can make" (Stewart, 1984, p. 203) and should be "the first consideration" (Shelley & Jones, 1993, p 78), and that "the process of turnaround is one of organizational learning" (Zimmerman, 1991, p. 274). This appears to be the case for a number of reasons. On the one hand, training is almost always required to help "build the infrastructure to support team building" (Mirvis, Ayas, & Roth, 2003, p. 84). In addition, studies regularly reveal that employees in failing firms lack the appropriate skills and abilities (Contino & Lorusso, 1982; Finkin, 1985) and that systems for correcting the deficiency are conspicuous by their absence (Umbreit, 1996). Furthermore, the transition at the heart of recovery often "requires extensive training" (Dewitt, Harrigan, & Newman, 1998). As a consequence of these various conditions, the need for new skills is quite high in most failing firms (Stopford & Baden-Fuller, 1990).

Again, without drilling deeply into the massive body of work on training and development, we can report that in failing firms moving toward recovery, continued professional development often highlights three issues. First, there is often a concerted effort to strengthen the skills of individual workers, "programs for individual development" (Mirvis, Ayas, & Roth, 2003, p. 20). Second, as discussed above, learning to support team building and the work of teams is often underscored (Mirvis, Ayas, & Roth, 2003). Finally, learning as an organizational phenomenon is often featured; that is, the skills needed to stimulate organizational learning are often promoted in development work (Short, Palmer, & Stimpert, 1998).

Creating a Productive Culture

In a turnaround, culture is vital. (Rindler, 1987, p. 221)

The pervasive impact of culture on every aspect of the business enterprise makes it a most important factor for sustaining a turnaround process. (Shelley & Jones, 1993, p. 71)

Every troubled company is embroiled in much the same crisis. How management goes about the task of relieving organizational stress by creating a climate for success makes all the difference whether those affiliated with the company begin to pull together or continue to pull the company apart. (Goldstein, 1988, p. 110)

Throughout each of the chapters to this point, we have examined the issue of rebuilding organizational culture in considerable detail. Here we simply highlight a few themes pertaining to culture in turn-around organizations that cut across those chapters. To begin with, and as discernible in the quotes above, in the recovery game changing culture is critical: it "isn't just one aspect of the game—it *is* the game" (Gerstner, 2002, p. 182). For turnarounds to succeed, leaders must "fully understand the cultural dimensions that inhibit or enhance the improvement process" (Shelley & Jones, 1993, p. 70). They must create "a new corporate culture" (Finkin, 1987, p. 4; also Breault, 1993) that becomes embedded in the "operating environment" (p. 4): "The turnaround leader must articulate a new set of values, recruit a managerial staff capable of practicing those values and help employees internalize them" (Rindler, 1987, p 221): "The crux of the problem [is] developing a new . . . culture" (Bratton & Knobler, 1998, p. 244).

We also reinforce a point visible most prominently in Chapters 4 and 5. That is, the problem with the culture in many troubled firms is that it is characterized by an inability or unwillingness of leaders to look at the shifting world objectively and to overhaul the culture to align with new realities (Gerstner, 2002), a not-surprising finding, given the tenacity of existing culture (Goodman, 1982; Zimmerman, 1991) and the fact that it is "the glue that [holds] the company together" (Slater, 1999, p. 87), especially in professional organizations (McDaniel & Walls, 1998): "Tradition makes it difficult to move from an orientation rooted in the past and the present to an orientation grounded in the potential opportunities and responsibilities for the future" (p. 133)—"as the world changes, the rules, guidelines, and customs lose their connections to what the enterprise is all about" (Gerstner, 2002, p. 184).

We resurface a "cultural" conclusion from the research on recovery that should be well ingrained by this point in the narrative; that is, "it [is] no easy matter to turn a company's culture around" (Shook, 1990, p. 186): "The most difficult and slowest change to make is one that involves a change in the corporation's culture" (p. 93). Or, as Gerstner (2002) observes about the successful turn-around at IBM in the 1990s: "The hardest part . . . was neither the technological nor the economic transformations required. It was the changing culture" (p. 177).

We also reintroduce the crosscutting finding that although there are many productive corporate cultures and many pathways to develop culture (Grinyer, Mayes, & McKiernan, 1988), cultures in most successful turnaround organizations underscore two avenues. One underscores changing both "mindsets" and "heartsets" (Mirvis, Ayas, & Roth, 2003, p. 85). The second highlights developing new recipes and scripts that permit the company to reorient itself (Castrogiovanni, Bahga, & Kidwell, 1992; Grinyer & Spender, 1979). Thus the great challenge in re-creating culture is to "reshape the beliefs and recipes of organizational members" (Castrogiovanni, Bahga, & Kidwell, 1992, p. 37).

Finally, we throw the spotlight once again on five interlinked elements from Chapters 4 through 9 that generally characterize the culture of organizations that successfully overcome their declining fortunes. First, these cultures are marked by an entrepreneurial spirit (Slater, 1999). Second, they promote change—"the hallmark of a successful turnaround is a culture where employees embrace change as a challenge to be met rather than as an obstacle to be overcome" (Shelley & Jones, 1993, p. 81)—and feature a "bias for action" (Grinyer, Mayes, & McKiernan, 1988, p. 105) or "an action orientation" (p. 114), what Grinyer and his team describe as "enthusiasm, commitment, determination to succeed, and courage" (p. 105). Third, and relatedly, the culture in a successful turnaround enterprise is characterized by a penchant for challenging the status quo as well as existing organizational recipes (Shook, 1990). Fourth, the DNA of the recultured organization is "excellence" (Slater, 1999, p. 15), a commitment to quality above all else. And finally, cultures in organizations that recover from decline are distinguished by a relentless commitment to continuous improvement (Shook, 1990). "Success involves continuous commitment, effort and relentless hunger for more success" (Grinyer, Mayes, & McKiernan, 1988, p. 129).

DIFFERENTIATED PRODUCTS AND SERVICES

In approaching a turnaround, there are numerous opportunities for improvement in the area of production strategies. (Goodman, 1982, p. 179)

[Where] price competition is not possible, what gives a company the edge is quality. (Grinyer, Mayes, & McKiernan, 1988, p. 125)

Product differentiation is an essential survival attribute well deserving of the attention of top management. (Zimmerman, 1991, p. 132)

The last of the five dimensions of recovery addresses "product-market reorientation" (Slatter, 1984, p. 123) and attends to the strategic work introduced in Chapter 8. This strategic activity is designed to work as a complement to the earlier cost containment moves and needs to be aligned with the changing ideology, structures, and personnel of turnaround organizations analyzed earlier. Innovation is the key construct here (Lohrke & Bedeian, 1998; Shuchman & White, 1995), with energy directed to "changes companies make in products and markets" (Short, Palmer, & Stimpert, 1998, p. 161), to "providing new products/services and/or entry into new markets" (Shook, 1998, p. 270). That is, strategic work in turnarounds "is built around key skills in marketing and production" (O'Shaughnessy, 1995, p. 4; also Ackley, 1989), on "invest[ments] in new markets, new products, new technologies, [and] new methods of operating" (Starbuck, Greve, & Hedberg, 1978, p. 131). The DNA of strategic work is product differentiation—the development of "products with distinguishing features, high reliability, and significant performance, exceptional product quality, and the development of long-term continuity with the markets being served" (Zimmerman, 1991, p. 12).

The research on turnarounds generally confirms the importance of strategic recovery work and product differentiation in troubled firms: "Strategic change is adaptive for firms suffering from performance declines and . . . failure to enact strategic change often explains why some firms are unable to turn around" (Barker & Duhaime, 1997, p. 14). And, as nearly everywhere else in this volume, we are again confronted by the importance of context. For example, Arogyaswamy and associates (1995) and Barker and Duhaime (1997) reveal how variables such as nature of the decline, industry type, leadership, and organizational size interact with strategic recovery moves. We also learn that product analysis is critical to strategic product-oriented work:

In order to win in the competitive marketplace, you have to start with an evaluation of your strengths and weaknesses in relation to the competition. Only then can you devise a program that might enable you to differentiate your company's offerings in terms of cost, product design, quality, and distribution. Decide which of your business segments or product areas are potentially viable. Determine which ones are intrinsically unprofitable. Those must be eliminated. For the potentially viable product segments, decide what strategic changes are needed to make them viable. Understanding must lead to action and include the market and what makes it work. In some cases everything else becomes secondary. (Finkin, 1987, p. 5)

Another lesson is that such analysis is, unfortunately, often underutilized in recovery: "What is surprising is how much effort and energy go into the attempted resurrection of companies in trouble without any serious investigation of the products being offered to the customers" (Zimmerman, 1991, p. 166). One indicator of this is the almost random focus on new product development and product acquisition with little regard for the core work of the organization.

We present our review of the research on product development and strategic change under the two headers of Conservative Entrepreneurship and Commitment to Quality.

Conservative Entrepreneurship

The key to the revival of a sick unit is the formulation of a new strategy that fits the unit's environment. (Khandwalla, 1983–1984, p. 12)

Troubled companies must be particularly cautious to select strategies consistent with the limited resources available and should err on the side of caution. (Goldstein, 1988, p. 102)

Collectively, findings on product differentiation of recovering organizations suggest that failing schools would be wise to pursue what we call a conservative entrepreneurial strategy. It calls, as a starting point, for turnaround organizations headed by chief executive officers who "know how their products work" (Zimmerman, 1991, p. 148) and an "intense focus on the market being served"

(p. 125). It entails innovation or "changes in a firm's domain or portfolio of business" (Barker & Duhaime, 1997, p. 24), to be sure, but innovation of a particular stripe. It means, primarily, improving the products and services at hand and, as a corollary, spending less time "seek[ing] entry into new markets" (Zimmerman, 1991, p. 117), of avoiding what Gerstner (2002) calls "acquisition fever" (p. 221), or more positively, pursuing what Zimmerman (1991) identifies as "market continuity" (p. 15).

> Market continuity can be briefly described as the predisposition of the firm to focus on providing products for one very familiar market before expanding into any new markets or into other new activities. (Zimmerman, 1991, p. 15)

Successful turnaround organizations concentrate on "issues such as product quality . . . and product differentiation . . . unsuccessful firms often on external expansion, acquisition, or financial restructuring" (Zimmerman, 1991, p. 259). The focus is on established, "familiar markets" (Zimmerman, 1991, p. 120).

Relatedly, conservative entrepreneurship necessitates (1) focusing on the organization's core products and services, as noted above, "because expanding weaknesses is a sure ticket to disaster" (Goodman, 1982, p. 145) and (2) avoiding a "focus on acquisition, restructuring, joint ventures, . . . and a variety of other activities not central to producing differentiated products" (Zimmerman, 1991, p. 206). In short, "a period of turnaround may not be the time for major shifts in the product portfolio" (Khandwalla, 1983–1984, p. 28). Rather, attention should be directed to "historical markets" (Zimmerman, 1991, p. 170) and "attention to the business the company [is] in at the time (p. 172)—on "mak[ing] improvements in products being offered to familiar markets" (p. 116). In addition, successful turnaround firms "actively preserve product identifiers, such as names, product colors, advertising, or product attributes that retain continuity with historical markets. Unsuccessful companies frequently change product identifiers" (p. 169).

Staying with this line of analysis, conservative entrepreneurship includes what Dewitt and colleagues (1998) describe as "strategic triage" (p. 25). That is, even within the confines of the core portfolio of services, the spotlight needs to be directed to those selected elements that can produce the most impressive results. Conversely, it entails a constant questioning of whether resources directed to certain products and services might "be put to more profitable use" (Goodman, 1982, p. 145). In particular, strategic triage throws into question the use of "custom-made products or frequent modifications to suit the needs of individual customers" (Slatter, 1984, p. 233). Indeed, this brand of "product-line rationalization" (p. 233) moves the organization to rely more on common delivery platforms (Zimmerman, 1991).

Conservative entrepreneurship also includes an emphasis on what Goldstein (1988) calls "organic growth" (p. 220), that is, growth "evolv[ing] from the strengths of the organization" (p. 220), and a movement away from "strategic drift" (Zimmerman, 1991, p. 162). This, according to Reisner (2002), necessitates "connect[ing] change initiatives to [the] core business" (p. 52). It also underscores a concept we examined in detail earlier—getting close to the customer or creating a "customer-first mentality" (Grinyer, Mayes, & McKiernan, 1988, p. 89). Finally, conservative entrepreneurship entails "concentrating on gradual incremental improvements" (Zimmerman, 1991, p. 163) rather than undertaking "significant and abrupt changes in market position" (p. 163).

Commitment to Quality

Successful firms put greater emphasis on product quality. Unsuccessful firms often neglected quality issues. (Zimmerman, 1991, p. 258)

The second dimension of product differentiation highlights the ability of successful turnarounds to generate and maintain a relentless commitment to quality, that is, the ability of these organizations to maintain a relentless focus on quality in a variety of places across the enterprise. We have already examined issues of quality in some detail in earlier chapters. Here we simply reinforce that analysis and add clarifying notes that show that in successful turnarounds, there is "a dramatic increase in levels of productivity and quality" (Taylor, 1982–1983, p. 8). Zimmerman (1991) puts his finger on the issue here when he observes that in organizations that successfully rebound from decline, "product quality is actively managed and constantly improved" (p. 15). There is, as Shook (1990) affirms, a "best-in-class philosophy" (p. 155) in play in these recovery firms. Indeed, "turnaround managers who are successful attend to quality problems with vigor and dispatch" (Zimmerman, 1991, p. 145). In unsuccessful turnaround situations, on the other hand, product quality is often either neglected altogether or oriented to cosmetic features rather than in-depth quality" (p. 147).

Successful turnaround organizations see everything through the lens of return on investment (Goodman, 1982). They set aggressive performance targets (Mirvis, Ayas, & Roth, 2003). They are adept at using world-class benchmarks to assess quality (Sumerin, 1993). Successful turnarounds often rely on reverse engineering to arrive at quality standards (Shook, 1990). They are also more likely to "invest in technology compared to nonturnarounds" (Arogyaswamy & Yasai-Ardekani, 1997, p. 9). And they use the research and development money primarily to improve existing products (Hegde, 1982) and enhance "product design" (Grinyer, Mayes, & McKiernan, 1988, p. 87).

PART V

Understanding Turnarounds in Schools

Across the states and districts, the following elements, in varied combinations, are most frequently associated with corrective action and school redesign: school improvement grants, professional development, new instructional materials, programmatic prescriptions (e.g., pacing plans, structured reading and math programs), new or extension of existing services (e.g., summer school, extended day, after school), on-site instructional specialists, evaluations or audits, intervention teams or individual change agents, bureaucratic pressures (e.g., reassignment of teachers, principals, external monitors, increased oversight), market pressures (e.g., vouchers, school choice, student reassignment, magnet schools), school reorganizations or reconstitutions, teacher recruitment incentives, teacher quality policies, school construction and repair programs, and changes of governance and authority (e.g., special districts, educational management organizations, charters, school takeover, district takeover). (Mintrop & Trujillo, 2005, pp. 3–4)

Assessing the roles of strong interventions for failing schools is quite complicated, even in the narrow sense, because the combination of intended and unintended consequences is difficult to sort out. (Fullan, 2005, p. 174)

CHAPTER TEN

Turning Around Failing Schools

The Landscape

Turning around a school is a complex process in which clear cause-effect relationships are difficult to isolate, but the recent interest has generated some useful research and thoughtful analysis. (Lashway, 2004, p. 25)

O̶ur investigation thus far has focused on turnaround writ large. In this chapter, we apply our investigatory tools to failure and turnaround in schools.

The concept of troubled schools is not new in American public education, but with the advent of and increase in high-stakes testing, the identification of failure and turnaround is growing more prominent in public education. The pressure emanating from failure generates turnaround efforts of various kinds and intensities—implemented and enforced at different levels. In this chapter, we examine these forces in some detail. We begin our analysis by setting the stage— with the development of and understanding of failing schools and education turnaround efforts. Then we examine the causes of school failure. Once we identify why schools fail, we consider various ways to view turnaround efforts—by type, level, and intensity. In Chapter 11, the evidence on turnaround strategies and overarching lessons is provided.

SETTING THE STAGE

> *While the research is clear on what an effective school should look like, there is considerably less research consensus on the process by which a low-performing school becomes high performing. In fact, research on process is only now beginning to appear in any quantity.* (U.S. Department of Education, 2001, p. 29)

We begin this chapter on turning around failing schools by discussing the key terms—failing schools and turnaround—as they have come to be understood in the education sector. To do so, we focus on three aspects of the education literature: understanding failing schools, understanding turnaround, and identifying turnaround schools.

Understanding Failing Schools

Four important themes emerge from the failing school literature that aid (or hinder) understanding school failure. Three themes—newness of the term, interchangeable terms, and undefined parameters—address directly the concept of failing schools, while the last theme—lack of research—deals with the story of the failing schools concept.

Newness of the Term

The term "failing school" appears to be a relatively new one, surfacing in the 1990s as the accountability movement began to take root. With schools now being graded based on student performance, the term "failing school" appears to be gaining prevalence as policymakers and researchers link student failure to school failure. Now that policies are designed to hold schools accountable for student achievement, the concept of school failure will likely become more prevalent.

Interchangeable Terms

Failing schools are "often characterized as dysfunctional or unstable" (Housman & Martinez, 2001, p. 2), but "precise definitions remain elusive" (Lashway, 2004, p. 25), as "each accountability system has created its own nomenclature" (Mintrop, 2003, p. 2).

Failing is used almost interchangeably with other terms that range from euphemistic substitutes to graphic descriptors, for example, needing help (Archer, 2006), in need of improvement (Mazzeo & Berman, 2003; Popham, 2004), needing improvement (U.S. Department of Education, 2001), underperforming (Bowles, Churchhill, Effrat, & McDermott, 2002), low-performing (Cibulka, 2003; Mintrop & Trujillo, 2005; U.S. Department of Education, 2001; Wolk, 1998), schools in decline (Mintrop, 2003), ineffective schools (Nicolaidou & Ainscow, 2005), troubled schools (Malen & Rice, 2004), corrective action schools (Mazzeo & Berman, 2003), special intervention schools (Wang & Manning, 2000), reconstitution-eligible schools (Mintrop, 2003), educational bankruptcy (Cibulka, 2003), and academic bankruptcy (Cibulka, 2003; Mazzeo & Berman, 2003; McRobbie, 1998; Wong & Shen, 2003).

Fuzziness: Undefined Parameters

Such a range of possible failing school terms "raises the question of whether failing schools are categorically different than bad schools that are not yet failing" (Spreng, 2005, p. 22). The literature indicates that this question is not definitively answered and that the labeling of a school is inexact. The criteria for identifying a failing school vary "considerably from state to state" (U.S. Department of Education, 2001, p. 4). Even differences in assessment cutoff scores vary considerably across states (Duffy, 2001). Ultimately, "where the line is drawn between schools that are deemed failing and those that are not is somewhat arbitrary" (Wolk, 1998, p. 4).

Lack of Research

Though "teachers, principals, and parents . . . can easily name the schools to avoid" (Lashway, 2004, p. 25), "there is little research available that looks closely at failing schools" (Nicolaidou & Ainscow, 2005, p. 230). Perhaps such limitations in research exist in part because of a lack of concreteness about what a failing school actually is. However, the quantification of school performance based on student achievement and the use of high-stakes testing found in state reforms and NCLB appear to be focusing failing school inquiry. For example, schools in the state of Florida receive letter grades from A to F based on assessment student achievement, and a school that receives an F is labeled as failing. The current failure specifications provided by various state and national policies seems likely to further failing school research.

Understanding Turnaround

The process of change requires sustained commitment and collaboration across community and governance structures. Further, the transformational process of turning around low-performing schools requires that leaders and stakeholders acknowledge and proactively address the context and complex set of factors influencing schools and communities. Organizing around a shared vision for coherence and deeper connectivity among educators, students, and families lays the foundation for the journey. (Housman & Martinez, 2001, p. 10)

Turnaround in education is a new concept and one that is not especially well defined. At the same time, with the rise of high-stakes accountability and subsequent increase in the number of schools deemed failing, turnaround efforts and accounts of these endeavors grow. Turnaround literature often mentions how unusually effective schools succeed despite being burdened, like failing schools, with limited resources and high levels of poverty; their successes have often been trumpeted for emulation by failing schools. However, the turnaround literature has recently begun to throw into question effective schools as good turnaround models, since "the wide range of attributes that characterize unusually effective schools suggests that turning a 'failing' school into an effective one is a complicated task, under the best of circumstances" (Arsen, Bell, & Plank, 2003, p. 3): "We know more about the characteristics of high-performing schools than about the process of transforming low-performing schools" (U.S. Department of Education, 2001, p. 6): "The process through which previously ineffective schools become effective remains mysterious" (Arsen, Bell, & Plank, 2003, p. 3), and "research on the process of turning a low-performing school into an effective school is much less plentiful and more difficult to interpret" (U.S. Department of Education, 2001, p. 27).

For some time now, "there have been schools that have failed to provide their students with the skills they need to become active and productive members of society" (Hassel & Steiner, 2003, p. 1). The idea behind intervening in these schools "is to transform [them] from failure to success" (Brady, 2003, p. 8), an idea that rests "on the heroic assumption that the fundamentals of a school's culture and practice can be changed via external pressure, professional development or new leadership" (Hassel & Steiner, 2003, p. 2). In Kowal and Hassel's view (2005), "in public schools, a successful turnaround produces a dramatic increase in student achievement in a limited amount of time" (p. 5). More comprehensively, according to Brady (2003), turnaround efforts to date have been based on the following five beliefs that

- All schools can succeed
- Some elements are missing and inhibiting school success
- The intervening body can provide what the school is missing
- School leadership and/or professionals lack the necessary skills to achieve success; and, to a lesser degree
- School administrators and staff lack the will to improve (pp. 8–9)

To be sure, "focusing on performance failures raises a host of complex issues . . . [like] what should be the nature of the intervention?" (Cibulka, 2003, p. 250), as "chronically low-performing schools . . . usually cannot engage in and sustain improvement without support from local and state infrastructures" (Housman & Martinez, 2001, p. 2): "There is no reason to believe that most 'failing' schools have the knowledge or capacity to pull themselves up by their bootstraps, even when faced with state sanctions" (Arsen, Bell, & Plank, 2003, p. 3). Perhaps most problematic, states currently lack the knowledge and resources to turn around failing schools (U.S. Department of Education, 2001), and determining responsibility for turning around a school and implementing the turnaround remain unclear.

As "researchers, analysts, and practitioners have . . . begun to study various strategies for fixing failing schools" (Wolk, 1998, p. 2), we have learned that "surprisingly little is known about what kinds of interventions are most likely to turn faltering schools into successful education institutions" (Brady, 2003, p. iii). At the same time, we know that "these efforts generally have the goals of (a) improving students' academic outcomes; and (b) encouraging high-quality, standards-based classroom instruction aimed at developing higher-order performances and cognitive skills" (Borman et al., 2000, p. 1). Similarly, the U.S. Department of Education's "initiative to turn around low-performing schools is to mobilize resources to improve the quality of school leadership and the teaching force and help low-performing schools implement coordinated, research-based reforms to improve student achievement" (p. 8). Even though "there are enough examples of failing schools being transformed into effective schools to prove that it can be done" (Wolk, 1998, p. 6), "there are no quick fixes for low-performing schools" (p. 7). We return to turnaround strategies below.

Identifying Turnaround Schools

At its simplest, a failing-school strategy decides how "failure" is to be defined and measured, and how the causes of failure are to be identified and corrected. The operating premise is that the worst schools will be identified, a plan for improvement will be adopted and pursued until the school improves, and the district or state will provide substantial assistance toward that end. (Wolk, 1998, p. 3)

Though some systems develop numerous indicators to identify failure and turnaround, generally two classes of measures—standardized test performance and other indicators—are used to identify turnaround schools.

Standardized Test Performance

Though student achievement as measured by state-mandated tests is the principal gauge in determining failing schools as well as turnaround success, efforts to turn around schools for "reasons of students' failure to achieve" (McRobbie, 1998, p. 2) is a fairly new development. Generally, "schools are targeted for [turnaround intervention] based on low test scores" (Adcock & Winkler, 1999, p. 1) stemming from "prolonged dismal performance" (Green & Carl, 2000, p. 58). More specifically, in their study of school reconstitution, Adcock and Winkler (1999) state that "the primary selection criteria for failing school status was [sic] low and declining performance in State mandated tests" (p. 3). Similarly, the Maryland district studied by Malen, Croninger, Remond, and Muncey (1999) established criteria that included "low test scores" and "uneven performance on state-mandated tests" (p. 5). Mac Iver, Ruby, Balfanz, and Byrnes (2003) report that "[Cooke Middle School] was flagged for showing an overall drop in students' test scores and for having an increasing proportion of students who were scoring below the Basic level of performance" (p. 260).

States often employ "two basic approaches to identifying schools for assistance: some focus on their weakest schools, while others identify a larger group of schools that fall below performance levels or miss growth targets" (Mazzeo & Berman, 2003, p. 8). Both choices are predicated on the failing schools' ability to turn around "their performance on indicators such as standardized test scores in specific subject areas and [close] achievement gaps within and across subsets of the student population" (Malen & Rice, 2004, p. 632). Such "ranking systems generally have three or more categories, with at least one category clearly identified for unacceptable or low performance" (Rudo, 2001, p. 1).

Other Indicators

When identifying failing schools to turn around, test data are a "central part of information-gathering" (Hassel & Steiner, 2003, p. 7), though probably not sufficient. For example, the Chicago Public Schools have added "increasing the high school graduation rate, . . . decreasing the dropout rate, and decreasing the number of schools on the (academic) watch list" (Hess, 2003, p. 301) as school- and district-level turnaround goals. Green and Carl (2000) list suspensions, expulsions, special educational placement, dropout rates, graduation rates, and teacher absenteeism as other indicators contributing to outside intervention. In the district Malen and her team (1999) studied, inadequate attendance, absentee and suspension rates, poverty indicators, diversity factors, and the availability of grant monies at the sites were listed as turnaround criteria. Green and Carl (2000) also point out that turnaround efforts occur with schools suffering from financial mismanagement and bureaucratic waste.

CAUSES OF FAILING SCHOOLS

In some schools, expectations of students are low, teachers and parents are frustrated, and academic performance is poor. Many problems, including poverty, limited resources, unqualified teachers, and unsafe learning environments, contribute to frustration, disillusionment, and discouragingly low levels of student achievement in such schools. (U.S. Department of Education, 2001, p. 7)

But it is what goes on inside these institutions that creates a tenacious culture of failure. There are no goals, no sense of mission, and little positive leadership. The schools are usually mismanaged, and use their resources inefficiently and unwisely. They are usually larger than average, with larger classes, and teachers know little about their students. Many of the teachers are inexperienced first-year novices who are ill-prepared for the challenge confronting them. Some will not finish the year, and as many as half of them will leave the school after only one year. Those who return usually transfer out as soon as seniority permits; those who stay, more often than not, do not know how to reach children who arrive in class unready to learn and often wounded. Some of these teachers simply go through the motions, counting the days to retirement. Some are true professionals who strive heroically to help their students learn. Parents are missing partners. (Wolk, 1998, p.1)

As is the case with organizational decline in other sectors (see Chapter 3), school failure stems from both external and internal causes, but seldom does a school fail solely due to either external difficulties or internal dysfunction. On one hand, the literature often focuses on the negative impact that external causes, such as community conditions, have on schools. For example, when Mintrop and MacLellan (2002) reviewed failing schools' school improvement plans, they found that "about 70% of all factors of decline mentioned in the 46 plans could be attributed to external factors" (p. 283). However, internal causes like the defeatist attitude shared by the community and the school staff, as noted by Picucci, Brownson, Kahlert, and Sobel (2002), also fuel decline (Goldstein, Kelemen, & Koski, 1998; Wolk, 1998). Below we review both sets of causes.

External Causes

Obstacles and challenges, such as high student mobility rates, an influx of non-English-speaking students, inadequate funding, . . .

neighborhood crime, or lack of social services in the community,
also must be taken into account. (American Federation of Teachers,
1999, p. 6)

The most prominent external causes contributing to school failure are urban setting, minority population, and low socioeconomic
status, although it is clear from the literature that these concepts are
highly correlated. Phenix, Siegel, Zaltsman, and Fruchter (2005) note
that "grim correlations among race, poverty and student achievement
. . . characterize most urban districts" and "academic performance
[is] especially poor and particularly highly correlated with indicators
of race and poverty" (p. 2). More specifically, failing schools "are
usually found in the poorest neighborhoods, where children are
mostly black and Hispanic or immigrants who are not proficient in
English" (Wolk, 1998, p. 1). For example, in a study of interventions
by Borman and his colleagues (2000), "all nine schools were located
in urban areas and served a majority population of students eligible
for the federal free or reduced-price lunch program" (p. 2). Students
enrolled in failing schools are "almost invariably poor and minority
children" (McRobbie, 1998, p. 2). The "true roots of the urban school
crisis lie much deeper [, however]—in poverty, family dysfunction,
urban abandonment, institutionalized racism, and the 'curse of low
expectations'" (Green & Carl, 2000, p. 63).

Urban Setting

Failing schools are most often located in urban and rural areas
(Hassel & Steiner, 2003), and the preponderance of these institutions are located in our central cities: "These schools are not ran-
domly or evenly distributed across the states, but in many instances
are clustered in districts that traditionally serve poor and disadvantaged minority populations" (Mintrop, 2003, p. 2). "Every big city
district has too many low-performing, persistently failing schools"
(Wolk, 1998, p. 1), and the "failure of local school districts [occurs]
particularly in urban areas" (Forster, 1997, p. 1). For example, as
noted above, in their research on low-performing schools, Borman
and his colleagues (2000) found most of the schools were located in
urban communities. Furthermore, in their study of Maryland, Mintrop
and MacLellan (2002) discovered that the "overwhelming majority,
five-sixths [of failing schools], were located in the state's largest
city" (p. 280).

Minority Status

Failing schools serve a disproportionate number of minority students (U.S. Department of Education, 2001) and "as a rule, have had high concentrations of poor and non-white students, especially African-American males" (Green & Carl, 2000, p. 57). Malen and Rice (2004) found in their work that the student bodies of failing schools were largely African American (65% to 95%). Mintrop and MacLellan (2002) reported similar findings, with over 80% African American enrollment in failing Maryland schools. In addition, Hassel and Steiner (2003) document an African American enroll-ment of 96% in their study of a failing elementary school. Immigrant groups and other minorities are also likely to attend failing schools. In the Malen and Rice (2004) research, "first-generation Spanish-speaking, Asian, African, and Caribbean students, along with a small percentage of Euro-American students, [make] up the remainder [%] of the student population" (p. 642). All nine schools in Borman and his colleagues' (2000) research on low-performing schools enrolled a predominantly minority student body.

Low Socioeconomic Status

Corallo and McDonald (2001) affirm that failing schools "are located in impoverished communities" (p. 3), which is consistent with a U.S. Department of Education (2001) report that concluded that failing schools are likely "to be located in communities with sig-nificant concentrations of poverty" (p. 4). The "presence of concen-trated poverty" (Picucci et al., 2002, p. 31) is a prevalent cause of failing schools. Borman and his colleagues (2000) note that failing Title I schools often exist within "challenging, high-poverty con-texts" (p. 1). Failing schools "serve disproportionately poor . . . students" (p. 1), which is "one major reason school failure is a con-cern [, as] it tends to disproportionately affect economically disad-vantaged children" (Spreng, 2005, p. 25). An American Federation of Teachers (1999) report calls this a "vicious cycle of poverty and failure" (p. 4). In research on turnaround middle schools, Picucci and associates (2002) reported that "all seven schools served—and still serve—economically depressed areas" (p. 32). Research indi-cates that while at least 50% of students qualify for free or reduced meals in most failing schools, it is not uncommon for these schools to enroll a student body in which 80% to 100% of students qualify for free or reduced meals (Mac Iver et al., 2003; Malen & Rice, 2004; Mintrop & MacLellan, 2002; Picucci et al., 2002; Wang & Manning, 2000). According to McColskey and Monrad (2004), these schools generally face two major challenges: "(1) they are often located in communities that have few economic resources and (2) the students who attend them come to school beset by problems associated with poverty that require significant services" (p. 6).

Lack of Prerequisite Knowledge

Students attending failing schools appear to be less likely than their peers to begin school ready to learn, as "American society still sees many of its children enter school ill-prepared to benefit from education" (Hart & Risley, 1995, p. 2). For example, in Hart and Risley's (1995) study of 42 American families in varied socioeconomic clusters, welfare parents spoke to their infant children (9 to 36 months old) significantly less than working-class and professional parents spoke to theirs. Furthermore, "in the welfare families, the utterances addressed to the children were both fewer in quantity and somewhat less rich in nouns, modifiers, verbs, past tense verbs, and clauses" (p. 125). In a similar vein, it is of little surprise that "children of poor families are at greater risk of literacy failure" (Snow, Barnes, Chandler, Goodman, & Hemphill, 1991, p. 2). Poor families are more likely to face stresses such as unemployment, marital discord and divorce, alcoholism, and so on, which can result in the lowering of self-worth, increasing the odds of psychiatric disorders, and increasing the chances of conduct disorders within children (Snow et al., 1991). Children in such circumstances enter school at a disadvantage.

Other External Causes

Other external explanations of school failure consistent with the themes noted above are also mentioned in the literature. The impoverished communities in which youngsters at failing schools often live "make it difficult for students to come to school prepared to learn" (Corallo & McDonald, 2001, p. 3). Such "social deprivation" (Willmott, 1999, p. 10) and "associated problems" (U.S. Department of Education, 2001, p. 4) lead to "high levels of violence and disruption" (American Federation of Teachers, 1999, p. 5), including gang conflicts, drug dealing, and prostitution (Mac Iver et al., 2003).

Failing schools have "a history of low student performance; chaotic and, in some instances, unsafe environments; and poor reputations" (Picucci et al., 2002, p. vii). Such "an environment . . . destabilizes home life, undermines support, and creates despair" (Lashway, 2004, p. 25), and these outside affairs undoubtedly make schooling more difficult (Brady, 2003). A student population that is in constant flux, due to either student mobility (Malen & Rice, 2004; McColskey & Monrad, 2004) or absenteeism caused by societal problems, is also presented as an explanation of school failure. For example, "in urban school systems, despite compulsory attendance laws, it is not uncommon for as many as a third of the high-school students enrolled to be absent on any given day" (Lipsky & Gartner, 1989, p. 152).

Internal Causes

The cause of this [school] failure is not considered to be some environmental or external force, but rather failure is caused by internal/organizational factors. . . . Such failure is intractable because it is a part of the organizational culture—the assumptions, shared beliefs, meanings and values of an organization. (Goldstein, Kelemen, & Koski, 1998, p. 4)

The internal forces that contribute to or represent failing schools are, as is the case with external causes, difficult to disentangle. Furthermore, internal explanations are difficult to extricate from external causes, as external rationales and internal conditions form combinations that are often toxic to school organizations. Nonetheless, identifying and understanding the internal reasons that schools fail is crucial to a turnaround effort. The following internal causes that promote an organizational culture of failure combine to produce an environment of distrust and demoralization: poor teacher quality, high teacher turnover, ineffective leadership, inadequate resources, and low morale.

Poor Teacher Quality

Teacher shortages; inadequate resources to compete with wealthier school districts for qualified teachers; teacher transfer policies that allow experienced teachers to leave impoverished

schools for more attractive teaching assignments; rigid, undif-
ferentiated pay schedules that inhibit recruiting teachers in crit-
ical shortage areas such as math, science, and special education
. . . [—]many of these inadequacies are deeply embedded in the
policies and practices of school systems. (Cibulka, 2003, p. 265)

Poor or inadequate teaching is the most cited internal cause of school failure in the literature. This is not always an indictment of teachers serving in failing schools, as some "have the potential to be great teachers given the right support" (Housman & Martinez, 2001, p. 6). However, "most teachers are being asked to do what they have not been able to do before, and in a context for which they have not been adequately prepared" (p. 6). Factors that contribute to poor-quality teaching include limited skills and knowledge, inexperience, and teaching out of specialty.

Limited Skills and Knowledge

"Limitations in teachers' skills and knowledge" (Mintrop & MacLellan, 2002, p. 283) are often evident in failing schools. Teachers there are often inadequately prepared for classroom teaching (Ediger, 2004; U.S. Department of Education, 2001) and are often "lower-skilled" (Mintrop & Trujillo, 2005, p. 18). Failing schools "dispropor-tionately serve economically poor students [and] tend to have the least qualified teachers" (Cibulka, 2003, p. 264). Furthermore, "schools most in need of skilled teachers are least likely to get them" (Goldstein, Kelemen, & Koski, 1998, p. 19). Therefore, teachers in failing schools are likely to "lack expertise in literacy, math, or more specialized subject areas" (Mazzeo & Berman, 2003, p. 22). As a result, youngsters "who often need the most help from the best teachers . . . are the ones most likely to be in classrooms with teachers who are less fully quali-fied" (U.S. Department of Education, 2001, p. 48), leading to "a high proportion of unsatisfactory teaching" (Willmott, 1999, p. 5). For example, one principal in the Borman and his colleagues (2000) study of low-performing schools reported filling eight vacancies in her first two years at the school with "long-term substitutes who were not pro-fessionally trained, certified teachers" (p. 12), serving notice that "state certification hasn't sufficed in the poorest schools" (Lenz, 2002, p. 84). Another school in the Borman and colleagues study (2000) employed 10 teachers with emergency credentials.

In addition, teachers in failing schools usually "have not been trained and supported to meet the needs of low-income children" (Lenz, 2002, p. 84). Furthermore, "only a handful [of colleges and universities] prepare beginning educators or assist veteran educators to teach in low-performing schools" (Mazzeo & Berman, 2003, p. 23), which is especially troubling, considering, as noted above, that "new teachers are more likely to be assigned to low-performing schools" (p. 23). For example, in the U.S. Department of Education (2001) report, in one failing school "teachers often felt overwhelmed and ill equipped to deal with their students' ESL needs" (p. 35). In another study, one teacher recalls having only one graduate class addressing multicultural or diverse students, and she reports not getting "any help with transferring it to the classroom" (Garcia & Guerra, 2004, p. 157).

Inexperience

Though students in failing schools most need sophisticated teaching practices, "these schools have the hardest time attracting qualified, experienced teachers" (McRobbie, 1998, p. 11). Instead, students in failing schools are much more likely than students not in failing schools to be taught by inexperienced teachers (Goldstein, Kelemen, & Koski, 1998; Lashway, 2004; Mintrop & Trujillo, 2005; U.S. Department of Education, 2001). Borman and his team (2000) note that one school in their study of low-performing schools "struggled to attract veteran teachers" (p. 22), while a principal of another school expressed that "she had a good faculty, [but] many of the teachers were inexperienced and in need of a great deal of support" (p. 28). Furthermore, a coordinator at a third school "felt that the teachers were inexperienced and not very good at using 'teacher judgment' or at 'thinking on their feet'" (p. 45).

Teaching Out of Specialty

Teachers in failing schools are also more likely to teach classes outside of their subject area specialties (Lashway, 2004). Many failing school teachers "have been assigned to teach courses for which they have no specialized training" (Mac Iver et al., 2003, p. 268) or given responsibilities that "are not always appropriate and in some cases do not match their expertise" (Willmott, 1999, p. 4). Beyond the curriculum, teachers in failing schools are also assigned to teach grade levels for which they have not been adequately prepared. For example, Mac Iver and his colleagues (2003) researched a failing middle school that hired numerous teachers certified for elementary school and had "not been trained specifically in middle grades content, curriculum and instruction" (p. 268).

High Teacher Turnover

The stresses of working in failing schools (Corallo & McDonald, 2001; Watts, 2000) cause such schools to "often suffer from extremely high rates of faculty turnover" (American Federation of Teachers, 1999, p. 8). In addition, Mac Iver and his associates (2003) report that failing schools have "difficulty in attracting and retaining teachers" (p. 261). Furthermore, Mazzeo and Berman (2003) suggest that "unsafe climates, poor attendance, low achievement, rundown facilities, and material scarcity also make it difficult for such schools to attract and retain good teachers qualified to teach at high levels in core subject areas" (p. 10).

Such "high faculty turn-over rates" (Malen, Croninger, Muncey, & Redmond-Jones, 2002, p. 119; also U.S. Department of Education, 2001) are common in failing schools. "Continual influx of new teachers" (Picucci et al., 2002, p. 33) in failing schools is common. Indeed, Mazzeo and Berman (2003) document that such schools "often face a labor force in which between 15 percent and 25 percent of their teachers turn over during a single school year" (p. 22). In their study, Borman and his colleagues (2000) unearthed teacher turnover rates of 75% and 80%. In a Maryland study, teachers felt as though their school was "a sinking ship" (Mintrop, 2003, p. 9), and highly motivated teacher leaders were as likely to leave the school as were lesser motivated teachers. In a similar vein, teachers who are effective in troubled schools are highly valued and are "often recruited to settings where they believe the conditions are more conducive for their success" (Mazzeo & Berman, 2003, p. 22), thus limiting investments "to improve the knowledge and skill of teachers . . . in these schools" (p. 22). Furthermore, such high teacher turnover, as Wang and Manning (2000) reveal, can leave a failing school "with an insufficient number of teachers" (p. 7).

Ineffective Leadership

According to Borman and his team (2000), success and failure depend on the leadership and culture of a school. As such, as is the case in other types of organizations, ineffective leadership is often reported as an essential internal cause of failure in schools (Mintrop & MacLellan, 2002; Watts, 2000). Indeed, like unsatisfactory teaching, ineffective leadership is one of the most consistent features of failing schools (Nicolaidou & Ainscow, 2005). Ineffective stewardship is often a product of inadequate training to meet the needs of low-income children (Lenz, 2002), a lack of leadership abilities (Ediger, 2004), or "timid leadership" (Lashway, 2004, p. 25).

Brady (2003) posits two assumptions about ineffective school leadership in failing schools: the leaders "lack the requisite skills to achieve success" and/or lack "the will to improve" (p. 9). Mazzeo and Berman (2003) make a similar observation in noting that few failing school principals "have the knowledge and skills needed to lead instructional improvement and develop better teachers" (p. 22). And Archer (2006), touching on the timidness issue, reported that North Carolina Judge Howard Manning recently ruled that unless failing schools are turned around quickly, principals will be fired. In a letter to the state superintendent, Manning warned, "There is simply no excuse today for a principal or superintendent to sit still and watch the world go by because they are either too lazy or too set in their ways to change" (p. 40).

High administrative turnover is also a common element of failing schools (Mintrop & Trujillo, 2005). For example, in their six-school study of low-performing schools, Wang and Manning (2000) reported two new principals and a new assistant principal by the second year of the study. High administrative turnover is hardly surprising, considering "principals under pressure of accountability often act as conduits of pressure, making for unsupportive working relationships between teachers and administration" (Mintrop & Trujillo, 2005, p. 18).

Inadequate Resources

Because, as we noted above, failing schools are generally in impoverished areas, resources in these schools are often stretched (Corallo & McDonald, 2001) and schools "typically lack the education resources that matter the most" (U.S. Department of Education, 2001, p. 4). Educators in these institutions often find the resources necessary for success to be conspicuous by their absence (Spreng, 2005; U.S. Department of Education, 2001). "Outdated, unattractive textbooks" and a "lack of being up to date on computer services" are just two examples (Ediger, 2004, p. 170). In Malen and Rice's (2004) research on school capacity, teachers maintained that they had "limited, often outdated or otherwise inadequate instructional materials, equipment, and supplies" (p. 642). In a reconstituting school studied by Borman and his colleagues (2000), no supplies and few textbooks and materials were available, as former teachers took them when they departed. In the same study, the authors illustrate how another school "had not [been] provided materials in a timely manner and funds were not provided for supplies" (p. 36).

Low Morale

Insufficient training, teacher turnover, weak leadership, and inadequate supplies and facilities, compounded by the external forces fueling school failure, often produce such low morale that staff feel as though "even the best teachers [cannot] succeed" (Picucci et al., 2002, p. 32). "Expectations of students are low" (U.S. Department of Education, 2001, p. 7), "staff [feel] that they [cannot] overlook the presence of poverty in their schools (Picucci et al., 2002, p. 32), and "educators are unwilling to assume responsibility for students' low achievement and failure" (Garcia & Guerra, 2004, p. 150), refusing to examine "the links between school practices and student outcomes" (p. 151). Failing schools lack "internal accountability on anything but the most basic expectations [and] show little or no evidence of consistent expectations about the quality of instruction or student performance" (Mazzeo & Berman, 2003, p. 10). Sense of ownership, especially within the school, is further diminished because of high teacher and administrator turnover (Mintrop & MacLellan, 2002). Furthermore, oftentimes "adults . . . assign responsibility for low student performance to families and communities rather than to themselves" (p. 10) as well as "project their frustration, failure and tedium onto students, while remaining complacent" (Nicolaidou & Ainscow, 2005, p. 230). Often, teachers "believe that the students and the families are at fault because, from their perspective, 'these children' enter school without the necessary prerequisite knowledge and skills and that so-called uncaring parents neither value nor support their child's education" (Garcia & Guerra, 2004, p. 151). At the same time, educators "who express low expectations for their students often feel demoralized by the fact that they lack the skills and tools to help these students learn" (Housman & Martinez, 2001, p. 6).

The "history and reputation of poor student performance" (Picucci et al., 2002, p. 31), combined with pervasive low morale within failing schools, is often reciprocated by the communities these schools serve: "The communities also [hold] low expectations for the schools" (Picucci et al., 2002, p. 32). Many failing schools develop a reputation and a history of poor student performance that induce a "low community opinion of the school" (p. 32). Such a stigma places additional stress on an already ailing school (Corallo & McDonald, 2001), as it is not unusual for parent participation to be sporadic or nearly nonexistent (U.S. Department of Education, 2001). The reputation of the school further demoralizes school staff and results in a shared defeatist attitude (Picucci et al., 2002) that ultimately leaves "teachers and parents [frustrated]" (U.S. Department of Education, 2001, p. 7) as well as pervasive "poor morale among school community members" (Ziebarth, 2002, p. 5)—the very spiral of decline we documented in Part I of the book.

Other Internal Causes

Additional internal causes consistent with the themes described above are also highlighted in the literature. Goldstein and colleagues (1998) conclude from their research that the school's organization, its staff and administrative composition, can be "the source of its inability to provide quality educational services to students" (p. 3). Mazzeo and Berman (2003) assert that failing schools "lack agreement on expectations for student learning and lack the means to influence classroom instructional practice in ways that result in improved student learning" (p. 10). Similarly, Housman and Martinez (2001) maintain that failing schools often "lack . . . a coherent plan (p. 3) and that they represent a "disconnected set of programs layered one on top of the other" (p. 3). The American Federation of Teachers (1999) argue that "unfocused curriculum or the lack of an effective discipline policy may be critical" (p. 6) to school failure. Finally, the fact that "teachers and principals in low-performing schools tend to work in isolation from one another rather than as colleagues in a professional learning community" (Housman & Martinez, 2001, p. 7) is surfaced as a cause of school failure.

RESPONSES TO FAILURE: TURNAROUND

These [failing] schools ... must improve results quickly to avoid dire consequences for students, but they lack a clear strategy focused on the most necessary—and rapidly attainable—reforms. (Kowal & Hassel, 2005, p. 9)

Turnaround efforts seek to improve failing schools and districts by pressuring them to raise standardized test scores and close achievement gaps (Malen & Rice, 2004). Many of these turnaround initiatives include the carrot of rewards and the stick of sanctions (Mac Iver et al., 2003), which typically are "applied in an escalating fashion" (Spreng, 2005, p. 43). We explore turnaround efforts below using three analytic frames: turnaround type, turnaround level, and intensity of turnaround effort.

Type

Since school failure varies (American Federation of Teachers, 1999), and because there is an assortment of philosophies about organizational recovery, numerous types of turnaround interventions exist currently, each "designed to address the failure of schools after they have been identified as being in need of change" (Spreng, 2005, p. 2). Turnaround types most often discussed and/or implemented in failing schools include school improvement planning, expert assistance, provision of choice, provision of supplemental services, adoption of a reform model, reconstitution, as well as other miscellaneous turnaround proposals.

School Improvement Planning

School improvement plans [SIP] ... are often a mandatory feature for schools put on probation by their accountability agency for persistently low performance. In many accountability systems, accountability agencies treat SIPs as central to a school's path back to healthy performance. Often, SIPs are extensive documents subject to official review and approval. Whether they are hastily thrown together or carefully crafted, these SIPs are vivid testimony to the way schools (and districts) think about the task of school improvement under the unusual conditions of probation. . . . SIPs are presumably of heightened concern for schools toiling under the stigma of decline or reconstitution, public labels with which accountability agencies signify a school's precarious condition. (Mintrop, MacLellan, & Quintero, 2001, pp. 197–198)

NCLB envisions that schools and districts will include one of several interventions in [SIP] plans. It identifies five examples. One is to provide professional development for the school's teachers and principal, targeted at the problems or shortcomings that caused the school to be low performing. Another is to implement a "comprehensive school reform" model in the school. . . . Yet other interventions contemplated for inclusion in the school improvement plan include strategies to promote effective parental involvement, the addition of instructional time (through before and after school, summer, and extended year programs), and the development of teacher mentoring programs. (Brady, 2003, p. 4)

In a number of states, "low-performing schools are required to submit self-studies and self-generated plans for improvement" (Linn, Rothman, & White, 2001, p. 4), often an initial consequence of failure (Duffy, 2001). By 2001, 34 states had established corrective planning for failing schools (Rudo, 2001), and in early 2002, No Child Left Behind mandated improvement planning for all Title I schools failing to make adequate yearly progress for two consecutive years (Mazzeo & Berman, 2003).

School improvement plans "are supposed to address the issues that led to the school's low performance" (Brady, 2003, p. 4) and to show "how the school will get from the present situation of probation to lofty external standards" (Mintrop & MacLellan, 2002, p. 278). These blueprints "codify a school's envisioned improvement design" (p. 275) by facilitating "an effective, internalized, and self-sustained process of school improvement" (p. 276). Ultimately, such plans provide tools "for the accountability agency to direct schools toward rational management of improvement and to translate external (i.e., state or district) expectations into schools' internal obligations" (p. 276). Ideally, "school accountability systems align system goals with school organizational goals and create coherence between incentives and instructional programs" (p. 277).

Schools on probation or academic watch are often "mandated to undergo a formal process of school improvement, which stipulates the formation of school improvement teams (SITs), compilation of school improvement plans (SIPs), and external monitoring of the plans' implementation" (Mintrop & MacLellan, 2002, p. 275). For example, in Maryland, "review panels and state monitors visit the school to help identify needs and oversee implementation of the plan" (pp. 279–280). Often, these mandates also provide schools with support; "schools have access to a set of supports to assist in their improvement efforts" (Goldstein, Kelemen, & Koski, 1998, p. 13), including administrative liaisons, discretionary resources, and access to management consulting services. For example, school improvement facilitators spend three years helping restructure failing schools in Washington, and school support specialists use data to identify weaknesses and to plan improvement in Massachusetts (Archer, 2006).

Scaffolding school improvement plans on external expectations can cause tension, as found in San Francisco. Goldstein and colleagues (1998) document that improvement plans in San Francisco were blurry, as schools and principals determined whether they were being challenged or threatened, as fears of job loss and stouter sanctions emerged as real possibilities for continued failure. Nonetheless, "a SIP makes sense as a management tool that helps a school reflect on how to align a system's performance demands with local practitioners' actions, and that helps external agencies monitor the school's actions" (Mintrop, MacLellan, & Quintero, 2001, p. 199).

Expert Assistance

As noted above, mandated assistance is often provided to failing schools as part of school improvement planning, especially in the form of expert help. Experts external to the failing school or district are able to "provide customized assistance" (Bowles et al., 2002, p. 4). The roles and specific responsibilities of the experts vary from state to state, but their goals are generally the same.

According to the U.S. Department of Education (2001), "one of the most important things that states and districts can provide to struggling schools is expertise . . . to provide assistance with the planning, implementation, and evaluation of reform efforts" (p. 37). For example, failing schools in West Virginia are assigned a Distinguished

Educator—a principal who is either retired or currently working in the West Virginia public education system who "may be given authority to make all decisions in the school (overriding the incumbent principal if necessary) or may work in partnership with the principal" (Bowles et al., 2002, p. 7). In Kentucky, Highly Skilled Educators typically focus on leadership and instructional practice (Bowles et al., 2002). Oregon's Distinguished Educator Program "provides free counseling and ongoing professional development" as well as instruction on "how to use school planning to improve student performance and how to use school data to assist in planning" (U.S. Department of Education, 2001, p. 38). In Texas, "the monitor or master will work at the district level with a school to increase the school's capacity to improve" (Bowles et al., 2002, p. 17), while in Illinois, the Teacher in Residence works "with non-Title I schools to support the development and implementation of the school improvement plan" (p. 20). North Carolina developed State Assistance Teams that "are made up of currently practicing teachers and staff, retired educators, representatives from the higher education community, school administrators, and others deemed appropriate by the State Board . . . to help school staff devise ways to improve student achievement" (U.S. Department of Education, 2001, p. 45). Assistance teams are placed in schools that ask for help and "in those that are required to have such help because of seriously declining performance" (Watts, 2000, p. 18).

Turnaround specialists offer a specific form of expert assistance that appears to be emerging as a viable option for failing schools. Neuman-Sheldon's (2006) study of turnaround in Maryland reveals that approximately 73% of failing schools implemented this strategy in the 2005–2006 school year. In these schools, specialists are given "limited powers over the school in regards to curriculum, staff development, and decision-making processes" (p. 3). Though no additional training or certification is required of turnaround specialists, they must meet the following state requirements:

- A master's degree in education or school administration
- A minimum of three documented years as a successful school leader (principal, academic coach, resource teacher, master teacher, etc.)
- Documentation of curriculum and instruction expertise
- Experience designing and implementing school-based professional development for teachers

- Experience with the school improvement planning process
- Experience using data to inform instruction and instructional practices
- Demonstrated knowledge and expertise in an underachieving performance area or subgroup (e.g., reading, math, special education, English language learners, low-income students)
- Evidence of success in improving student achievement at a low-performing school (Neuman-Sheldon, 2006, p. 5)

Still, the tasks, services, and time that turnaround specialists provide failing schools vary significantly, though they are expected to be with school principals and school improvement teams two or three days a week.

Provision of Choice

[Under NCLB], parents of students in Title I schools identified for improvement will have the option to transfer to another public school in the district not in school improvement. (Advocates for Children, 2003, p. 6)

If a Title I school fails to make its AYP target for two consecutive years, its students are supposed to be offered "public school choice." The local district is to provide each student with a choice of alternative public (including charter) schools that are *making adequate yearly progress.* (Hess & Finn, 2004, p. 35)

A 2001 report from the U.S. Department of Education reveals that "federal and state policies increasingly require school districts to provide students in Title I schools identified as needing improvement with the choice of attending a higher performing public school within the district" (p. 7). Prior to NCLB, "thirteen states allow[ed] students in low-performing schools to transfer to other public schools, often providing the funds for these students' transportation" (Rudo, 2001, p. 2). In Florida, "if a school fails to improve its grade of 'F' under the state system of accountability for two out of four consecutive years, students in the school are able to attend any public school that scored a 'C' or better" (Duffy, 2001, p. 15). More recently, the federal No Child Left Behind Act mandated that districts "allow children in persistently failing schools to transfer to public schools that perform better" (Brownstein, 2003, p. 40).

Specifically, districts must provide "students in failing schools with the option to transfer to other public schools within the district, including charter schools" (Brady, 2003, p. 5). According to Hess and Finn (2004), the choice provisions in NCLB were designed to "give students in failing schools access to other places and service providers whereby they could learn reading and math . . . and . . . to give failing schools an incentive to improve" (p. 36) through the dual threat of enrollment and budget reductions.

Provision of Supplemental Services

If a student's school fails to make AYP for three consecutive years, the district is supposed to provide that child with the opportunity to enroll in "supplemental educational services"— which in practice typically amount to about 30 hours of free after-school tutoring. (Hess & Finn, 2004, pp. 35–36)

"Portrayed as a panacea for assisting poor students in failing schools [to] succeed" (Advocates for Children, 2003, p. 1) as well as a life raft (Hess & Finn, 2004), NCLB also mandates that districts offer students who have attended a failing school for three or more years "the opportunity to obtain extra tutoring from parent-selected and state-approved providers" (Brady, 2003, p. 5). "Services include tutoring, remediation, and academic intervention, and are provided free of cost to those who are eligible" (Advocates for Children, 2003, p. 7), with the goal of increasing "the academic achievement of low-income students, particularly in the areas of reading, language arts and mathematics" (p. 7). Such services are to be offered during "off-school hours" (p. 7), including after-school and weekend tutoring (Brownstein, 2003).

Currently, the literature suggests that "students aren't taking advantage of tutoring options under the No Child Left Behind Act" (Davis, 2006, p. 31). In particular, schools are "faltering when it comes to notifying parents about school transfer options under the law" (p. 31). According to Olson (2005), "11 states reported that 20 percent or more of eligible children received supplemental educational services" (p. 1). Eighteen states "had fewer than 10 percent of eligible students receive such services last school year" (p. 2). In the meantime, "the number of Title I schools identified as needing improvement has nearly doubled in recent years" (Davis, 2006, p. 31):

"As more students become eligible for afterschool services, and as word of the program spreads throughout disadvantaged communities, federal officials expect [the] number [of students receiving services] to . . . soar" (Peterson, 2005, p. 44).

Adoption of a Reform Model

Some turnaround interventions offer "a thorough program designed to change multiple key curricular, planning, communications, and other processes in schools in coordinated fashion around a coherent school design or philosophy" (Brady, 2003, p. 4). These interventions often call for the adoption of comprehensive reform models that "typically include elements of school-based planning, targeted professional development, increased parental engagement, and other strategies" (p. 14). Ideally, Comprehensive School Reform (CSR) based "school improvement must be comprehensive in scope and depth, so that changes in curriculum and instruction help all students and are aligned with and supported by appropriate school management, collaborative planning, and parental involvement" (Zuckerman, 2002, p. 1).

The use "of externally developed, schoolwide reform models is . . . being adopted by rapidly growing numbers of schools and districts" (Borman et al., 2000, p. 31). Zuckerman (2002) notes CSR-based turnaround in New York's District Number 2, as well as "the transformation of six low-performing districts into exemplars of achievement" (p. 2). In 1996, the District of Columbia Public School superintendent "asked the Laboratory for Student Success (LSS) . . . to assist the District in designing a comprehensive school reform initiative to help its lowest performing schools to significantly improve their capacity to increase student achievement" (Wang & Manning, 2000, p. 2). And the state of Nevada intervened with low-performing schools "to assess their needs and select an appropriate remedial program from one of 26 state-approved, research-based instructional programs" (Mazzeo & Berman, 2003, p. 24).

Reconstitution

Although school reconstitution can take a variety of forms, generally speaking, this strategy involve[s] removing a school's incumbent administrators and teachers (or large percentages of them) and replacing them with educators who, presumably, are more capable and committed. At heart, reconstitution is a human capital reform grounded in the assumption that upgrading the human capital in low-performing schools will improve the performance of those schools. (Rice & Malen, 2003, p. 635)

Despite the dramatic verbiage, reconstitution, while it has in a few cases led to major change, usually means little more than hiring a new principal and asking teachers whether they would like to remain on the staff or move somewhere else in the district. (Peterson, 2005, p. 43)

Of turnaround efforts, Duffy (2001) finds reconstitution to be "by far the most severe and controversial sanction available to states" (p. 16), a "get-tough" reform policy (Borman et al., 2000, p. 17). As such, reconstitution is often seen as a last resort, and "in most states [has] not been implemented [, although] "it is becoming more popular across the nation" (Rudo, 2001, p. 2). Beginning in San Francisco in 1983 (Cibulka, 2003), reconstitution has been embraced as an education reform strategy by select state governments and local districts (Malen et al., 1999). The No Child Left Behind Act "in effect 'nationalized' the concept of reconstitution, potentially altering the way existing state policies operate and also extending the policy to new states" (Cibulka, 2003, p. 262). Nonetheless, this turnaround strategy remains relatively new (Goldstein, Kelemen, & Koski, 1998), and "the practice of reforming failing schools through school reconstitution is one of the latest challenges for school district directors of evaluation and accountability" (Adcock & Winkler, 1999, p. 1).

Generally, reconstitution involves the following four components:

- Identifying failing schools according to state- or district-set measures
- Vacating staff and administrative positions
- Appointing a new principal
- Establishing a new school team, with some rehired and some new teachers (Peterson, 1999, p. 21)

In addition, it is important to note that other reform elements sometimes get wrapped up in reconstitution efforts, as Goldstein and colleagues (1998) reveal in portraying the eight components of San Francisco's reconstitution initiative:

(1) Vacating the adults and hiring new staff committed to the Consent Decree's vision; (2) implementing a set of philosophical tenets drawn up by the District; (3) implementing delineated student outcomes; (4) providing technology-rich environments; (5) encouraging flexibility in adult-student ratios; (6) providing staff development associated with items 1, 2, & 3; (7) selecting an instructional focus; and (8) involving parents. According to the District, to reconstitute a school in San Francisco means implementing all eight components. (p. 2)

"Reconstitution reforms, by definition and design, dismantle the organizational infrastructure of schools" (Rice & Malen, 2003, p. 647): "Most states agree that reconstitution includes creating a new philosophy and making severe staffing changes" (Rudo, 2001, p. 2) in order to "deliberately disassemble professional networks in hopes that more productive networks will be forged" (Rice & Malen, 2003, p. 650). And there is a growing body of literature that attests to the removal of significant percentages (if not all) of teachers from reconstituted schools (Adcock & Winkler, 1999; Borman et al., 2000; Cibulka, 2003; Malen et al., 1999; Peterson, 1999; Wolk, 1998; Ziebarth, 2004b). In addition to the removal and replacement of teachers, reconstituted schools often replace their administrators (Cibulka, 2003). In their study of failing schools in an urban district, Malen and her team (2002) found that "new principals were appointed in five of the six [reconstituted] schools" (p. 117). Also, the removal of building support staff (e.g., custodians, secretaries) is possible (Adcock & Winkler, 1999).

Under reconstitution, dismissed school employees generally have the opportunity to reapply for their positions (Borman et al., 2000). Malen and her colleagues (2002) report:

Teachers who wanted to continue to work in those schools, no matter their experience, preference, or history, had to (a) reapply for their position, (b) sit for a formal interview with a committee comprised of the new principal, district administrators and/or intermediate-level administrators, and (c) accept the verdict of that selection committee. (p. 117)

Those who reapply are "in some cases . . . rehired" (Borman et al., 2000, p. 17). For example, in its report on turnaround, the U.S. Department of Education (2001) notes that one reconstituted school rehired one-third of its original staff. Often, teachers not rehired or who do not reapply for their positions are transferred to nonfailing schools in the district (Adcock & Winkler, 1999). In the Borman and colleagues (2000) study, "tenured educators [were] guaranteed a teaching position somewhere in the district" (p. 17).

Research regularly shows that "the placement of better teachers in a school is one of the most influential determinants to student achievement" (Adcock & Winkler, 1999, p. 2). A central tenet "of reconstitution is that requiring all staff to reapply for their positions can both rid schools of weak [teachers] . . . and replenish schools with strong teachers" (Malen et al., 2002, p. 119).

The reform seeks to remove people who have done the work of the school and replace them with people who are not familiar with, and hence are not bound to (some would say blinded by) past practices. In essence, the reform "guts" a school in hopes that the reconstituted staff will create a more effective set of arrangements. (Malen et al., 1999, p. 15)

Because the source of failure is internal to the organization, reconstitution [, it is argued,] will remove the source of failure and breathe new life into the organization."(Goldstein, Kelemen, & Koski, 1998, p. 4)

Miscellaneous Turnaround Proposals

Other less discussed and researched interventions do exist and warrant mention. Some of these strategies represent more general reform ideas, while others are narrower in scope but have had limited implementation as turnaround interventions. These strategies include parent involvement, added school time, professional development, financial assistance, school reorganization, leader replacement, site-based reform, small schools, curriculum change, bringing teachers out of retirement, outsourcing, contracting out management of and/or running of the school, switching to "charter" status, and school closure:

- Forming "partnerships and fostering communication with parents and teachers" (U.S. Department of Education, 2001, p. 38) develops social and human capital and "would constitute [a turnaround] intervention in the school" (Spreng, 2005, p. 39). For example, a troubled elementary school in Atlanta initiated parent programs to "hone [the parents'] skills and improve their knowledge about the school curriculum" (U.S. Department of Education, 2001, p. 39), enabling them to help their children with homework. Afterward, parent involvement grew "at an astounding rate" (p. 39).

- Another common turnaround strategy is to add instruction time (U.S. Department of Education, 2001). Lengthening the school day increases teacher collaboration, principal and teacher development, and student learning. For example, adding school time at one overcrowded school in Washington, D.C., cultivated a feeling among teachers that "academics were the true focus of the school, and relations between classroom teachers and specialists improved because of their collaboration during the reading block" (U.S. Department of Education, 2001, p. 37).

- Financial assistance is sometimes provided directly to failing schools (Mazzeo & Berman, 2003). For example, in Kirby, Naftel, Berends, and McCombs's report (2005), approximately 34% of failing schools identified in the National Longitudinal Survey of Schools (NLSS) "reported receiving additional technical assistance . . . from outside agencies" (p. 9).

- School reorganization is a staff-led effort to turn around schools by reorganizing school "governance, decision-making processes, personnel assignments, and teaching practices" (Brady, 2003, p. 13) to raise student achievement. For example, a failing school in Kentucky instituted "teacher-led teams around each cognitive area (e.g., reading, mathematics, and science)" (p. 13). These teams, consisting of staff, parents, students, and others, applied "learning activities across the curriculum" (p. 13) and implemented regular self-evaluations.

- Another common intervention is leader replacement. For example, under a judge's order in North Carolina, principals of schools that fail for five years will be replaced (Archer, 2006).

- Site-based reform is a decentralized process in which many aspects of school management occur at the school (Murphy & Beck, 1995). Borman and his colleagues (2000) researched two midwestern schools attempting turnaround through site-based reform. One school implemented site-based management through professional control while the other troubled school primarily implemented administrative control, but the goal for both schools "was to shift major authority to the schools with the hope that the increased local activism would lead to such things as stronger school leadership, more parent and community involvement, and improved facilities (Borman et al., 2000, p. 6).

• The creation of small schools in hopes of "creating smaller learning communities to enhance personalism" (Hess, 2003, p. 312) is another intervention for troubled schools. For example, the Maryland state board approved options that partition "large urban high schools into smaller learning communities" (Neuman-Sheldon, 2006, p. 4). Similarly, in Chicago, small schools "were typically organized with students physically colocated in a set of specific divisions in an isolated section of the building, [the original school,] and their classes were taught by a faculty which was mostly devoted to those students alone" (Hess, 2003, p. 312).

• Curriculum change, especially in line with standardized testing, is another turnaround strategy employed in a few schools. This intervention "is one in which a district involuntarily imposes a notably different curriculum on a school" (Brady, 2003, p. 17). For example, in Paterson, New Jersey, failing schools were instructed by their district superintendent to implement a curriculum "focused exclusively on reading, writing, and mathematics" (p. 17). Occasionally, schools can impose such changes as noted in California and Maryland, where some failing schools are focusing on reading and mathematics as "intensive skills courses" (Manzo, 2004, p. 1; also Neuman-Sheldon, 2006) in place of other courses.

• Bringing teachers out of retirement is another improvement strategy gaining traction. For example, one of North Carolina's turnaround strategies "has been to bring high quality retired teachers back into the workforce" (Housman & Martinez, 2001, p. 2).

• The outsourcing "of a school's or district's operations to an outside provider" (Brady, 2003, p. 17) is another turnaround strategy. For example, in 1989, "the Massachusetts legislature voted to take over the Chelsea Public Schools and turn the management of the district over to Boston University" (Brady, 2003, p. 17; also Forster, 1997). More recently in Maryland, "the state board of education proposed to engage third party contractors to assume governance" (Neuman-Sheldon, 2006, p. 4) of four failing schools in Baltimore.

- Contracting out management of and/or running of the school in the form of Education Management Organizations (EMOs) is another turnaround strategy, potentially serving as an "intermediary institution to assist 'failing' schools" (Arsen, Bell, & Plank, 2003, p. 19). For example, in 2000, as part of the reconstitution process for three failing Baltimore schools, the state "hired Edison, Inc., a private for-profit firm, to operate them" (Cibulka, 2003, p. 260). However, EMOs appear handcuffed due to administrative and political constraints, leading to student achievement improvement to be "about the same as in comparable district schools" (p. 21).

- Switching to charter school status is another intervention sometimes applied to troubled schools (Arsen, Bell, & Plank, 2003). Unlike general public schools, charter schools "enjoy greater autonomy to hire and fire teachers, set salaries, and implement their programs" (p. 20). Furthermore, innovation is easier for a charter school, though determining whether or not charter schools "actually provide a better education via 'more effective programs' is, as yet, unknown" (Hacsi, 2004, pp. 15–16). Under Louisiana state law, failing schools are placed in the Recovery School District, at which point the state invites "nonprofit organizations to apply to run the schools as charter schools" (Steiner, 2005, p. 18). Moreover, NCLB allows the reopening of a failing school as a charter school as an option "designed to completely revamp the school" (Neuman-Sheldon, 2006, p. 2). Charter schools "can use very different policies and practices from district schools without asking special permission" (Hassel, Hassel, Arkin, Kowal, & Steiner, 2005, p. 7), gaining a great deal of autonomy (Ziebarth, 2004a). The district decides who will operate the school and monitor their performance while maintaining the authority to "take away the charter if the school does not improve learning enough" (Hassel et al., 2005, p. 7). The option of closing and reopening a school as a charter has not flourished. For example, in Michigan, 69 schools facing NCLB-sanctioned restructuring chose noncharter alternatives (Ziebarth, 2004a). However, three San Diego schools were closed in 2004 and have been reopened as charter schools since (Robelen, (2006).

- A final intervention is school closure, "by far the most severe and controversial sanction available to states as a way to address the needs of [failing] schools that seem incapable of improving their performance" (Duffy, 2001, p. 16). In Houston, two high schools receiving the state's lowest test rating for four consecutive years (and a middle school for three consecutive years) are now facing a new policy that declares schools failing for four years must close (Gewertz, 2006).

- Other turnaround strategy types mentioned by Brady (2003) but without concrete examples are redirection of funds, withholding of funds, and district closure.

Level

Whether fueled by an array of state policies or by recent federal legislation, high-stakes accountability initiatives have become a primary lever for policy makers seeking dramatic improvements in school performance. Despite the variation in design, high-stakes accountability initiatives share a common goal. They all seek, in one way or another, to pressure public schools, particularly those labeled failing or low-performing schools, to improve their performance on indicators such as standardized test scores in specific subject areas and achievement gaps within and across subsets of the student population. (Malen & Rice, 2004, p. 632)

Since the release of *A Nation at Risk* in 1983, "policymakers at state, local, and federal levels have enacted a variety of policies to improve the quality of the nation's public school system" (Cibulka, 2003, p. 252; see also Murphy, 1990; Murphy & Adams, 1998). As discussed above, these general policies have led to turnaround strategies ranging from additional planning to reconstitution (Rudo, 2001). Recovery efforts can be implemented at the federal, state, city (mayoral), and district levels.

Federal

The NCLB Act was signed into law on January 8, 2002. It included five basic education reform principles: (1) requiring states to create education plans that include standards for what a child should know and learn in each grade and testing to determine whether students progress toward those standards;

(2) increasing public awareness of school performance by requiring public reporting of state education standards and test scores; (3) providing parents a variety of tools to hold schools that continually fail to make adequate progress toward meeting the standards accountable; (4) improving teacher quality and emphasizing teaching methods with a proven track record; and (5) providing states with greater flexibility to determine the allocation of federal education grants. (Fine, Hsu, King et al., 2003, p. 10)

Although states and districts are central actors in helping failing schools to improve, "the federal government also has an important part to play" (U.S. Department of Education, 2001, p. 46). As noted earlier, the No Child Left Behind Act effectively nationalized sanctions such as reconstitution, "potentially altering the way existing state policies operate" (Cibulka, 2003, p. 262). NCLB mandates "states to implement reform plans with rapid timelines and to show academic achievement data in disaggregated formats" (Donlevy, 2003, p. 335), requiring "states to establish a single statewide accountability system based on rigorous content and performance standards" (Kirby et al., 2005). Furthermore, each state must develop and implement an accountability plan that ensures that all local educational agencies and public schools meet NCLB's adequate yearly progress (AYP) demands (Fine et al., 2003) for all students in Grades 3 through 8 in reading and math (Hess & Finn, 2004). Thus, "while images of failed schools have long been a motivating force in educational reform, the passage of No Child Left Behind (NCLB) has created a new sense of urgency" (Lashway, 2004, p. 25), putting federal "pressure on states and districts to identify and improve these low performing schools. The intensity of these pressures means that every state and district is now considering how to raise student achievement in the most challenged schools" (Hassel & Steiner, 2003, p. 1) even though "the rigor of performance demands and intervention burdens differ across states" (Mintrop & Trujillo, 2005, p. 4).

Though "the impetus for identifying and assisting [failing] schools did not start with NCLB" (McColskey & Monrad, 2004, p. 5), NCLB has codified the movement "towards the new accountability [statewide performance standards and testing] into a federal law" (Spreng, 2005, p. 11): according to the legislation, "a school that fails to make AYP is identified as being in need of improvement because the school failed to make AYP for its students as a whole or for one of several NCLB-designated subgroups" (Popham, 2005, p. 6), as "a key goal . . . is to close the achievement gap between subpopulations of students" (Picucci et al., 2002, p. 2). NCLB requires states "to quickly scale-up their school improvement strategies" (Mazzeo & Berman, 2003, p. 6) or face "progressively more serious consequences" (p. 7):

> Students attending schools that miss their performance targets for two consecutive years must be offered the option of moving to a higher-performing public school within the school district. Schools must also develop an improvement plan that sets performance targets by academic subject, uses 10 percent of the school's Title I funds for professional development, and incorporates a teacher mentoring program. After three years of missing the state performance target, parents of children in these schools must be offered the option of using federal Title I dollars to purchase supplemental educational services from an approved provider on the open market. After four years of missing the state performance target, the school becomes subject to 'corrective action,' which requires the district to formulate an improvement plan for the school. That plan could include replacing staff, decreasing management authority at the school level, appointing outside experts to advise the school, lengthening the school day or year, or restructuring the school. (Mazzeo & Berman, 2003, p. 7)

NCLB's "goals, mechanisms, and remedies do not fit neatly into the status quo [but] ask states and school districts to engage in unfamiliar, even unnatural, acts" (Hess & Finn, 2004, p. 35).

State

In recent years . . . state actions have focused attention on holding schools more accountable for students' academic achievement. The state has pressured the district largely through the enactment of mandatory state testing policies, threats of state takeovers, and calls for greater accountability, continuous school improvement, implementation of research-based practices, and development of a teacher corps that is fully certified. (Malen et al., 1999, pp. 5–6)

*States have addressed the task of turning around "failing"
schools in a variety of ways. Some have taken over schools or
school districts, or assigned control to municipal governments.
Some have sent teams of experts into "failing" schools to provide
assistance, or encouraged districts to award control over "failing" schools to private companies. Some states have tried more
than one approach, typically on an ad hoc basis.* (Arsen, Bell,
& Plank, 2003, p. 1)

*Direct interventions by state agencies to improve performance
in "failing" schools face a number of critical obstacles. First,
state education agencies typically serve hundreds of districts
and thousands of schools, most of which are geographically distant from the capital. They consequently have little local knowledge of schools and communities. . . . Second, state interventions
in local school districts are almost invariably triggered by crisis, so school districts rarely enter into a relationship with the
state freely or as a partner. The consequent lack of trust may
require state officials to overcome deep local resistance in order
to establish the legitimacy necessary to assist "failing" schools.*
(Arsen, Bell, & Plank, 2003, p. 16)

States serving as the fulcrum of turnaround is not a new concept.
As of 1998, "23 states ha[d] policies for intervening and mandating
major changes in chronically low-performing schools" (Borman
et al., 2000, p. 1), providing "state intervention along a continuum
that ranges from warnings to temporary leadership replacement to
takeover" (McRobbie, 1998, p. 3). After two decades of reform,
Cibulka (2003) notes that dissatisfaction with public schools and distrust of educators remain common trends that have fostered "a more
or less steady strengthening of state (and now federal) control"
(p. 254). Furthermore, "state intervention in local school districts
has not developed spontaneously and in isolation at state levels [but]
is an outgrowth of a long history of numerous unsuccessful attempts
at educational reform in failing school districts and a steady decrease
in public confidence in the system of public education" (Forster,
1997, pp. 19–20).

Since state governments possess the authority to demand change,
the power to reallocate resources, the scale to employ specialists, and
the ability to spread the costs of technical assistance, "the agencies of

state government are strong candidates for turning around 'failing' schools" (Arsen, Bell, & Plank, 2003, p. 15). However, "many states have been relatively slow to institute their own policies and mechanisms for intervening in low-performing schools" (U.S. Department of Education, 2001, p. 5), and the prevailing belief is that "states . . . must assume a larger role in assisting low-performing schools and have a specific plan and resources to support each school that needs it" (p. 6).

In an attempt to assume a larger role, "in 1999, the vast majority of states ratified new legislation or amended previous legislation to hold schools and school districts accountable for student performance" (Rudo, 2001, p. 2). In addition, some states have added "key elements" to their accountability programs (Watts, 2000, p. 6). Such components have the potential to "influence and encourage schools and districts to reallocate federal, state, and local funds in a focused, strategic way" (Housman & Martinez, 2001, p. 4) as well as to "successfully motivate a chronically low-performing school to initiate schoolwide improvement efforts" (p. 4).

Generally, "the first intervention by a state is to work with those at the school level to identify causes of under-performance and to develop an improvement plan" (Bowles et al., 2002). In addition, "many states use experts external to the under-performing school or district to provide customized assistance based on information from the diagnostic intervention" (p. 4). According to Duffy (2001), five pillars of state-level interventions are

1. On-site audits or monitoring by state officials

2. Probationary status or placement on a state's warning list

3. Suspension or loss of state accreditation status

4. Transfer or replacement of instructional or administrative staff at the school and/or district level.

5. Optional transfer of students. (p. 15)

Because of growing skepticism about the ability of districts to reverse failure, "several state governments have sought to shift administrative control of local education systems from school boards to other agencies" (Arsen, Bell, & Plank, 2003, p. 15). Indeed, fueled by "the continued failure of most educational reforms, inducements and sanctions at the hands of local school authorities, the ultimate intervention—the takeover and full operation of failing school districts by the state—has become a major educational and political issue in the last decade" (Forster, 1997, p. 1) and "will likely continue to take on greater significance within the larger context of educational reform until public expectations for student achievement are met" (pp. 4–5).

"*Takeover* is the common term used to refer to one remedy of sanction, although in practice takeover can mean different things. It may involve varying degrees of state oversight and management of the district [or school], depending on the violation, and the duration may be indefinite or time-specific, with more severe sanctions imposed over time" (Cibulka, 2003, p. 253): "State takeover of a local school district is viewed as a major reform initiative—a catalyst for educational change and improvement intended to break the failure cycle" (Forster, 1997, p. 2) and can be seen as "the ultimate reform initiative" (p. 21).

A state takeover can disrupt the cycle of failure and "provide an opportunity for a district to improve under new leadership" (Forster, 1997, p. 21), depending on the amount of state support and level of new leadership skill. "Takeover as a school reform model focuses on district-level capacity to reduce institutional fragmentation and raise academic accountability" (Wong & Shen, 2003, p. 91). Under state takeover, "the state legislature, the state board of education or a federal court charges the state department of education or another designated entity, such as a mayor, with managing a school district" (Ziebarth, 2004b, p. 1). According to Cibulka (2003), "the governance strategy used in [these] takeovers also has varied. In some cases, the state has actually run the school district" (p. 255), while in others, "states have not always taken such a top-down approach to interventions" (p. 256). Ultimately, state takeover "is a means to an end, not an end unto itself—a point which is critical to one maintaining proper perspective on the topic and understanding both its potential and its limitations" (Forster, 1997, p. 2).

Nonetheless, "in most states that identify low-performing and failing schools, officials are taking a softer tack, moving away from the 'ultimate sanctions' like state takeovers in favor of more collaborative efforts to encourage change and boost student performance" (Linn, Rothman, & White, 2001, p. 4). It is increasingly argued that "the state . . . has a strong incentive to go well beyond enforcer, instead partnering with the school and district to oust complacency, marshal combined talents and foster innovation and risk taking" (McRobbie, 1998, p. 2). Often, in such circumstances, "the *threat* of intervention—including, possibly, takeover—is harnessed as a motivational force" (p. 2), as "only a few states have exercised such authority" (Linn, Rothman, & White, 2001, p. 4). Indeed, "states increasingly view such measures more as tools to prod schools into action rather than as viable options to turn around their worst performers" (p. 4). Of 23 states with the legal right to take over schools, only 5 "have chosen to exercise their right to do so" (Steiner, 2005, p. 5).

City (Mayoral)

Mayoral takeovers generally involve some kind of state interventions, because states have constitutional responsibility for public education and therefore must authorize any change of governance arrangements. At the same time, after the initial involvement in authorizing a change, the state typically turns over fiscal control and political authority to the mayor, who is expected to be the "change agent" who will turn around a failing school system. (Cibulka, 2003, pp. 257–258)

The ways in which mayors have become more engaged with schooling have varied—from low involvement (for example, trying to influence traditional school board elections) to high involvement (gaining formal control over the schools or appointment of school board members). (Kirst, 2002, p. 1)

Over the last decade, "governors have turned to mayors to assist in turning around chronically failing school districts" (Linn, Rothman, & White, 2001, p. 4). State takeovers and mayoral control represent "two different approaches to reform, because the first relies primarily on external intervention, while the second seeks to replace one form of local governance with another" (Cibulka, 2003, p. 253). Yet the difference "between 'mayoral' and 'state' takeover is not always clearly delineated. State legislatures, for example, must approve legislation to give mayors more control. Furthermore, the cooperation of both state and local authorities is frequently seen in these cities" (Wong & Shen, 2003, p. 97).

Takeovers by mayors are "almost entirely an urban strategy that has emerged to address the substantial performance problems of urban school systems" (Cibulka, 2003, p. 258), which "share at least one characteristic: a perceived need to install new leadership into educationally and financially troubled districts" (Green & Carl, 2000, p. 58). The literature in this area suggests that "there are compelling reasons why mayors might be able to improve public school performance" (Cibulka, 2003, p. 258). Specifically, mayors are "geographically close to the schools. City boundaries are often coterminous with school district boundaries. Mayors have deep local knowledge, and their familiarity with local actors and their understanding of local politics can be useful in building trust among local educators" (Arsen, Bell, & Plank, 2003, p. 17): "As the chief executive of the city, a mayor can build a broad citywide coalition of stakeholders as an antidote to the highly fragmented politics of urban education" (Cibulka, 2003, p. 258) as well as "leverage other city services to assist schools" (p. 258). Furthermore, a mayor's longer tenure in comparison to that of an urban superintendent allows for more leadership stability (Cibulka, 2003) while providing "a single point of electoral accountability, greater integration of children's services with schools, and better pupil attainment" (Kirst, 2002, p. 3).

One significant "barrier facing mayors, however, is their lack of knowledge about schools, teaching, and learning" (Arsen, Bell, & Plank, 2003, p. 17). In addition, "school district boundaries and municipal boundaries are not always coterminous" (Cibulka, 2003, p. 259), which would "diminish local control for some of these jurisdictions" (p. 259). Furthermore, "opponents to mayoral control assert that a school board appointed by the mayor will result in less democracy because voters have fewer electoral choices" (Kirst, 2002, p. 3). Still another "problem with mayoral takeovers is that most mayors—like most school boards—are deeply embedded in a turbulent political environment . . . present[ing] serious obstacles to accomplishing the academic improvement that would justify the takeover" (Arsen, Bell, & Plank, 2003, pp. 17–18).

School District

School districts are the most likely candidates to do the work of turning around "failing" schools. These schools fall under the direct authority of district administrators, who are consequently in a strong position to amend rules, change procedures, and redistribute resources in order to turn them around. Many large districts employ specialized professional staff with the expertise and local knowledge to provide effective assistance. (Arsen, Bell, & Plank, 2003, p. 12)

Recent turnaround work "has emphasized the role of the school district in supporting instructional improvement" (Arsen, Bell, & Plank, 2003, p. 12), and districts with low scores or inequity in education outcomes do sometimes attempt to reform themselves. For example, in San Francisco "the purpose of the Comprehensive School Improvement Project (CSIP) . . . is to target underperforming schools that serve large numbers of African American and Hispanic student[s]" (Mintrop, MacLellan, & Quintero, 2001, p. 204). In New York City, the chancellor's effort to force improvement in failing schools "represents an [*sic*] historic departure from three decades of unobstructed local sub-district control" (Phenix et al., 2005, pp. 2–3). Implementing a turnaround design, "the School District of the District of Columbia agreed to . . . provide a full-time facilitator for each of the five schools to assist the principals and teachers in achieving a high degree of program implementation" (Wang & Manning, 2000, p. 4), among other things.

One well-documented example of district-level recovery occurred in the late 1990s when a district superintendent in Maryland announced that six schools in his district would be reconstituted. According to Rice and Malen (2003), "the district superintendent, local board members, and key central office staff believed that rapid, 'dramatic,' and 'decisive' action was required to avert a state takeover and to quell local discontent" (pp. 642–643).

Intensity

Though each state and district has its own way of responding to low performing schools, most responses fall into a basic pattern of escalating intervention. The first stage is one of assessment and reporting. Student test scores allow the district or state to rate each school's performance, perhaps categorizing schools by their level of achievement or growth. Next, schools that fall below some threshold receive assistance. An expert team may visit the school and offer recommendations; a coach may work with the school's leaders to develop a school improvement plan. Finally, more drastic intervention comes to schools that continue to lag. The expert team or coach becomes more directive;

perhaps a new principal comes in. Much more rarely, the state or district replaces a significant portion of the staff or "takes over" the school. (Hassel & Steiner, 2003, pp. 1–2)

From the descriptions of turnaround types and levels above, patterns of intensification emerge. For example, turnaround efforts become more severe the longer a school or school district is in a turnaround situation. In addition, sanctions delivered from higher levels appear to be more severe than those emerging from individual schools and districts. In working through these issues, Brady (2003) asserts, "the most efficient way to classify these interventions is in terms of their intrusiveness" (p. 10). He divides interventions into three levels of intrusiveness: mild, moderate, and strong.

Mild

The least aggressive "interventions do not significantly disrupt the basic structure of the school" (Brady, 2003, p. 10). Such strategies "attempt to add elements to the operations of the school that may promote the effectiveness of the existing structures and processes. The additional programs or initiatives are typically implemented by the existing staff" (Spreng, 2005, p. 39). Brady (2003) lists the following as mild interventions: identification, planning, technical assistance, professional development, parent involvement, and tutoring.

Moderate

More moderate reforms "typically retain existing staff but call on them to adjust to changes in some of the basic structures and processes in the schools" (Brady, 2003, p. 10). According to Brady (2003), "moderate interventions . . . are mostly implemented by or with the help of existing staff, but they often involve outside experts that assist with and enforce the required changes in the way the school operates" (Spreng, 2005, p. 40). Brady (2003) enumerates the following as moderate interventions: added school time, school reorganization, comprehensive school reform, and principal replacement.

Strong

The most severe interventions generally "result in changes in school staff and always result in significantly changed school structures or processes" (Brady, 2003, p. 10). Here we find that "structures in the school are deemed beyond repair. Changes are mandated and carried out by people or entities outside the school. Strong interventions signal the government's belief that the school failed and cannot be improved in its current form" (Spreng, 2005, p. 41). According to Spreng, "only the most broken schools are subject to the most severe interventions" (p. 41). Brady (2003) classifies the following as strong interventions: reconstitution, school takeover, district takeover, school closure, choice, curriculum change, outsourcing, redirection of school or district funds, and withholding of school or district funds.

CHAPTER ELEVEN

Turning Around Failing Schools

The Evidence

It is even more difficult to assess the effectiveness of a specific program relative to other differently structured programs without a common metric that would allow us to compare in a straightforward way. (Mintrop & Trujillo, 2005, p. 3)

At worst, a failing-school strategy may give the appearance of making progress without fundamentally changing the culture of schools to enable real teaching and learning. (Wolk, 1998, p. 10)

E ven though "deciding how to measure school success and school failure is complicated, and yardsticks vary from state to state" (Linn, Rothman, & White, 2001, p. 2), state designs remain fairly similar. For example, in researching Maryland and Kentucky, Mintrop, MacLellan, and Quintero (2001) find that both states' accountability designs "are driven by a few quantitative performance indicators, center on a largely performance-based test, have highly ambitious growth targets for all schools, focus on student achievement, and bestow rewards to and impose sanctions on schools based on quantitative performance records" (p. 205). Measuring improvement, much like determining school failure, is dependent upon student academic growth. Increased academic achievement "is the primary goal" (Adcock & Winkler, 1999, p. 1) or the "first standard" (Borman et al., 2000, p. 5) in judging school improvement. For many failing schools and districts, "the success of their efforts—developing and implementing a comprehensive improvement plan with programs and resources aligned around a shared vision—will be determined by student scores on statewide standardized assessments" (Housman & Martinez, 2001, p. 4). In their study of reconstitution, Malen and her colleagues (2002) note that the "ultimate aim . . . is a substantial and sustained improvement in student achievement, as measured by gains on the state or district tests" (p. 125). According to Bowles and her team (2002), in North Carolina, "evidence of turnaround (exit criteria) within a school is broader than the initial criteria used to identify the school as [failing]" (p. 11). Such evidence includes

- Improvement on student test scores, meeting improvement goals set by the state
- School capacity, building on the strengths of school leaders, faculty and staff
- Continuous improvement plan showing an ability to improve and sustain improvement
- Data-driven decision making occurring at all levels of the school. (p. 11)

We return now to the types and the levels of turnaround intervention in order to inspect the effectiveness of turnaround initiatives. We begin with this very important caveat, however. As noted in Chapter 10, turnaround is a new idea in education. Because of that, very little impact data are available. And in no case has anything close to a consensus picture begun to emerge. Data are uneven at best. Context issues are rarely investigated. And the methods employed to investigate effects often leave a good deal to be desired.

TURNAROUND FINDINGS

Type

We report turnaround findings in this section by the following previously discussed turnaround types: school improvement planning, expert assistance, provision of choice, provision of supplemental services, adoption of a reform model, reconstitution, and miscellaneous turnaround proposals.

School Improvement Planning

Data on school improvement planning as a turnaround vehicle largely predate No Child Left Behind (NCLB) legislation. Perhaps the emergence of NCLB and its ratcheting up of sanctions as schools fail multiple years consecutively reduced the importance of school improvement planning as a turnaround intervention. It also appears difficult to disentangle the influence of school improvement plans (SIPs) and of the looming, escalating sanction(s) in line behind them.

Research on SIPs as a potential turnaround mechanism illustrates more talk than substance, as affirmed by Mintrop and colleagues' (2001) assessment of three state accountability systems in which "content analysis showed that the number of activities planned by schools on probation for the school year was staggering" (p. 208) and the number of intended activities in many schools "represented a substantial load, if not overload" (Mintrop & MacLellan, 2002, p. 287). Furthermore, such plans "have been found to be unrealistically comprehensive and full of minutiae rather than focused and strategic" (p. 276). In addition, plan goals seldom consider site conditions and realistic growth expectations but instead tend to be "boilerplate, conventional, and to cast a wide net" (Mintrop, MacLellan, & Quintero, 2001, p. 212).

"Broad teacher participation in planning is not common" (Mintrop, MacLellan, & Quintero, 2001, p. 200), leading to a "general lack of ownership of the plans [and] little evidence that the plans are internalized" (Mintrop & MacLellan, 2002, p. 296). Borman and his colleagues' (2000) study of a failing school implementing a SIP corroborates Mintrop and MacLellan's (2002) observation that unless the principal pushes, "most teachers ignore the plan despite professed compliance" (p. 296).

Nonetheless, some data indicate that SIPs can have positive effects, as seen in Pinellas County Schools, Florida, where the alignment of curriculum, standards, assessment, leadership, human resource development, and information systems with the strategic goals of the school system has contributed to "the number of students scoring at or above grade level on the Comprehensive Test of Basic Skills [increasing] significantly in writing, reading, and mathematics in all grades tested [as well as] on state standardized exams" (U.S.

Department of Education, 2001, p. 33). However, for reasons such as NCLB legislation, increasing sanctions, and low buy-in, Borman and his associates' (2000) findings of stagnant attendance rates, noticeable reading achievement decreases, and only slight math achievement increases could be more representative of SIPs as an engine of turnaround.

Expert Assistance

Highly qualified individuals or teams of teachers and/or other personnel positioned in failing schools to assist with turnaround often produce positive results. In Kentucky, the assistance provided through the Highly Skilled Educator Program has been found to be effective (McColskey & Monrad, 2004). South Carolina reports positive findings with regard to their teacher specialists. Indeed, approximately 90% of principals and teachers surveyed in the 17 participating schools reported improved teacher effectiveness as well as an overall improvement in instruction, although concerns with ownership and best practices remained (McColskey & Monrad, 2004). Teams in North Carolina are generally viewed as successful (Mintrop & Trujillo, 2005), and "the majority of schools served thus far have managed to maintain their improvement" (U.S. Department of Education, 2001, p. 45). However, in California teams have worked with mixed success, "encountering much resistance at the school level" (Mintrop & Trujillo, 2005, p. 10). Though academic assistance appears to be positive, "limited reporting . . . in terms of the kinds of strategies that work well or don't work well or the level of intensity of intervention that is needed" (McColskey & Monrad, 2004, p. 13) remains a problem. So too does a reliance on perceptual data.

In Neuman-Sheldon's (2006) research of turnaround in Maryland, the decision to use turnaround specialists was made at the district level. The time and the services that turnaround specialists provide failing schools vary significantly. "It is also unclear to what extent turnaround specialists affect [failing] schools" (p. 10), but "principals and teachers rarely mentioned the turnaround specialist when they were asked about strategies to improve student performance" (p. 11).

Provision of Choice

School districts large and small report that hardly any students in failing schools are using the choice provisions of the federal

law to move to other public schools. Even in some of the
nation's largest cities, the number of kids traveling across town
to attend better schools on any given morning might not fill a
single school bus. (Brownstein, 2003, p. 40)

"Practical experience has shown that the hope of choice proponents, in regards to school failure, is only partially fulfilled"
(Spreng, 2005, p. 18), and "it is still too early to evaluate [choice's]
impact" (p. 19). According to Brownstein (2003), three salient points
appear to limit the choice provision thus far:

1. Parents' inertia, lack of knowledge, or reluctance to upset
   routines and friendships by removing their children from
   neighborhood schools

2. Lack of high-quality public school alternatives within reasonable driving distance of many a failing urban school

3. Little evidence that suburban schools are opening their doors
   to refugees from the urban systems. (p. 40)

In Kirby and her colleagues' study (2005) using National
Longitudinal Survey of Schools (NLSS) data, "authorizing transfers
of students to other public schools occurred very infrequently, in less
than 5 percent of the schools" (p. 13). Faced with such limitations,
"failing schools may well continue to operate without being affected
[by choice] in the expected way" (Spreng, 2005, p. 37).

Provision of Supplemental Services

*Over 80% . . . of survey respondents indicated through anec-
dotes that they did not think that parents were sufficiently
informed about the availability of SES [Supplemental Education
Services] and encountered many parents who had heard about
the program through other parents or service providers, but had
never received eligibility letters from the district.* (Advocates for
Children, 2003, p. 15)

An experimental study of a representative sample of students
participating in Hillsborough County (Florida) School District's
one-to-one tutoring program "showed that second-graders who
received tutoring improved their composite assessment scores by

274 percent, more than double the rate of increase for non-tutored students [and] were also three times more likely than their non-tutored counterparts to be reading at the third-grade level" (U.S. Department of Education, 2001, p. 41). Though the Hillsborough County study is encouraging, research on supplemental services as a turnaround intervention is quite limited. Limitations similar to choice provision exist: according to Davis (2006), a Department of Education report released in April 2006 "found that only 17 percent of eligible students nationwide signed up for the free tutoring that Title I schools are required to offer after not meeting educational targets for three years in a row" (p. 31). From their survey of parents of students in New York City failing schools, Advocates for Children (2003) reports that some eligible parents never receive SES information. When the information is presented, it is often given with a "hurried timeline" (p. 4) and sometimes not presented in the parents' primary language. Moreover, some service providers are unable to accommodate English language learners and students with disabilities.

Adoption of a Reform Model

Thus, as an intervention strategy, CSR [Comprehensive School Reform] can and does work, but the best evidence suggests that it does so about half the time. (Brady, 2003, p. 25)

Adoption of a model did not by itself increase a school's chances of getting out [of failing status]. (Kirby et al., 2005, p. 16)

Despite all the attention focused on schoolwide reform as the answer to improving students' academic success, comprehensive reform remains "promising but unproven." (McChesney & Hertling, 2000, p. 10)

Although the adoption of a comprehensive school reform model yields mixed results overall, there are clear success stories. For example, Avery County High School in Newland, North Carolina, began using the Tech Prep Program in partnership with a local community college. Five years later, Avery County also joined High Schools That Work (HSTW), a program combining challenging academic courses with vocational training. "The changes made through Tech Prep and HSTW have raised students' scores on both the SAT and the North Carolina End of Course Exams. The number of students taking the SAT nearly doubled between 1996 and 1998, even as average scores rose" (U.S. Department of Education, 2001, p. 40). In addition, Wang and Manning (2000) report the following findings for Community for Learning (CFL) implemented in failing Washington, D.C., schools:

- Many staff were able to achieve a moderate to high degree of program implementation within less than 6 months.

- As the degree of program implementation improved, a concomitant pattern of positive changes in the classroom processes and teacher and student classroom behaviors was observed.

- Teachers spent more time interacting with students for instructional rather than managerial purposes.

- Teachers expressed more positive perceptions about their ability to provide for student diversity when survey results from preimplementation and postimplementation periods were compared.

- Achievement scores suggested that students functioning in the program for a greater period of time performed better than their peers who had less time in the program.

- Positive changes in student achievement were also reflected when comparing the fall 1996 and spring 1997 Stanford Achievement test . . . results.

- There was a consensus among the principals and program facilitators that a kindred sense of accomplishment was evident among the staff. (pp. 9–11)

Borman and his colleagues (2000) also report positive turn-around implications for the adoption of reform models, but their assessment of the turnaround results in two failing schools uncovers potential limitations as well. In both schools, teachers rationalized the compromising of their creativity "as worthwhile sacrifices because of the evidence" (p. 40) of student improvement, so teacher buy-in was generally high in each school. In one school, attendance rates increased slightly, and large increases in both reading and mathematics achievement were recorded. However, in the other school, attendance rates remained constant, and reading and mathematics scores improved much less significantly. In Memphis, researchers found added value with the first test group of schools, but the second test group of schools "did not demonstrate similar gains" (Brady, 2003, p. 25).

For comprehensive school reform models as turnaround interventions to be successful, faculty, staff, and parents must support them (McChesney & Hertling, 2000), a difficulty that often "lies in the paradox of creating a common vision among people with different beliefs and assumptions about education" (p. 11). In Kentucky, for example, Picucci and her associates (2002) establish the importance of teacher buy-in, specifically with regard to turnaround. In two turnaround schools, "since significant time to plan was available to these schools, and there [were] no strong traditions for doing things a certain way, staff members were able to implement major reforms simultaneously and contribute to the new direction for these schools" (p. 46). McChesney and Hertline (2000) suggest the following for "sustaining schoolwide reform programs past the initial stage of enthusiasm":

- Strong leadership
- Freely chosen designs
- Parent involvement with site councils, planning teams, and accreditation committees. (p. 11)

Reconstitution

Anecdotal evidence suggests [reconstitution has] brought a much-needed sense of order and stability to some schools, along with an increase in parent and community involvement. (Ziebarth, 2004b, p. 5)

Although some anecdotal evidence suggested that reconstitution efforts have removed ineffective staff members and brought in staff who are eager to take on the challenge of working in chronically unsuccessful schools, the anticipated gains in student achievement scores and other student performance indicators have been sporadic. (Rudo, 2001, p. 3)

Overall, it is clear that reconstitution as a policy initiative is different in every setting where it has been implemented. (Peterson, 1999, p. 21)

In reviewing reconstitution turnaround findings, Brady (2003) offers three assumptions regarding reconstitution from which decision makers typically work:

1. That reconstitution will create more capable (skilled) and committed (willing) school faculty and staff

2. That the new faculty and staff will, based on their skills and commitment, redesign the failing school

3. That the redesigned school will improve student achievement. (p. 26)

Indeed, many of the reconstitution findings are reported with the assumptions listed above as the guiding framework.

"In some schools, [reconstitution] turnaround efforts have brought order and stability, as well as an increase in parent and community involvement" (Kowal & Hassel, 2005, p. 7; also Rudo, 2001). In their study of two reconstituted schools, Borman and his colleagues (2000) found "some evidence that reconstitution had the intended effects of ridding the schools of staff who may have held prejudices and who may have been less than committed" (p. 56), but such changes are "not without a cost to the stock of human capital at sites" (Rice & Malen, 2003, p. 645). In Chicago, for example, good teachers "were reluctant to transfer to [reconstituted] schools for fear the school would eventually be closed and their faculties would be fired" (Hess, 2003, p. 307). In their study of Prince George County (PGC), Maryland, Malen and her team (2002) discovered that reconstitution "may not secure more capable and committed staff [as] negative sentiments prompted some reputedly excellent teachers to accept positions in other schools and in other districts" (pp. 120–121). Therefore, in PGC "the majority of the staff in the new schools came from outside the district" (Brady, 2003, p. 28), raising concerns about teacher commitment.

Hope High School in Providence experienced substantial staff turnover, "including three new administrators and 50 teachers" (Steiner, 2005, p. 6). Such staff overhaul can lead to many teachers operating with emergency credentials (Borman et al., 2000). In PGC, where the "infusion of inexperienced teachers was not a one-time occurrence" (Rice & Malen, 2003, p. 646), teacher and administrator qualifications declined. Three of the six reconstituted school "principals were not only new to the school but also relatively new to this role" (p. 123; Brady, 2003). Furthermore, "principal and teacher replacements, on average, had less experience and fewer teaching credentials than the previous faculties" (Rice & Malen, 2003, p. 645). Even experienced teachers can feel "'ill-prepared' for and 'overwhelmed' by the many classroom management, instructional development and major organizational challenges confronting them" (Malen et al., 2002, p. 122). In San Francisco, it was "not clear that the evidence fully supported the expansion of all aspects of reconstitution as a remedy. It is particularly not clear that vacating the adults led to heightened performance" (Goldstein, Kelemen, & Koski, 1998, pp. 9–10).

Results of redesigning the school and implementing change on the heels of reconstitution seem site-specific, that is, context-dependent. In Hess's (2003) study in Chicago, there was relatively little staff change in the reconstituted schools and hence "little change in the culture and structure of [the] schools" (p. 318). Borman and his colleagues (2000) report high buy-in by veteran and new teachers in one reconstituted school where staff voted for a reform model. However, at the second school in the study, the district mandated a reform that the teachers "hated" (p. 23). The PGC schools show "little evidence that major programmatic changes accompanied the new staff" (Brady, 2003, p. 28). According to Malen and her associates (2002), minimal redesign in reconstituted schools is understandable:

> Reconstitution creates major changes in the personnel component of the schools, but these personnel changes may not be sufficient to overhaul a school. Rather reconstitution may create disruptions and intensify pressures that consume new staffs and deny them opportunities to redesign schools. . . . New staffs may be quickly and repeatedly "swept into a survival mode" that necessitates the restoration of familiar routines and stifles the prospects for meaningful reform. (p. 124)

In PGC, reconstitution "contributed to organizational dynamics in ways that undercut productivity and diluted capacity for meaningful school improvement" (Malen & Rice, 2004, p. 650), as "the recurrent pattern of administrative reassignments and staff departures meant that site actors were having to repeatedly reinvent the wheel" (Rice & Malen, 2003, p. 649).

For all of the school-level changes, academic progress among reconstituted schools remains mixed (Kowal & Hassel, 2005), "effective in improving student achievement in some schools, but yielding little or no improvement in others" (Brady, 2003, p. 28). Ziebarth (2004b) reports that "academic progress, as measured by standardized test scores, is uneven in reconstituted schools" (p. 5). "Nonetheless, it is clear that some schools have been turned around through reconstitution and that some previously dysfunctional schools are now better serving their students" (Peterson, 1999, p. 22). Kowal and Hassel (2005) report that one elementary school in Houston "has become a model turnaround, consistently gaining ratings of Acceptable or higher on the Texas grading system" (p. 8) since being reconstituted in the early 1990s. At Humboldt Elementary in Portland, Oregon, student scores on state tests have risen by approximately 50 percentage points in reading for both third and fifth graders, and math improvement for fifth graders has been even more dramatic (U.S. Department of Education, 2001). In early San Francisco reconstitution interventions, a "review panel found . . . that school restructuring had enhanced students' achievement, and the panel recommended expansion of the . . . policy" (Kowal & Hassel, 2005, p. 7).

However, both reconstituted schools in the Borman and colleagues (2000) study declined considerably in reading achievement, and one declined significantly in mathematics, while the other increased slightly. Furthermore, while the seven reconstituted schools in Chicago "made modest gains in reading achievement" (Hess, 2003, p. 318), such improvements were only about half of the citywide gains. Moreover, more eighth- and ninth-grade students scored at national norms, but this occurred only after enforcement of promotion gates. Several New York City Schools Under Registration Review (SURR) schools have undergone a version of reconstitution, and about half of the them appear to be turning around. However, Brady (2003) asserts that these findings are hollow, "as another half of its schools do not improve and, for those that do, these improvements do not assure that anywhere near enough of their students possess sufficient academic skills to pass, much less excel, in state tests" (pp. 22–23).

Over three years of reconstitution in PGC, "two of the six schools strongly outpaced the average gain for the state. A third school . . . gained ground commensurate with the state gain. But the remaining three schools lagged behind statewide gains" (Brady, 2003, p. 28). Such erratic patterns in PGC "suggest that the relationship between reconstitution . . . and gains in student achievement is neither direct nor dependable" (Malen et al., 2002, p. 126). According to Cibulka (2003), "only a small number of Maryland's schools under local reconstitution have improved enough to be removed from the state list" (p. 266). Even when students at a reconstituted school do perform markedly better, it remains "unclear which aspects of the policy generated improved student performance and that vacating alone did not do so" (Goldstein, Kelemen, & Koski, 1998, p. 21).

The effects of reconstitution could create a school climate that inhibits student achievement, since "the decision to reconstitute schools has a profound impact on a school community" (Goldstein, Kelemen, & Koski, 1998, p. 17). In addition to pedagogical and other limitations often associated with young and inexperienced teachers, Borman and his team (2000) found "clear tensions between the new teachers and the pre-reconstitution veterans who were hired back" (p. 56). Also, returning teachers "often feel *personally* blamed when a school is reconstituted" (Goldstein, Kelemen, & Koski, 1998, p. 17); in some PGC reconstituted schools, returning teachers "mourned the loss of colleagues and friends who were no longer a part of the school" (Rice & Malen, 2003, p. 655). In Chicago, the reputation of the reconstituted schools drove many students away as "the seven reconstituted schools lost 17.6[%] of their students between the fall of 1997 and the following spring" (Hess, 2003, p. 308). As for the students who remain in reconstituted schools, Borman and his team (2000) note that some feel as though reconstitution is their fault.

More broadly, studies on reconstitution are few, and results "offer no conclusive effects" (Cibulka, 2003, p. 266; also Hassel & Steiner, 2003), though Peterson (1999) offers the following early lessons:

1. The reconstitution process is an enormously complex and difficult process of school reform—perhaps more difficult than initially was thought. It is difficult to successfully reconstitute schools.

2. There have been extremely varied approaches to reconstitution across districts and states. This makes comparison of results difficult and simple replication ill-advised.

3. The outcomes in terms of student achievement are quite varied: Some schools improve while others remain unproductive. Reconstitution does not guarantee improved student learning.

4. This approach to school reform requires an enormous reservoir of resources, skills, knowledge, and leadership that the district must provide in a continuous and coordinated effort. Districts will need to commit some of their best people and many resources to support reconstitution.

5. Care and attention to each stage of reconstitution seems important if this reform is to succeed. Schools need help while preparing to reconstitute, during the implementation stage, and finally, in the institutionalization stage when the school is no longer under district watch.

6. Highly qualified, skilled school leadership remains crucial to success. Good principals are needed in these schools as they rebuild.

7. Before employing this reform technique, districts need to consider the range of unintended consequences from reconstitution including political conflict, lowered teacher morale, and a flood of inexperienced teachers into reconstituted schools. These can swamp any success. (pp. 21–22)

"Given the swift rise of reconstitution as a policy tool, and given the dramatic nature of the policy, it is surprising how little we know about the efficacy of reconstitution" (Goldstein, Kelemen, & Koski, 1998, p. 1) as well as "disappointing that research on the effects of reconstitution . . . is so very limited" (Rudo, 2001, p. 3). Even with marginal student achievement improvement in places such as Chicago (Hess, 2003), it seems "too soon to dismiss [reconstitution] without further thought" (Hassel & Steiner, 2003, p. 4) while it "remains an open, empirical question" (Malen et al., 2002, p.127). Reporting on reconstitution in San Francisco, Goldstein and colleagues (1998) report that no clear evidence of vacating the staff and administration increased student performance in failing schools. However, they also "want to be clear that there is no conclusive evidence that it was not a necessary part of the . . . reforms" (p. 11).

Miscellaneous Turnaround Proposals

In this subsection, we note the quite limited findings for some miscellaneous turnaround strategies: parent involvement, site-based reform, contracting out management of and/or running of the school, and switching to "charter" status.

• According to the U.S. Department of Education (2001), simply involving parents as a turnaround intervention can provide a path to improvement. Burgess Elementary School in Atlanta, Georgia, has increased parent involvement in the school substantially. This involvement has "had an effect on student performance" (p. 39), including over a 30-percentage point increase on the Iowa Test of Basic Skills in both reading and mathematics in three academic years.

• In Borman and his team's (2000) study of site-based turnaround, the failing school implementing professional control raised the attendance rate and substantially increased both reading and math achievement scores, perhaps due to the high occurrence of authentic instruction. On the one hand, the failing school implementing administrative control was unable to substantially raise attendance rates, reading scores, or math scores. Teachers there were much more limited in options, and authentic instruction was relatively low. Generally, effective site-based intervention advances democratic ideals, but "such an effort is difficult to replicate at other schools" (Borman et al., 2000, p. 55).

• According to Mintrop and Trujillo (2005), "takeover by management companies has helped in some cases, but is not universally positive" (p. 8). For example, preliminary data from Philadelphia suggest that the quality and content of turnaround differ substantially. Similarly, results of three such schools under Education Management Organizations (EMOs) in Baltimore show that "only one [failing school] saw consistent gains, one performed unevenly, and one was not improving" (p. 8). However, Spreng (2005) notes that some initial reports "suggest that . . . EMO schools show promising progress on the state exams" (p. 50).

• "While the research base on charter schools is expanding" (Mintrop & Trujillo, 2005, p. 9) and "charter schools' impact on student achievement reveals a mixed picture" (Ziebarth, 2004a, p. 3), "little is known about charter school conversion" (Mintrop &

Trujillo, 2005, p. 9) as a means of turnaround. Some converted charter schools "have managed to increase the standardized test scores of their students, but others have not" (Hacsi, 2004, p. 16). In one Sacramento high school, the school's test score index has risen 20 points (Arkin & Kowal, 2005), while in one San Diego high school, "attendance rates are up, suspensions are down, and grades have improved" (Robelen, 2006, p. 8). A Colorado middle school "made mixed progress in raising student achievement" (Arkin & Kowal, 2005, p. 7). In a Brown Center study, "conversion charters scored more highly than their public school counterparts and start-up charters . . . [but] anecdotal evidence from Philadelphia suggests that charter school conversion without the benefit of an external provider model may be the least successful conversion of the ones tried there" (Mintrop & Trujillo, 2005, p. 9).

Level

Looking at individual failing schools redirects the attention almost invariably to the policy environment in which they function. Despite a focus on individual schools, much of any identified failure can be traced back to challenges facing the entire districts, or state, in which they are located. (Spreng, 2005, p. 48)

Turnaround findings can be examined at the federal, state, city (mayoral), and district levels.

Federal

Although NCLB creates some uniformity in states' approaches to low performance by demanding adequately yearly progress towards a proficiency ceiling, the rigor of performance demands and intervention burdens differ across states. (Mintrop & Trujillo, 2005, p. 4)

Following NCLB legislation, some early reports indicate achievement gains. The U.S. Department of Education concluded that students in subgroups most often associated with failing schools generally had slight achievement gains in reading and mathematics from the 2000–2001 to the 2002–2003 school year (Davis, 2006). However, the same report also found that students in failing schools are more likely than their peers "to be taught by teachers who did not meet the law's 'highly qualified' criteria" (p. 31). Research remains incomplete, and many find that "it's premature to gauge NCLB's 'success'" (Hess & Finn, 2004, p. 34).

More broadly, assessing student achievement gains and turnaround interventions at the federal level will be complicated, considering that NCLB's remedy provisions rely "on state and district educators to police themselves" (Hess & Finn, 2004, p. 38). Whether states or districts have the capacity and knowledge to turn around failing schools is debatable, and "a general lack of detailed information at the national level" (Kirby, Naftel, Berends, & McCombs, 2005, p. 1) means that the question is still open. For example, Kirby and her colleagues (2005) found that many failing school principals were unaware of or disagreed with their schools' failing status and/or how long the school had been identified. Moreover, NCLB "does not explicitly address what the state should do after state officials have taken over a school; it merely suggests that under some circumstances the district might choose to turn the school over to the state" (Steiner, 2005, p. 4). "Meanwhile, many states are not identifying in a timely fashion the schools that are eligible, not providing effective guidance on fulfilling the mandates of the law, or not supporting the creation of new options" (Hess & Finn, 2004, pp. 38–39). Since under NCLB, states, cities (mayors), and districts determine turnaround interventions, perhaps little meaningful federal-level data will be forthcoming.

State

Direct interventions by state agencies to improve performance in "failing" schools face a number of critical obstacles. First, state education agencies typically serve hundreds of districts and thousands of schools, most of which are geographically distant from the capital. They consequently have little local knowledge of schools and communities. Under these circumstances, political and bureaucratic exigencies make it difficult for them to tailor their interventions to the specific local needs of individual schools and districts. Second, state interventions in local school districts are almost invariably triggered by crisis, so school districts rarely enter into a relationship with the state freely or as a partner. The consequent lack of trust may require state officials to overcome deep local resistance in order to establish the legitimacy necessary to assist "failing" schools. (Arsen, Bell, & Plank, 2003, p. 16)

[State takeover] has yielded no conclusive research findings to support their effectiveness in reversing school district failure and improving student achievement. (Forster, 1997, p. 2)

Student achievement still oftentimes falls short of expectations after a state takeover. In most cases, academic results are usually mixed at best, with increases in student performance in some areas and decreases in student performance in other areas. The bottom line is that state takeovers, for the most part, have yet to produce dramatic and consistent increases in student performance, as is necessary in many of the school districts that are taken over. (Ziebarth, 2004b, p. 2)

"The results of several long-term state experiments in intervening in failing school districts have been mixed" (Linn, Rothman, & White, 2001, p. 4). Furthermore, "school/district takeovers have been found to have inconsistent results for student performance" (Rudo, 2001, p. 5). Still, the "need for the intervention never stops being questioned and debated" (Forster, 1997, p. 27).

Highly centralized state takeovers in New Jersey seem to have improved academic achievement slightly, as indicated by eighth-grade students scoring at or above state standards in reading and mathematics, but resulted "in tension between state officials and the local community" (Cibulka, 2003, p. 255). Furthermore, "survival, jobs and power emerged as the predominant cultural themes in the organization" (Forster, 1997, p. 18), with student education relegated to a lower level of importance. The most significant gains in New Jersey appear to be in financial management (Cibulka, 2003). In many other state takeovers, as in New Jersey's, interventions "seem to be yielding more gains in central office activities than in classroom instructional practices" (Ziebarth, 2004b, p. 2; also Rudo, 2001). Five years removed from the original takeover, Forster (1997) feels that "it is too soon to determine complete success or failure of the takeover as an intervention which brings about effective reform or direct educational benefit to students" (p. 4).

In Compton, California, since the state takeover, there has been "small but steady progress" (Bushweller, 1998, p. 4) in the district's test scores, dropout rates, and measures of campus crime. Student academic performance is improving in some failing schools as well (Wong & Shen, 2003). However, the top-down approach to intervention has been resisted strongly (Cibulka, 2003), and when state takeovers "produce administrative and political turmoil, student achievement suffers" (Wong & Shen, 2003, p. 110) perhaps due in part to staff resentment of external influence (Cibulka, 2003). Thus, in Compton, many teachers have left the district, approximately 40% of the current teachers operate under emergency credentials, and the school board is the root of "some of the biggest troubles" (Bushweller, 1998, p. 4).

Not all state takeover initiatives are so highly centralized. In Maryland, a city-state partnership was created as an "alternative to state takeover when [the state] intervened in Baltimore City" (Cibulka, 2003, p. 257). In the same vein, local and state authorities worked collaboratively in Logan County, West Virginia, where state officials attributed standardized test score gains "to the fact that the state did not dissolve the school board and worked to win local support for the reforms" (p. 265). Instead of attempting to repair everything at once, 8 to 10 problems were identified for improvement yearly. When West Virginia returned the Logan County district to local control, "all of the schools were scoring above the 50th percentile and had attendance rates of 90 percent or better" (Bushweller, 1998, p. 2). Some general lessons from Jersey City, Compton, and Logan County include the following:

- Align the local curriculum with state standards and test.
- Involve teachers from the outset.
- Work to prevent turnover in key administrative positions.
- Pick a realistic number of problems to address each year.
- Open lines of communication with the community.
- Work to maintain consistency on the board.
- Seek formal board training. (Bushweller, 1998, p. 7)

In addition, Linn and colleagues (2001) provide governors with the following policy-action suggestions:

- Demand Results-Based Accountability.
- Ensure Efficient Use of Resources.
- Invest in Quality Professional Development.
- Support Extra Learning Opportunities.
- Create Incentives to Reward Performance. (pp. 6–7)

Data from "Kentucky, North Carolina, and other states suggest that providing intensive support is an essential part of these states' success in turning around [failing] schools" (Mazzeo & Berman, 2003, p. 14), but too many state turnaround efforts "have not provided remedies for the continuing failure of school districts and low student achievement" (Forster, 1997, p. 1). "Research on state interventions has suggested that states often lack the capacity needed to intervene successfully in [failing] schools" (Steiner, 2005, p. 7), and new burdens imposed by NCLB and added or recurrent state budget deficits will further inhibit state capacity to turn around failing schools in the future (Arsen, Bell, & Plank, 2003).

It is important to remember that "there is no magic in a takeover" (Forster, 1997, p. 21). "State efforts to turn around [failing] schools will not succeed in isolation" (Mazzeo & Berman, 2003, p. 22), and as such, all of their education policies and resources will need to be carefully assembled. Even then, the complexities of implementing turnarounds "are just as great, if not greater, after the takeover" (Forster, 1997, p. 21), as it is not unusual for student achievement to remain inadequate after takeover, with some school systems "worse off than they were before the takeover" (Rudo, 2001, p. 5). And "unfortunately, there is limited information about how much and what type of support is most effective" (Steiner, 2005, p. 20). Furthermore, schools lose many of the resources used to implement successful turnaround soon after making adequate progress (Neuman-Sheldon, 2006). Nonetheless, some maintain that after a period of adjustment, "state takeovers may also be able to produce positive achievement gains" (Wong & Shen, 2003, p. 112).

City (Mayoral)

Assessing the results of urban school takeovers is a complex, controversial, and as yet [an] inconclusive matter. (Green & Carl, 2000, p. 66)

Just as each city is different, so are the impacts (such as can be determined) of governance change. Most importantly, it is difficult to link these governance shifts to improved instructional practices or outcomes. (Kirst, 2002, p. 1)

Some mayors, as has been the case in Cleveland, have taken a hands-off approach to troubled schools, while others, such as those in Boston and Chicago, have "responded with strong leadership"

(Cibulka, 2003, pp. 265–266), as "each city presents a somewhat different scenario" (p. 259). Sacramento, California, possibly the most successful city-school turnaround, "has no formal mayoral appointment power, but was galvanized by the election of a mayoral-endorsed slate of candidates" (Kirst, 2002, p. 3). Cibulka (2003) contends that strong civic capacity could be the key to turnaround success in cities like Pittsburgh, Boston, and Chicago that have received the most academic scrutiny while enjoying some academic success. Polls indicate that citizens of each city are more pleased with mayoral control than with the school boards that were replaced (Kirst, 2002). "Mayoral takeovers in Chicago and Boston [also] appear to be more productive in terms of academic improvement" (Wong & Shen, 2003, p. 117) than state takeovers have been. In Chicago, "mayoral takeover led to improved student achievement, particularly at the elementary level" (Cibulka, 2003, p. 265). After examining mayoral takeover as it unfolded in Boston and Chicago, Wong and Shen (2003) provide the following three general conclusions:

1. Mayoral takeover is linked to increases in student achievement at the elementary grades.

2. Gains in achievement are especially large for the lowest performing schools.

3. Mayoral takeover seems less effective for the upper grades. (pp. 107–109)

Though the takeover in Chicago led to some success, other mayoral takeovers have not (Green & Carl, 2000). "Mayors perhaps have the least impact where the mayor's powers are least clear, as in Oakland and Detroit" (Kirst, 2002, p. 9), leaving the mayors vulnerable to "significant resistance from some stakeholder groups" (Cibulka, 2003, p. 259). In Detroit, Mayor Archer was opposed strongly by the teachers' union and a divided black community. In Baltimore, the mayor was forced to surrender control of the schools to the state after years of dismal pupil attainment and public dissatisfaction (Kirst, 2002).

Like the federal- and state-level turnarounds discussed above, "mayoral interventions are not a panacea" (Cibulka, 2003, p. 265), and "the verdict on urban school takeovers is somewhat mixed"

(Green & Carl, 2000, p. 66). Even failing districts and schools that show improvement typically "remain far below state and national averages" (p. 67) on achievement indicators. Though "the impact of enhanced mayoral influence on instruction remains tenuous and unclear" (Kirst, 2002, p. 15), there are some positive signs, including "early evidence that [mayoral] takeover initiatives may be stimulating positive developments in nonacademic areas of school performance and operations" (Green & Carl, 2000, p. 67). Ultimately, mayors are able to "help balance the budget, improve buildings, and increase school supplies, but intervention in the classroom is more difficult" (Kirst, 2002, p. 15).

District

The strategies that school districts could adopt to accomplish [turnaround] are increasingly well known, but their track record in improving performance in these schools is poor, for several reasons. Most districts are too small to offer effective assistance, and few are able to marshal the breadth and depth of technical expertise that is needed to bring about lasting improvements in teaching and learning. In other cases, the best efforts of district administrators are undermined by political turbulence, or by long histories of "policy churn," broken promises, and a consequently deep distrust on the part of local educators. (Arsen, Bell, & Plank, 2003, pp. 14–15)

Turnarounds in San Diego and Community District #2 in New York City serve as "evidence that districts can act as 'agents of instructional change'" (Arsen, Bell, & Plank, 2003, pp. 12–13). In Community District #2, lessons learned include "focusing on instruction, sharing expertise, focusing on district-wide improvement, and setting clear expectations" (Fullan, 2005, p. 177). After their examination of New York City's Chancellor's District, Phenix and her colleagues (2005) maintain that such initiatives could be "a harbinger of the newly emerging emphasis on the district as the necessary locus of school change" (p. 20), though the components that led to the turnaround remain elusive.

The mixed results from district turnarounds need to be understood in the context of "a large body of research that argues that districts are generally ill prepared to support improvement in 'failing' schools" (Arsen, Bell, & Plank, 2003, p. 13). Available evidence indicates that few districts have the capacity to implement such vast turnaround initiatives as was the case in Community District #2, where failing schools received considerable help, "including replacement of principals, external support, monitoring, and feedback" (Fullan, 2005, p. 177). Instead, failing schools are often located in failing or struggling districts, where problems include limited technical expertise, lack of deep commitment to professional learning, and mistrust between the district and its schools (Arsen, Bell, & Plank, 2003). Research confirms that efforts to turn around failing schools "will be hampered or derailed entirely without a supportive and complementary district context within which to implement reforms" (Mazzeo & Berman, 2003, p. 17).

GENERAL TURNAROUND INSIGHTS

No one strategy alone is the "magic bullet" for turning around all low-performing schools. In the process of ongoing improvement, creativity, innovation and full participation are key ingredients. From the many examples offered, it is clear that low-performing schools require unique and multiple strategies to address the context and complexity of the school and its community. (Housman & Martinez, 2001, p. 7)

Decades of experience with turning around low performing schools, however, suggests that the rate of success is unlikely to be 100%. (Hassel & Steiner, 2003, p. 1)

Indeed, the only sure way to transform dysfunctional schools into effective schools is to build capacity in them—to provide smart, strong leadership, a mission clearly and intensely focused on children's learning, highly competent committed teachers, clean lines of responsibility, adequate financial resources, and an environment that fosters collaboration, trust, and continuous learning. (Wolk, 1998, p. 7)

Complicated Implementation

As noted above and seen in Chapters 6 through 9, the real work of turnaround begins after policy is enacted (Forster, 1997), since any turnaround initiative is a "complex process in which clear cause-effect relationships are difficult to isolate" (Lashway, 2004, p. 25). "There are no one-size-fits-all solutions to turning around . . . failing schools" (Linn, Rothman, & White, 2001, p. 7), and most studies "suggest that it is far easier to clean up district-level finances and management practices than it is to make a dent in student achievement" (Wong & Shen, 2003, p. 96). Even when turnarounds are successful, experts have difficulty isolating which aspects of reform explain the turnaround (Goldstein, Kelemen, & Kosko, 1998; Lashway, 2004). Furthermore, once a turnaround effort has proven successful, sustaining momentum is difficult (Brady, 2003). Overall, "lack of dramatic or immediate results is not surprising" (Lashway, 2004, p. 26).

Inconclusive Evidence

A variety of turnaround initiatives have been tried, "but none stick out as universally effective or robust enough to overcome the power of local context" (Mintrop & Trujillo, 2005, p. 10; see also Chapter 5). "The prevailing [turnaround] approaches will work for some schools, but others will be left behind" (Hassel & Steiner, 2003, p. 3), and "the research base offers many instances where interventions that are successful in one setting fail in another" (Brady, 2003, p. 30). Cibulka (2003) finds research on state takeovers, mayoral takeovers, and reconstitution to be limited; not all aspects of effectiveness are addressed, and "the outcomes of such approaches have been mixed at best. Some successes can be found, but counterexamples are evident as well" (p. 266). Wong and Shen (2003) aver that many examples of student achievement improvements exist after both city and state takeovers, but "there are also many counterexamples of recent decline" (p. 102). As such, "it is not clear that gains in performance can be attributed directly to takeovers themselves" (Green & Carl, 2000, p. 67). Strong interventions like reconstitution and takeover continue to be implemented on a limited basis due to the controversy and difficulties that follow, which, perhaps implicitly, make the costs of these turnaround interventions "exceed the potential benefits" (Brady, 2003, p. 19). In addition, some schools in large cities get off the watch list only to see "in the long-term these student achievement gains [level] off" (Hassel & Steiner, 2003, p. 2).

Combining Turnaround Strategies

"Schools fail for a variety of reasons, and [turnaround] strategies need to be tailored to fit the needs of individual schools" (Kirby et al., 2005, p. 16; also Brady, 2003; U.S. Department of Education, 2001). Interventions typically follow a graduated pattern, but turnaround initiatives often devise "multiple simultaneous intervention strategies" (Brady, 2003, p. 10) and are implemented as groups in order to "mix and match various strategies . . . most appropriate [for a] particular school" (p. 31). Turnaround efforts in New York's SURR include several strategies working simultaneously: "identification, planning, technical assistance, professional development, more time, and the threat of closing schools" (p. 21).

Building Capacity

The key to understanding any organization lies in understanding its human and social dimensions. (Forster, 1997, p. 23)

Policies that incorporate the provision of material and human resources and establish a climate of support and leadership seem to have a much better chance of improving student performance. (Rudo, 2001, p. 7)

According to Fullan (2005), a turnaround intervention that combines accountability—although Mintrop and Trujillo (2005) contend it is a "double-edged sword and not as promising as perhaps originally perceived" (p. 6)—and capacity-building strategies result in school improvement to a point. With such a combination and with capacity building acting as the "main driver" (Fullan, 2005, p. 176), achievement scores often increase to a point, though in these cases it is usually "a move from poor scores to adequate ones" (p. 176). Similarly, Mac Iver and his team (2003) suggest that the success of turnaround interventions depend upon "the cooperative nature of the effort" (p. 286). According to the U.S. Department of Education (2001), research to date suggests that "capacity is the major issue in turning around low-performing schools [considering those schools] are usually the ones least likely to be in a position to turn themselves around" (p. 30).

Leaders must garner control and commitment while creating a healthy organizational climate that promotes problem solving and productivity (Forster, 1997). Linn and colleagues (2001) assert that principals are "the key to the success of any schools, but especially in turning around" failing schools (p. 5). "In most instances where a [failing] school made real gains, a strong and typically experienced principal" (Brady, 2003, p. 31) was a "crucial success factor" (Mazzeo & Berman, 2003, p. 22). "The right leader can effect enormous improvements no matter how low the odds of success" (Steiner, 2005, p. 9). Hence, as we saw in other sectors and industries, strong leadership appears to be a necessary condition for turning around failing schools (U.S. Department of Education, 2001), and "without strong, supportive, visionary leadership, . . . school capacity is seriously undermined" (Kirby et al., 2005, p. 17). Still, turnaround leadership "must be put in perspective with and connected to comprehensive strategies" (Fullan, 2005, pp. 180–181), as "programs must be able to replicate even without a colossus at their helm" (Wang & Manning, 2000, p. 21).

Cibulka (2003) suggests that failure to provide students in failing schools with qualified teachers "may be a powerful explanation for the limited impact of many takeover and reconstitution policies" (p. 264). For example, in Goldstein and colleagues' (1998) study of reconstitution in San Francisco, the authors aver that successful turnaround is attributable to "a commitment to staff development and individual learning" (p. 8). Similarly, Mac Iver and his colleagues (2003) maintain that one of the keys to turnaround gains appears to "lie in the focus on improving instruction" (p. 286). As noted in various sections above, teacher buy-in seems critical for successful turnaround. "Without the initial 'buy-in' and commitment of teachers, change is far less likely to be successful" (Borman et al., 2000, p. 67); therefore, turnaround interventions "should be done *with* local participants, not *to* them" (Bowles et al., 2002, p. 3). In Picucci and her colleagues' (2002) study of failing schools, turnaround initiatives "were most effective when they were made by staff who understood the direction of the improvement process and were committed to making this vision a reality" (p. 48). On the other hand, mandated reforms "tend to result in low teacher buy-in" (p. 28), and teachers who feel "helpless to affect improvement . . . sometimes perceive rewards as unfair and/or unattainable" (Mazzeo & Berman, 2003, p. 13).

OVERARCHING LESSONS

> *It appears that comprehensiveness is a key characteristic that makes [turnaround] interventions sufficiently different from all other things that schools have tried before and that makes corrective action programs effective.* (Mintrop & Trujillo, 2005, p. 17)

Since so much of the early literature on turnarounds in education is exploratory, many findings are broad in nature. In general, successful turnaround efforts "appear to share a four-step process involving a needs assessment, a planning phase, an implementation phase, and a period of assessment and evaluation" (U.S. Department of Education, 2001, p. 29). To conclude their study of various turnaround interventions, Borman and his colleagues (2000) determine five characteristics that consistently shape turnaround effort results:

1. How the reform model was implemented

2. Teachers' beliefs, both before and during implementation, that the reform would make a difference for their students

3. Fiscal resources

4. Community outreach and support

5. Use of a nationally proven school reform model (pp. 61–62)

In reviewing turnaround literature, Brady (2003) lists the following 10 general conclusions:

1. Some turnaround efforts have improved schools.

2. Success is not the norm.

3. No particular intervention type appears clearly more successful than any other.

4. Standard cost-benefit analyses of interventions may be misplaced.

5. School leadership is a common thread in successful turnarounds.

6. Stronger intervention strategies are difficult and costly.

7. Most decision makers accept failure rather than intervene.

8. Interventions are typically implemented as packages, not discrete actions.

9. Interventions are hard to sustain.

10. Interventions are uneven in implementation and unpredictable in practice. (pp. 30–32)

In the same vein, Mintrop and Trujillo (2005) record eight overarching lessons:

1. Sanctions and increasing pressures are not the fallback solution.

2. No single strategy has been universally successful.

3. Staging should be handled with flexibility.

4. Intensive capacity building is necessary.

5. A comprehensive set of strategies seems promising.

6. Relationship-building needs to complement powerful programs.

7. Competence reduces conflict.

8. Strong state commitment is needed to create system capacity. (pp. 5–20)

And Spreng (2005) adds the following "common conclusions [drawn from] a number of different reports" (p. 45):

1. The evidence of turnaround is mixed, as "providing the right circumstances . . . is very hard to do." (p. 45)

2. The two components that matter most are the capacity of the turnaround body and the leadership of the turnaround school.

3. The balance between supporting the failing school and sanctioning the failing school is crucial but difficult to maintain.

4. The "management of expectations is key" (p. 46), and though results should be expected, they should not be demanded immediately.

Furthermore, Brady (2003) provides six implications for decision makers who will be considering when, how, and with what strategies to intervene in a failing school:

1. The specific intervention strategy is not important. What's important is having the right mix of people, energy, timing, and other elements—particularly school leadership—that together contribute to success.

2. Interventions come in many forms and flavors, and for each circumstance a different package might be appropriate.

3. Don't hesitate to mix and match.

4. Stick around. . . . Where interventions have been associated with success, it is typically two to three years before these results manifest themselves in test scores.

5. You will be criticized and sometimes vilified. Your efforts may be discarded when you leave. But know that you do have colleagues who are fighting the same fight and taking on the same battles.

6. Don't expect anything to work every time or everywhere. (p. 32)

With similar observations, Mazzeo and Berman (2003) present five suggestions:

1. Not all low-performing schools are the same.

2. Capacity-building must be part of the solution.

3. Districts are essential collaborators in efforts to turn around schools.

4. Be prepared for the long haul.

5. Assistance to low-performing schools should be part of a larger strategy of school improvement. (pp. 10–22)

From the education turnaround literature, we find that eight key lessons emerge:

1. Turnarounds can work, although success is not guaranteed. Of the turnaround initiatives, no one intervention appears to be significantly more successful than others. Such interventions are difficult to sustain, especially stronger ones that seem to be more difficult to manage as well as more costly. Still, some reports suggest that turnaround attempts are successful about half of the time.

2. Since single turnaround interventions do not always succeed, mixing and matching to develop a comprehensive approach seems promising. A comprehensive approach to turnaround failing schools allows for contextualized packages that are able to address specific concerns for a given school.

3. Successful turnaround schools almost always have good, if not exceptional, principals. As a common strand across successful school turnarounds, leadership is crucial. The principal typically sets the turnaround agenda while leading teachers, involving the community, and building general capacity—all important individual lessons discussed below.

4. Capacity building appears to be an imperative component of turning around failing schools. Developing relationships is integral in creating a positive environment in which to learn and in

establishing a shared vision. Cooperation and human development are two elements of capacity building that failing schools sometimes lack but need to move forward.

5. Teachers must believe in the turnaround intervention being implemented. Their opinions should be weighed when deciding upon turnaround strategies, especially considering their role in implementing the plans. When teachers do not buy in to the turnaround intervention(s), failing schools do not improve. Therefore, teachers should probably be seen as partners and facilitators in the turnaround process.

6. Connecting with parents is another important aspect of school turnaround. Since many of the students in failing schools face disruptive factors to learning outside of school, turnaround initiatives should engage parents on some level.

7. Failing schools need ample fiscal resources to turn around. Some failing schools lack these resources at the outset, while some others receive significant financial support immediately after being deemed failing. However, there are cases where the additional financial resources have ended too soon for the schools to completely implement their interventions fully.

8. In their attempts to turn around, failing schools should consistently assess themselves, especially considering it is not unusual for standard cost-benefit analyses of interventions to be misplaced. State and federal measures do not address some aspects of failure. Self-analysis enables failing schools to monitor successes as well as focus on areas that continue to lag.

References

Ackley, S. (1989). Tribune Company. In M. A. Wahba (Ed.), *Crisis management: Cases of success and failure of turnaround strategies* (pp. 3–76). New York: Hofstra University Yearbook of Business.

Adcock, E. P., & Winkler, L. (1999, April). *Jump higher or else! Measuring school reconstitution.* Paper presented at the annual meeting of the American Educational Research Association, Montreal, Canada.

Advocates for Children. (2003, October). *Serving those most in need or not? A report on the implementation of the NCLB's supplemental education services in New York City.* New York: Author.

Allmendinger, J., & Hackman, J. R. (1996). Organizations in changing environments: The case of East German symphony orchestras. *Administrative Science Quarterly, 41*(3), 337–369.

Altman, E. I. (1983). *Corporate financial distress: A complete guide to predicting, awarding, and dealing with bankruptcy.* New York: John Wiley & Sons.

Amburgey, T. L., Kelly, D., & Barnett, W. P. (1993). Resetting the clock: The dynamics of organizational change. *Administrative Science Quarterly, 38*(1), 51–73.

American Federation of Teachers. (1999). *Redesigning low-performing schools: It's union work.* Washington, DC: Author.

Anheier, H. K., & Moulton L. (1999a). Organizational failures, breakdowns, and bankruptcies: An introduction. In H. K. Anheier (Ed.), *When things go wrong: Organizational failures and breakdowns* (pp. 3–14). Thousand Oaks, CA: Sage.

Anheier, H. K., & Moulton, L. (1999b). Studying organizational failure. In H. K. Anheier (Ed.), *When things go wrong: Organizational failures and breakdowns* (pp. 273–290). Thousand Oaks, CA: Sage.

Anheier, H. K., & Romo, F. P. (1999). Stalemate. In H. K. Anheier (Ed.), *When things go wrong: Organizational failures and breakdowns* (pp. 241–270). Thousand Oaks, CA: Sage.

Archer, J. (2006). Proposed grants for improvement highlight key new role for states. *Education Week, 25*(24), 1, 40.

Argenti, J. (1976). *Corporate collapse: The causes and symptoms.* London: McGraw-Hill.

Arkin, M. D., & Kowal, J. M. (2005). *Reopening as a charter school.* Naperville, IL: North Central Regional Educational Laboratory.

Armenakis, A. A., & Fredenberger, W. B. (1998). Diagnostic practices of turnaround change agents. In L. W. Foster & D. Ketchen (Eds.), *Turnaround research: Past accomplishments and future challenges* (pp. 39–55). London: JAI Press.

Armenakis, A., Fredenberger, W., Cherones, L., & Field, H. (1995). Symbolic actions used by business turnaround change agents [Special issue]. *Academy of Management Journal,* 229–234.

Arogyaswamy, K., Barker, V. L., & Yasai-Ardekani, M. (1995). Firm turnarounds: An integrative two-stage model. *Journal of Management Studies, 32*(4), 493–525.

Arogyaswamy, K., & Yasai-Ardekani, M. (1997). Organizational turnaround: Understanding the role of cutbacks, efficiency improvements, and investment technology. *IEEE Transactions on Engineering Management, 44*(1), 3–11.

Arsen, D., Bell, C., & Plank, D. N. (2003, August). *Who will turn around "failing" schools? A framework for institutional choice* (Working Paper No. 12).

Ashmos, D. P., & Duchon, D. (1998). Participation in the midst of a turnaround: Using connections to make successful adaptations. In L. W. Foster & D. Ketchen (Eds.), *Turnaround research: Past accomplishments and future challenges* (pp. 223–236). Stamford, CT: JAI Press.

Austin, J. E. (1998). Business leadership lessons from the Cleveland turnaround. *California Management Review, 41*(1), 86–106.

Baehr, R. A. (1993). Introduction. In R. A. Baehr (Ed.), *Engineering a hospital turnaround* (pp. 1–11). Washington, DC: American Hospital Publishing.

Barker, V. L., & Duhaime, I. M. (1997). Strategic change in the turnaround process: Theory and empirical evidence. *Strategic Management Journal, 18*(1), 13–38.

Barker, V. L., & Mone, M. A. (1998). The mechanistic structure shift and strategic reorientations in declining firms attempting turnarounds. *Human Relations, 51*(10), 1227–1258.

Barker, V. L., Mone, M. A., Mueller, G. C., & Freeman, S. J. (1998). Does it add up? An empirical study of the value of downsizing for firm turnaround. In L. W. Foster & D. Ketchen (Eds.), *Turnaround research: Past accomplishments and future challenges* (pp. 57–82). Stamford, CT: JAI Press.

Barker, V. L., & Patterson, P. W. (1996). Top management team tenure and top manager causal attributions at declining firms attempting turnarounds. *Group and Organizational Management, 21*(3), 304–332.

Baum, J. A. C., & Oliver, C. (1991). Institutional linkages and organizational mortality. *Administrative Science Quarterly, 36*(2), 187–218.

Benjaminson, P. (1984). *Death in the afternoon: America's newspaper giants struggle for survival.* Kansas City, MO: Andrews, McMeel, & Parker.

Bennis, W., & Nanus, B. (1985). *Leaders: The strategies for taking charge.* New York: Harper & Row.

Bibeault, D. B. (1982). *Corporate turnaround: How managers turn losers into winners.* New York: McGraw-Hill.

Billings, R. S., Milburn, T. W., & Schaalman, M., L. (1980). A model of crisis perception: A theoretical and empirical analysis. *Administrative Science Quarterly, 25*(2), 300–316.

Borman, G. D., Rachuba, L., Datnow, A., Alberg, M., Mac Iver, M., Stringfield, S., et al. (2000). *Four models of school improvement: Successes and challenges in reforming low-performing, high-poverty Title I schools* (Report No. 48). Baltimore: Center for Research on the Education of Students Placed At Risk.

Boulding, K. F. (1975). The management of decline. *Change, 7*(5), 8–9, 64.

Bowles, S. A., Churchhill, A. M., Effrat, A., & McDermott, K. A. (2002). *School and district intervention: A decision-making framework for policymakers.* Amherst, MA: Center for Education Policy.

Boyle, R. D., & Desai, H. B. (1991). Turnaround strategies for small firms. *Journal of Small Business Management, 29*(3), 33–42.

Boyne, G. A. (2004). A "3Rs" strategy for public service turnaround: Retrenchment, repositioning and reorganization. *Public Money & Management, 24*(2), 97–103.

Bozeman, B., & Slusher, E. A. (1979). Scarcity and environmental stress in public organizations: A conjectural essay. *Administration and Society, 11*(3), 333–355.

Brady, R. C. (2003). *Can failing schools be fixed?* Washington, DC: Thomas B. Fordham Foundation.

Bratton, W., & Knobler, P. (1998). *Turnaround: How America's top cop reversed the crime epidemic.* New York: Random House.

Breault, P. C. (1993). Case study: Turning around an independent community hospital. In R. A. Baehr (Ed.), *Engineering a hospital turnaround* (pp. 197–207). Washington, DC: American Hospital Publishing.

Brenneman, G. (1998). Right away and all at once: How we saved Continental. *Harvard Business Review, 76*(5), 162–179.

Brightman, J. (1995, Nov/Dec). The best products turnaround. *American Demographics,* 46–47.

Brinkley, D. (2003). *Wheels for the world: Henry Ford, his company, and a century of progress—1902–2003.* New York: Viking.

Brownstein, R. (2003). Locked down. *Education Next,* Summer, 40–46.

Bushweller, K. (1998). Under the shadow of the state. *American School Board Journal, 185*(8), 16–19.

Caldwell, D. F., & O'Reilly, C. A. (1982). Responses to failure: The effects of choice and responsibility on impression management. *Academy of Management Journal, 25*(1), 121–136.

Cameron, K. (1983). Strategic responses to conditions of decline: Higher education and the private sector. *Journal of Higher Education, 54*(4), 359–380.

Cameron, K. S., Kim, M. V., & Whetten, D. A. (1988). Organizational effects of decline and turbulence. In K. S. Cameron, R. I. Sutton, & D. A. Whetten (Eds.), *Readings in organizational decline: Frameworks, research, and prescriptions* (pp. 207–224). Cambridge, MA: Ballinger.

Cameron, K. S., Sutton, R. I., & Whetten, D. A. (1988). Issues in organizational decline. In K. S. Cameron, R. I. Sutton, & D. A. Whetten (Eds.), *Readings in organizational decline: Frameworks, research, and prescriptions* (pp. 3–19). Cambridge, MA: Ballinger.

Cameron, K. S., & Whetten, D. A. (1988). Models of the organizational life cycle: Applications to higher education. In K. S. Cameron, R. I. Sutton, & D. A. Whetten (Eds.), *Readings in organizational decline: Frameworks, research, and prescriptions* (pp. 45–61). Cambridge, MA: Ballinger.

Cameron, K. S., Whetten, D. A., & Kim, M. V. (1987). Organizational dysfunctions of decline. *Academy of Management Journal, 30*(1), 126–138.

Cameron, K. S., & Zammuto, R. F. (1988). Matching managerial strategies to conditions of decline. In K. S. Cameron, R. I. Sutton, & D. A Whetten (Eds.), *Readings in organizational decline: Frameworks, research, and prescriptions* (pp. 117–128). Cambridge, MA: Ballinger.

Carrington, H., & Aurelio, J. M. (1976). Survival tactics for the small business. *Business Horizons, 19*(1), 13–24.

Castrogiovanni, G. J., Bahga, R. B., & Kidwell, R. E. (1992). Curing sick businesses: Changing CEOs in turnaround efforts. *Academy of Management Executive, 6*(3), 26–40.

Chaffee, E. E. (1983, March). *Turnaround management strategies: The adaptive model and the constructive model.* Paper presented at the annual meeting of the Association for the Study of Higher Education, Washington, DC.

Chakraborty, S., & Dixit, S. (1992). Developing a turnaround strategy: A case study approach. *International Journal of Management Science, 20*(3), 345–352.

Chan, P. S. (1993). Managing successful turnarounds: Lessons from global companies. *Management Decision, 31*(3), 29–33.

Chesley, J. A., & Huff, A. S. (1998). Anticipating strategic turnaround: The systems and structures that enable/constrain change. In L. W. Foster &

D. K. Ketchen (Eds.), *Turnaround research: Past accomplishments and future challenges* (pp. 177–204). Stamford, CT: JAI Press.

Chowdhury, S. D., & Lang, J. R. (1993). Crisis, decline, and turnaround: Test of competing hypotheses for short term performance improvement in small firms. *Journal of Small Business Management, 31*(4), 8–17.

Cibulka, J. G. (2003). Educational bankruptcy, takeovers, and reconstitution of failing schools. In W. L. Boyd & D. Miretzky (Eds.), *American educational governance on trial: Change and challenges* (pp. 249–270). Chicago: National Society for the Study of Education.

Clarke, L., & Perrow, C. (1999). Prosaic organizational failures. In H. K. Anheier (Ed.), *When things go wrong: Organizational failures and breakdowns* (pp. 179–196). Thousand Oaks, CA: Sage.

Clausen, A. W. (1990, Winter). Strategic issues in managing change: The turnaround in BankAmerica Corporation. *California Management Review,* 98–105.

Contino, R., & Lorusso, R. M. (1982). The theory Z turnaround of a public agency. *Public Administration Review, 42*(1), 66–72.

Corallo, C., & McDonald, D. (2001). *What works with low-performing schools: A review of research literature on low-performing schools.* Charleston, WV: Appalachia Educational Laboratory.

Crandall, R. (1995). *Turnaround strategies for the small church.* Nashville, TN: Abingdon Press.

Cummings, L. L. (1988). Organizational decline from the individual perspective. In K. S. Cameron, R. I. Sutton, & D. A. Whetten (Eds.), *Readings in organizational decline: Frameworks, research, and prescriptions* (pp. 417–424). Cambridge, MA: Ballinger.

D'Aunno, T., & Sutton, R. I. (1992). The responses of drug abuse treatment organizations to financial adversity: A partial test of the threat-rigidity thesis. *Journal of Management, 18*(1), 117–131.

D'Aveni, R. A. (1989). The aftermath of organizational decline: A longitudinal study of the strategic and managerial characteristics of declining firms. *Academy of Management Journal, 32*(3), 577–605.

Davis, M. R. (2006). Report: Schools could improve on NCLB tutoring, choice. *Education Week, 25*(31), 31.

Devos, D., & Hampden-Turner, C. (2002). Recapturing the true mission: Christian Majaard, LEGO. In F. Trompenaars & C. Hampden-Turner (Eds.), *21 leaders for the 21st century* (pp. 141–158). New York: McGraw-Hill.

Dewitt, R. L., Harrigan, K. R., & Newman, W. H. (1998). Downsizing strategically. In L. W. Foster & D. Ketchen (Eds.), *Turnaround research: Past accomplishments and future challenges* (pp. 21–36). Stamford, CT: JAI Press.

Donlevy, J. (2003). No Child Left Behind: Failing schools and future directions. *International Journal of Instructional Media, 30*(4), 335–338.

Duffy, M. C. (2001, April). *America's reform inferno: The nine layers of accountability.* Paper presented at the annual meeting of the American Educational Research Association, Seattle, WA.

Ediger, M. (2004). What makes for failing schools? *Journal of Instructional Psychology, 31*(2), 170–175.

Fine, L. R., Hsu, T. P., King, K., et al. (2003). *Education: Federal rights and racial equity, adequacy, and standards in K–12 education.* Washington, DC: Lawyers' Committee for Civil Rights Under Law.

Fink, S., Beak, J., & Taddoo, K. (1971). Organizational crisis and change. *Journal of Applied Behavioral Science, 7*(1), 15–37.

Finkin, E. F. (1985). Company turnaround. *Journal of Business Strategy, 5*(4), 14–24.

Finkin, E. F. (1987). *Successful corporate turnaround: An agenda for board members, financial managers, financial institutions, and other creditors.* New York: Quorum.

Ford, J. D. (1980). The occurrence of structural hysteresis in declining organizations. *Academy of Management Review, 5*(4), 589–598.

Ford, J. D. (1983). The management of organizational crises. *Business Horizons, 24*(3), 10–16.

Ford, J. D. (1985). The effects of causal attributions of decision makers' responses to performance downturns. *Academy of Management Review, 10*(4), 770–786.

Ford, J. D., & Baucus, D. A. (1987). Organizational adaptation to performance downturns: An interpretation-based perspective. *Academy of Management Review, 12*(2), 366–380.

Forster, E. M. (1997, April). *State intervention in local school districts: Educational solution or political process?* Paper presented at the annual meeting of the American Educational Research Association, New York.

Fredenberger, W. B., Lipp, A., & Watson, H. J. (1997). Information requirements of turnaround managers at the beginning of engagements. *Journal of Management Information Systems, 13*(4), 167–192.

Fullan, M. (2005). Turnaround leadership. *Educational Forum, 69*(2), 174–181.

Gainer, R. (1999). In the land of the king: Reflections on the acquisition of a facility plagued by controversy. *Residential Treatment for Children and Youth, 17*(1), 13–20.

Garcia, S. B., & Guerra, P. L. (2004). Deconstructing deficit thinking: Working with educators to create more equitable learning environments. *Education and Urban Society, 36*(2), 150–168.

Gerstner, L. V. (2002). *Who says elephants can't dance: Inside IBM's historic turnaround.* New York: Harper Business.

Gewertz, C. (2006). 3 Houston schools fight to keep doors open. *Education Week, 26*(1), 1, 20.

Goldstein, A. S. (1988). *Corporate comeback: Managing turnaround and troubled companies.* New York: John Wiley & Sons.

Goldstein, J., Kelemen, M., & Koski, W. (1998, April). *Reconstitution in theory and practice: The experiences of San Francisco.* Paper presented at the annual meeting of the American Educational Research Association, San Diego, CA.

Goldston, M. R. (1992). *The turnaround prescription: Repositioning troubled companies.* New York: Free Press.

Goodman, S. J. (1982). *How to manage a turnaround: A senior manager's blueprint for turning an ailing business into a winner.* New York: Free Press.

Green, R. L., & Carl, B. R. (2000). A reform for troubled times: Takeovers of urban schools. *Annals of the American Academy, 569,* 56–70.

Green, R., & Hanson, T. (1993). Case study: Turning around a multi-hospital system. In R. A. Baehr (Ed.), *Engineering a hospital turnaround* (pp. 186–195). Washington, DC: American Hospital Publishing.

Greenhalgh, L. (1983). Organizational decline. In S. B. Bacharach (Ed.), *Research in the sociology of organizations* (pp. 231–276). Greenwich, CT: JAI Press.

Grinyer, P. H., Mayes, D. G., & McKiernan, P. (1988). *Sharpbenders: The secrets of unleashing corporate potential.* Oxford, England: Basil Blackwell.

Grinyer, P., & McKiernan, P. (1990). Generating major change in stagnating companies [Special issue]. *Strategic Management Journal, 11,* 131–146.

Grinyer, P. H., & Spender, J. C. (1979). Recipes, crises, and adaptation in mature businesses. *International Studies of Management and Organizations, 9*(3), 113–133.

Grzymala-Busse, A. (2002). The programmatic turnaround of communist successor parties in East Central Europe, 1989–1998. *Communist and Post-Communist Studies, 35*(1), 51–66.

Hacsi, T. A. (2004). *Innovation and accountability: Vouchers, charters, and the Florida virtual school* (Policy Brief). Tempe, AZ: Education Policy Studies Laboratory.

Hager, M., Galaskiewicz, J., Bielefeld, W., & Pins, J. (1999). "Tales from the grave": Organizations' accounts of their own demise. In H. K. Anheier (Ed.), *When things go wrong: Organizational failures and breakdowns* (pp. 51–69). Thousand Oaks, CA: Sage.

Hall, W. K. (1980). Survival strategies in a hostile environment. *Harvard Business Review, 58*(5), 75–80.

Hamblin, R. L. (1958). Leadership and crisis. *Sociometry, 21*(4), 322–335.

Hambrick, D. C. (1985). Turnaround strategies. In W. D. Guth (Ed.), *Handbook of business strategy* (pp. 10-1–10-32). Boston: Warren, Gorham, & Lamont.

Hambrick, D. C., & D'Aveni, R. A. (1988). Large corporate failures as downward spirals. *Administrative Science Quarterly, 33*(1), 1–23.

Hambrick, D. C., & Schecter, S. M. (1983). Turnaround strategies for mature industrial-product business units. *Academy of Management Journal, 26*(2), 231–248.

Hardy, C. (1990). *Strategies for retrenchment and turnaround: The politics of survival.* Berlin, Germany: Walter de Gruyter.

Harrigan, K. R. (1988). Strategies for declining industries. In K. S. Cameron, R. I. Sutton, & D. A. Whetten (Eds.), *Readings in organizational decline: Frameworks, research, and prescriptions* (pp. 129–149). Cambridge, MA: Ballinger.

Hart, B., & Risley, T. R. (1995). *Meaningful differences in the everyday experiences of young American children.* Baltimore: Paul H. Brookes.

Hassel, B. C., & Steiner, L. (2003). *Starting fresh: A new strategy for responding to chronically low performing schools.* Chapel Hill, NC: Public Impact.

Hassel, E. A., Hassel, B. C., Arkin, M. D., Kowal, J. M., & Steiner, L. M. (2005). *School restructuring under No Child Left Behind: What works when? A guide for education leaders.* Chapel Hill, NC: Public Impact.

Haveman, H. A. (1992). Between a rock and a hard place: Organizational change and performance under conditions of fundamental environmental transformation. *Administrative Science Quarterly, 37*(1), 48–75.

Hegde, M. (1982). Western and Indian models of turnaround management. *Vikaipia, 7*(4), 289–304.

Henderson, L. J. (1993). Baltimore: Managing the civics of a "turnaround" community. *National Civic Review, 82*(4), 329–339.

Hess, F. M., & Finn, Jr., C. E. (2004). Inflating the life rafts of NCLB: Making public school choice and supplemental services work for students in troubled schools. *Phi Delta Kappan, 86*(1), 34–58.

Hess, G. A. (2003). Reconstitution—three years later: Monitoring the effect of sanctions on Chicago high schools. *Education and Urban Society, 35*(3), 300–327.

Hofer, C. (1980). Turnaround strategies. *Journal of Business Strategy, 1*(1), 19–31.

Honig, C. A. (1987). *Organizational failure: A multidisciplinary approach to description and prediction.* Unpublished doctoral dissertation, Bowling Green State University, Bowling Green, OH.

Housman, N. G., & Martinez, M. R. (2001). *A brief for practitioners on turning around low-performing schools: Implications at the school, district, and state levels.* Washington, DC: National Clearinghouse for Comprehensive Reform.

Jackson, M. (2001). Bringing a dying brand back to life. *Harvard Business Review, 79*(5), 53–61.

Kanter, R. M. (2003). Leadership and the psychology of turnarounds. *Harvard Business Review, 81*(6), 58–67.

Kaufman, H. (1991). *Time, change, and organizations: Natural selection in a perilous environment* (2nd ed.). Chatham, NJ: Chatham House.

Khandwalla, P. N. (1983–1984). Turnaround management of mismanaged complex organizations. *International Studies of Management & Organizations, 13*(4), 5–41.

Kierulff, H. E. (1981). Turnarounds of entrepreneurial firms. In K. H. Vesper (Ed.), *Frontiers of entrepreneurship research* (pp. 483–495). Proceedings of the 1981 Conference on Entrepreneurship at Babson College, Babson Park, MA.

Kirby, S. N., Naftel, S., Berends, M., & McCombs, J. S. (2005). *Schools identified as in need of improvement under Title I* (Working Paper). Washington, DC: Rand Education.

Kirst, M. W. (2002). *Mayoral influence, new regimes, and public school governance* (Report No. RR-049). Philadelphia: Consortium for Policy Research in Education.

Kowal, J. M., & Hassel, E. A. (2005). *Turnarounds with new leaders and staff.* Naperville, IL: Learning Point Associates/North Central Regional Educational Laboratory.

Kramer, R. (1987). *Restructuring and turnaround: Experiences in corporate renewal.* Geneva, Switzerland: Business International Research.

Krantz, J. (1985). Group process under conditions of organizational decline. *Journal of Applied Behavioral Science, 21*(1), 1–17.

Lashway, L. (2004). The mandate: To help low-performing schools. *Teacher Librarian, 31*(5), 25–27.

Lawrence, P. R., & Dyer, D. (1983). *Renewing American industry.* New York: Free Press.

Lenz, L. (2002). Been there, done that, Mr. President. *Journal of Staff Development, 23*(4), 84.

Levine, C. H. (1978). Organizational decline and cutback management. *Public Administration Review, 38*(4), 316–325.

Linn, D., Rothman, B., & White, K. (2001). *State strategies for turning around low-performing schools* (Issue Brief). Washington, DC: National Governors Association for Best Practices.

Lipsky, D. K., & Gartner, A. (1989). Overcoming school failure: A vision for the future. *Academy of Political Science, 37*(2), 149–158.

Lohrke, F. T., & Bedeian, A. G. (1998). Managerial responses to declining performance: Turnaround investment strategies and critical contingencies. In L. W. Foster & D. Ketchen (Eds.), *Turnaround research, past accomplishments and future challenges* (pp. 3–20). Stamford, CT: JAI Press.

Lorange, P., & Nelson, R. T. (1987). How to recognize—and avoid—organizational decline. *Sloan Management Review, 28*(3), 41–48.

Lubatkin, M., & Chung, K. (1985). *Leadership origin and organizational performance in prosperous and decline firms.* Paper presented at the Academy of Management Best Paper Proceedings.

Mac Iver, D. J., Ruby, A., Balfanz, R., & Byrnes, V. (2003). Removed from the list: A comparative longitudinal case study of a reconstitution-eligible school. *Journal of Curriculum and Supervision, 18*(3), 259–289.

Malen, B., Croninger, R., Muncey, D., & Redmond-Jones, D. (2002). Reconstituting schools: "Testing" the "theory of action." *Educational Evaluation and Policy Analysis, 24*(2), 113–132.

Malen, B., Croninger, R., Redmond, D., & Muncey, D. (1999, October). *Uncovering the potential contradictions in reconstitution reforms: A working paper.* Paper presented at the annual meeting of the University Council for Educational Administration, Minneapolis, MN.

Malen, B., & Rice, J. K. (2004). A framework for assessing the impact of education reforms on school capacity: Insights from studies of high-stakes accountability initiatives. *Educational Policy, 18*(5), 631–660.

Manzo, K. K. (2004). Troubled high school narrows courses. *Education Week, 23*(40), 1, 26.

Mayntz, R. (1999). Organizational coping, failure, and success: Academics of sciences in Central and Eastern Europe. In H. K. Anheier (Ed.), *When things go wrong: Organizational failures and breakdowns* (pp. 71–87). Thousand Oaks, CA: Sage.

Mazzeo, C., & Berman, I. (2003). *Reaching new heights: Turning around low-performing schools.* Washington, DC: National Governors Association Center for Best Practices.

McArthur, A. A. (1993). An exploration of community business failure. *Policy and Politics, 21*(3), 219–230.

McChesney, J., & Hertling, E. (2000). The path to comprehensive school reform. *Educational Leadership, 57*(7), 10–15.

McColskey, W., & Monrad, D. M. (2004). Assisting low-performing schools in the Southeast. *International Journal of Educational Policy, Research, & Practice, 4*(4), 3–24.

McDaniel, R. R., & Walls, M. F. (1998). Professional organizations stuck in the middle: A complex adaptive systems approach to achieving organizational turnaround in adverse situations. In L. W. Foster & D. Ketchen (Eds.), *Turnaround research: Past accomplishments and future research* (pp. 131–152). Stamford, CT: JAI Press.

McKelvey, B. (1988). Organizational decline from the population perspective. In K. S. Cameron, R. I. Sutton, & D. A. Whetten (Eds.), *Readings in organizational decline: Frameworks, research, and prescriptions* (pp. 399–410). Cambridge, MA: Ballinger.

McKinley, W. (1993). Organizational decline and adaptation: Theoretical controversies. *Organization Sciences, 4*(1), 1–9.

McNeil, L., & Thompson, J. D. (1971). The regeneration of social organizations. *American Sociological Review, 36*(4), 624–637.

McRobbie, J. (1998). *Can state intervention spur academic turnaround?* San Francisco: WestEd.

Meyer, A. D. (1982). Adapting to environmental jolts. *Administrative Science Quarterly, 27*(4), 515–537.

Meyer, A. D. (1988). Organizational decline from the organizational perspective. In K. S. Cameron, R. I. Sutton, & D. A. Whetten (Eds.), *Readings in organizational decline: Frameworks, research, and prescriptions* (pp. 411–416). Cambridge, MA: Ballinger.

Meyer, M. W. (1999). Permanent failure and the failure of organizational performance. In H. K. Anheier (Ed.), *When things go wrong: Organizational failures and breakdowns* (pp. 197–211). Thousand Oaks, CA: Sage.

Meyer, J., & Rowan, B. (1977). Institutionalized organizations: Formal structures as myth and ceremony. *American Journal of Sociology, 83*, 340–363.

Meyer, M. W., & Zucker, L. G. (1989). *Permanently failing organizations.* Newbury Park, CA: Sage.

Milburn, T. W., Schuler, R. S., & Watman, K. H. (1983a). Organizational crisis. Part I: Definition and conceptualization. *Human Relations, 36*(12), 1141–1160.

Milburn, T. W., Schuler, R. S., & Watman, K. H. (1983b). Organizational crisis. Part II: Strategies and responses. *Human Relations, 36*(12), 1161–1180.

Miles, R. E., Snow, C. C., & Meyer, A. D. (1978). *Organizational strategy, structure, and process.* New York: McGraw-Hill.

Miles, R. H. (1980). Findings and implications of organizational life cycle research: A commencement. In J. Kimberly & R. M. Miles (Eds.). *The organizational life cycle: Issues in the creation, transformation, and decline of organizations* (pp. 430–449). San Francisco: Jossey-Bass.

Miller, D. (1977, November). Common syndromes of business failure. *Business Horizons,* 43–53.

Mintrop, H. (2003). The limits of sanctions in low-performing schools: A study of Maryland and Kentucky schools on probation. *Education Policy Analysis Archives, 11*(3). Retrieved September 8, 2005, from http://epaa.asu.edu/epaa/v11n3.html

Mintrop, H., & MacLellan, A. (2002). School improvement plans in elementary and middle schools on probation. *Elementary School Journal, 102*(4), 275–300.

Mintrop, H., MacLellan, A., & Quintero, M. F. (2001). School improvement plans in schools on probation: A comparative content analysis across three accountability systems. *Educational Administration Quarterly, 37*(2), 197–218.

Mintrop, H., & Trujillo, T. (2005). Corrective action in low performing schools: Lessons for NCLB implementation from first-generation accountability systems. *Education Policy Analysis Archives, 13*(48), 1–30.

Mirvis, P., Ayas, K., & Roth, G. (2003). *To the desert and back: The story of the most dramatic business transformation on record.* San Francisco: Jossey-Bass.

Modiano, P. (1987). Made in Great Britain: Lessons from manufacturing turnarounds. *European Management Journal, 5*(3), 174–179.

Mohrman, S. A., & Mohrman, A. M. (1983). Employee involvement in declining organizations. *Human Resource Management, 22*(4), 445–465.

Motroni, H. (1992). A turnaround: Putting the customer first. *Journal of Business and Industrial Marketing, 7*(4), 29–32.

Murphy, J. (1990). The educational reform movement of the 1980s: A comprehensive analysis. In J. Murphy (Ed.), *The reform of American public education in the 1980s: Perspectives and cases* (pp. 3–55). Berkeley, CA: McCutchan.

Murphy, J., & Adams, J. E. (1998). Educational reform in the United States: 1980–2000. *Journal of Educational Administration, 36*(5), 426–444.

Murphy, J., & Beck, L. (1995). *School-based management as school reform: Taking stock.* Thousand Oaks, CA: Corwin Press.

Musfeldt, C., & Collier, T. (1993). Medical staff issues in a turnaround. In R. Baehr (Ed.), *Engineering a hospital turnaround* (pp. 125–132). Washington, DC: American Hospital Publishing.

Neuman-Sheldon, B. (2006). *Building on state reform: Maryland school restructuring* (Report). Washington, DC: Center on Education Policy.

Nicolaidou, M., & Ainscow, M. (2005). Understanding failing schools: Perspectives from the inside. *School Effectiveness and School Improvement, 16*(3), 229–248.

O'Neill, H. M. (1981). *Turnaround strategies in the commercial banking industry.* Ann Arbor, MI: UMI Research.

O'Neill, H. M. (1986a). An analysis of the turnaround strategy in commercial banking. *Journal of Management Studies, 23*(2), 165–188.

O'Neill, H. M. (1986b). Turnaround and recovery: What strategy do you need? *Long Range Planning, 19*(1), 80–88.

O'Shaughnessy, N. J. (1995). Tactics for turnaround. *Management Decision, 24*(3), 3–6.

Olson, L. (2005). NCLB choice option going untapped, but tutoring picking up. *Education Week, 24*(27), 1–2.

Oviatt, B. M., & Bruton, G. D. (1994). Turnarounds of distressed entrepreneurial firms. *Entrepreneurship, Innovation, and Change, 3*(2), 125–143.

Pearce, J. A., & Robbins, D. K. (1993). Toward improved theory and research on business turnaround. *Journal of Management, 19*(3), 613–636.

Pearce, J. A., & Robbins, D. K. (1994a). Entrepreneurial recovery strategies of small market share manufacturers. *Journal of Business Venturing, 9*(2), 91–108.

Pearce, J. A., & Robbins, D. K. (1994b). Retrenchment remains the foundation of business turnaround. *Strategic Management Journal, 15*(5), 407–417.

Peterson, K. D. (1999). Reconstitution and school reform: Issues and lessons. *Newsletter of the Comprehensive Center Region—VI, 4*(2), 21–22.

Peterson, P. E. (2005). Making up the rules as you play the game. *Education Next, 5*(4), 42–8.

Phenix, D., Siegel, D., Zaltsman, A., & Fruchter, N. (2005). A forced march for failing schools: Lessons from the New York City Chancellor's District. *Education Policy Analysis Archives, 13*(40), 1–27.

Picucci, A. C., Brownson, A., Kahlert, R., & Sobel, A. (2002). *Driven to succeed: High-performing, high-poverty, turnaround middle schools: Vol. I. Cross-case analysis of high-performing, high-poverty, turnaround middle schools.* Austin: The University of Texas, The Charles A. Dana Center.

Pincus, J. D., & Acharya, K. (1988). Employee communication strategies for organizational crises. *Employee Responsibilities and Rights Journal, 1*(3), 181–199.

Popham, W. J. (2004). *America's "failing" schools: How parents and teachers can cope with No Child Left Behind.* New York: Routledge Falmer.

Popham, W. J. (2005). "Failing" schools or insensitive tests? *School Administrator, 3*(6). Retrieved November 17, 2005, from http://www.findarticles.com/p/articles/mi_m0JSD/is_3_62/ai_n13467072

Reich, R. B., & Donahue, J. D. (1985). *New deals: The Chrysler revival and the American system.* New York: Times Books.

Reisner, R. A. F. (2002). When a turnaround stalls. *Harvard Business Review, 80*(2), 45–52.

Renn, S. C., & Kirk, O. A. (1993). Identifying the financially distressed hospital. In R. A. Baehr (Ed.), *Engineering a hospital turnaround* (pp. 13–44). Washington, DC: American Hospital Publishing.

Rice, J. K., & Malen, B. (2003). The human costs of education reform: The case of school reconstitution. *Educational Administration Quarterly, 39*(5), 635–666.

Rindler, M. E. (1987). *Managing a hospital turnaround: From crisis to profitability in three challenging years.* Chicago: Pluribus Press.

Robbins, D. K., & Pearce, J. A. (1992). Turnaround: Retrenchment and recovery. *Strategic Management Journal, 13*(4), 287–309.

Robelen, E. W. (2006). School reopened as charter under NCLB winds up year 1. *Education Week, 26*(24), 8–9.

Rosenblatt, Z., Rogers, K. S., & Nord, W. R. (1993). Toward a political framework for flexible management of decline. *Organizational Sciences, 4*(1), 76–91.

Ross, J. E., & Kami, M. J. (1973). *Corporate management in crisis: Why the mighty fail.* Englewood Cliffs, NJ: Prentice Hall.

Rudo, Z. (2001). *Corrective action in low-performing schools and school districts.* Austin, TX: Southwest Educational Development Laboratory. Retrieved November 12, 2005, from www.sedl.org/pubs/catalog/items/p0191.html

Schendel, D. E., & Patton, G. R. (1976). Corporate stagnation and turnaround. *Journal of Economics and Business, 28*(3), 236–241.

Schendel, D., Patton, G. R., & Riggs, J. (1976) Corporate turnaround strategies: A study of profit decline and recovery. *Journal of General Management, 3*(3), 3–11.

Seibel, W. (1999). Successful failure. In H. K. Anheier (Ed.), *When things go wrong: Organizational failure and breakdowns* (pp. 91–105). Thousand Oaks, CA: Sage.

Shelley, S., & Jones, L. (1993). The turnaround process: Management, board, and cultural changes. In R. A. Baehr (Ed.), *Engineering a hospital turnaround* (pp. 69–81). Washington, DC: American Hospital Publishing.

Shook, C. L. (1998). Turning around turnaround research: The value of process in advancing knowledge. In L. W. Foster & D. J. Ketchen (Eds.), *Advances in applied business strategy* (pp. 261–280). Stamford, CT: JAI Press.

Shook, R. L. (1990). *Turnaround: The new Ford Motor Company.* New York: Prentice Hall.

Short, J. C., Palmer, T. B., & Stimpert, J. L. (1998). Getting back on track: Performance referents affecting the turnaround process. In L. W. Foster & D. J. Ketchen (Eds.), *Advances in applied business strategy* (pp. 153–176). Stamford, CT: JAI Press.

Shuchman, M. L., & White, J. S. (1995). *The art of the turnaround: How to rescue your troubled business from creditors, predators, and competitors.* New York: American Management Association.

Siegel, J. G. (1981, April). Warning signs of impending business failure and means to counteract such prospective failure. *National Public Accountant,* 9–13.

Silver, A. D. (1992). *The turnaround survival guide: Strategies for the company in crises.* Chicago: Dearborn Financial.

Slater, R. (1999). *Saving big blue: Leadership lessons and turnaround tactics of IBMs Lou Gerstner.* New York: McGraw-Hill.

Slatter, S. (1984). *Corporate recovery: A guide to turnaround management.* Harmondsworth, Middlesex, England: Penguin Books.

Sloma, R. S. (1985). *The turnaround manager's handbook.* New York: Free Press.

Smart, C., & Vertinsky, I. (1984). Strategy and the environment: A study of corporate responses to crises. *Strategic Management Journal, 5*(3), 199–213.

Smith, R. A. (1963). *Corporations in crisis.* New York: Doubleday.

Snow, C. E., Barnes, W. S., Chandler, J., Goodman, I. F., & Hemphill, L. (1991). *Unfulfilled expectations: Home and school influences on literacy.* Cambridge, MA: Harvard University Press.

Spreng, C. P. (2005). *Policy options for interventions in failing schools.* Doctoral dissertation, Pardee Rand Graduate School, 2006. Santa Monica, CA: RAND Corporation.

Starbuck, W. H., Greve, A., & Hedberg, B. L. T. (1978). Responding to crisis. *Journal of Business Administration, 9*(2), 111–137.

Staw, B. M., Sanderlands, L. E., & Dutton, J. E. (1981). Threat-rigidity effects in organizational behavior: A multilevel analysis. *Administrative Science Quarterly, 26*(4), 501–524.

Steiner, L. M. (2005). *State takeovers of individual schools.* Naperville, IL: Learning Point Associates/North Central Regional Educational Laboratory.

Stephens, J. E. (1988). Turnaround at the Alabama Rehabilitation Agency. *Public Productivity Review, 11*(3), 67–84.

Stewart, J. (1984). *Managing a successful business turnaround.* New York: American Management Associates.

Stopford, J. M., & Baden-Fuller, C. (1990). Corporate rejuvenation. *Journal of Management Studies, 27*(4), 399–415.

Sumeren, M. V. (1993). Cost reduction and quality improvement. In R. A. Baehr (Ed.), *Engineering a hospital turnaround* (pp. 111–123). Washington, DC: American Hospital Publishing.

Sutton, R. I. (1990). Organizational decline processes: A social psychological perspective. In B. M. Staw & L. L. Cummings (Eds.), *Research in organizational behavior* (pp. 205–253). Greenwich, CT: JAI Press.

Sutton, R. I., Eisenhardt, K. M., & Jucker, J. V. (1986). Managing organizational decline: Lessons from Atari. *Organizational Dynamics, 14*(4), 17–29.

Taylor, B. (1982–1983). Turnaround, recovery and growth: The way through crisis. *Journal of General Management, 8*(2), 5–13.

Thompson, J. D. (1967). *Organizations in action.* New York: McGraw-Hill.

Thurow, L. (2003). *Fortune favors the bold: What we must do to build a new and lasting global prosperity.* New York: Harper Business.

Trompenaars, F., & Hampden-Turner, C. (2002a). The balance between market and product: Anders Knutsen, Bang and Olufsen. In F. Trompenaars & C. Hampden-Turner (Eds.), *21 leaders for the 21st century* (pp. 159–170). New York: McGraw-Hill.

Trompenaars, F., & Hampden-Turner, C. (2002b). Remedy for a turn-around: Phillippe Bourguignon, Club Med. In F. Trompenaars & C. Hampden-Turner (Eds.), *21 leaders for the 21st century* (pp. 121–139). New York: McGraw-Hill.

Tushman, M. L., Newman, W. H., & Romanelli, E. (1988). Convergence upheaval: Managing the unsteady pace of organizational evolution. In K. S. Cameron, R. I. Sutton, & D. A. Whetten (Eds.), *Readings in organizational decline: Frameworks, research and prescriptions* (pp. 63–74). Cambridge, MA: Ballinger.

Tushman, M. L., & Romanelli, E. (1985). Organizational evolution: A metamorphosis model of convergence and reorientation. In L. L. Cummings & B. M. Staw (Eds.), *Research in organizational behavior* (pp. 171–222). Greenwich, CT: JAI Press.

Umbreit, W. T. (1996). Fairmont Hotels' turnaround strategy. *Cornell Hotel & Restaurant Administration Quarterly, 37*(4), 50–57.

U.S. Department of Education. (2001, January). *School improvement report: Executive order on actions for turning around low-performing schools.* Washington, DC: Office of Elementary and Secondary Education.

Wang, M. C., & Manning, J. (2000). *Turning around low-performing schools: The case of the Washington, DC, schools* (Report No. 143). Washington, DC: Office of Educational Research and Improvement.

Watts, J. (2000). *Getting results with accountability: Rating schools, assisting schools, improving schools* (Report). Atlanta, GA: Southern Regional Education Board.

Weitzel, W., & Jonsson, F. (1989). Decline in organizations: A literature integration and extension. *Administrative Science Quarterly, 34*(1), 91–109.

Whetten, D. A. (1988a). Organizational growth and decline processes. In K. S. Cameron, R. I. Sutton, & D. A. Whetten (Eds.), *Readings in organizational decline: Frameworks, research, and prescriptions* (pp. 27–43). Cambridge, MA: Ballinger.

Whetten, D. A. (1988b). Sources, responses, and effects of organizational decline. In K. S. Cameron, R. I. Sutton, & D. A. Whetten (Eds.), *Readings in organizational decline: Frameworks, research, and prescriptions* (pp. 151–174). Cambridge, MA: Ballinger.

Whitney, J. O. (1987). Turnaround management every day. *Harvard Business Review, 65*(5), 49–55.

Willmott, R. (1999). Structure, agency and school effectiveness: Researching a "failing" school. *Educational Studies, 25*(1), 5–18.

Wilson, D., Hickson, D. J., & Miller, S. J. (1999). Decision overreach as a reason for failure. In H. K. Anheier (Ed.), *When things go wrong: Organizational failures and breakdowns* (pp. 35–49). Thousand Oaks, CA: Sage.

Wolk, R. (1998). Strategies for fixing failing public schools. *Education Week, 18*(12). Retrieved September 8, 2005, from http://secure.edweek.org/ew/vol-18/12pew.h18

Wong, K. K., & Shen, F. X. (2003). Measuring the effectiveness of city and state takeover as a school reform strategy. *Peabody Journal of Education, 78*(4), 89–119.

Yates, B. (1983). *The decline and fall of the American automobile industry.* New York: Empire Books.

Yukl, G. (2002). *Leadership in organizations* (5th ed.). Upper Saddle River, NJ: Prentice Hall.

Zammuto, R., & Cameron, K. S. (1985). Environmental decline and organizational response. In L. L. Cummings & B. M. Staw (Eds.), *Research in organizational behavior* (pp. 223–262). Greenwich, CT: JAI Press.

Ziebarth, T. (2002). *State takeovers and reconstitutions* (Report). Chicago: Education Commission of the States.

Ziebarth, T. (2004a). *Closing low-performing schools and reopening them as charter schools: The role of the state* (Policy Report). Denver, CO: Education Commission of the States. Retrieved December 20, 2006, from http://www.ecs.org/clearinghouse/54/25/5425.htm

Ziebarth, T. (2004b). *State takeovers and reconstitutions* (Policy report). Denver, CO: Education Commission of the States.

Zimmerman, F. M. (1991). *The turnaround experience: Real-world lessons in revitalizing corporations.* New York: McGraw-Hill.

Zuckerman, D. (2002). *Comprehensive school reform and district- and school-based improvement* (Digest No. 710). Philadelphia: Temple University Laboratory for Student Success.

Index

CORWIN PRESS

The Corwin Press logo—a raven striding across an open book—represents the union of courage and learning. Corwin Press is committed to improving education for all learners by publishing books and other professional development resources for those serving the field of PreK–12 education. By providing practical, hands-on materials, Corwin Press continues to carry out the promise of its motto: **"Helping Educators Do Their Work Better."**

NSDC's mission is to ensure success for all students by serving as the international network for those who improve schools and by advancing individual and organization development.

The American Association of School Administrators, founded in 1865, is the professional organization for more than 13,000 educational leaders across America and in many other countries. AASA's mission is to support and develop effective school system leaders who are dedicated to the highest quality public education for all children.

DATE DUE

#47-0108 Peel Off Pressure Sensitive